Theories of Crime

SECOND EDITION

Theories of Crime

Daniel J. Curran
Claire M. Renzetti

St. Joseph's University

Allyn and Bacon

Boston • London • Toronto • Sydney • Tokyo • Singapore

Editor-in-Chief: *Karen Hanson*
Acquisitions Editor: *Jennifer Jacobson*
Series Editorial Assistant: *Sarah McGaughey*
Marketing Manager: *Jude Hall*
Production Editor: *Annette Pagliaro*
Editorial Production Service: *Kathy Smith*
Composition Buyer: *Linda Cox*
Manufacturing Buyer: *Megan Cochran*
Cover Administrator: *Kristina Mose-Libon*
Electronic Composition: *Publishers' Design and Production Services, Inc.*

Library of Congress Cataloging-in-Publication Data

Curran, Daniel J.
    Theories of crime / Daniel J. Curran, Claire M. Renzetti.—2nd ed.
      p.   cm.
    Includes bibliographical references and index.
    ISBN 0-205-27588-5
    1. Criminology.   I. Renzetti, Claire M.   II. Title.
HV6018.C87   2000
364—dc21

                                         00-060586

Printed in the United States of America

10 9 8 7 6 5   05 04

CONTENTS

PREFACE

This second edition has been far too long in coming. We are grateful to colleagues and students who encouraged us to revise and update the book, and who patiently awaited the revision. There are far too many of you to name individually, although we make an attempt at the end of this preface. We apologize now for any oversights; please know we are grateful to all of you.

As we noted in the preface to the first edition, it has been said that there are as many theories of crime as there are criminals. This is an overstatement, but we don't think it is stretching the truth too far to say that there are as many textbooks about theories of crime as there are theories of crime. When we wrote this book, we certainly did not want to add to the existing pile of paper, but rather contribute something new. We offer no new theory of our own, but instead a balanced presentation of the major theories in our field.

We wrote this book with three goals in mind. Our first goal stems from our knowledge of the audience likely to use the book: undergraduate and graduate students in criminology and criminal justice courses. Students who take criminological theory courses are typically social science majors, including sociology, criminal justice, and pre-law. But students from other majors, such as education and business, may also enroll. For many graduate students in criminology and criminal justice, the criminological theory course is one of the first courses of their graduate school careers. It provides them with a pivotal introduction to the discipline, even if as undergraduates they were sociology or criminal justice majors.

All of these students share an interest in—some might even say a fascination with—crime, although most have limited direct personal experience with it and, for many, their perceptions and understanding of crime may be based largely on media presentations. Consequently, our first goal was to write a book that is accessible to such a diverse group. In examining specific theories of crime, we discuss the empirical research that supports or refutes particular positions as well as the practical implications of each theory. This approach gives students a better understanding of the theory and also helps them distinguish the myths and realities of crime. At the same time, it demonstrates the interrelatedness of theory and practice.

Our second goal follows from the first: to encourage students to view crime, law, and theories about crime and law as criminologists do. Students (and some criminologists) may see crime and law as absolutes; that is, crime is something "wrong" or "bad" and law is a set of regulations that stipulates what is "wrong" or "bad." Criminological theories are simply explanations of why people do "wrong" or "bad" things. In contrast, we present the view that crime, law, and the theories that explain them are social products. They reflect the social, political, and economic conditions of the historical period during which they were created. This book, therefore, is designed to teach students that theories of crime, as well as who and what are defined and studied as criminal, are outgrowths of a social process that is affected not only by structural conditions, but also by the personal characteristics of the researchers and the researched.

Our third goal is to teach students that crime is not just a problem in the United States and that, consequently, it cannot be fully explained by culture-bound theories. We have found during our combined thirty-eight years of teaching criminology and criminal justice courses that when students think of crime in foreign countries, they think only in terms of how it might impact the United States—for example, how terrorism affects U.S. citizens abroad. We hope to expand students' views by introducing them to cross-cultural research, which empirically tests theories developed in the United States in societies different from our own. We also seek to expose students to some of the ways that issues raised by various theories (such as the death penalty and the insanity defense) are handled in other countries.

How do we realize these goals in this text? First, we provide our readers with a balanced presentation of the major theoretical perspectives on crime and law. We begin by introducing the concepts of *theory* and *paradigm* in Chapter 1, where we also explain criteria for evaluating the explanatory power of a theory. In addition, in Chapter 1 we present the assumptions and central principles of the major schools of criminological thought—the classical school, positivism, and Marxism. In subsequent chapters, we systematically evaluate criminological theories rooted in biology/physiology (Chapter 2), psychology/psychiatry (Chapter 3), and sociology (Chapters 4–7). In this second edition, we have expanded our coverage to include routine activities theory in Chapter 4, control balance theory in Chapter 5, and peacemaking and postmodern theories in Chapter 6. Also new to this edition is a full chapter on feminist criminology (Chapter 7), which we see as having a major impact on shaping the future of the discipline.

Each chapter contains a boxed feature entitled *Controversy and Debate*, highlighting a controversial issue raised by the propositions of a specific theory. Although this feature appeared in the first edition, many of the issues covered in this edition are new, such as the prosecution of pregnant drug users and education as a crime prevention strategy. Each chapter also contains a boxed feature entitled *How the World Sees It*, which examines various ways that a practical issue raised by a specific theory is addressed in other countries. This feature, too, was included in the first edition, but topics new to this edition include sex tourism and violence against women as a human rights issue.

In each chapter, key concepts are highlighted in bold print within the chapter narratives and are grouped alphabetically with definitions at the end of the chapter. A summary and concluding statement, along with an annotated list of suggested readings, also appear at the end of each chapter.

Because a substantial amount of empirical research is discussed in the text, we thought it would be helpful to include an appendix on research methodologies. Here students with little or no background in research methods will find a brief explanation of fundamental methodological concepts and procedures, such as reliability and validity, sampling, cross-sectional versus longitudinal designs, and the differences between and problems associated with official data versus self-report data. Students well-versed in research methods do not need to review the appendix, but those students who have little training in methods or who lack confidence in their methodological abilities have told us they appreciated having the appendix available.

Finally, an instructor's manual is available for this text. This supplement contains a test bank with multiple choice, true/false, and essay questions; film and video suggestions; and web sites, listservs, and e-mail addresses. We hope instructors will find the manual helpful in preparing and evaluating their classes.

As we noted at the outset, we were helped in preparing this edition by many people who offered us feedback on the first edition, shared their own and others' research or simply encouraged us. You know who you are, but at risk of missing someone, we especially wish to thank: Patrick Carr, St. Joseph's University; Patrick Donnelly, University of Dayton; David Kauzlarich, Southern Illinois University at Edwardsville; Lawrence Walsh, St. Joseph's University; and the following reviewers: Mary G. Almore, The University of Texas at Arlington; Stephen J. Bahr, Brigham Young University; Ellen G. Cohn, Florida International University; Guy Guzzo, Kent State University; and Christine S. Sellers, University of South Florida. We also want to acknowledge the following individuals who reviewed the manuscript for the first edition: Stephen Bahr, Brigham Young University; Bruce L. Berg, University of Massachusetts—Boston; Thomas Calhoun, Ohio University; Dennis Hoffman, University of Nebraska—Omaha; Billy Hu, Missouri State University; William Kelly, University of Texas at Austin; David Simon, San Diego State University; Ellwyn Stoddard, University of Texas at El Paso; and Victoria Swigert, College of the Holy Cross.

We also want to thank the production and sales staff at Allyn and Bacon—such patience and support few authors are privileged to experience. Kathy Smith continues to amaze us with her ability to take our projects through the production process with incredible skill, grace, and good humor. Karen Hanson, editor-in-chief of social sciences at Allyn and Bacon, is a fabulous editor and an even better friend. We're grateful to work with you, Karen. But the grand prize for patience and support goes to our sons, Sean and Aidan, who over the last eleven years have selflessly shared us with Allyn and Bacon and all of you. Boys, your generosity, warmth, and intelligence light up our lives.

1 Theoretical Perspectives in Criminology

Criminologists use a variety of methods to study crime, law creation, and other topics that interest them. These are methods of data collection; they yield *empirical observations* (see Appendix). However, the data do not speak for themselves; they must be interpreted. In other words, criminologists seek to understand the meaning of the data. This typically proves more challenging—and often, more frustrating—than the task of collecting data. Criminologists, then, are not satisfied with simply describing what's "out there"; they also wish to *explain* it. This is where *theory* comes in. An overly simplistic definition of a theory—but one that serves our purpose for the time being—is that it is an explanation of something.

In the chapters that follow, we will discuss some of the theories that have been developed to explain criminal as well as law-abiding behavior. There are many theories, and students are sometimes overwhelmed by the numerous names and concepts they feel obligated to memorize. We organize the theories broadly into "types" (including biological, psychological, and sociological) and "subtypes," recognizing, of course, that all such categorizations are imperfect. We also examine the theories in the social and intellectual contexts in which they were developed. Hopefully, both strategies will make learning about these theories not only more manageable but also more interesting.

Before we undertake the study of specific theories, however, it would be useful to know more about theory in general as well as theoretical traditions or schools of thought. This will be our primary objective in Chapter 1. Let's begin by taking a closer look at what a theory is and what its role is in scientific disciplines such as criminology.

The Importance of Theory in Criminology

Theory, whether we realize it or not, is a fundamental part of our everyday lives. We all draw on theory to make our lives safer, simpler, and less uncertain, although we rarely stop to think that this is what we are doing. Suppose, for example, that you invite several friends to a dinner at which you plan to serve chicken. You do the grocery shopping the day before the dinner and keep the chicken in the refrigerator until you're ready to cook it. Why wouldn't you just leave the chicken on the kitchen counter until dinnertime? The reason is that you understand the relationships between temperature and the growth of bacteria, and between bacteria and disease. Theories have just saved you and your friends from serious illness and hours of discomfort.

More specifically, then, what is a theory? A **theory** is a set of interconnected statements or propositions that explain how two or more events or factors are related to one another. Many of the theories that we use in our everyday lives are derived from personal experience, common sense, or from someone who has passed the knowledge on to us. In any event, these theories help bring order to our lives because they expand our knowledge of the world around us and suggest systematic solutions to problems we repeatedly confront. Without the generalizable knowledge provided by theories, we would have to solve the same problems over and over again, largely through trial and error. Theory, therefore, rather than being just a set of abstract ideas, is quite practical. It is *useable knowledge*.

Criminologists use theories for much the same reason noncriminologists do—for problem solving. Theories that explain the causes of crime suggest methods for solving the crime problem. Unlike some of the theories that we use to organize our daily lives, however, criminologists employ *scientific* theories. A scientific theory is *logically sound* and, more important, *empirically verifiable* (grounded in systematic observation). As Earl Babbie (1998, p. 63) explains, "*Logic alone is not enough, but on the other hand, the mere observation and collection of empirical facts does not provide understanding—the telephone directory, for example, is not a scientific conclusion.*"

This is not to say that scientific theory never springs from intuition or imagination. Indeed, some have argued that greater progress toward understanding crime would be made if criminologists exercised their imaginations more in research and theory development (Christie, 1997; Williams, 1984). In addition, observation and experience often provide the starting point for the development of scientific theory. Some criminologists (Christie, 1997, for example) even argue that we should draw much more on our personal experiences in developing theory. When theory is developed *after* systematic observation, through the analysis of data, the process is called *inductive* theory construction. In *deductive* theory construction, on the other hand, the theory is developed and subsequently tested through empirical observation. Of course, deductive theory construction does not take place in a vacuum; ideas are generated from one's own and others' observations. Thus, the distinction between inductive and deductive theory construction is less clear cut than it at first appears. However, whatever the source of the theory, to qualify as scientific it must satisfy at least the two criteria of logical integrity and empirical verifiability.

We have noted already that criminologists have developed numerous theories, each purporting to explain crime or criminals or both. To confuse the matter further, all of these theories may be considered scientific. Should we conclude, therefore, that all theories are created equal? Is there any way to determine if one theory is better than another? These are questions we will address next.

Bad Theory, Good Theory, Better Theory: How Do We Judge?

Scientists use several criteria to assess the superiority of one theory relative to competing theories of the same phenomenon. If, in fact, you were to ask a group of scientists how they make such a judgment, you would likely find little variation in their answers. One might reply, for instance, that she evaluates the *parsimony* of each theory—that is, the simplicity of its structure. The theory based on the fewest assumptions and requiring the fewest statements or propositions to delineate the explanation is the most parsimonious and generally is considered the superior theory. Another scientist may say that he favors a theory that sensitizes people to things they otherwise would not have noticed or that causes them to see a phenomenon in a new way. Despite these minor variations, probably every scientist would also cite the two criteria of scope and accuracy.

The scope of a theory is sometimes called its *pervasiveness*. This refers to the range of phenomena that a theory can explain. **Accuracy** refers to the extent to which the theory matches empirical reality and, therefore, allows us to make correct predictions about the occurrence of the phenomenon in question. For instance, a theory stating that criminal behavior is the result of growing up in a broken home would lead us to predict that individuals reared in broken homes are more likely than others to engage in crime. Thorough empirical testing would provide us with a measure of the correctness of this prediction and, consequently, of the accuracy of the theory.

As a general rule, the theory that can explain the widest range of phenomena with the greatest degree of accuracy is considered better than alternative theories. Singleton and his associates (1988) use an example from physics to illustrate this principle:

> From Newton's theory it is possible to explain (or deduce) Kepler's laws describing the motion of the planets, Galileo's law of free fall, and the law of the tides, in addition to the motion of numerous objects that these laws cannot explain. . . . And so, once constructed, Newton's theory covered more ground and was more accurate than the existing laws that it explained. Later Einstein formulated his general theory of relativity, which explained and improved Newton's theory and also made new predictions about the motion of light near massive objects. (p. 25)

Social scientists, including criminologists, rarely construct theories that conform to the formal propositional model common in the physical and natural sciences, and social science theories seldom approach the level of accuracy of those developed in these other fields. Yet this does not mean that scope and accuracy are not applicable to the development of social science theories. Consider our earlier example regarding the effect of growing up in a broken home on the probability of subsequently committing a crime. The theory is logically sound and it may withstand empirical testing—we may in fact find that individuals reared in broken homes more often engage in crime than individuals raised in intact families. However, an alternative theory—say a theory of economic inequality—may explain not only the likelihood of committing crime, but also the breakdown of marital and family relations. Thus, the alternative theory is more pervasive (broader in scope) and research may show it to be more accurate as well.

The use of terms such as "probability" and "likelihood" in the preceding discussion alerts us to another important issue to remember when evaluating criminological theories in the chapters that follow. Scientific predictions derived from theories are *probabilistic*, not absolute. When researchers test a theory, they measure the regularity with which the predicted behaviors or events occur. They look for patterns of behavior, but they always find exceptions. For instance, let's return one last time to our theory of crime and broken homes. It is not necessarily damaging to the theory's accuracy that some individuals from broken homes are law-abiding and some from intact families are criminal if we find that *overall*, individuals from broken homes are *more likely* than individuals from intact families to commit crimes; what is important is that we observe a general or probabilistic pattern. Therefore, a theory is not deemed inaccurate simply because it is not confirmed by 100 percent of the observable cases.

When one of your authors enrolled in her first criminology course many years ago, she expected to know by the end of the semester what causes crime. But in class after class, theory after theory was carefully scrutinized and found wanting on some grounds. There was, she found, no one correct answer. Those of you who have similar expectations will reach the same conclusion after reading this text, for little has changed in this respect. We may have more data than we did twenty-five years ago, but instead of a pat explanation, we still only have bad, good, and better theories of crime.

Finally, although it is not typically examined as a criterion for evaluating scientific theories, there is an ideological component in making such judgments. Understanding this requires some knowledge of *paradigms*. We turn now to a discussion of what a paradigm is and how paradigms are used in the social sciences. Then we will examine specific criminological paradigms.

Paradigms

Sometimes, when we read about a particular study or hear a research presentation, we come away feeling that the researcher was *biased*. Most of us would argue, in fact, that research is supposed to be conducted *objectively*. In reality, however, no study is characterized by complete objectivity. The research process is always influenced by the researcher's values as well as a host of other sources of bias and constraint. The research process, in other words, is both subjective *and* objective. In deciding what to study, how to study it, and what to do with their findings, researchers draw on their personal value systems; this is a subjective dimension of research. This does not mean, though, that if their findings turn out not to support their hypotheses, the hypotheses should be changed to conform to their perspective. It is during the data analysis that researchers must remain objective.

One especially important constraining factor in the research process is the set of assumptions or organizing principles that provide the foundation of a researcher's work. Michalowski (1977) refers to this set of organizing principles as a *perspective*, and likens it to formulas for understanding the world around us. Any particular occurrence will be interpreted in a way that is fairly consistent with our basic assumptions about human nature and how the world operates. Michalowski states that:

> At the level of scientific inquiry, general perspectives on how that particular part of the world being studied functions leads to the development of relatively consistent bodies of knowledge which reflect the accumulation of past applications of that perspective to

a particular phenomenon. As this "scientifically" produced body of knowledge about a particular phenomenon begins to grow and coalesce into a relatively consistent set of understandings, it becomes a paradigm. (p. 20)

A **paradigm,** in other words, is a school of thought within a discipline. It provides the scientist with a model for choosing the problems to be analyzed, the methods for analyzing them, and the theoretical framework for explaining them.

All scientists, including criminologists, use paradigms to guide their work. However, while paradigms provide an essential structure to the scientific enterprise, they simultaneously act to constrain it. Because a paradigm defines what should be studied and how it should be studied and interpreted, it blinds the researcher to other relevant problems, methods, and explanations. The scientist, in effect, does not "see" certain puzzles to be solved, or labels them unimportant. There is a tendency not to use certain tools for puzzle solving or even to consider some solutions to particular puzzles because they appear unreasonable in the context of the paradigm in which the scientist is working (Christie, 1997; Kuhn, 1970; Ritzer, 1980). A number of different theories that explain a phenomenon may be developed by scientists working within the same paradigm, but as we will see in subsequent chapters, all will reflect the basic organizing principles of that paradigm.

How, then, are advances in a scientific discipline made? Usually, during any given period, one paradigm or school of thought dominates a science in that it has the greatest number of adherents. Knowledge about a phenomenon or problem accumulates as scientists working within the paradigm build on one another's work and previous findings. This is what Kuhn (1970) refers to as "normal science" and it fits best with the popular or ideal image of scientific advancement.

Sometimes, though, contradictory evidence or anomalies are discovered that are difficult to explain in terms of the currently dominant paradigm. For a time, the paradigm may be modified to account for them but, sooner or later, the dominant paradigm becomes stale or "wears out." That is, it becomes inadequate for explaining new problems and changing conditions without compromising its basic organizing principles in some fundamental ways (Harding, 1979). When this happens, a *scientific revolution* is likely: The inadequate dominant paradigm is displaced by another paradigm that is incompatible with the dominant paradigm's basic assumptions, but better able to account for prevailing conditions and observations.

The significance of a scientific revolution is that it promotes advances in a discipline. "Led by a new paradigm, scientists adopt new instruments and look in new places. Even more important, during revolutions scientists see new and different things when looking with familiar instruments in places they have looked before" (Kuhn, 1970, p. 111).

In sum, while the paradigm has been considered by some to be the "broadest unit of consensus" within a science (Ritzer, 1980), not all practitioners in a discipline necessarily use the dominant paradigm to guide their work. There typically exist other competing paradigms for studying the same phenomenon. This is certainly the case in criminology, as it is in most other disciplines. Let's examine, then, the major paradigms or schools of thought that historically have informed criminological research and theory building. We will discuss three: the classical school, the positivist school, and the Marxist/radical school.

Classical Criminology

The **classical school** of criminology is exemplified in the writings of *Cesare Beccaria* (1738–1794) and *Jeremy Bentham* (1748–1832). Both were heavily influenced by the philosophical arguments of the social contract thinkers of their day, including Locke, Hobbes, Voltaire, and Rousseau, who emphasized hedonism, rationality, and free will as the underlying bases of human action. According to the social contract philosophers, people come together and form a society because the social stability and protection such an arrangement affords is worth more to them than the piece of personal freedom they must lose in exchange. Beccaria (1963/1764) himself best summed up the argument when he wrote:

> Weary of living in a continual state of war, and of enjoying a liberty rendered useless by the uncertainty of preserving it, they [independent individuals] sacrificed a part so that they might enjoy the rest of it in peace and safety. The sum of all those portions of liberty sacrificed by each for his own good constitutes the sovereignty of a nation, and their legitimate depositary and administrator is the sovereign. But merely to have established this deposit was not enough; it had to be defended against private usurpations by individuals each of whom always tries not only to withdraw his own share but also to usurp for himself that of others. Some tangible motives had to be introduced, therefore, to prevent the despotic spirit, which is in every man, from plunging the laws of society into its original chaos. These tangible motives are the punishments established against infractors of the laws. (pp. 11–12)

These words were written during a period in which social life can be most aptly characterized as chaotic and tyrannical. Church leaders and the aristocracy formed a corrupt and repressive union against the peasants and the rising middle class. The great inequalities engendered by the political economic system were conspicuous, but the common people tended to explain their lot in terms of superstition and the divine right of traditional authority. Of course, the powerful did little to dispel such myths since they served to reinforce their advantageous position in the society.

Monachesi (1955) describes how the criminal justice system worked at that time:

> Secret accusations were in vogue and persons were imprisoned on the flimsiest of evidence. Torture, ingenious and horrible, was employed to wrench confessions from the recalcitrant. Judges were permitted to exercise unlimited discretion in punishing those convicted of crime. The sentences imposed were arbitrary, inconsistent and depended upon the status and power of the convicted. (p. 441; see also Foucault, 1977)

Not surprisingly, protests against such conditions were voiced by many Enlightenment thinkers, but one of the most effective was Cesare Beccaria.

Cesare Bonesana, Marquis of Beccaria. In 1764, when he was just twenty-six years old, Beccaria published anonymously the essay *On Crimes and Punishments* (*Dei delitie delle pene*). This slim volume, according to most reviewers, became the model for penal reform. It contains practically all of the reforms that we associate with the administration of criminal justice and penology in contemporary Western societies.[1]

Laws, according to Beccaria, are the embodiment of the social contract. It is legislators, chosen by the members of a society to represent them, who are charged with the responsibility of enacting laws and establishing the penalties to be imposed if they are broken. This was an important point, for with it Beccaria was emphasizing that it was not within the authority of judges to make laws and set penalties—a practice that we already have noted was common in the operation of the criminal justice system at that time. Instead, Beccaria argued, it is the judge's duty to determine the guilt or innocence of the accused and to do so on the basis of fact, impartially and uniformly, without regard for individual circumstances or intentions, or for the individual's social status. If the accused is found guilty, then the judge should impose the penalty prescribed by law, again with impartiality and uniformity.

Punishment is necessary, Beccaria maintained, because human beings are naturally self-serving and, if left unrestrained, they will always try to maximize their personal pleasure even if this means violating the rights and freedom of others. Thus, in his view, the function of punishment is not revenge or retribution, but rather deterrence. However, if punishment is to successfully deter crime, it must have particular characteristics: It must be *swift* and *certain*, and it must be *proportionate* and *appropriate* to the seriousness of the crime.

More specifically, Beccaria argued that punishment is most effective not when it inflicts tremendous pain and suffering, but rather when it is inescapable. "The certainty of a punishment, even if it be moderate, will always make a stronger impression than the fear of another that is more terrible but combined with the hope of impunity" (Beccaria, 1764/1963, p. 58). At the same time, an individual accused of a crime should be tried as quickly as possible and, if found guilty, receive the penalty promptly. This minimizes the length of time between commission of a crime and punishment. "I have said that the promptness of punishment is more useful because when the length of time that passes between the punishment and the misdeed is less, so much the stronger and more lasting in the human mind is the association of these two ideas, *crime and punishment*" (Beccaria, 1764/1963, p. 56).

Beccaria's discussion of the certainty and swiftness of punishment also hints at his concern over the extreme harshness and cruelty of the penalties commonly inflicted in his day. According to Beccaria, any punishment should always be appropriate to the seriousness of the crime committed, and the true measure of a crime's seriousness is the harm it does to society. He delineated three categories of crime presented in order of seriousness according to this criterion: crimes against the state and its representatives, crimes that injure the security and property of individuals, and crimes that disrupt the public peace. However, even the most serious crimes should be punished with a penalty that inflicts suffering "only to exceed the advantage derivable from the crime." Anything more severe he saw as tyrannical. In fact, he argued that extreme punishments promote crime. The offender reasons that he or she will be punished harshly for a single crime, so why not commit others and enjoy oneself as much as possible while one can? According to Beccaria, "The countries and times most notorious for severity of penalties have always been those in which the bloodiest and most inhumane deeds were committed, for the same spirit of ferocity that guided the hand of the legislators also ruled that of the parricide and assassin" (Beccaria, 1764/1963, p. 44).

It is for these reasons that Beccaria opposed the death penalty. Capital punishment, he said, has no deterrent effect because even though it shocks and appalls witnesses to it, it leaves no permanent impression on them. "It is not the intensity of punishment that has the greatest effect on the human spirit, but its duration, for our sensibility is more easily and more permanently affected by slight but repeated impressions than by a powerful but momentary action" (Beccaria, 1764/1963, pp. 46–47). More important, however, he argued that the death penalty itself is homicide and therefore unjust. "It seems to be absurd," Beccaria wrote, "that the laws which are an expression of the public will, which detest and punish homicide, should themselves commit it, and that to deter citizens from murder, they order a public one" (1764/1963, p. 50).

While Beccaria viewed punishment—sure, swift, and proportionate punishment—as an effective deterrent, he also maintained that the laws themselves could prevent crime. To do this, though, they had to have the full support or approval of the members of the society. This support, he reasoned, would be forthcoming if first, the laws were widely publicized so that all people were aware of them. Second, the laws must be written clearly and simply so that all could understand them. And third, the laws must be fair and impartial.

Several reviewers have noted that Beccaria's ideas were not entirely original; many had been suggested by other humanitarian reformers (Monachesi, 1955; Newman & Marongiu, 1990). However, in *On Crimes and Punishments*, Beccaria made an impassioned argument for penological reform that was taken up by many of his contemporaries. Certainly his ideas appear quite radical for the time, although his work often reflects the constraints of the social position from which he was writing. For example, even though Beccaria acknowledged that inequality might cause crime, he did not see the equitable redistribution of property as a tenable solution. Thus, in discussing the appropriate punishment for thieves, many of whom, he recognized, were poor, he argued simply that capital punishment should be replaced with long imprisonment at hard labor "in order to oblige him [the thief] to repair by this dependence, the unjust despotism he usurped over the property of another and his violation of the social compact" (quoted in Taylor et al., 1973, p. 6). Being a member of the propertied classes himself, Beccaria logically defended the institutions of private property. In his view, inequality of authority and social rank were not in themselves problematic; problems would arise if such inequalities were abused (Newman & Marongiu, 1990; Radzinowicz, 1966).

Still, Beccaria's impact on law and penology was far-reaching. Before we examine this influence, though, we will look briefly at the work of another writer in the classical tradition, Jeremy Bentham.

Jeremy Bentham.   Jeremy Bentham, a British contemporary of Beccaria, has been described as an eccentric personality whose idiosyncrasies are reflected in his work. Unlike Beccaria, it has been said that Bentham's writing is not likely to "impress the present-day criminologist with its immediate relevance, particularly in the sphere of criminological theory" (Geis, 1955, p. 160; but for a different view, see Newman & Marongiu, 1990). Nevertheless, we will soon see strains of Bentham's thought in some contemporary economic theories of crime and the rational criminal, so it is worthwhile for us to examine it here.

Actually, Bentham shared much in common with Beccaria. He wrote in response to the cruel and inconsistent practice of criminal justice in his society with the goal of bringing order to the chaotic legal system. He also accepted the premises of social contract philosophy. He argued that all human action stems from a single motivation: the pursuit of pleasure and the simultaneous avoidance of pain. Naturally, humans would engage in rampant criminality to maximize their personal pleasure if they were not controlled by sanctions on their behavior. These sanctions or punishments are established by law and serve to align the individual's pursuit of personal happiness with the collective interests of the whole society. "Punishment is considered an evil, but a necessary evil to prevent greater evils being inflicted on the society and thus diminishing happiness" (Geis, 1955, p. 166).

Like Beccaria, then, Bentham saw the purpose of punishment as deterrence, not vengeance. Moreover, he argued that a punishment should be only so severe as to produce just enough pain to outweigh the pleasure to be derived from committing the forbidden act. Bentham even went so far as to claim that his pleasure/pain ratio can be measured using his *felicity calculus.* Felicity calculus was a pseudo-mathematical model developed by Bentham that really had as its basis no criteria other than his personal estimate of the utility of an act.

Bentham maintained that punishment should be avoided if the end result—deterrence from crime—could be achieved effectively by less painful means, such as education. Bentham opposed punishments that were groundless either because no real crime had been committed (such as in cases of sexual acts involving consenting adult partners) or because more good than evil was accomplished by an offense (such as in cases of homicide in self-defense). He also denounced situations in which the evil of the punishment exceeded the evil of the offense. It was chiefly for this latter reason that he, too, opposed capital punishment.

Neither Bentham nor Beccaria explored in detail the question of why some individuals commit crimes and others do not. For them this issue was irrelevant; criminal motivation was a given. Their primary concern was social control. Consequently, Vold and Bernard (1986, p. 25) refer to their work and the classical school in general as "administrative and legal criminology." Clearly it was in the area of jurisprudence that their writing had its greatest impact.

Neoclassical Criminology.   Attempts were made to implement the principles of the classical school in the everyday operation of a number of countries' criminal justice systems. The French Code of 1791, for instance, relied heavily on Beccaria's work. The

Code treated everyone equally, without regard for individual circumstances, and imposed standardized punishments based on the harm done by specific actions, not on offenders' personal characteristics, motives, or intentions. It was not long, however, before the practical limitations of the classical position became evident. "It was impossible in practice to ignore the determinants of human action and to proceed as if punishment and incarceration could be easily measured on some kind of universal calculus" (Taylor et al., 1973, pp. 9–10). As a result, classical criminology underwent revision.

The revisionists—Rossi, Garaud, Joly—are known as the *neo-classicists*, and their principles are known as the **neo-classical school**. Essentially, the neo-classicists introduced three major modifications of the classical position. First, although they continued to ignore the issue of motivation in criminal behavior, they argued that an individual's free will could be constrained by certain circumstances. Thus, they allowed the court to consider as mitigating factors the physical and social environments in which individual offenders lived. Second, the courts were encouraged to take into account an offender's record. Finally, the neo-classicists recognized that certain groups of individuals—including children, the insane, the mentally retarded—are less capable or totally incapable of exercising adult freedom of action and, therefore, should be given special treatment by the courts.

These changes led, in turn, to revisions in the philosophy and practice of punishment. The neo-classicists recognized that a particular sentence would have varying effects depending on the individual characteristics of offenders. In addition, they pointed out that incarceration placed offenders in an environment that in itself influenced their future likelihood to commit crimes. A direct consequence of these revisions was that punishment increasingly was viewed in terms of its conduciveness to rehabilitation. This does not mean, however, that environment was seen as the determinant of behavior. Rather, environment was viewed simply as a factor that might influence an individual's ability to make the correct moral choices (Taylor et al., 1973).

The principles of the classical and neo-classical schools figure prominently in contemporary discussions of how the various branches of the criminal justice system should operate. It is the model that continues to be the major framework for understanding human behavior adhered to by criminal justice agencies in the majority of advanced industrial countries throughout the world. It is also the model that dominated criminology for about one hundred years until it was displaced by the positivist school which we will discuss shortly. Meanwhile, though, we will take note of the recent resurgence of this tradition in some contemporary criminological theories.

Contemporary Strains of Classicism.   As we will soon see, the positivist school of criminology focuses on isolating the causes of crime, either within the individual or in his or her environment. Emphasis is placed on treating the offender rather than on punishing him or her. However, by the late 1970s, a number of criminologists had become disillusioned with this perspective. For one thing, despite years of trying, researchers still had not pinpointed the specific causes of criminality. What is more, none of the numerous treatment strategies that had been tried in the prisons and by other agencies of social control appeared to be successful, at least if success is measured by *recidivision rates* (rates of reoffending). These factors, along with a conservative political climate, have contributed to a "get-tough" approach to crime, making a return to classicism appealing to some criminologists.

Contemporary classicists work in a variety of disciplines, including sociology, psychology, and economics. For example, several economists, such as Gary Becker (1968) and Peter Schmidt and Ann Witte (1984), have tried to quantify criminal decision making. They argue that the decision to commit a crime is like any other decision in that the individual weighs the benefits of carrying out the action against the costs to be incurred. Both benefits and cost may be material as well as psychological, but most economic models translate them into monetary terms so that a cost/benefit ratio can be computed. Schmidt and Witte, for instance, provide a formula for this calculation that is essentially a time allocation model—that is, a model for determining the amount of time in a twenty-four-hour period that an individual will spend on legal versus illegal activities. Figuring into the calculation are such factors as the amount of income that can be obtained through legitimate activities, the amount of income to be made from illegitimate activities, the probability of being arrested for a particular crime, the probability of conviction if arrested, the probability of being imprisoned if convicted, or the cost of a fine if convicted. Also considered are personal tastes, convenience, psychic costs (shame, guilt), and psychic benefits (satisfaction, excitement). Once the potential offender has made these computations, he or she will choose the course of action that yields the highest return. The decision, though, may be the wrong one; that is, the offender may have miscalculated the costs and/or benefits of a particular action, and suffers the consequences (jail) as a result. "The basic economic assumption does not maintain that people do not make mistakes but rather that they do their best given their reading of present and future possibilities and given their resources" (Sullivan, 1973, p. 142).

Another popular neo-classical theory of crime is *rational choice theory*, which was developed most extensively by *Derek Cornish* and *Ronald Clarke* and accepts the classical position that humans are rational beings who exercise free will in deciding on a course of action. "Its starting point [is] an assumption that offenders seek to benefit themselves by their criminal behavior; that this involves the making of decisions and choices, however rudimentary on occasion these processes might be; and that these processes exhibit a measure of rationality, albeit constrained by limits of time and ability and the availability of relevant information" (Cornish & Clarke, 1986, p. 1). Even crimes that appear to be purely impulsive or caused by some individual pathology are seen as having rational components.

These assumptions lead rational choice theorists to focus on crimes rather than on criminals. Their approach, moreover, is *crime-specific*. That is, they argue that different crimes may meet different needs for different offenders. In addition, situational factors and available information also may vary among types of offenses. Consequently, relatively fine distinctions should be made among types of crimes if we are to fully understand them and develop effective strategies for dealing with them.

> For example, it may not be sufficient to divide burglary simply into its residential and commercial forms. It may also be necessary to distinguish between burglaries committed in middle-class suburbs, in public housing, and in wealthy residential enclaves.

> Empirical studies suggest that the kinds of individuals involved in these different forms of residential burglary, their motivations, and their methods all vary considerably. (Cornish & Clarke, 1986, p. 2)

An emphasis on offenses does not mean that rational choice theorists ignore offenders altogether. Instead, they maintain that each offender has specific individual needs and skills and that these intersect with particular offense characteristics to impinge on an offender's choices. In other words, offender characteristics combine with offense characteristics in shaping criminal decisions. Rational choice theorists refer to this process as *choice structuring* (Clarke & Cornish, 1985).

Finally, rational choice theorists distinguish between types of criminal decisions. *Involvement decisions* are multistage and are made over an extended period of time. These include the initial decision to engage in criminal activity as well as subsequent decisions to continue one's involvement or to desist. As Figure 1.1 shows, involvement decisions are influenced by a wide range of factors and information. In contrast, *event decisions* typically are made quickly, utilizing more particularlistic information about immediate circumstances. Thus, the decision to engage in crime is followed by a series of decisions that includes selecting a place to commit the crime and choosing a suitable target.

Of course, a good question at this point is whether this is really the way people conduct their everyday lives. Before you act, especially before you do something others may disapprove of, do you usually plan ahead, taking into account your past experiences, your "generalized needs," the rewards to be gained from the behavior, the chances of getting caught and punished, and so on? Sometimes you might, but we're willing to bet that typically you don't. Most rational choice theorists are careful to point out that much behavior is only partly rational, limited by inaccurate information as well as ingrained moral values and a host of other constraints. Nevertheless, their emphasis is on the rationality of criminal behavior: Most offenders engage in some planning of their crimes, know quite well what they are doing and that it is wrong, and yet do it anyway. An important implication of rational choice theory, then, is that the criminal justice system must make offending less rewarding by making apprehension and punishment more certain and severe (see, for example, Newman, 1983; but for a different view, see Beres & Griffith, 1988).[2] Also implicit in this theory is the idea that offenders *deserve* to be punished because they knowingly did wrong (see also Box 1.1 on pages 14–15).

Critics of rational choice theory (and economic models in general) think that this position overstates the extent to which individuals calculate the costs and benefits of deciding whether to commit a crime. Consider, for example, the research by criminologist Ray Paternoster (1989), who examined the effects of certainty and severity of punishment on decisions to commit specific delinquent acts in a longitudinal study of 1,250 high school students. He found that although the perceived certainty of punishment influences some offending decisions, the perceived severity of punishment has no significant impact on decisions to engage in delinquent acts. More important, though, is his finding that the social costs of offending, such as perceived peer or parental sanctions, carry greater weight in the delinquency decision-making process than the perceived certainty of formal legal punishment. He also reports that youths who decided

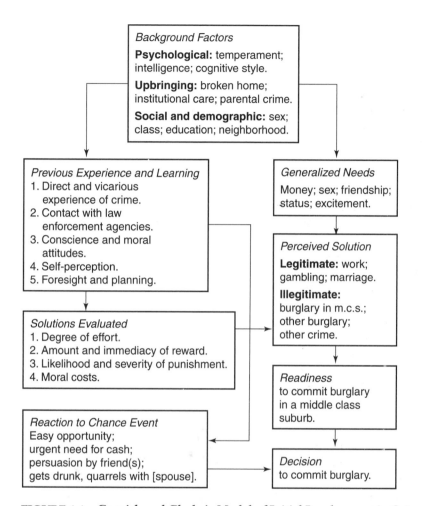

FIGURE 1.1   Cornish and Clarke's Model of Initial Involvement in Crime*

*Cornish and Clarke use burglary in a middle-class suburb to illustrate their model.

Source: D. Cornish and R. Clarke (eds.) (1986). *The Reasoning Criminal.* New York: Springer-Verlag, p. 3. Used with permission.

to desist from offending after previous involvement did so for reasons other than the perceived risk of punishment. Elsewhere, Paternoster (1987) presents an extensive review of deterrence research and concludes that there is little support for the proposition that fear of punishment inhibits people from engaging in crime (see also Bachman et al., 1992).

A related criticism is that rational choice theorists, like early classical thinkers, fail to recognize that one plausible solution to the crime problem may be a more equitable distribution of resources in society. For instance, they would indeed be correct in predicting that an unemployed inner-city youth will probably conclude that more can be

---

BOX **1.1**   **HOW THE WORLD SEES IT**
The Death Penalty

The death penalty, a punishment widely supported in the United States for crimes such as murder, has been abolished in most other industrialized countries in the world. At least thirty-five countries, including Australia, France, Denmark, and Sweden, abolished the death penalty for all crimes. In eighteen others (including Canada, Spain, and Great Britain), the death penalty has been abolished for all but a few unusual crimes, such as crime under military law and crimes committed in exceptional circumstances such as wartime. There are at least twenty-seven countries, including Greece and Ireland, where the death penalty for ordinary crimes remains on the books, but where the courts have been abolitionist in practice, not executing anyone in ten or more years. Of the 100 countries and territories that retain the death penalty for ordinary crimes such as murder and drug offenses, only three are economically developed, industrialized countries: the United States, Japan, and South Africa (Amnesty International, 1989/1999).

In countries and territories that continue to impose and carry out the death penalty, exceptions are usually made for certain groups of offenders. For example, most countries exempt children under the age of eighteen, although since 1970, at least four countries, including the United States, have executed juveniles. Most also exempt the elderly (people over age seventy) and the mentally retarded or incapacitated (although in 1986, a U.S. court allowed the execution of James Roach, a seventeen-year-old who was found at trial to be mentally retarded). Most countries exempt pregnant women and new mothers from execution, and women are sentenced to death less often than men. However, the United States has shown an increased willingness to execute women in recent years. Although the ratio of men to women living on death row in the United States is 70:1, more women than ever before are being sentenced to death, and the dominant attitude among the general public appears to be that an offender's sex should have no bearing on whether she or he is executed (Verhovek, 1998).

Supporters of the death penalty give three main reasons for retaining it. One reason is *incapacitation*; that is, the offender is put to death to ensure that she or he never repeats the crime. Certainly, the death penalty accomplishes incapacitation, but a flaw in the logic of this argument is that it assumes that *all* offenders so sentenced would repeat their crimes if they were allowed to live—a questionable assumption at best. A second reason offered in support of the death penalty is *deterrence*: The possibility of being executed and the spectacle of an execution dissuade others from committing crimes for which the penalty is death. There are several problems with this argument, too. For one thing, research indicates that few if any offenders consider the prospect of being put to death for their crimes prior to committing them; most carry out their crimes in the heat of passion, under the influence of drugs or alcohol, or under the assumption that they will not be caught. At the same time, there is no evidence that the death penalty reduces the crime rate in those countries that retain it, or that crime increases after abolition. In fact, studies show that certain types of homicides actually increase with the reinstatement of the death penalty and following media coverage of executions (Bailey, 1998; Cochran et al., 1994). These findings are explained by the *brutalization hypothesis*: "inhibitions against the use of lethal violence to solve problems created by 'unworthy' others are reduced by executions," so that the death penalty actually *incites* some types of homicide (Bailey, 1998, p. 712).

The final reason offered in support of the death penalty is *retribution*: The offender pays for the crime with his or her life. The crime is so terrible that justice demands that the offender be executed. This reason receives strong popular support, but this support is showing some signs of weakening in the United States as increasing evidence shows that the death penalty is sometimes imposed on innocent people or is used in discriminatory ways. For instance, the availability of DNA testing has identified a number of cases in which innocent people have been wrongly convicted and sentenced to death. In addition, those defendants sentenced to death are typically poor and Black and have received shoddy legal representation. Since 1973, eighty-seven death row inmates have been freed because of wrongful convictions or serious legal errors (Holmes, 2000; Kifner, 2000; U.S. Gen-

eral Accounting Office, 1990). In fact, one analysis of all death penalty convictions in the United States from 1973 to 1995 showed that 68 percent were plagued by legal errors serious enough to warrant reversals or retrials. Of those retried, 82 percent of the defendants received a lesser sentence and 7 percent were acquitted (Liebman et al., 2000). Nevertheless, about 66 percent of the general public in the United States still favors the death penalty and more than 3,600 people remain on death row in this country (Holmes, 2000; Rimer & Bonner, 2000).

gained from selling drugs than from working full time in a fast-food restaurant for the minimum wage. However, it does not logically follow that increasing the threat and severity of punishment would successfully deter such youth from crime when few, if any, reasonable alternatives are available.

We will return to these issues later. For now, though, it is important to note that the value of contemporary classicism is its depiction of the offender as a rational social actor rather than a passive receptor of internal or external forces over which he or she has little control. Such determinism is characteristic of the positivist school of criminology, to which we turn our attention now.

The Positivist School

The **positivist school** of criminology developed during the second half of the nineteenth century. As Vold and Bernard (1986) point out, advances in the physical and natural sciences played a direct role in the emergence of positivist criminology:

> Animal experimentation was becoming an accepted way of learning about humans in physiology, medicine, psychology, and psychiatry. Humans were beginning to appear to scientists merely as one type of creature, with no special links to divinity. Even more important, humans were beginning to be understood as creatures whose conduct was influenced, if not determined, by biological and cultural antecedents rather than as self-determining beings who were free to do what they wanted. (p. 36)

In short, the development of positivism initiated a scientific revolution in criminology.

There is some disagreement today over who founded positivist criminology. Many writers give the credit to Cesare Lombroso and his students Enrico Ferri and Raffaele Garofalo, whose work we will discuss in Chapter 2. Others claim that Franz Joseph Gall was the first "scientific criminologist," and still others claim the honor for Adolphe Quetelet, A. M. Guerry, and Willem Bonger (see, for example, Beirne, 1987;

Hagan, 1985; Savitz et al., 1977; Sylvester, 1982). We will discuss Gall's ideas in Chapter 2 and Bonger's theories in Chapter 6. Of more immediate concern, however, is not who said what first, but rather what positivist criminologists have to say in general.

Positivist criminologists focus on criminals, not on crimes as classical criminologists do. Their goal is to discover the underlying causes of criminal behavior. As we will learn in forthcoming chapters, the causes may be biological, psychological, social, or some combination of these. (The latter is referred to as *multiple factor causation*.) Consequently, positivists reject the classical doctrine of human behavior in general, and criminal behavior in particular, as the end products of individuals' rational exercise of their free will. Instead, they see behavior as more or less determined by factors within the individual or in his or her external environment. Indeed, a hallmark of positivism is the assumption of *determinism*.

In undertaking the search for the causes of criminality, positivists have adopted the techniques of the physical and natural scientists—the *scientific method*. They denounced the classical school as "armchair criminology." For them, the study of crime must be framed in terms of a set of causal propositions that can be operationalized as empirically testable variables. Ferri's comparison of the positivist and classical schools is enlightening on this point:

> We speak two different languages. . . . For them [the classicists], the facts should give place to syllogisms; for us [positivists] the fact governs and no reasoning can occur without starting with facts. For them science needs only paper, pen and ink and the rest comes from a brain stuffed with more or less abundant reading of books made with the same ingredients. For us science requires spending a long time in examining the facts one by one, evaluating them, reducing them to a common denominator, extracting the central idea from them. For them a syllogism or an anecdote suffices to demolish a myriad of facts gathered by years of observation and analysis; for us the reverse is true. (quoted in Taylor et al., 1973, pp. 21–22)

As our discussion at the outset of this chapter indicates, the demand for scientific or empirical analysis remains a fundamental component of contemporary criminology. There is, as John Hagan puts it, "an enduring commitment to measurement" (1985, p. 78).

The assumption that human behavior is both determined and measurable has important implications with regard to the appropriate responses or solutions to the crime problem. More specifically, if crime is not the result of a rational decision freely made by the offender, but rather is produced by forces that, to some extent at least, are beyond the offender's control, then punishment will be ineffective at best. Positivists maintain that instead of being punished, offenders should undergo *treatment* with the goal of *rehabilitation*. Since their behavior can be measured, experts can assess their initial condition and conduct ongoing evaluations of their progress as treatment proceeds. Not surprisingly, positivist criminologists opposed the policy of standardized fixed sentences advocated by the classical school. They called for more flexible correctional strategies such as *indeterminant sentencing*, in which an offender is institutionalized for the period of time necessary to effect his or her rehabilitation. This, in turn, is depending on the offender's condition on admission, personality, and other individual factors.

The differences between the positivist and classical schools of criminology are clear. There is one area, however, in which these two paradigms are alike: their views of the law. You will recall that classicists conceptualize law in terms of a social contract; laws are essentially agreements among the members of a society that they will not physically harm one another or usurp each other's property in the pursuit of personal pleasure or gain. Law, in other words, represents the collective interests of the society. Similarly, positivists conceptualize law as the embodiment of a set of values and norms shared or agreed on by a majority of the members of a society. This approach is known as the *consensual model* of law; law is the codification of societal consensus. Crime is a violation of this consensus. In committing a crime, therefore, an offender transgresses not only against an individual victim, but also against the whole society.

Taylor, Walton, and Young (1973) nicely characterized the difficulty that confronts positivists because of their consensual view of crime and law: They call it "the problem of multiple realities." What they mean is that there typically are a number of different ways of looking at or defining a situation, including what may be considered criminal. As an example, they quote political activist Angela Davis, who has said that "The real criminals in this society are not all the people who populate the prisons across the state, but those people who have stolen the wealth of the world from the people." Positivists cannot account for such diversity in definition except to label it deviant. But while it is true that in any society certain definitions and ideas dominate the culture, we need to consider the role that power plays in legitimating and institutionalizing those dominant definitions of behavior. As we will find labeling theorists doing in Chapter 5, it is perhaps best not to ask why a person is deviant, but rather to ask from what does the person deviate and by whom is he or she considered deviant? Because of their consensual view of crime and law, positivists tend to overlook the issue of power.

Others have critiqued the positivist school for its tendency to rely on official statistics to study crime and criminals. Since most of the theories we examine in this text are more or less positivist, we will postpone a detailed analysis of specific criticisms until we assess individual theoretical perspectives derived from this model. Instead, at this point we will refocus the discussion onto a third paradigm for which the issues of power and inequality are central. This is the Marxist or radical paradigm.

The Marxist Paradigm

It is difficult to sketch out the **Marxist paradigm** in criminology because *Karl Marx* (1818–1883), after whom it is named, never made law or crime primary topics in his theorizing. Consequently, one must piece together Marx's ideas about crime and law from his mention of them in sections of many different works. Sometimes his discussion is extensive enough to make his point clear, but more often he simply alludes to these phenomena and it is left to the reader to discern his meaning. To complicate the matter further, scholars frequently treat his references to law and crime that are scattered among his various works as additive, "as if their central concerns were the same," when in fact Marx wrote differently about law and crime at different times in his career and depending on what it was more specifically that he was analyzing (Cain, 1982). Not surprisingly, this has led to considerable debate among criminologists about what Marx "really said" and, as we will see in Chapters 6 and 7, it has given rise to a number of criminological theories that all claim to be Marxist.

What did Marx have to say about crime and law? To outline his major propositions we will rely heavily on the analysis of Maureen Cain, who, with Alan Hunt (1979), has completed one of the most thorough surveys of Marx's writings on law and crime. However, to understand Marx's conceptions of crime and law, one also must understand his general theory of social organization and production, particularly in capitalist societies, because the two are inseparable.

An Overview of Marx's Social Theory.   In developing his theory of social organization and behavior, Marx begins with the materialist premise that the most basic human activity is laboring to meet one's survival needs or, as we would say today, "making a living." To do this, humans enter into a relationship with nature; they transform nature to meet their needs for food, shelter, and so on. The specific ways that they carry out this transformation or *production process* depend to a large extent on such factors as the resources available in their environment, the tools and technology they have developed, and their current knowledge and skills—factors that together Marx referred to as the *means of production*. Thus, in any society in any given historical period, one system of production necessarily will be most widely used. Marx called the dominant system of production in a society the *mode of production*; we typically call it the *economy*.

People do not make their living in isolation, but rather in association with other people. In other words, the production process is not just physical or material, it is also social. "The relations [people] establish with nature through their labor are reflected in their social relationships" (Coser, 1977, p. 55). Marx called these social relationships the *relations of production* or property relations. According to Marx, throughout history, in all societies except the earliest least technologically developed ones, the relations of production have been fundamentally social class relations. A *social class* is a group of people who hold the same position in the production process. For example:

> In the society of ancient Greece and Rome, the economy was organized around slavery; hence the basic classes were those whose living came from owning slaves (the patricians or citizens), the slaves themselves, and those who were neither slaves nor slave holders (the plebians or freemen). In the feudal society of the Middle Ages the basis of the economy was the manor; the main class was the nobility, who owned the land and the services of the peasants attached to it, and the serfs or peasants, who provided the agricultural labor. In modern or bourgeois [capitalist] society the economy is organized around industrial production and commercial exchange; and the main classes comprise the capitalists, who own the factories, the banks, and the goods to trade, and the proletarians, who own nothing but their own labor power. (Collins & Makowsky, 1989, p. 36)

A society organized into social classes is inherently unequal; different groups of people have differential access to societal resources and rewards, both material and social. Marx was especially interested in how membership in a social class shapes a group's experiences and behavior. He believed that a person's place on the social class hierarchy—from wealthy to poor—will cause that person to develop specific interests. Members of a particular social class will act according to these interests; that is, their ideas and behavior will reflect their relative class position.

Those at the top of the hierarchy will act to preserve the privileges they have acquired largely through their exploitation of those at the bottom. But the dominance of the rich does not go unchallenged: Those at the bottom of the hierarchy, the proletariat or working class, are engaged in an antagonistic struggle with the capitalist class to overcome their exploitation and oppression. However, Marx did not think of social classes as monolithic; he also identified divisions within classes and recognized that the members of a social class, particularly within the capitalist class, may compete against one another.

Marx frequently has been accused of *economic determinism* or *reductionism*—of seeing all elements and institutions of society (what he called the *superstructure*) as being simply a reflection of the economy. If this was the case, then "all knowledge of the superstructure can be 'reduced' to, or derived from, or read off from, the base [the economy]" (Cain & Hunt, 1979, p. 49). What this charge ignores, however, is Marx's emphasis on the *dialectic* nature of social organization: People are born into a set of social and environmental conditions that to some extent constrain them, but they can react to, act back on, and change these conditions as well. Marx himself responded to this criticism:

> The political, legal, philosophical, literary, and artistic development rests on the economic. But they all react upon one another and upon the economic base. It is not the case that the economic situation is the *sole active cause* and that everything else is merely a passive effect. There is, rather, a reciprocity within a field of economic necessity which *in the last instance* always asserts itself. (Marx & Engels, 1962, p. 304)

Elsewhere he wrote:

> According to the materialist conception of history, the *ultimately* determinant element in history is the production and reproduction of real life. . . . Hence if somebody twists this into saying that the economic element is the *only* determining one, he transforms that proposition into a meaningless, abstract, and senseless phrase. The economic situation is the basis, but the various elements of the superstructure . . . also exercise their influence upon the course of the historical struggle and in many cases preponderate in determining their *form*. (Marx & Engels, 1962, p. 488, author's emphasis)

Keeping these quotes in mind, let's examine Marx's writing on law and crime.

Marx on Law. As we have already noted, it is perhaps inappropriate to refer to *the* Marxist paradigm in criminology, since Marx's work contains no fully developed direct theorizing on law and crime. There is, in a sense then, only the *potential* for a criminological paradigm. Still, as Cain and Hunt (1979) point out, Marx's writings on these subjects are considerable even if they are scattered.

Whereas the focus of the classical school is on social control and punishment and that of the positivist school is on the causes of criminality, the focus of the Marxist paradigm is on law. However, Marx never explicitly defined law. He, along with his friend and collaborator *Frederick Engels*, "build their argument on the common sense view that we all know what law means" (Cain, 1982, p. 65). Instead, the concern is with how law is created and how it operates.

In light of Marx's broader theory of society, it is hardly surprising that he examines laws and the legal system in the context of the particular mode of production in which they have developed. "Legal relations," he tells us, "as well as form of state are to be grasped neither from themselves nor the so-called development of the human mind, but rather have their roots in the material conditions of life" (Marx & Engels, 1962, p. 362). Given the class character of the capitalist mode of production, the law and the legal system in such a society will reflect an inherent inequality. In fact, law and the legal system will preserve this inequality in that they function to preserve the capitalist system as a whole. Thus, one of the roles of law under capitalism is legitimation. In legitimating capitalism, law simultaneously serves to mystify the true class character of the social structure.

> The most persistent theme that emerges is that the state, as an apparatus under the general domination of the economically dominant class, gives the class interests which it protects and advances the form of the "general" or "universal will." Law is central to this process; its mode of operation is specifically characterized by its universal form. Legal rights and duties are not attached to classes or statuses, rather they pertain to "the citizen," devoid of rank and title, all formally equal. The law protects the property of all, and in so doing . . . obliterates or obscures the real relations between social classes. (Cain & Hunt, 1979, pp. 147–148)

We must be careful not to conclude from all this, as some contemporary theorists have (see Chapter 6), that law is simply a tool or an instrument of a united and malevolent ruling class. We have already noted that divisions within the capitalist class itself may compete with one another. At the same time, there are numerous instances of law creation that benefit the working class as much as, and sometimes more than, the capitalist class. Consequently, it appears that what Marx was arguing is that rather than directly serving the immediate interests of one class, the primary purpose of law and the legal system is to preserve the relations of capitalism in the long run. "Thus, on any particular issue, including the enactment and enforcement of criminal laws, the actions of the state may serve other interests besides those of the capitalist class" (Vold & Bernard, 1986, p. 311). The capitalist class retains its dominant position, however, and because of its greater economic and political power relative to other classes, it does have the ability to get its interests disproportionately represented in law and protected by law enforcement.

Marx on Crime.   Similar to their perspective on law, Marx and Engels see crime as self-evident; the process of defining crime is unproblematic for them. Quite simply, there are certain behaviors that are inherently "criminal." We must await the work of contemporary Marxist theorists for a critique of the concept of crime itself (see Chapters 6 and 7).

There are at least three ways that Marx (and Engels) viewed crime. The first can be found in their discussions of the *lumpenproletariat.* Who is the lumpenproletariat?

> The "dangerous class," the social scum, the passively rotting mass thrown off by the lowest layers of the old society, [it] may, here and there, be swept into the movement by a proletarian revolution, its conditions of life, however, prepare it more for the part of a bribed tool of reactionary intrigue. (Marx & Engels, 1948, p. 20)

The lumpenproletariat is made up of thieves, extortionists, beggars, prostitutes, and others who live by illegitimate means. It is, in short, a criminal class.

Marx and Engels warn the working class not to trust the lumpenproletariat and not to count on its support in the struggle against the capitalists. Indeed, they see the lumpenproletariat as an enemy of the workers. Although some analysts have dismissed this as Victorian moralizing, Paul Hirst (1975) cites two compelling reasons for this harsh position:

> First, as a parasitic class, living off productive labor by theft, extortion and beggary, or by providing "services" such as prostitution and gambling [the lumpenproletariat's], class interests are diametrically opposed to those of the workers. They make their living by picking up the crumbs of capitalist relations of exchange . . . Secondly, they are open to the bribes and blandishments of the reactionary elements of the ruling classes and the State; they can be recruited as police informers and the armed elements of reactionary bands and "special" State forces. . . . Marx and Engels's strong language and their strong opposition to the criminal classes and the demi-monde, far from expressing an idiosyncratic moralism, stems from a definite theoretical-political point of departure. (pp. 216–217)

Marx and Engels's two other views of crime are also politically based. One of these is referred to as the "*primitive rebellion thesis.*" This is the position that some crime is a form of revolt, either individual or collective, against the ruling class and the capitalist system. This argument is presented most explicitly in Marx and Engels's *The German Ideology* (1845–46) and Engels's *The Condition of the Working Class in England* (1945). However, as we will learn in Chapter 6, most Marxist theorists today reject this position.

Marx and Engels's third view of crime is more widely accepted. It sees crime as a result of the *demoralization* produced by living as one of the "have-nots" in the capitalist system. "The conditions of labor, recreation and family life spawned by industrial capitalism lead to the brutalization and degradation of life; the advance of crime is a direct index of this process" (Cain & Hunt, 1979, p. 149). For example, a central

feature of capitalism is competition. A mark of success is having more material posses-
sions than others. This, Marx and Engels maintain, fosters crime, especially theft.

Unlike the classical school, then, which placed responsibility for crime on the
individual, the Marxist paradigm sees some criminal behavior at least as a rational
response to dehumanizing conditions. Marx and Engels rejected the deterrence doctrine of the classical school and posited instead that the only effective means to eliminate crime is to change the social system. "The emphasis on the relation between
crime and class society is underlined by their view that in the classless society of the
future, crime will disappear with the creation of fully social conditions" (Cain & Hunt,
1979, p. 149). Although, as Box 1.2 indicates, the relationship between the economy
and the crime rate is hotly debated today, we will see later in the text that a number of
recent studies have found a strong correlation between the level of inequality in a society and the rate of certain types of crimes (see Chapters 6 and 7).

BOX **1.2**   **CONTROVERSY AND DEBATE**
Do Changes in the Economy Affect the Crime Rate?

At the close of the twentieth century, the U.S.
economy was booming. The inflation rate (the
rate of increase in the cost of goods and services
as well as production expenses) was low: 3 percent in 1998 compared to 6 percent in 1990.
Moreover, the unemployment rate (the percentage of the civilian labor force over the age of 16
that is out of work but actively looking for a job)
was the lowest it had been since 1970: 4.1 percent in 1998 compared to 10.6 percent in 1982
and 7.4 percent in 1992 (U.S. Department of
Commerce, Bureau of the Census, 1998). In
some areas of the United States, the unemployment rate was below 2 percent.

One group experiencing a sharp increase
in employment since the early 1990s is young
men between the ages of 16 and 24, a group that
accounts for a high percentage of crime as well.
Young men in this age group who were not still
in school or were not in prison had a 6 percent
gain in employment from 1992 to 1998, from
74 percent to 80 percent. Even more dramatic
were the employment gains of young, African

American men: Between 1992 and 1998, Black
men aged 16 to 24 who were not in school or in
prison had a 12 percent increase in employment,
from 52 percent to 64 percent (Fagan &
Freeman, 1999). For criminologists interested
in the relationship between the economy and
crime, these circumstances offer a good opportunity to test the hypothesis that the crime rate
is affected by economic conditions. If, for example, unemployment and the poverty it causes
motivate young men to commit crimes as Marxist criminologists propose, then we would expect
the crime rate to decline during periods of economic prosperity when these men have less difficulty finding jobs.

There is research that supports this
hypothesis. For instance, Jeffrey Fagan and
Richard Freeman (1999) analyzed data for 332
U.S. metropolitan areas, comparing places
where the unemployment rate had dropped by 5
percent or more from 1992 to 1997 with areas
where it had remained higher than 7 percent
during this period. Their findings showed that

although the crime rate had declined in most areas they studied, it was in areas with the strongest job growth that the crime rate had fallen the most. According to Fagan and Freeman, in these areas, even if they had less than a high school education and a prison record, young men—particularly young Black men—were more likely to find work at the end of the 1990s than they were at the start of the 1990s. Moreover, the jobs they obtained, although still low-skilled, paid higher wages. Not surprisingly, say Freeman and Rodgers, we see a corresponding drop in crimes committed by these young men.

Although the data offer support for the Marxist paradigm, they raise several concerns, regardless of one's theoretical perspective. First, observers point out that despite the drop in unemployment and crime, young men aged 16 to 24 are still more likely than older men to be unemployed or in prison and, when race is taken into account, we find that most of those who are unemployed or in prison are young men of color. Racism interacts with economic factors to produce specific outcomes, whether they are job opportunities or criminal convictions (see Chapter 6). There are more people in prison in the United States today than ever before. The healthy economy appears to be unsuccessful in reducing incarceration even if it does help lower crime. Second, what do these data tell us about the future? It appears that as long as the economy is strong and labor markets tight, we will enjoy a safer society, but should the economy sour and unemployment rates rise we can expect crime to go up as well, perhaps even more dramatically than in the past since those who have moved from the margins of society toward the center will likely be hardest hit and have fewer safety nets thanks to welfare "reform." These are concerns that both criminologists and politicians need to consider as they develop research and policy for the twenty-first century.

Summary and Conclusion

Table 1.1 on page 24 summarizes each of the three paradigms presented in this chapter. As we have noted repeatedly, a large number of diverse theories have developed out of these schools of thought, particularly the positivist and Marxist schools.

Most criminologists today identify more or less with one of these three schools of thought, although not all who call themselves neo-classicists, positivists, or Marxists necessarily agree with others who share the same self-label. Our goal in this chapter has not been to depict criminologists as working in distinct, nonoverlapping theoretical camps, but rather simply to present the core organizing principles of the major criminological paradigms. Now you can undertake your examination of specific theories with an understanding of the assumptions that underlie each one. In addition, we have provided two criteria—scope and accuracy—that you may use to assess the superiority of these theories relative to one another.

Let's begin our examination of individual theories, then, by turning first to the biological, physiological, and biosocial theories of crime, which are framed squarely in the positivist tradition.

TABLE 1.1   Summary of Three Criminological Paradigms

	Classical	Positivist	Marxist
Developed by:	Cesare Beccaria Jeremy Bentham	Franz Joseph Gall Cesare Lombroso Enrico Ferri Raffaele Garofalo Adolphe Quetelet A. M. Guerry	Karl Marx Frederick Engels
Assumptions about human nature:	Human beings are rational hedonists; they seek out the greatest pleasure at the least cost to themselves.	Human behavior is more or less determined by internal factors or external environmental factors. Human behavior is measurable/quantifiable.	Humans are natural workers. The most basic human activity is laboring to meet one's survival needs. While humans are born into particular circumstances that shape their behavior, they are capable of acting back on and reshaping these conditions.
Focus:	criminal acts	criminals	law

Core concepts:	punishment
	deterrence
	social control
		scientific method
		indeterminate
		  sentencing
		rehabilitation
			means of production
			relations of
			  production
			mode of production/
			  economy
			social class
			dialectic

Major themes:	Laws are the embodiment of the social contract and also serve to prevent crime if they have the full support of the members of society. The criminal justice system determines guilt and imposes punishments that are swift, sure, and proportionate.	Crime is not a product of free will, but rather is determined by factors within the individual or by factors in his or her environment. Because behavior is determined, punishment is ineffective at best. Consequently, the criminal justice system should treat offenders to rehabilitate them.	Laws and the legal system in an inherently unequal society reflect that inequality and function to preserve it. Some crime in capitalist societies is a rational response to the dehumanizing conditions of these societies. The only effective means to eliminate crime is to bring about a classless society.

KEY TERMS

accuracy of a theory—the extent to which a theory matches or is supported by empirical reality.

classical school—a paradigm in criminology that focuses on crime and criminal justice rather than the criminal. Classicists assume that human beings have free will and, therefore, are responsible for their behavior, including crime. They support the use of punishment, but maintain that to be effective, punishment must be swift, certain, and proportionate to the crime.

Marxist/radical school—a paradigm that sees law as well as crime reflecting the mode of production of a society. Consequently, capitalist societies will have a legal system that is inherently unequal, and much crime in such societies will be a result of this inequality.

neo-classical school—a revision of the tenets of the classical school in that neo-classicists emphasized the importance of considering mitigating factors, including individual characteristics of the offender, in determining criminal responsibility and arriving at a just punishment.

paradigm—a school of thought within a discipline that provides the scientist with a model for choosing the problems to be analyzed, the methods for analyzing them, and the theoretical framework for explaining them.

positivist school—a paradigm that focuses on criminals rather than crime. Positivists seek to discover the causes of crime, which may be biological, psychological, and/or social. Given their determinist stance, they emphasize treatment of offenders rather than punishment.

scope of a theory—its pervasiveness or how much it can explain.

theory—a set of interconnected statements or propositions that explain how two or more events or factors are related to one another.

SUGGESTED READINGS

Beirne, P. (1993). *Inventing criminology: Essays on the rise of* homo criminalis. Albany: State University of New York Press. Not an easy read, but certainly a careful and insightful analysis of the origins of the discipline.

Cain, M., & Hunt, A. (1979). *Marx and Engels on law*. London: Academic Press. Still one of the best analyses of Marx's and Engels's theorizing on crime, criminality, and law.

Foucault, M. (1979). *Discipline and punish: The birth of the prison*. New York: Vintage. An acclaimed historical study of punishment that provides a chilling glimpse at how the criminal justice system functioned at the time Beccaria developed his critique.

NOTES

1. For a critical assessment of Beccaria and this treatise, see Newman and Marongiu, 1990. Interestingly, in his analysis of *On crimes and punishments*, Beirne (1991, 1993) questions the very existence of a distinctive school of classical criminology.
2. One popular manifestation of this "get tough" philosophy is the enactment of "three strikes and you're out" laws, which impose lengthy mandatory sentences—in some cases, life sentences for repeat offenders who commit serious crimes. For a review of different types of "three strikes" laws across 24 states as well as a discussion of their effects, see Clark et al., 1997. For an empirical evaluation of the effect of California's three strikes law on the crime rate in that state, see Beres and Griffith, 1998. And for an analysis of the costs of three strikes laws and the potential for abuses, see Greenwood et al., 1994.

2 The Born Criminal: Biological and Physiological Theories of Crime

Everyone probably has heard the old sayings, "Appearances are deceiving", and "You can't judge a book by its cover." Yet it is also a fact of everyday life that we often judge others, at least initially, by how they look. We may try to strike up a conversation with someone because we find him or her attractive. Or we may deliberately avoid another person because he or she is physically unappealing to us. We may hear someone described as "shifty looking," or when the photograph of a suspected thief is flashed on our television screens, we may say he or she "looks like a crook." Most defense attorneys even coach their clients on how they should dress and groom themselves for court so jurors will get the impression they are not the "type" of person who would commit a crime (Crist, 1997). In short, we frequently make inferences about another person's *character* based on his or her *appearance*.

This is nothing new. In fact, the notion that an individual's character could be read from a physical examination dates back to the ancient Greeks and Romans. Known as *physiognomy,* practitioners of this "science" studied faces, skulls, and other physical features that they believed revealed a person's natural disposition. For example, physiognomists warned against trusting beardless men and bearded women, and individuals with "the peculiar dark and pallid complexion" were judged to be naturally violent and envious. In the Medieval period there was even a law that specified that if two people were suspected of having committed the same crime, the uglier one should be regarded as more likely the guilty party (Ellis, 1915).

By the middle of the eighteenth century, however, physiognomy had fallen into disrepute—so much so that a British statute "made all persons pretending to have skill in physiognomy liable to be whipped as rogues and vagabonds" (Mannheim, 1965, p. 213). Nevertheless, the idea that physical structure determines personality and behavior died hard—if, indeed, it ever did die out completely—particularly among those interested in understanding the causes of crime.

In this chapter we examine a variety of theories that explain crime, at least in part, in biological or physiological terms. We begin with a discussion of physical type theories and then review a number of other theories that focus on biological or physiological factors: heredity, chromosomal abnormalities, hormones, brain disorders, and diet or nutrition.

Many of the early theories of this genre were based on obviously flawed research and may appear somewhat silly from the vantage point of hindsight. However, while contemporary biological and physiological theories are being tested with greater methodological sophistication and most now take into account the important role environment plays in shaping our behavior, they rest on many of the same assumptions that underlie the earlier theories. They also raise serious concerns with respect to legal policy and crime control programs.

Physical Type Theories

Phrenology: Grandparent of the Physical Type Perspective

Savitz, Turner, and Dickman (1977) have singled out phrenology as the starting point for the scientific study of crime. **Phrenology**, a term coined by Thomas I. Forster in the nineteenth century, has been defined rather amorphously as "the science of the mind." A more precise definition can be derived from one of phrenology's major propositions: that the development and shape of the brain affects personality and social behavior. As Savitz and his colleagues (1977) point out, unlike the armchair theorizing of the classicists, phrenologists developed their theoretical propositions through scientific experimentation in anatomy and physiology using the scientific rules and procedures that were the standard at that time.

Franz Joseph Gall (1758–1828) is considered the founder of phrenology. Gall, a physician, is credited with the discovery that the various functions of the brain are localized. In other words, specific areas of the brain control particular types of behavior and personality traits. In addition, Gall theorized that the more important the brain area (which he also called an "organ" or "faculty" of the brain), the greater its size. One could study the brain through surgery and dissection, of course, but short of that one could examine and measure the cranium or skull. According to Gall, the skull formed a perfect cover over the cranial cortex. Therefore, any organ that was dominant in an individual would grow to produce "protuberances"—that is, bumps—on the skull that could easily be felt by a skilled phrenologist.

Gall identified twenty-six distinct faculties or organs. (Some later phrenologists listed as many as thirty-five.) These, in turn, were found in three major regions or compartments of the brain. There were the intellectual faculties, the moral faculties, and the lower, base or animal faculties. Not surprisingly, it was this last group, which included such traits as destructiveness and secretiveness, that were thought to be overdeveloped in criminals. The faculty of destructiveness, for instance, which was localized in the area of the brain found slightly over the ear, was linked to violent behavior, such as homicide.[1]

Although Gall perceived crime as having biological causes, he was fairly optimistic about the possibility of preventing or inhibiting criminal behavior. According to Gall, an individual's higher moral and intellectual faculties could be developed and strengthened through careful training and exposure to a good social environment so that they would control or suppress the lower, criminal faculties. Consequently, Gall and other phrenologists supported punishments designed to rehabilitate criminals and generally opposed the death penalty and the practice of exiling prisoners, both of which they saw as serving no useful purpose, not even deterrence (Fink, 1938; Savitz et al., 1977).

Phrenology enjoyed considerable popularity in Europe, England, Australia, and especially in America, from about 1807 to 1845. Among those credited with having won phrenology a sizeable following were *Johann Gaspar Spurzheim* (1776–1873), a student of Gall and, for a time, his friend and collaborator; *Charles Combe* (1788–1858), who wrote the first book on phrenology printed in England; and *Charles Caldwell* (1772–1853), who wrote the first American textbook on phrenology, *Elements of Phrenology*, which was published in 1824. Caldwell is also notable for his study of twenty-nine women who had been convicted of infanticide. Among them he claimed to have found twenty-seven in whom the faculty of philoprogenitiveness (love of offspring) was poorly developed—an idea to which we will return in our discussion of another biological/physiological theorist, Cesare Lombroso.

The scientific decline of phrenology is said to have begun in the 1840s. It lost support in the academic community for several reasons, including personality and political conflicts among various scientists and the opposition of a number of religious groups who viewed as morally dangerous the assertion that the brain, rather than the heart, is the center of reason. In addition, in the 1830s, empirical phrenological studies began to decrease, and eventually the scientists were displaced by charlatans who practiced a popularized version of phrenology in which they "read" heads much the same way other fortune tellers read palms (Savitz et al., 1977).

Savitz and his colleagues (1977) claim that phrenology did not fall into disfavor because empirical data disproved it. Certainly many criminologists would dispute them on this, but, for whatever reason, phrenology came to be regarded as "unscientific" by some and as an embarrassment by others. Instead, the work of Cesare Lombroso, dubbed the "founder of criminal anthropology," captured the attention of the academic community.

Atavism

In his biographical essay on *Cesare Lombroso* (1835–1909), Marvin Wolfgang (1973) remarked that:

> More has been written by and about Lombroso than any other criminologist . . . The depth and breadth of his investigations permit a post–Lombrosian contemporary approach to the etiology of crime to proceed in Europe without suffering from a unilateral perspective. On the other hand, his emphasis on certain biological traits of

criminal identification has provided sufficient fuel for continuous attacks from many critics who no longer take the time to read his works. (p. 232)

What in this man's work is so provocative?

Lombroso was an Italian physician who, early in his career, developed a keen interest in psychology, psychiatry, and the anatomy of the brain. Like Gall, he emphasized the importance of studying human behavior through scientific means and he rejected the philosophizing of the classical school. In fact, as we noted in Chapter 1, it is Lombroso who is usually identified as the founder of positivism.

Lombroso's central thesis was that the criminal was a biological degenerate, a "throwback" to an earlier evolutionary stage, more ape-like than human. He called this degeneracy **atavism**. Atavism manifested itself, according to Lombroso, in certain physical characteristics that he called **stigmata**. The stigmata did not cause criminality; atavism did. But the stigmata were useful for identifying atavists, or "born criminals" as Lombroso's colleague and son-in-law, *Enrico Ferri*, called them.

Lombroso presented a long list of stigmata that included: "ears of unusual size, or occasionally very small, or standing out from the head as do those of the chimpanzee"; fleshy, swollen and protruding lips; receding or protruding chin; premature and abundant wrinkling of the skin; an inability to blush; "anomalies of the hair, marked by characteristics of the hair of the opposite sex"; supernumerary fingers, toes, or nipples; ambidexterity, or "greater strength in the left limbs"; insensitivity to pain; and tattooing including, in men, tattooing of the penis (Becker, 1994; Gould, 1981; Wolfgang, 1973). The tattoos were significant to Lombroso not only because of the excessive number atavists typically had, but also because of the obscene nature of their depictions and messages. To Lombroso, the tattoos stood as evidence of both insensitivity to physical pain and immorality (Becker, 1994).

After examining 383 Italian men convicted of various crimes, Lombroso reported that 21 percent had just one atavistic trait, but 43 percent had five or more. He concluded that the presence of five or more stigmata indicated atavism. Subsequently, Lombroso conducted numerous studies using his anthropometric methods, as well as historical and anecdotal data, to compare criminals with noncriminals.

Lombroso's first major presentation of these ideas was *L'Uomo delinquente (The Criminal Man)*, originally published in 1876. Gould (1981, pp. 132, 135) writes that "Lombroso's theory of atavism caused a great stir and aroused one of the most heated scientific debates of the nineteenth century. . . . Criminal anthropology was not just an academician's debate, however lively. It was *the* subject of discussion in legal and penal circles for years." On the positive side, his supporters saw him as a "scientific Columbus who opened up a new field for exploration." He was praised as a "great instigator of ideas in criminology, he created systems and conceived of ingenious and bold hypotheses" (quoted in Wolfgang, 1973, pp. 287–288).

At the same time, his critics were many and, for the most part, their opposition was well-founded. A number of scientists, especially in France, criticized Lombroso for ignoring social and economic causes of crime. As a result, in subsequent editions of *L'Uomo delinquente* and in another work, *Crime: Its Causes and Remedies* (1912). Lombroso explored the role of a wide range of social and economic factors, such as poverty, alcohol abuse, urbanization, population density, religion, and education. He expanded his criminal typology beyond atavists to include those who were criminals because of insanity and epilepsy; criminals of passion, which included political criminals; and "occasional criminals." This last criminal category consisted of three subtypes: (1) *pseudocriminals*—those who committed crimes involuntarily (such as in self-defense or to defend family honor); (2) *criminaloids*—those whose predisposition to crime is activated by particular environmental circumstances or opportunities; and (3) *habitual criminals*—those who become criminal because of poor education or weak parental training. Moreover, he revised his original estimate of the proportion of atavists among the criminal population from 65 to 100 percent to about 30 to 33 percent (Becker, 1994; Wolfgang, 1973).

Nevertheless, despite these revisions, Lombroso remained committed to his original thesis that criminal behavior has biological roots. As Gould points out:

> At first glance, this distinction of occasional from born criminals has the appearance of a compromise or retreat, but Lombroso used it in an opposite way—as a claim that rendered his system immune to disproof. . . . All criminal acts are covered: a man with stigmata performs them by innate nature; a man without stigmata by force of circumstances. By classifying exceptions within his system, Lombroso excluded all potential falsification. (1981, p. 132)

Eventually, Lombroso claimed that many social factors were really organic anyway (Becker, 1994; Wolfgang, 1973).

However, the most damaging criticisms of Lombroso's work were methodological. To his credit, Lombroso did utilize control groups in most of his studies, but the representativeness of these groups was dubious. One comparison group, for example, was composed of Italian soldiers. To what extent are such men representative of the general "noncriminal" population? Lombroso utilized large samples, often reporting thousands of measurements, but sample size does not ensure representativeness.

A second methodological difficulty was his use of statistics. Even though rigorous statistical techniques were not yet available, Lombroso frequently drew unwarranted conclusions from the statistics he did have. For instance, in one comparison of 121 male criminals with 328 "upright" men, the data actually show no significant difference in the average cranial capacity of the two groups. What difference did exist could have been the result of the larger number of noncriminal men, since the more people you sample, the higher the probability of including extremes. Still, Lombroso claimed that the data clearly revealed that criminals have smaller brains than "normal" people. Often, when confronted with data that undeniably contradicted his theory, "he performed some mental gymnastics to incorporate it within his system" (Gould, 1981, p. 126).

It has been said that the demise of atavism came in 1913 when Charles Goring published *The English Convict*. Goring compared 3,000 English convicts with large groups of noncriminal (unconvicted) Englishmen. Utilizing more sophisticated statistical techniques, he found no significant differences between the two groups in terms of physical measurements or the presence of physical anomalies. (The exceptions were that the criminals tended to be shorter and to weigh less than the noncriminals.) He concluded that *"there is no such thing as a physical criminal type"* (p. 173, author's emphasis), and the rigorousness of his research quickly convinced other scientists.

Nevertheless, as we noted earlier, Lombroso's work had a significant impact, for better or for worse, not only on the academic community, but also on the legal community. Lombroso was often called to testify as an expert witness at criminal trials, and the presence of stigmata in defendants was not infrequently admitted as evidence. We will never "know how many men were condemned unjustly because they were extensively tattooed, failed to blush, or had unusually large jaws and arms" (Gould, 1981, p. 138). We do know that Lombroso and his followers, especially Enrico Ferri, lobbied successfully for a number of criminal justice reforms. One of the most notable of these was the indeterminate sentence. In addition, they supported the death penalty, in particular for born criminals since they were naturally evil and punishment of any other kind would therefore have been ineffective (Gould, 1981).

Typically, this is where most contemporary discussions of Lombroso end. However, there is one other aspect of his work that deserves our attention: his application of the theory of atavism to female criminals. Criminology historically has ignored female criminals or downplayed the importance or seriousness of their crimes. Lombroso was one of a handful of criminologists writing prior to the 1970s who gave any attention to the female offender. Let's see, then, what he had to say about this subject.

The Criminal Woman.   Lombroso observed that in official records, women had a far lower crime rate than men. On one hand, he felt that these official statistics were misleading. Women probably engaged in more criminal activity than the records showed and, if prostitution were included as an offense category, their crime rate would equal if not surpass that of men.

On the other hand, Lombroso used his theory of atavism to explain the criminal *and* noncriminal behavior of women. In *La donna delinquente (The Female Offender)*, published in 1893, he argued that women, as a group, are less evolved than men. This is evidenced by the presence of various "primitive" traits in women. For example, women, according to Lombroso, are naturally vengeful and jealous; their moral sensibilities are deficient; and they are less sensitive to pain than men. Ordinarily, these defects are neutralized by other feminine traits, such as passivity, physical weakness, low intelligence, and a maternal "instinct." However:

> when a morbid activity of the psychical centers intensifies the bad qualities of women, and induces them to seek relief in evil deeds; when piety and maternal sentiments are wanting, and in their place are strong passions and intensely erotic tendencies, much muscular strength and a superior intelligence for the conception and execution of evil, it is clear that the innocuous semi-criminal present in the normal woman must be transformed into a born criminal more terrible than any man. (Lombroso, 1893, p. 150)

In short, the normal woman is an atavist. The criminal woman is masculine, but masculinity is good only in men; it transforms women, as Lombroso put it, into "monsters." Consequently, in *Crime: Its Causes and Remedies*, Lombroso argued against giving women the same education and occupations as men since these only "give them the means and opportunity to commit crimes against the laws of the Press, and swindling" (1912, p. 54).

Since Lombroso's research on the female offender was conducted in much the same way as his studies of male offenders, it is subject to the same criticisms, which are unnecessary to repeat here. Lombroso's writings on the female offender are worth singling out, however, because later social scientists interested in female crime shared many of his assumptions about the physical and psychological nature of women. This is an issue to which we will return repeatedly throughout the text. For now, though, we will continue our discussion of physical type theories of criminality, bearing in mind that they are based on research that utilized male subjects almost exclusively.

Earnest A. Hooton: Lombroso Revisited

It has been argued that Lombroso's initial popularity, especially in the United States, was largely the result of "a chance association of the newly burgeoning Italian/anthropological/positivist school, with the simultaneous rise in the late nineteenth century of biological evolutionary thought, racism, and the science of physical anthropology" (Savitz et al., 1977, p. 41). Although Goring's work, along with the development of other criminological theories that we will be discussing in this book, did much to weaken academic support for the Lombrosian perspective, Lombroso's major proposition—that structure determines function—was never extinguished completely. It has periodically resurfaced in the twentieth century in a number of guises.

Perhaps the best example of twentieth century criminology cut from the Lombrosian mold is that of *Earnest A. Hooton*, a Harvard anthropologist. In two books—*Crime and the Man* (1939a) and *The American Criminal* (1939b)—Hooton presented the results of his twelve-year study of the relationship between physiology and criminality. The research involved more than 17,000 subjects from ten states who, Hooton claimed, represented the racial and ethnic diversity of the U.S. population. Almost 14,000 male prisoners were anthropometrically measured, along with 3,203 "civilians" who composed a control group.

According to Hooton (1939a, p. 252), his research indicated that "within every race it is the biologically inferior, the organically unadaptable, the mentally and physically stunted and warped, and the sociologically debased—who are responsible for the majority of crimes committed." He claimed that on nineteen out of thirty-three measurements there were significant differences between the criminals and the controls, and that for nearly all physical measures, the criminals were inferior to the controls. Criminals have "straighter hair, more mixed patterns of eye color, more of the various kinds of skin folds in the upper eyelid, lower and more sloping foreheads, more pointed chins, more extreme variations in the projection of cheek bones, ears with less roll of the rim, and a greater frequency of Darwin's tubercle—a cartilagenious module on the free margin of the ear" (1931a, p. 238). In addition, echoing Lombroso, Hooton pointed out that tattooing was more common among criminals than among civilians. He went on to argue that one could even distinguish between different types of criminals based on their physical characteristics. For instance, tall thin men, he claimed, tended to be murderers and robbers, whereas tall heavy men, besides killing, were also prone to forgery and fraud.

Hooton carried his biological argument to its logical conclusion in terms of public policy. In the last paragraph of *The American Criminal*, he wrote:

> Criminals are organically inferior. Crime is the resultant of the impact of environment upon low grade human organisms. It follows that the elimination of crime can be effected only by the extirpation of the physically, mentally, and morally unfit, or by their complete segregation in a socially aseptic environment. (1939b, p. 309)

The response to Hooton's work from the scientific community was mostly negative. At the center of the criticism were Hooton's statistical analyses and the inferences he drew from them. Perhaps the most systematic (and damning) critique of Hooton's research came from sociologist Robert Merton and anthropologist M. F. Ashley Montagu (1940). Merton and Montagu's first concern was with Hooton's samples. Hooton dismisses as "stupid" the objection to his work that incarcerated offenders are unrepresentative of the entire criminal population; they are simply those who have been caught. Although Merton and Montagu agreed that incarcerated offenders usually are the only criminal subjects available for study, they emphasized that researchers must take into account that certain groups—such as racial and ethnic minorities, the poor, those with little education—are disproportionately represented among the incarcerated at least in part because of selective arrests and sentences. "It is at least possible, then, that some of the apparent sociological and physical differentials between criminals and civilians would be eliminated, were allowances made for the selective elements in commitment" (Merton & Montagu, 1940, p. 386). Merton and Montagu were even more doubtful of the representativeness of Hooton's control groups. More than half of the controls were Tennessee fire fighters or members of the Massachusetts militia. Given that both of these groups have physical qualifications for membership, neither is likely to be representative of the general noncriminal population.

Merton and Montagu also objected to the racism and ethnocentrism that infuses Hooton's work. Hooton's publications are peppered with assertions about the biological inferiority and "retarded" culture of people living in "primitive" societies. Nowhere, however, does he provide empirical support for these claims. The empirical data, in fact, suggest just the opposite of Hooton's position—that people in pre-industrial societies are at least as perfectly adapted to their environments as modern industrial peoples are to theirs.

Hooton's judgment of inferiority is no less problematic with respect to the physical and biological traits he identifies. We have already listed some of the characteristics Hooton found to be more common among the incarcerated criminals than the civilians. But the question remains: What makes these traits inferior? Hooton's response is a classic example of a *tautology*—circular reasoning. A trait is considered inferior if it is more often found in the criminal sample than in the civilian sample. What makes people commit crimes? Their biological inferiority as evidenced by these traits. In other words, Hooton "use[d] criminality to discover the inferiority, then

•

turn[ed] around and use[d] the inferiority to explain or account for the criminality" (Vold & Bernard, 1986, p. 57).

To better evaluate Hooton's research, Merton and Montagu (1940) reanalyzed his data using a criterion independent of criminality to judge inferiority. They deemed as "primitive" or inferior any trait that is more apelike than human. Similarly, "advanced" characteristics were those furthest removed from the apes. The results of this re-examination are telling. "We conclude . . . that the aggregate characters which the criminals exhibit more frequently than the civilian group comprise a very high percentage of advanced characters, and significantly lower proportions of primitive and indifferent characters as compared with the civilians" (p. 400). Moreover, with regard to differences among offenders, they reported:

> Apparently one must be in the vanguard of evolutionary development to commit first degree murder and heavily weighted with primitive characters in order to execute second degree murder. Forgers and frauds must roost near the top of the "evolutionary scale," whereas rapists and assaulters must inhabit the lower regions. Yet, even the lowly rapists are more often characterized by the possession of advanced characters than civilians. Clearly on the basis of such findings . . . one cannot speak of the criminal as "organically inferior." (p. 398)

Elsewhere Hooton has been criticized for not looking into the offense histories of the criminal sample. At least half the men had previous convictions, but for crimes other than the ones for which they were imprisoned at the time of the study. Therefore, it was inappropriate to classify these offenders, as Hooton did, simply as "robbers" or "forgers," etc. More important, had Hooton controlled for the prisoners' records, "most of his type differences would have been compromised, if not dissipated entirely" (Vold & Bernard, 1986, p. 57).

These and other serious weaknesses in Hooton's work led many criminologists to reject it rather quickly. Nevertheless, some continued the search for the "criminal type."

Body Build and Crime

Similar to the idea that criminals can be identified by certain anatomical traits was the notion that criminals tend to have a particular physique or body build. Essentially the argument was that one's body build is related to one's personality or temperament.

One frequently cited promoter of this perspective was the German psychiatrist *Ernst Kretschmer*. Kretschmer delineated three body types: (1) the *leptosome* or *asthenic* type, who was tall and thin with long limbs, narrow shoulders, weak muscles, and tended to age prematurely; (2) the *athletic* type, who was the opposite of the first, well developed physically and very muscular; and (3) the *pyknic* type, described as small and round, friendly and sociable, with a tendency to put on weight easily. In addition, he named a special category, *dysplastic*, for individuals characterized by certain glandular disorders, but he noted that mixed physical types were common (Mannheim, 1965).

In his early research in the 1920s, Kretschmer wanted to determine if there was a relationship between physique and specific mental disorders. Using correlation techniques, he reported finding that leptosomes, athletics, and some dysplastics were prone to schizophrenia, while pyknics tended to be manic-depressives. Later, he applied his typology to a study of criminals. Overall, he reported, the criminal population appears to have the same frequency distribution of body types as the general population (although it cannot be determined how he arrived at this conclusion since he presents no specific comparisons with a noncriminal control group). In addition, he tells us that leptosomes begin and end their criminal activity at an early age, whereas athletics have a relatively stable pattern of criminality until age 55. Pyknics, because they are socially more adaptable, do not engage in crime until relatively late in life and recidivate less than the other types.

Finally, with regard to types of crimes, Kretschmer claimed that leptosomes tend to be thieves and swindlers, pyknics are prone to fraud, and athletics are heavily represented among violent offenders. It is among serious habitual criminals, however, that we find a high proportion of dysplastics. Thus, as one evaluator of Kretschmer's work noted, he does not "pretend to be able to predict whether an individual will become criminal [as Lombroso and others did], but only which forms his criminal activities are likely to assume *if* he should become one" (Mannheim, 1965, p. 239, author's emphasis).

The work of *William Sheldon* in the United States made less modest claims. Sheldon's theory, known as **somatotyping**, was somewhat more elaborate than Kretschmer's. He began with the proposition that the human body is made up of three components: (1) *endomorphy*—soft roundness; (2) *mesomorphy*—square masculinity and skeletal massiveness; and (3) *ectomorphy*—linearity and frailty.[2] Each of these components is found, more or less, in everyone, and a person's body can be typed by a trained observer using a seven-point scale Sheldon developed. A rating of seven indicates maximum presence of the component, whereas a one would mean that it was minimally present. A typed individual, therefore, received a three-digit score; for instance, an extreme endomorph would be scored 7-1-1. Sheldon recognized that different parts of the body might have different amounts of each component, so he divided the body into five regions: (1) head, face, and neck; (2) thoracic trunk; (3) shoulders, arms, and hands; (4) abdominal trunk; and (5) legs and feet. To get a somatotype rating for the entire body, he then averaged the regional scores.[3]

From here Sheldon made the quantum leap to *constitutional psychology*. As Sheldon (1949) states, "Constitutional [psychologists] interpret and explain an individual's personality against the frame of reference of his or her physical constitution. We find no break—no discontinuation—between what is physical and what is mental. We find no '*psyche*' and '*soma*', no mind-body problem; no conscious *versus* unconscious. We find only structure and behavior, which seem to make a functional continuum" (p. 4, author's emphasis). Consequently, Sheldon developed a corresponding temperament or personality type for each of his three body types. These are summarized in Table 2.1.

According to Sheldon, endomorphs typically are *viscerotonic*—they are relaxed and sociable; they love physical comfort, food, affection, approval, and the company of others. Mesomorphs are mainly *somatonic*—they are active, assertive, aggressive, and noisy; they lust for power and love to dominate others. In contrast, ectomorphs are most often *cerebrotonic*—they are private, restrained, inhibited and "hyperattentive."

TABLE 2.1   William Sheldon's Typology of Somatotypes

Body Build	Associated Temperament
endomorph: soft and round; a tendency to put on fat due to a well-developed digestive system; well nourished; floats easily in water	*viscerotonic:* relaxed in posture and movement; loves physical comfort; slow to react; loves eating; loves polite ceremony; seeks affection and approval; tolerant; complacent
mesomorph: massive strength and muscular development; "solid"; athletic; large heart and blood vessels; skin seems thick because of heavy reinforcement of underlying connective tissue; less buoyant, but good swimmers	*somatotonic:* assertiveness in posture and movement; loves physical adventure; energetic; needs and enjoys physical exercise; loves to dominate; lusts for power; loves risk and chance; boldly direct in manner; competitively aggressive; ruthless; callous; indifferent to pain
ectomorph: predominance of skin and appendages; little body mass and great surface area leading to greater sensory exposure to the outside world; flat and fragile body; lean	*cerebrotonic:* restrained in posture and movement; loves privacy; secretive; inhibited and sociophobic; chronically fatigued; hypersensitive to pain; quiet; agoraphobic

Source: Adapted from W. Sheldon. (1949). *Varieties of Delinquent Youth*, New York: Harper and Brothers, pp. 15–30.

Sheldon utilized this theory to explain criminality in his best-known work, *Varieties of Delinquent Youth* (1949). There he reports the findings of his research at the Hayden Goodwill Inn, a small private home for boys in Boston, Massachusetts. Over a ten-year period, Sheldon examined and somatotyped 200 youths who had resided at the Inn. Compared with a group of 4,000 male college students he had examined previously, these young men were high in mesomorphy and low in ectomorphy. There was no significant difference between the two groups on endomorphy; both were moderately endomorphic.

One may conclude from Sheldon's findings that there is a relationship between mesomorphy and crime, or at least juvenile delinquency. However, Sheldon drew more far-reaching inferences. After comparing the "delinquency scores" of his subjects with those of their parents, he concluded that the tendency to become criminal is hereditary—an idea that has been more or less popular up to the present time, as we shall see. As Sheldon put it, "Whatever else may be true of the delinquency I saw in Boston, it was mainly in the germ plasm" (Sheldon, 1949, p. 45).[4] This prompted him to argue fervently for "selective breeding" or *eugenics*. According to Sheldon:

> In the present situation, which is purely a human arrangement . . . reproduction has been made so easy and so safe that even the weakest and least gifted of the species can

spawn. The consequence is that those not only participate in but tend to monopolize the spawning business. . . . This is merely to say that bad reproduction drives out good. In consequence, under conditions soft and unregulated, our best stock tends to be outbred by stock that is inferior to it in every respect. (1949, p. 836)

He therefore urged governments to adopt stringent birth control programs that prevent the "bad stock" from reproducing and encourage the "good stock" to multiply. "It would not be difficult to find out who are the biologically best," Sheldon (1949, p. 879) writes. "If standardized photographic records of even a few hundred thousands [sic] of a well-sampled population were to be kept for so short a time as half a dozen generations, together with biographical summaries embracing the physiological, psychiatric, and social adventures of this sample population, it might be possible to define both medical delinquency and biological superiority in one operational frame of reference." But if we choose to continue to remain complacent about this problem, he warns, we are "scheduled for such inconveniences as social chaos, wars of increasing and crescendic violence, general frustration, and the confusion necessarily attendant upon the pathology of increasing urbanization and loss of zest in human life" (Sheldon, 1949, pp. 837–838).

It is ironic that in one of the passages we have quoted we see Sheldon calling for good sampling of the population, since one of the major criticisms of his work focused on his sample. Of the 200 youths he examined at the Inn, at least twenty-two had no known criminal record or had engaged in very minor violations. What, then, was Sheldon's definition of delinquency? As Sutherland (1951, p. 11) pointed out, "He defines delinquency as 'disappointingness' and the feelings of Dr. Sheldon are obviously the criterion of disappointment." Clearly, any measure or score of delinquency based on such a definition would be so subjective and unreliable as to be meaningless. Indeed, as Sutherland (1951, p. 11) noted, "No other investigator with Sheldon's data and instructions would be likely to make a close approximation to his scores and it is doubtful whether he could duplicate his own scores." As Merton and Montague did with Hooton's data, Sutherland undertook a reanalysis of Sheldon's data using a more objective measure of delinquency: the seriousness and consistency of the subjects' legal violations. He reported, "The general conclusion is that in this group of 200 youths the variations in civil delinquencies are not significantly related to variations in Sheldon's indexes of constitutional psychology" (1951, p. 13).

William Sheldon's theory and research were met with little enthusiasm in the academic community and, fortunately, they were largely ignored by public policymakers although, as we will see in Chapter 3, many states already had passed eugenics or "defective delinquency" laws. Still, some clinics and social agencies adopted the practice of somatotyping their clients (see Snodgrasse, 1951), and several criminologists continued to collect data on the body builds of their research subjects. Among the latter were *Sheldon* and *Eleanor Glueck*. In 1950, the Gluecks published *Unraveling Juvenile Delinquency*, a comparison on a number of different factors of 500 persistently delinquent adolescent boys with 500 nondelinquent adolescent boys. Included as an appendix was a detailed morphological study conducted for the Gluecks by a physical anthropologist named Carl C. Seltzer. Seltzer reported findings similar to those of

Sheldon that were discussed previously: Among the delinquents, there was a predominance of mesomorphs, but few ectomorphs or extreme endomorphs.

Subsequently, in 1956, the Gluecks published *Physique and Delinquency*, in which they explored further the body build variable not, they stated, "because of any belief in the preponderant criminogenic role of the bodily structure, but only as one of several studies to follow up the results of *Unraveling*" (quoted in Mannheim, 1965, p. 241). Here they report that 60 percent of the delinquents were mesomorphs compared with just 30.7 percent of the controls. They then correlated somatotype with sixty-seven personality traits and forty sociocultural factors for both the delinquents and the controls. As Mannheim (1965, p. 241) has noted, "The results are very complicated and not always revealing. Only a minority of the traits and factors they examined were found to vary in their relationships to different somatotypes."

The Gluecks did find that the mesomorphs tended to be insensitive, relatively uninhibited, and prone to express anger and frustration physically—factors that might make them more likely to commit violent offenses. The delinquent mesomorphs also typically came from homes that had "careless household routines" and lacked family recreational facilities and activities. However, unfavorable sociocultural conditions appeared to contribute less to the delinquency of mesomorphs than it did to the delinquency of the other two somatotypes. The Gluecks maintained that their data help to explain mesomorphs' greater susceptibility to delinquency. "The final conclusion, however, is that there is no specific combination of physique, character and temperament to be found which would determine whether an individual becomes a delinquent" (Mannheim, 1965, p. 241).

The Gluecks have been criticized for using only incarcerated youths in their delinquent sample and for determining somatotypes using visual assessments of the boys' photographs rather than precisely measuring them. In addition, it has been pointed out that the Gluecks failed to take into account how the process of social selection may have contributed to their findings. "In other words," as Gibbons (1970, pp. 75–76) argues, "it is not unlikely that recruits to delinquent conduct are drawn from the group of more agile physically fit boys, just as 'Little League' baseball or 'Pop Warner' league football players tend toward mesomorphy. Fat delinquents and fat ball players are uncommon because the social behavior involved in these cases puts fat, skinny, or sickly boys at a disadvantage. If so, the findings reflect the workings of social factors, not biology."

At least one researcher took exception to Gibbons's argument. *Juan B. Cortes* (1972) claims that Gibbons himself provides support for biological/physiological explanations of crime when he points out that certain people are physically disadvantaged in certain activities. Therefore, Cortes argues, they are socially *and* biologically selected out.

Cortes's (1972) own research involves the somatotyping of 100 delinquent boys (70 in institutions and 30 on probation or under suspended sentence), 20 incarcerated adult felons, and 100 male high school seniors with no official record of delinquency. Virtually all of the adult felons were clearly mesomorphic. Among the youths, 57 percent of the delinquents compared with only 19 percent of the high school seniors were highly mesomorphic. Cortes then examined the relationship between physique and temperament and found, just as Sheldon would have predicted, that the mesomorphs were highly somatonic. Lastly, Cortes correlated subjects' body build with their need for achievement and their desire for power.[5] He reported that mesomorphs, both delinquent and nondelinquent, showed significantly higher achievement motivation than individuals with the other two body types. In addition, delinquent mesomorphs showed an especially high need for power. Cortes concluded:

> Criminal and delinquent behavior are the result of a negative imbalance within the individual, in the interaction between (a) *the expressive* forces of his biological and psycho-impulses, and (b) the *normative forces* of familial, religious, and sociocultural factors. (1972, pp. 348, 351, author's emphasis)

Vold and Bernard (1986) are critical of Cortes for arriving at such sweeping generalizations in light of his data. They emphasize that this research never establishes a direct link between delinquency/criminality and temperament and motivation. It just shows that delinquency/criminality are related to mesomorphy, while mesomorphy is related to particular temperaments and motivations.[6] They also question Cortes's method of measuring temperament—subjects' self-assessments—and the inference drawn from the analysis that those who perceive themselves as energetic are more likely to behave aggressively than others (such as the ectomorphs who tended to describe themselves as tense and anxious). Finally, any observed differences between delinquents and nondelinquents may be the result of differences in their relative social class positions. Cortes failed to control for the important variable of socioeconomic status.

Some readers by now probably consider physical type theories of crime more akin to fortune telling than science. However, we should keep in mind that such ideas still may have some influence within the criminal justice system. For instance, not long ago, a popular magazine reported on a behavioral psychologist who is paid thousands of dollars by prestigious attorneys to assist them in jury selection. What does he do? This psychologist assesses a potential juror's temperament by looking at his or her eyes (for example, close-set eyes indicate intolerance), nose and nostrils (for example, narrowly flared nostrils are a sign of low self-reliance), and hair (for example, fine hair indicates sensitivity) (Greene, 1986). For the most part, though, biological theories have grown more sophisticated than this, as the following sections will show.

It Runs in the Family: Crime and Heredity

Most readers probably have been told at one time or another that they not only physically resemble a particular relative, but also that they behave like certain relatives. It may be said, for instance, that you are "stubborn like your father" or "ambitious like your mother." And sometimes heredity can be a great excuse—for example, we may rationalize that the increasingly snug fit of our jeans is due to the large bone structure characteristic of our mother's side of the family, rather than our recent overindulgence in ice cream.

Undoubtedly, the idea that genetics is responsible for who we are socially, as well as physically, is appealing. Not surprisingly, therefore, it has also been popular as an explanation for criminal behavior. Most early theorists who postulated a relationship between crime and genetics saw criminality as a direct manifestation of hereditary defects. More contemporary theories, however, attempt to take into account how environmental factors may interact with hereditary predispositions to produce criminality. Research to test these theories has largely been of three different types: general pedigree or family studies, twin studies, and adoption studies.

General Pedigree or Family Studies

One way of trying to determine if heredity plays a part in inducing crime is to look for similarities in the behavior of individuals who are genetically related to one another. This is the purpose of *general pedigree* or *family studies*, which are based on the assumption that since family members share a common genetic heritage, behaviors that are genetically determined should correlate more strongly among family members than among unrelated individuals (Walters & White, 1989).

One of the first family studies was published in 1877 by *Richard Dugdale*. Dugdale examined the criminal history of one family, the Jukes, who in 1874 had six members incarcerated in a New York county jail. Tracing their family history back about 200 years, Dugdale found a high incidence of criminality, which he explained in terms of the "degenerate nature" of this family. Since that time, a number of more rigorously designed family studies have been conducted, including several during the second half of the twentieth century. Most of these examine the arrest or conviction records of a group of parents and their offspring, with the common finding that criminal parents tend to have criminal offspring (Butterfield, 1992; Ellis, 1982; Rowe et al., 1898; Walters & White, 1989).

The major difficulty with family studies is that they cannot disentangle the relative contributions of genetics and environmental factors to behavior. While parents and their children share genetic material, they also live in the same environment. Consequently, "unless a trait is simply due to the actions of a single gene and virtually no environmental factors are involved in determining its expression (both rare, especially with respect to behavioral traits), the only conclusion to draw from general pedigree studies, if close genetic relatives are found to more closely resemble one another in a particular characteristic than do nonrelatives, is that a substantial variation in the trait is due to the genetics *or* to the environment family members share with one another— as opposed to the environment they do not share" (Ellis, 1982, p. 45).

Many family studies do not use appropriate control groups, so it is difficult to determine if the arrest and incarceration rates of children with criminal parents are actually higher than the arrest and incarceration rates of children with noncriminal parents. In at least one study that did use a control group, the researchers found that delinquent boys had more criminal relatives than nondelinquent boys, but the difference between the groups was small. In general, then, "no matter how well designed, these studies are widely regarded as a very weak, nonexperimental design" (Ellis, 1982, p. 42; see also Rowe, 1995).

Twin Studies

There are two types of twins. *Monozygotic* (MZ or identical) *twins* are the more rare type. They originate from a single fertilized egg and so share all (100 percent) of their genes. They look very much alike and, obviously, they are the same sex. *Dizygotic* (DZ or fraternal) *twins*, on the other hand, develop when two separate eggs are fertilized by two separate sperm. DZ twins share the same amount of genetic material as nontwin siblings, about 50 percent. They tend to resemble one another as much as nontwin siblings do, and they may or may not be the same sex.

Researchers study the role of genetics in criminal behavior by determining the degree of *concordance*—similarity—in the behavior of MZ twins and comparing it with the concordance of DZ twins' behavior. Richard Herrnstein (1982a) explains further:

> The logic of the twin method is that identical twins share more of their genes than fraternal twins while sharing roughly equal environments. Their environments are equal because they shared the uterine environment at the same time in their mother's life, they were born at the same time, and grew up contemporaneously. They experienced all of the major, and many of the minor, events of their time at the same time in their lives. Thus, to the extent that fraternal and identical twins differ in how much they resemble each other, it is assumed to be due to the difference in their genetic overlap. (pp. 8–9)

In other words, researchers using this method view it as having some built-in control for environmental factors, an assumption that we shall see has been challenged, causing some researchers to modify this position.

The first criminological twin study was conducted in the late 1920s by Johannes Lange and since then, many more twin studies have been reported. Among the most famous of the recent twin studies is that by *Karl O. Christiansen* (1974) in Denmark, which examined 3,586 twin pairs born between 1870 and 1920 who were listed in the Danish Twin Register. After searching police, court, and prison records, Christiansen discovered that 926 individuals from 799 twin pairs had committed at least one offense. Subsequently focusing on serious crimes (violent and/or sexual offenses), Christiansen found that among the 18 MZ twin pairs with serious records, 5 were concordant, yielding a concordance rate of 28 percent. In contrast, of the 27 DZ pairs with serious records, only 3 were concordant, a rate of 11 percent. In fact, Christiansen reports that the more serious the crime and criminal career, the greater the similarity between MZ twins compared with DZ twins.

Recent research in the United States conducted by David C. Rowe and colleagues (Rowe, 1986, Rowe, 1995; Rowe & Gulley, 1992; Rowe & Osgood, 1984) supports Christiansen's findings. In one study, for example, Rowe (1986) used the self-report method to survey 265 pairs of twins in the eighth to twelfth grades in Ohio from 1978 to 1980. He found that the concordance rates for self-reported delinquency by MZ twins, both male and female, were higher than those of DZ twins. In addition, he showed that MZ twins have a higher concordance rate for self-reported delinquent associations—number of delinquent friends—than DZ twins. This led him to conclude that there is not only a genetic component to delinquency, but also that genetics may predispose some individuals to selecting friends who are delinquent (see also Grove et al., 1990; Rowe, 1995).

On the face of it, then, twin studies seem to provide fairly strong support for the notion that criminality is heritable. However, these studies also are fraught with methodological difficulties. For example, there is wide variation among twin studies in terms of definitions of criminality and offense severity, the techniques of statistical analysis used, and the care and methods employed to determine zygosity. Thus, studies with similar findings may not be comparable. At the same time, there are sampling problems. Rowe (1986), for instance, excluded Ohio's inner city school districts from his sample. Although he states that his final sample was composed of families "from across the social class spectrum" (Rowe & Osgood, 1984, p. 531), one may nevertheless question its representativeness. Only 50 of the 530 individuals who completed the questionnaire were African Americans, and Rowe's overall return rate was less than 50 percent.[7]

Another serious problem with twin studies stems from the assumption of the environmental equality of MZ and DZ twins. Research indicates that MZ twins are treated more alike by others and also tend to spend more time together than DZ twins. Consequently, the greater similarity in the behavior of MZ twins compared with DZ twins may be the result of these environmental factors rather than genetics. Rowe (1986) did consider this by asking respondents how many activities they shared with their twins. He reports that concordance rates for self-reported delinquency were unrelated to the number of activities shared by MZ twins or by DZ twins.[8] However, another study of 139 pairs of male Norwegian twins found that differences in the concordance rates for delinquency between MZ and DZ twins disappeared when the twins' closeness to one another was taken into account (Dalgaard & Kringlen, 1976). Other researchers have attempted to control for the effects of mutual identity by comparing the behavior of MZ twins separated at an early age and reared apart. However, because these cases are so rare, the findings have been inconsistent and inconclusive (Christiansen, 1974).

In light of these methodological issues, Christiansen (1974, p. 75) has argued that twin studies do not necessarily provide a measure of heredity. Instead, they simply tell us "something about the impact of the similarities of twins, whether these are determined by environmental factors or factors in the personality, which is itself a product of heredity and environment. Consequently, a greater frequency of concordance among MZ than among DZ twins means only that similar hereditary factors and/or similar prenatal, natal or postnatal environmental conditions result in a greater probability of similarities in social behavior than do disparate hereditary factors and/or disparate environmental conditions." Rowe (1995), however, is more specific about the impact of genetics and environment on criminality. He argues that "criminality has a biological basis that results when genetically-disposed individuals are both exposed to and find environments that encourage crime" (p. 301; see also Mednick et al., 1987; Rowe, 1994).

Adoption Studies

Adoption studies represent a third attempt to sort out the relative contributions of genetics and environment to human behavior. In these studies, the behavior of individuals separated from their biological parents at an early age and reared by unrelated adoptive parents is examined relative to the behavior of both the biological and adoptive parents. If a trait such as criminality is genetically transmitted, adoptees should more closely resemble their biological parents than their adoptive parents with respect to this trait.

A number of adoption studies have been conducted during the last twenty-five years in the United States and abroad, primarily in Sweden and Denmark. One of the most frequently cited studies was conducted by Mednick and his colleagues (1987), who analyzed the conviction records of 14,427 Danish adoptees relative to the recorded criminality of both their biological and adoptive parents. For adopted sons, they found that among those with neither a criminal biological parent nor a criminal adoptive parent, only 13.5 percent had convictions themselves. When at least one adoptive parent had a criminal conviction but the biological parents did not, only 14.7 percent of the sons had convictions. If, however, at least one of the biological parents had a criminal conviction but neither of the adoptive parents did, the percentage of convicted sons rose to 20.0 percent. The highest percentage of convicted sons, 24.5 percent, occurred among the group in which at least one biological parent *and* at least one adoptive parent had criminal convictions.

Mednick and his colleagues (1987) are quick to point out that these data by themselves do not prove a genetic basis for criminality since they cannot tell us how criminogenic an adoptee's environment has been. What the data do show is that "sons with a convicted biological parent have an elevated probability of being convicted." To these researchers, this finding "suggests that some biological characteristic is transmitted from the criminal biological parent that increases the son's risk of obtaining a court conviction for a criminal law offense" (Mednick et al., 1987, p. 79).

Mednick et al. (1987) see their data on sex differences in conviction rates as lending further support to this conclusion. They note that females as a group have a far lower criminal conviction rate than males. From this they speculate that "those women who do exhibit a level of criminal behavior that prompts a court conviction must have a severe predisposition for such behavior" (p. 84). Thus, we may expect that the relationship between biological mothers' convictions and adoptees' convictions will be stronger than that between biological fathers' convictions and adoptees' convictions. This is, indeed, what their analyses showed, especially with regard to adopted daughters, although they do recognize that this finding may simply be an artifact of the relatively small number of female convictions in the sample.

Several U.S. studies obtained similar results. Crowe (1972) examined the arrest records of fifty-two adoptees in Iowa who had been separated from their incarcerated biological mothers at a young age and compared them with the arrest records of adoptees whose biological mothers had no record of criminality. He found that eight adoptees (15.4 percent) in the former group compared with only two (3.8 percent) in the latter group had arrest records. Later he reported that more of the adoptees with convicted biological mothers, when compared with controls, had been diagnosed as having antisocial personalities (Crowe, 1975). In another Iowa study, Cadoret (1978) reported that, based on responses to a structured diagnostic questionnaire, adoptees whose biological parents had been diagnosed as antisocial were themselves more likely to be antisocial. And Rowe (1994) reports no significant correlations between adoptive parents and adoptive children, and also between unrelated siblings reared together, for a variety of personality traits, such as extroversion, as well as more problematic adolescent behaviors (see also Loehlin & Rowe, 1992). In fact, Rowe (1994) goes so far as to claim that the data indicate that except in the most pathologically extreme cases, parental child rearing and family environment have virtually no impact on the behaviors and traits a child ends up exhibiting as an adolescent or adult.

In their careful review of adoption research, Walters and White (1989, p. 473) conclude that such studies "appear to represent the best strategy available for determining the independent contributions of environment and heredity relative to human behavior. Unfortunately, the current body of adoption research serves more to cloud than to clarify the relevant issues." This is primarily due, once again, to methodological problems. For instance, like researchers in twin studies, adoption researchers do not utilize a consistent definition of criminality. Some employ diagnostic categories, such as antisocial personality, which often are determined by questionable criteria (such as using "bad language" or spending money "irresponsibly"). Others use behaviors that some observers may consider problematic—for example, cigarette smoking or having sexual intercourse—but not necessarily "antisocial" or "delinquent" (see, for instance, Rowe, 1994). Even those who use arrest, conviction, or incarceration records, however, present problems. For example, in Crowe's (1972) study discussed previously, the children of incarcerated women comprised the research sample on the assumption that women who had been sentenced to prison could appropriately be considered criminals. But as Walters and White (1989) reveal, among these forty-one incarcerated mothers, five had been convicted of prostitution, three of desertion, three of adultery, two of lewdness, one of bigamy, and one of transmitting venereal disease. "One can only speculate about how a more realistic definition of criminality may have influenced Crowe's results" (Walters & White, 1989, pp. 473–474, see also Walters, 1992).

A second serious shortcoming in these studies stems from the amount of time children spend with their biological parents before being relocated to new homes. For research purposes, the ideal condition would be to examine children who were separated from their biological parents at birth. In most adoption studies, though, the length of biological parenting before separation varies. In the Mednick et al. (1987) study, about half the children were separated from their biological mothers within several weeks after birth, while the other half were separated some time between several months and one year after birth. In Crowe's (1972) study, the separation occurred within six months of birth for half the children, but anywhere from six to eighteen months for the other half. And in Cadoret's (1978) study, the children were separated from their biological mothers at birth, but 40 percent spent at least three months in an institution or foster care before being adopted.

The research also shows that the offspring separated from their mothers at a later age and those who spend more time in institutions are more likely to be diagnosed antisocial or to have criminal records. Thus, it may be that the quality of early parenting, rather than genetics, influences criminal behavior. Another important factor may be the trauma induced by separation itself and/or the experience of institutionalization. Finally, one also must consider that being an adoptee may affect an individual's self-concept and consequently his or her behavior (Walters, 1992; Walters & White, 1989).

So, is criminality inherited? In light of the research we have reviewed here, our answer must be a cautious maybe. Although there are indications that criminality may have a genetic component, at least for some individuals, the research methods and designs at our disposal are still too flawed or unsophisticated to control for all the likely environmental influences that could be involved. It may be, as some have argued, that criminality is a heritable trait, but one that becomes manifest only when triggered by particular environmental conditions (such as poverty, parental neglect or abuse, or living in a crime-ridden neighborhood). What is more clear is that, given present methodological as well as ethical limitations, we are a long way from knowing for certain. Yet, if one argues that crime is not inherited, this does not necessarily mean that one thinks there is no relationship between biology and criminality. Let's consider some other biological theories of crime.

Faulty Chromosomes

Normally, a person is born with forty-six chromosomes arranged in twenty-three pairs, one of each pair contributed by the individual's mother and one by his or her father. One pair of chromosomes—designated pair twenty-three by scientists—is composed of the *sex chromosomes* because they play the primary role in determining whether a fertilized egg will develop into a male or a female fetus. The sex chromosomes of a genetically normal male consist of one X and one Y chromosome, whereas genetically normal females have two Xs. Thus, since the mother of a child always contributes an X to the sex chromosome pair, it is the father's genetic contribution that determines the child's sex.

Unfortunately, mishaps sometimes occur. One type of mishap, called *nondisjunction*, may occur during the production of sperm. When sperm are produced, a process called *meiosis* takes place in two stages. During meiosis, the chromosomes divide and duplicate themselves, thereby producing two kinds of sperm—sperm with an X chromosome and sperm with a Y chromosome. Nondisjunction refers to a failure of the sex chromosomes to divide properly. If it occurs during the first stage of meiotic division, the two kinds of sperm produced are those with both an X and a Y chromosome, and those with no sex chromosomes. If one of these defective sperm subsequently fertilizes a normal egg, the offspring will have either XXY sex chromosomes or XO sex chromosomes (the O representing the failure of the father's sperm to contribute a sex chromosome). But nondisjunction may also occur during the second stage of meiotic division, in which case three kinds of sperm are produced: those with no sex chromosomes, those with two X chromosomes, and those with two Y chromosomes. If one of these sperm fertilizes a normal egg, the offspring may be XO, XXX, or XYY.[9] Figure 2.1 illustrates each of these problems.

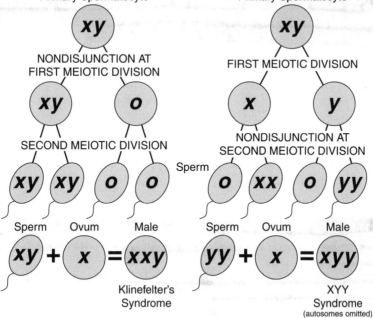

FIGURE 2.1   Nondisjunction of Sex Chromosomes in Male Meiosis

Source: M. F. A. Montagu. (1968, October). "Chromosomes and Crime," *Psychology Today*, p. 47. Reprinted with permission from the author.

Researchers have long been interested in the physical and potential behavioral effects of these chromosome abnormalities. For instance, *Turner's syndrome* is the name given to the XO condition. Individuals with Turner's syndrome are female, but they have no gonadal tissue so they cannot produce sex hormones. Scientists have studied Turner's syndrome females to learn if those physical problems impact on their gender identification (Baker, 1980). Scientists have studied the XXY condition, known as *Klinefelter's syndrome*, for similar reasons. Individuals with Klinefelter's syndrome are male because of the presence of the Y chromosome, but usually they have small penises and testicles, secrete very low levels of the male sex hormone testosterone, are sterile, and may show breast development at puberty. They also may have some mental impairment and often are confused about their gender identity (Hoyenga & Hoyenga, 1993).

Several studies conducted in the 1960s and 1970s using small samples found higher rates of criminality among XXY males compared with normal XY males (Ellis, 1982). But the chromosomal abnormality that most captured the attention of criminologists is undoubtedly XYY syndrome.

XYY Syndrome

Individuals with **XYY syndrome** tend not to have major physical problems probably because the Y chromosome appears to carry relatively little genetic information. However, XYY males have a high incidence of internal and external genital abnormalities, they tend to be above average in height and below average in intellectual ability, and they often develop severe facial acne during adolescence. The incidence of XYY syndrome in the general population is estimated at about one per 1,000–2,000 males.

In 1965, Patricia Jacobs and her colleagues at Western General Hospital in Edinburgh, Scotland, reported that in their study of 197 inmates of a maximum-security hospital, 7 men (3.5 percent) were XYY. Several subsequent studies also found a disproportionately high incidence of XYY syndrome among institutionalized and incarcerated men, with some reporting a frequency ten to twenty times greater than that in the general population. In addition, the offenders in at least two well-publicized murders—Daniel Hugon in France and Richard Speck in the United States—reportedly had XYY syndrome, so it is not surprising that this chromosome abnormality attracted the attention of both the scientific and lay communities.[10] By 1970, more than 200 scientific articles and books had been written on XYY syndrome (Ellis, 1982).

How does the extra Y chromosome contribute to criminality? Originally, the answer to this question rested on the fact that the presence of a Y chromosome signals the secretion of the male sex hormone, testosterone. Evidence from animal studies has linked testosterone with aggression. Thus, it was hypothesized that an extra Y chromosome would lead to elevated testosterone levels which, in turn, would increase the likelihood of aggressive behavior. In support of this argument, early reports emphasized the violent nature of the crimes committed by XYY males (see, for example, Montague, 1968). Subsequent studies, however, showed rather conclusively that XYY males were not predictably aggressive. Rather, as a group they appeared somewhat less aggressive than XY males. Typically they are convicted of petty property offenses

(Herrnstein, 1988a; Sarbin & Miller, 1970). In addition, there is a considerable body of research that calls into question a direct relationship between testosterone and aggression in humans.[11]

It does appear that, given the low incidence of the abnormality in the general population, XYY males are disproportionately represented among the institutionalized. Some analysts have argued, though, that this may be because of psychological or social factors, rather than biological ones. Sarbin and Miller (1970), for example, suggest that since XYYs tend to be unusually tall, police officers, judges, and juries may be biased toward arresting, convicting, and institutionalizing them because they look "dangerous" and capable of violence. Kessler and Moos (1970) maintain that social class biases may be at work instead. If the rate of chromosome abnormalities is higher among the poor and working class due perhaps to the unavailability or unaffordability of prenatal care, an adequately nutritional diet, and so on, then the disproportionate number of institutionalized XYY males is simply a reflection of the class bias of the criminal justice system. The poor and the working class are significantly more likely than members of the middle and upper classes to be processed through the system. Finally, other researchers (for example, Witkin et al., 1976) hypothesize that the high institutionalization rate of XYY males may be due to their low intellectual ability, an issue we will take up again in Chapter 3.

Some scientists (see, for instance, Wilson & Herrnstein, 1985) are interested in XYY syndrome because it may reveal a genetic component of crime that is not hereditary, although there is some evidence that a tendency toward nondisjunction is itself heritable (Montague, 1968). Nevertheless, most studies of XYY males have utilized small, selective samples, which may seriously compromise the findings (Ellis, 1982). More importantly, even if criminality is associated with this abnormality, XYY syndrome can account for only a tiny portion of crime. The vast majority of crimes are still committed by chromosomally normal XY males. This fact has led Rowe (1995) to speculate on why the presence of the Y chromosome elevates a person's likelihood of committing a crime. He suggests that the reason significantly more men than women commit crimes has to do with hormonal sex differences triggered by the Y chromosome that affect brain development. We'll discuss the role of hormones and brain functioning in the etiology of crime shortly.

Other Potential Biological Contributors to Crime Causation

A variety of additional biological factors have been studied with respect to the etiology of criminal behavior. Some factors are thought to be heritable. Some are hypothesized to be the result of prenatal difficulties, such as fetal developmental problems, the interuterine exposure of the fetus to harmful substances, or even birth trauma. And others are the result of a physical injury suffered during childhood or adulthood, or the product of a hormonal or nutritional imbalance. Let's begin by looking at hormones.

Hormonal Imbalance and Crime: "My Hormones Made Me Do It"

For more than a century, scientists have been studying the potential impact that hormones may have on behavior. **Hormones** are chemicals secreted by the body to regulate the activities of specific cells or organs. Most studies of the relationship between hormones and crime have focused on one kind of hormone, the sex hormones, especially testosterone.

Although both males and females secrete testosterone, testosterone is referred to as a male sex hormone because males secrete significantly more of it than females do. As we noted earlier, research on animals has shown a relationship between testosterone secretion and aggressive behavior. Typically, in these experiments, laboratory animals (rats, mice, or monkeys) are injected with testosterone. The usual outcome is that, regardless of their sex, the animals show a significant increase in impatience, rough-and-tumble play, and fighting. A variation on this theme is to castrate newborn animals, with the result that as they mature, they display little aggressive behavior. Certainly, one of the strongest behavioral differences between human males and females is their rates of criminal offending, especially violent offending. For example, the number of men arrested for violent crimes (murder, manslaughter, forcible rape, robbery, and aggravated assault) is more than five times greater than the number of women arrested for violent crimes (U.S. Department of Justice, Bureau of Justice Statistics, 1998). Not surprisingly, then, such findings have led some criminologists to examine whether male criminals, particularly those who are aggressive or violent, secrete excessively high levels of testosterone.

One way that scientists have researched this possibility is by first determining testosterone levels from blood samples of a group of subjects, then seeing how these correlate with the results of various psychological tests of hostility or aggressiveness and/or with the actual commission of violent offenses. Taken together, the findings are mixed. For instance, studies of normal male teenagers (healthy nonoffenders) "indicate that there is no consistent correlation between various measures of hostility, aggression, and similar behavior, as determined both by rating scales and observed behavior, and circulating testosterone levels" (Rubin, 1987, p. 245). Some studies, though, indicate that among normal male youths, testosterone level is related to both verbal and physical aggression manifested in response to a perceived provocation, such as unfair treatment or a threat (Olewus, 1987; see also Van Goozen et al., 1994). Schalling's (1987) description is apropos here: "The picture is rather one of a highly assertive and self-assured boy who is able to defend himself when provoked and who can show anger when necessary" (p. 288).

Research using samples of prisoners has shown fairly consistently a relationship between increased testosterone and violent offenses. In most of these studies, violent offenders (such as rapists and armed robbers) had higher testosterone levels in their blood than did nonviolent offenders and/or nonoffenders. Nevertheless, in all subjects testosterone levels were within the normal range (Rubin, 1987). Other studies have found that drugs that lower testosterone levels are successful in treating men with certain sexual problems (including pedophiles, masochists, and exhibitionists). However, the drugs seem to be useful only for reducing sexual behavior and do not appear to be effective in controlling nonsexual violent outbursts (Dirks-Linhorst & Laster, 1998; Rubin, 1987).

Although research with humans does show that high levels of circulating testosterone are correlated with edginess, competitiveness, and anger—in both men and women—empirical support for the hypothesized relationship between testosterone and crime appears to be equivocal at best. One of the reasons that scientists have not been able to better pinpoint how testosterone affects specific behaviors such as crime is that the hormone fluctuates dramatically over the course of a day and in response to environmental stimuli (Blum, 1997). For instance, we noted that testosterone has been correlated with competitiveness and aggressive responses to perceived challenges, with the traditional hypothesis being that high testosterone makes a person more competitive and aggressive. But recent research shows that testosterone levels rise and fall *in response to* competitive challenges. In one study, for example, researchers found that testosterone rises in male tennis players before a match, goes down as the match is being played, and then rises dramatically in players who win, but drops just as dramatically in players who lose (Booth et al., 1989; Mazur & Lamb, 1980; see also Mazur et al., 1992). Thus, elevated testosterone levels may be the *product* rather than the cause of aggression.

Another reason scientists have had difficulty specifying the relationship between testosterone and human aggression, violence, and crime is that testosterone is only one of several chemicals interacting in the body that affect human behavioral response. Other important chemicals are *neurotransmitters*. Research on the relationship between neurotransmitters and criminal behavior shows more promise than the hormonal research. Before we discuss studies of neurotransmitters and crime, it is important to point out that testosterone is not the only hormone that has been thought to be associated with criminality. The female sex hormones—estrone, estradial, estriol, and progesterone—have also been implicated in the commission of crimes, especially violent crimes, by women.

We've all heard stories and jokes about changes in women's personality and behavior that result from the fluctuation of hormones in their bodies every month, particularly just before the onset of their menstrual periods. The stereotype of the premenstrual women is a woman out of control, depressed, and easily enraged. The idea that women's personality and behavior are dictated by their hormones is an old one. For instance, the word *androgen*, the collective name for the male sex hormones, comes from the Greek word for "man," while *estrogen*, one of the female sex hormones, comes from the Greek word for "frenzy" (Blum, 1997). It has only been in the last few decades, however, that women's premenstrual personality and behavioral changes have been officially renamed *premenstrual syndrome* or *PMS*.

The relationship of PMS to women's violent crime entered the public spotlight in the 1980s, largely as a result of media coverage of two British homicide trials. The first case in 1980 involved a thirty-seven-year-old woman who drove her car at full speed directly at her boyfriend, pinning him to a telephone pole and killing him. She was subsequently convicted of manslaughter instead of murder and was released on probation because of a mitigating factor in her case: At the time of the crime, her defense attorney argued, this woman was suffering from PMS, which may have caused her to behave violently. Also in 1980, a twenty-nine-year-old woman was convicted of killing a coworker at the London pub where she tended bar, but she too was sentenced to probation on the basis of the PMS defense. As a condition of their probation, both women were required to receive monthly hormone injections to control their PMS symptoms (Glass, 1982; Parlee, 1982).

Understandably, these cases generated considerable controversy, not only in Great Britain, but also in the United States, Canada, and Australia. Some criminologists and legal scholars expressed concern that the courts would be flooded with cases in which female defendants would try to escape punishment for serious crimes by claiming their behavior was a product of the stress caused by the onset of their monthly periods. These worries proved to be unfounded, although to a lesser extent than originally expected. Reduced responsibility because of PMS has been argued successfully as a mitigating factor at pretrial hearings to reduce female defendants' charges and at sentencing hearings to reduce the severity of their sentences (Easteal, 1991). However, regardless of how it is used and the extent to which it is used successfully, the question remains as to whether it *should* be used as a legitimate criminal defense. Is there a causal connection between PMS and criminal behavior in women?

One of the difficulties in answering this question is that much of the research on PMS is plagued by serious methodological problems. For instance, the majority of studies rely on subjects' self-reports in determining the onset of premenstrual symptoms (see, for example, Thys-Jacobs et al., 1995). This method is unreliable because subjects' recall may produce exaggerated results (Koeske, 1980; Sommer, 1983), or their recall may be selective, focusing only on those changes that occurred during the premenstrual phase of their cycles (Hardie, 1997; Widom & Ames, 1988).

A second difficulty in causally linking PMS with crime is that studies examining actual behavioral or personality changes related to the menstrual cycle, particularly the premenstrual phase, have produced inconsistent results. Some of the research on mood swings, for example, has found that women tend to feel less able to cope with everyday problems during the premenstrual phase of their cycles (Friedman et al., 1980). Others report that negative changes in mood, as well as physical changes, may have more to do with stressful external events (e.g., the triple burden of housework, caregiving, and work outside the home) than with the phase of the menstrual cycle (Golub, 1992; Hardie, 1997; Ripper, 1991). A few studies even show improved task performance premenstrually (Parlee, 1983), although most show no relationship between task performance and menstrual cycle (Chrisler, 1991; Morgan et al., 1996). Some researchers have observed a relationship between menstrual cycle phase and a number of psychophysiological functions, such as visual, auditory, and olfactory sensitivity; galvanic skin response; and spontaneous body movement. "However, the variations among the findings are such that one could select studies to support almost any hypothesis one chose" (Sommer, 1983, p. 82).

Premenstrual syndrome is not the only hormonal condition that has been linked with female crime. There have been cases, for example, in which menopause and its concomitant symptoms have been cited as mitigating factors for female defendants

(Easteal, 1991). *Postpartum depression syndrome* has also been used as a criminal defense. Symptoms of postpartum depression syndrome typically appear from two weeks to three months after a woman has given birth and may last from several weeks to several months. Depression after the birth of a baby is not uncommon and is thought to be caused by the sudden drop in the hormone progesterone following childbirth. In the United States, 50 to 80 percent of women report feeling sad, tense, or irritable during the first two weeks following the birth of their babies. For most women, these feelings disappear quickly, often within just a few days. About 10 to 20 percent of women who give birth report more severe symptoms, including feelings of inadequacy, guilt, extreme fatigue, and an inability to care for the baby. And a very small number of women—1 to 2 percent who give birth—experience very severe symptoms, including hallucinations, mental confusion, panic attacks, suicide attempts, and attempts to kill their babies (Giovannini, 1992; Taylor, 1996). For instance, in January 1989, Tanya Dacri, a twenty-year-old American woman, reported to police that her seven-week-old son had been kidnapped by two men at a shopping center. Within twenty-four hours, though, Ms. Dacri had been charged with murdering the infant; she had drowned him in the bathtub, dismembered his body, and disposed of the various parts in area rivers. Her defense was postpartum depression syndrome. By the time Dacri went to trial, there were about twenty-five similar cases in the United States, less than half of which successfully used this defense. In England and Canada, however, a woman charged with killing her infant within one year of its birth cannot be found guilty of murder if it is determined that she was suffering from postpartum depression syndrome. Instead, she may be found guilty of a special category of infanticide similar to manslaughter, which carries a less severe sentence (Conrad, 1989; Easteal, 1991).

Although as we have noted, postpartum depression syndrome is thought to be caused by a sharp and sudden decline in progesterone after childbirth (Gitlin & Passnau, 1990), other researchers point out that the exceptionally low incidence of postpartum depression in cross-cultural studies indicates that sociocultural or environmental factors are also important contributors to the disorder. For example, there is research that shows that the incidence and severity of postpartum depression are directly related to the amount of social support available to new mothers, as well as the amount and type of socioenvironmental stressors (e.g., financial or housing difficulties, marital problems, the number and ages of other children in the household) to which new mothers are exposed. Women who are isolated in their homes, lack family and social support networks, and are exposed to serious and prolonged stress are more likely to experience postpartum depression syndrome (Giovannini, 1992; Gjerdingen et al., 1990; Taylor, 1996).

In sum, our review of studies of the relationship between various hormones and crime indicates that considerably more research is needed before we can confidently link hormonal levels or changes with either male or female criminality. However, these studies do point to a strong interaction between biological processes and socioenvironmental conditions that may help to produce criminality. Neurological studies also support this link, so let's turn our attention now to research on brain functioning and its potential role in the etiology of crime.

Crime and the Brain

As we learned in our discussion of phrenology, the brain has long been studied for its role in shaping human behavior, including criminal behavior. Early scientific research was devoted largely to "mapping" the brain, that is, identifying discrete areas of the brain and pinpointing their functions. Figure 2.2 shows one human brain map. Studies of both animals and humans indicated that individual areas of the brain were responsible for particular functions, an idea known as *functional localization*. A competing perspective—*globalization*—depicted the brain in more holistic terms as a set of interrelated, interdependent parts functioning together. Thanks largely to advances in medical technology, especially those developed since the 1960s, scientists now know that the latter position is more accurate. Although various parts of the brain specialize in particular functions (e.g., vision, speech), the model typically used nowadays to describe the structure and workings of the brain is that of a complex, interconnected network. In fact, one neuroscientist likens the brain to "a teeming, dynamic modern city; a collective of interconnected communities of neurons, each characterized by a distinct architecture, style, and local population. . . . In this expanded model of the relationship between structure and function, an event that occurs in one neighborhood has the potential to affect all, and injuries that 'break the link' at different points often trigger similar behavioral consequences" (Niehoff, 1999, pp. 82–83). Despite how far we have progressed in our ability to study the brain, the precise links between brain structure and functioning and many behaviors, such as crime, are still not well understood. Let's consider first research on brain structure and then turn to research on brain chemistry, keeping in mind that although we are separating these issues for discussion, they are interrelated rather than discrete.

Brain Structure.   A number of researchers have investigated whether damage to a specific part of the brain could precipitate criminality. Much of this research has focused on the frontal lobe and the temporal lobe (see Figure 2.2). The frontal lobe is important for regulating and inhibiting behavior. If this area is damaged, a person may exhibit impulsive behavior, a lack of self-control, an inability to evaluate behavioral consequences, and a loss of feelings of guilt or remorse. Similarly, the temporal lobe plays an important role in subjective consciousness, emotionality, and response to environmental change. It is not difficult to see why researchers would associate criminal behavior, especially violence, with damage to these parts of the brain.

In recent studies examining the brain damage/crime relationship, researchers have used computed tomography (CT scans) and magnetic resonance imaging (MRI), which allow them to see damage caused by injury or disease in living human beings in their laboratories. Some researchers also use positron emission tomography (PET scans) and single photon emission computed tomography (SPECT scans), which allow them to not only find damage, but also trace brain activity in a snapshot fashion within seconds after it occurs (Niehoff, 1999).

However, studies using these sophisticated tools have not convincingly demonstrated that brain damage leads to criminal behavior. In fact, some critics have characterized this work as "digital phrenology," in which researchers look at "bumps on the

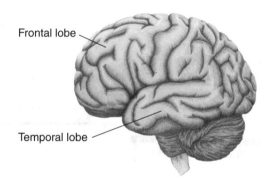

Frontal lobe

Temporal lobe

FIGURE 2.2   The Human Brain

inside rather than bumps on the outside" of the head (quoted in Niehoff, 1999). In one study, for instance, researchers found distinct differences in both the temporal and frontal lobes when they compared the brains of violent offenders with the brains of a nonviolent control group composed of individuals of the same sex and age (Volkow & Tancredi, 1987). In a subgroup of violent offenders who expressed no remorse for their crimes, the PET images showed loss of neural activity in the frontal lobe and reduced blood flow and glucose utilization in the left temporal lobe. In a subgroup of violent offenders who did express remorse for their crimes, loss of neural activity was evident only in the temporal lobe. Nevertheless, none of the violent offenders' brain scans revealed any structural defects that could have produced these differences. In another study (Raine, 1993), PET and SPECT technology was used to compare the brain activity of homicide offenders with that of a nonviolent control group. Again, glucose utilization in the frontal lobe was significantly lower in the homicide offenders than in the controls.

Provocative though these studies are, critics point out that they rely on very small samples; Volkow and Tancredi (1987), for example, had only two subjects in each of their three test groups, while Raine (1993) collected data from just twenty-two subjects in each of his groups. The nature of the observed relationship in these studies has also been questioned: Are the observed differences a *cause* of the criminal behavior or are they the *result* of engaging in violence or even of being arrested and incarcerated? Research findings that underline the importance of addressing this question come from studies of crime *victims*, which show that the trauma of being violently victimized may cause structural brain defects that in turn affect brain functioning by, for example, reducing short-term memory (Bremner et al., 1997; Stein et al., 1997). Given additional research that shows that incarcerated offenders—both women and men—are often survivors of child physical and sexual abuse (see, for instance, Chesney-Lind, 1997; Fishbein, 2000), these findings raise the intriguing possibility that early violent victimization may lead to changes in brain structure and function that could later contribute to criminality.

We are a long way from being able to definitively test this hypothesis, but some researchers are already exploring how exposure to various traumas or stressors early in life, even prenatally, can affect the brain's development and thereby increase the risk of antisocial or criminal behavior as a person matures (Fishbein, 2000). For instance, fetal exposure to nicotine, alcohol, and other drugs has been correlated with a number of risk factors for antisocial behavior, such as hyperactivity and attention deficits (Gibson & Tibbetts, 1998; Lou et al., 1994). Babies who experience prenatal trauma that impairs their development are born with *minor physical anomalies (MPAs)*—that is, congenital abnormalities of the body.[12] A high number of MPAs at birth is strongly predictive of later behavioral problems, including hyperactivity, attention deficits, and other learning disabilities. Studies show such a strong association between learning disabilities and delinquent and criminal behavior that some criminologists recommend infant physical exams for MPAs to allow early identification of those at greatest risk of growing up to be offenders (Buikhuisen, 1987; Fishbein, 2000; Fiske, 1989; Krouse & Kauffman, 1982).

Learning disabilities, however, do not directly cause delinquency and crime (Murray, 1976). Instead, learning disabilities appear to be indirectly related to delinquency through a complex chain of intervening social events and conditions. For example, one study found a strong relationship between MPAs, hyperactivity, and later criminality only if an offender grew up in an unstable family (Mednick et al., 1988). Additionally, research shows that because the brain continues to develop during infancy, an enriched and stimulating early childhood environment can improve brain functioning and offset deficits incurred prenatally (Fishbein, 2000). Such findings have important policy implications. At a time when many states, as well as the federal government, are allocating funds to fight crime with larger police forces and more prison cells, these studies indicate that the money would be better spent on prenatal care programs, programs to teach parenting skills, quality day care centers, Head Start and other early childhood education programs, as well as increased funding for our nation's underresourced schools. As some observers have pointed out, the cost of a year in prison is about the same as the cost of a year's tuition at some of the best U.S. colleges and universities (Center on Crime, Communities and Culture, 1997; Fiske, 1989). As Box 2.1 suggests, perhaps if federal spending on education were increased instead of federal spending for the expansion of the prison system, more youth might end up in college than in the criminal justice system.

Brain Chemistry.   The structure of the brain is made up of cells called *neurons*, which communicate with one another by way of chemical messengers called **neurotransmitters**. Neurotransmitters are chemical compounds found between nerve cells that send signals from one neuron to another, thus having a direct impact on behavior, emotion, moods, and learning (Niehoff, 1999). Our bodies produce many different neurotransmitters, at least fifty of which have been studied extensively (Lefton, 2000). Those of greatest interest to criminologists are: norepinephrine, a "watchdog" chemical that helps us respond to perceived threats or danger; dopamine, a chemical involved in feelings of pleasure and reinforcement or reward; and serotonin, a chemical that regulates impulsivity and reactions to sensory information (Niehoff, 1999).

BOX **2.1** **CONTROVERSY AND DEBATE**

Lowering the Crime Rate by Improving Educational Opportunities for Offenders

About 40 percent of juveniles doing time in correctional facilities have a learning disability (Gemignani, 1994). On average, these youth read at a fourth-grade level, although the median age is 15.5 years. "More than one-third of all juvenile offenders of this age group read below the fourth-grade level" (Center on Crime, Communities and Culture, 1997). Once released from detention, most juvenile offenders who are 16 or older do not return to school. Among the strongest correlates of high levels of criminal activity are low levels of educational attainment (Center on Crime, Communities and Culture, 1997).

With these statistics in mind, many experts have called for significant educational reforms, including increased funding to under-resourced schools in high-crime neighborhoods, expansion of education programs in juvenile and adult correctional facilities, and the establishment of programs to help youth transition from correctional facilities back to school. Youth Out of the Education Mainstream (YOEM), established in 1996, is one such federally funded effort, focusing on at-risk youth who are afraid to go to school because of the threat of violence, truants, those who have been suspended or expelled from school, and detainees who need help reentering the school system. YOEM is not a single program, but rather is made up of a number of innovative programs operating in various school and correctional systems throughout the United States (Stephens & Arnette, 2000).

Although YOEM is relatively new and evaluation research has yet to gauge many programs' success in preventing crime and lowering reoffending, other studies suggest that education is more effective in reducing recidivism than more punitive approaches such as shock incarceration or boot camps. For example, nationally, the recidivism rate for juveniles is between 60 and 84 percent. However, among juvenile offenders who were enrolled in quality reading instruction programs, recidivism was reduced by at least 20 percent (Center on Crime, Communities and Culture, 1997). Similarly, among adult offenders, the more education received in prison, ranging from literacy training to advanced degrees, the lower the recidivism rate (Center on Crime, Communities and Culture, 1997).

Despite these promising findings, however, the political rhetoric of "getting-tough" on criminals by not "coddling" them in prison has contributed to a reduction in funding for many prison-based programs, including educational programs, in some parts of the country. In some cases, prison higher education programs have been eliminated (Center on Crime, Communities and Culture, 1977). Nevertheless, in other jurisdictions, lawsuits brought on behalf of prisoners have resulted in court-ordered expansion of educational programming (see, for example, Forero, 2000).

It remains to be seen whether the "get-tough" advocates will win out over the education advocates, but one thing is clear: Education is less expensive than more punitive correctional methods, a fact that should appeal to taxpayers, even politically conservative ones.

Even in a hypothetical situation with a comparatively expensive correctional higher-education program ($2,500 per year, per inmate in New York State) and one of the highest recorded rates of recidivism upon completion of such a program (15%), the savings of providing higher education are still substantial: The cost of incarcerating 100 individuals over 4 years is approximately $10 million. For an additional 1/10 of that cost, or $1 million, those same individuals could be given a full, four-year college education while incarcerated. Assuming a recidivism rate of 15% (as opposed to the general rate of 40–60%), 85 of those initial 100 individuals

(continued)

BOX 2.1   Continued

will not return to prison, saving U.S. tax-payers millions of dollars each year. (Center on Crime, Communities and Culture, 1997, pp. 9–10).

Additional savings come from eliminating costs to crime victims and the courts and lost wages to

people while incarcerated, including reducing the economic dependency of an inmate's family. In light of these data it is no wonder that many experts consider correctional education programs a "bargain."

With respect to norepinephrine, the traditional hypothesized relationship was that excessive levels of the chemical circulating in the body could induce individuals to engage in aggressive, violent, or other types of antisocial and high-risk behavior. However, while some studies support this hypothesis, others contradict it. For instance, some studies of incarcerated violent criminals (see, for example, Woodman et al., 1977) show these offenders to have abnormally high levels of norepinephrine. Other studies, however, indicate that violent offenders produce abnormally low levels of norepinephrine (Virkkunen et al., 1987).[13] Raine (1996) and others (Raine et al., 1997) have found that violent individuals have slower than normal reaction times when confronted with distressing visual images or other unpleasant stimuli as measured by their heart rate and galvanic skin conductance. These findings suggest that violent crime may be one result of a failure in the part of the nervous system responsible for inhibiting bad behavior, that is, the system that produces—in these cases, too little—norepinephrine.

One reason for the inconsistency in the norepinephrine findings, however, may be that the relationship between the chemical and criminal behavior is not one of direct cause and effect, but is rather a *reciprocal interaction effect*, where fluctuations in the chemical contribute to certain behaviors, but engaging in specific behaviors or having particular experiences also produces fluctuations in norepinephrine production (Niehoff, 1999). Thus, specific behavioral outcomes associated with norepinephrine levels may very depending on an individual's unique social *and* biological history.

The second neurotransmitter that has been linked to criminal behavior, especially violence, is dopamine. The production of dopamine is part of our body's internal reward system; our brain associates particular behaviors with positive outcomes, thereby *reinforcing* those behaviors (i.e., increasing the likelihood that those behaviors will be enacted again when we are confronted by similar circumstances in the future) (Niehoff, 1999). Some behaviors are more reinforcing than others. Any behavior that contributes to our survival, for example, is highly rewarding. Too much dopamine, however, can produce a "self-defensive overreaction" (Niehoff, 1999, p. 132)—in short, hostility, verbal or physical sparring, violence.

Though interesting, research on the effects of dopamine on behavior must be interpreted cautiously, since nearly all has been conducted in laboratories with animals, not humans. Moreover, the role of dopamine production as cause or effect is unclear.

Once again, studies indicate that although rises in dopamine can trigger violence, a violent encounter can also increase dopamine production. For example, researchers have found that dopamine increases dramatically in mice the first time they are confronted with an intruder in their laboratory cages. However, by their tenth encounter with intruders, their dopamine levels are the same as those of mice not exposed to intruders (Haney et al., 1990; Miczek & Tornatzky, 1996). As Niehoff (1999, p. 133) explains, "Over time, repeated encounters are characterized not by a static neurochemistry that 'causes' behavior, but by a dynamic readjustment in dopaminergic activity that represents a progressive reshaping of the dopamine system by experience."

It is the neurotransmitter serotonin, however, that has generated the greatest interest among criminologists. Serotonin is a neurotransmitter that inhibits impulsivity; it induces you to reflect before you actually do something. Consequently, low serotonin levels have been strongly linked to impulsive crimes, such as arson, unpremeditated murders and attempted murders, and also to self-inflicted violence, including attempted or completed suicide (Coccaro, 1992; DeFeudis & Schauss, 1987; Fishbein, 2000; Linnoila & Virkkunen, 1992). Still, like much of the research on norepinephrine and dopamine, the serotonin research is conducted largely with laboratory animals, and the precise relationship between serotonin levels and crime is not well understood. For instance, in a study that allowed researchers to observe changes in rats' serotonin levels as they occurred, the findings showed that serotonin decreased in the aggressor *after* an attack, not before (van Erp & Miczek, 1996). As Niehoff (1999, p. 145) concluded, "This important study warns that we ignore the circular relationship between brain and behavior at our peril, that correlations are clues but not necessarily causes. Alterations in brain chemistry show us where the brain has been as well as where it is going next, as it collaborates with the environment to shape responses that ensure survival."

One link between serotonin and environment has been found in studies of children exposed to drugs, such as cocaine, prenatally. The research shows that such children have abnormally low serotonin levels which, in turn, have been associated with such problems as an inability to calculate the consequences of their actions, impaired logical thinking, difficulty following instructions, difficulty in abstract thinking, and memory and learning deficiencies (Gorio et al., 1992; Guerra, 1998; but for a critique of the fetal cocaine exposure research see Humphries, 1999). As we have noted, these problems are further associated with delinquent and criminal behavior. Prenatal exposure to cocaine has also been shown to cause a depletion of dopamine and an increase in norepinephrine, along with damage to neurological receptors and a reduction in blood flow. According to Fishbein (2000), in some major U.S. cities, between 10 and 15 percent of women of childbearing age use cocaine. Not surprisingly, these findings have raised public policy questions about how to best reduce women's, especially pregnant women's, use of cocaine and thereby prevent later antisocial or criminal behavior in their offspring. Some advocates have called for better drug treatment programs, which for women have been sorely lacking. But as we see in Box 2.2 on pages 60–61, others in the criminal justice system have taken a more punitive approach, prosecuting pregnant drug users for endangering the well-being of their unborn children.

BOX 2.2   HOW THE WORLD SEES IT
Drug Abuse During Pregnancy: The Effects on Offspring

During the late 1980s and early 1990s, crack cocaine use peaked in the United States. In 1988, the national news media focused the country's attention on pregnant crack users and the effects of the drug on their babies, who were quickly dubbed "crack babies" (Humphries, 1999). Early research reports summarized in the popular media indicated that babies exposed to cocaine *in utero* exhibited various congenital defects, including malformations of the genitourinary tract, as well as serious neurobehavioral problems that persisted from infancy through the toddler years (see, for example, Chasnoff, 1991).

In 1991, however, a team of Canadian researchers pooled the data from 20 clinical studies in order to pinpoint more specifically what effects, if any, cocaine had on babies exposed to the drug *in utero* (Lutiger et al., 1991). These researchers conducted three sets of comparisons: They looked at women who had used only cocaine relative to women who had used no drugs, women who had used cocaine as well as other drugs relative to women who had used no drugs, and women who had used only cocaine relative to women who had used other drugs but not cocaine. This study showed that cocaine use during pregnancy was unrelated to a wide variety of fetal and infant problems with which it had been previously associated; cocaine use did not cause heart malformations, sudden infant death syndrome (SIDS), or placental bleeding and detachment. Cocaine use, however, was related to smaller head size in infants, premature delivery, and low birth weight and length, although no more so than other drugs. In fact, another Canadian research team found a large number of studies that showed no detrimental effects to offspring from prenatal cocaine exposure, but argued that such studies were less likely to be published than those showing detrimental effects because of biases in the scientific community and funding agencies (Koren et al., 1989).

According to Humphries (1999), it is difficult to accurately evaluate the effects of prenatal cocaine exposure because of serious flaws in much of the research. For example, many studies use very small samples of women selected on the basis of convenience, which makes generalizing the results to the general population risky at best. In addition, the methods that the researchers use to determine a pregnant woman's drug use status are sometimes questionable in terms of their reliability. Most studies also do not or cannot specify the timing, dose, and duration of individual prenatal exposures. Finally, and perhaps most important, none of the studies has been able to isolate the effects of cocaine exposure from other risk factors "that themselves adversely affect pre- and postnatal development . . . such as poverty, violence, abandonment, homelessness, short-term foster placements, and inadequate or abusive parenting" (Humphries, 1999, p. 62; see also the Appendix).

In light of these methodological problems, it is not surprising that researchers who observed prenatally exposed infants in hospital nurseries did not see widespread manifestations of the toxic effects of the drug. Instead, "most exposed infants presented in the nursery as remarkably normal and asymptomatic" (Hutchings, 1993, p. 283). Nevertheless, most criminal justice officials in the United States have uncritically accepted the idea that cocaine causes lasting deficits in children exposed to the drug prenatally. Many have sought ways to prosecute pregnant addicts for endangering the welfare of their children. In South Carolina, for example, pregnant women who were suspected drug users were tested when they sought prenatal care or gave birth. This program officially ended in the mid-1990s, but advocates for addicted women contend that the drug testing is still common because South Carolina's child endangerment law applies to viable fetuses as well as children (Greenhouse, 2000). In other states, such as

Florida, prosecutors charged pregnant addicts with child abuse, arguing that the women were delivering illegal drugs to their babies through the umbilical cord (Boyd, 1999; Humphries, 1999). Whereas in most other countries drug addiction is considered an illness, in the United States pregnant addicts have been criminalized, a practice that is unlikely to prove helpful to either them or their children since so few women's correctional facilities offer drug treatment programs.

Diet and Crime: You Are What You Eat?

The production and efficient utilization of neurotransmitters by the body is also to some extent dependent on diet. For instance, serotonin is produced from tryptophan, which is an amino acid found in high-protein foods, such as eggs, fish, dairy products, and some types of meat. The production of both dopamine and norepinephrine depends on the amino acid tyrosine, which is also found in most protein foods. Consequently, it has been suggested that certain behavior problems, such as aggression due to low serotonin levels, may be correctable through a high-protein diet (Cronkhite, 1996; Fishbein & Pease, 1988; Mawson & Jacobs, 1978).

There are, however, several other ways that diet is thought to be related to antisocial and criminal behavior. One theory that received considerable attention in the popular media focuses on diets high in refined carbohydrates (white rice and flour; sugar and high-sugar foods, such as cake, candy, and soft drinks; and most "junk" foods, such as potato chips). The problem apparently arises because of the way our bodies process refined carbohydrates compared with complex carbohydrates.

More specifically, complex carbohydrates are processed relatively slowly because of their natural bulk. As they are digested, they convert to glucose, which enters the bloodstream and, in turn, causes the pancreas to secrete insulin. It is insulin's job to facilitate the cells' absorption of the glucose, which can be used for energy. However, because refined carbohydrates lack bulk and break down quickly, the process goes somewhat awry. A large amount of glucose enters the bloodstream, triggering the rapid release of insulin.

> In the body's effort to control the rapid influx of glucose, excessive amounts of insulin may be released, causing a sharp decline in blood sugar level which seriously deprives the brain of needed glucose. . . . Hence the individual feels hungry again and/or craves sweets to raise the blood sugar level and the process starts over again. . . . If blood glucose falls to subnormal levels, the brain registers a crisis and causes the release of hormones such as adrenalin, prolactin, cortisol, and ACTH. . . . Increases in these hormones have been associated with irritability, agitation, and anxiety. Also, the neurotransmitter dopamine rises and exacerbates behavioral and psychological disruptions. These symptoms may compromise individuals' ability to control their behavior. (Fishbein & Pease, 1988, pp. 14–15, see also Cronkhite, 1996)

Chronically low blood sugar constitutes a medical condition known as *hypoglycemia*. Among the behavioral symptoms of hypoglycemia are irritability and nervousness, depression, and destructive outbursts. Hypoglycemic individuals, therefore, may be prone to acting out, violence, or other forms of antisocial behavior of obvious interest to criminologists.

The study of the relationship between blood sugar levels and crime is not all that new. However, popular and academic interest peaked in the late 1970s when the theory was used as a defense in a criminal trial. Now often referred to as the "Twinkie defense," the case involved former San Francisco city supervisor Dan White, who admitted to killing mayor George Moscone and fellow supervisor Harvey Milk. Although the evidence indicated premeditation, which called for a first degree murder conviction, White's attorney argued that, at the time of the murders, the defendant suffered from diminished capacity because of severe depression made worse by his excessive consumption of junk foods, such as Twinkies and sodas. White was convicted of manslaughter.[14]

Despite the success of the "Twinkie defense" in Dan White's case, scientific research on blood sugar levels has not demonstrated a clear relationship to crime. Several intervention studies, in which the diets of various samples of criminal offenders were modified to reduce the intake of refined carbohydrates, have shown that such dietary changes appear to produce measurable positive effects on violent or antisocial behavior (Cronkhite, 1996; Schoenthaler, 1983 & 1984; Virkkunen, 1987). However, these studies have serious methodological flaws that do not allow researchers to rule out other competing factors as the causes of the observed behavioral changes (Fishbein & Pease, 1988; Gray, 1986).

Still other ways that diet may be related to criminal behavior have to do with food allergies or sensitivities, the toxic effects of certain minerals in food, reactions to food dyes or other food additives, and vitamin deficiencies. For example, prolonged exposure to lead and cadmium can damage brain tissue and alter the production of neurotransmitters. Cadmium levels are especially high in refined carbohydrates. Thus, the potential negative effects of a diet dominated by refined carbohydrates may be exacerbated by the increased exposure to cadmium in such foods. In addition, some individuals are especially sensitive to certain naturally occurring or added substances in foods, such as monosodium glutamate (MSG), caffeine, and phenylethylemine (found in chocolate). Reactions to such substances in sensitive or allergic individuals include hyperactivity, hostility, and aggressiveness, which, in turn, could lead to criminal behavior (Cronkhite, 1996; Fishbein & Pease, 1988; Schauss, 1980).

Once again, though, we must be careful not to jump too quickly to any conclusions here. The research methodologies in studies testing the relationship of food sensitivities to crime frequently are flawed and the findings are inconsistent, often contradictory. Some researchers simply rely on reports of a few case studies to support their claims (Cronkhite, 1996; Rapp, 1981; Schauss, 1980). Unfortunately, as we have already noted, this has not prevented the introduction of these theories into the courtroom. Besides the Dan White case, for instance, there was the more recent case of a Virginia man who was acquitted of burglary charges on the basis of a vitamin deficiency defense (Gray, 1986).

Summary and Conclusion

In this chapter, we have reviewed a wide variety of theories that, though different in many ways, share the basic premise that the causes of crime lie at least to some extent *within* the individual. From Lombroso's notion of atavism to contemporary studies of genes, hormones, the brain, and diet, each of these theories sees the criminal as suffering from some biological defect. While early research on biology and crime was obviously faulty on methodological grounds, better designed studies in recent years still have failed to produce consistent findings. Though much of this work is provocative, it remains to be seen whether criminologists of this tradition can provide us with any conclusive answers to our continuing questions about crime causation.

The history of biological criminology is tainted by bad science and misguided campaigns such as the eugenics movement. Fear of the policy implications of some biological theories—for example, altering people's genes, brain structure, or brain chemistry to prevent crime—has led many criminologists today to simply reject these theories outright. However, we have seen in this chapter that most contemporary biological research on crime causation recognizes that human behavior is the product of a complex interaction between biological factors and environmental or social conditions. "Behavior is . . . a dialogue—between past and present, experience and physiology" (Niehoff, 1999, p. 116). Our biology provides a foundation or starting point for our development and imposes constraints on what we can accomplish, but only within extraordinarily wide boundaries. In turn, our culture and living conditions, as well as our unique experiences as individuals, shape who we are and who we become not only socially, but also biologically. It is deciphering the workings of this continual feedback loop between biology and environment, physiology and experience, that holds the greatest challenge, but also perhaps the greatest promise for biological criminologists.

KEY TERMS

atavism—a concept developed by Lombroso to refer to the evolutionary degeneracy of born criminals.

hormones—chemicals secreted by the body to regulate the activities of specific cells or organs.

neurotransmittors—chemical compounds found between nerve cells that send signals from one neuron to another, thus having a direct impact on behavior, emotion, moods, and learning.

phrenology—one of the earliest biological theories of crime, which argued that the development and shape of the brain affects personality and social behavior.

somatotyping—Sheldon's system of classifying criminals (and others) according to the presence of endomorphy, ectomorphy, and mesomorphy in their physique.

stigmata—the physical signs or traits that Lombroso used to identify atavists.

XYY syndrome—a chromosomal abnormality that during the 1960s was believed to predispose men with the extra Y chromosome to criminality, especially violent crime.

SUGGESTED READINGS

Fishbein, D. H. (Ed.). (2000). *The science, treatment and prevention of antisocial behaviors: Applications to the criminal justice system*. Kingston, NJ: Civic Research Institute. A compendium of the latest research on biological and physiological factors that may contribute to delinquent and criminal behavior.

Humphries, D. (1999). *Crack mothers: Pregnancy, drugs, and the media*. Columbus, OH: Ohio State University Press. A careful analysis of the social construction of the "crack mom," which includes a thorough review of the research on the effects of prenatal exposure to cocaine and other drugs.

Niehoff, D. (1999). *The biology of violence*. New York: Free Press. A readable—indeed, enjoyable—explanation of very complex research on the role of brain structure, function, and chemistry in the etiology of violent behavior.

NOTES

1. Interestingly, Savitz and his colleagues (1977, pp. 53–54) report that "modern brain surgery has, admittedly with moderate success, reduced extremely aggressive, uncontrollably hostile behavior in some individuals by destroying very restricted areas of the amygdala and the hippocampus . . . and these are precisely within the 'Destructive' organ area. One might speculate that Gall's anatomical studies of the brain early revealed to him one major area involved in human violent behavior."

2. According to Vold and Bernard (1986, p. 59), "Sheldon took his underlying ideas and terminology of types from the fact that a human life begins as an embryo that is essentially a tube made up of three tissue layers, namely an inner layer (or endoderm), a middle layer (or mesoderm), and an outer layer (or ectoderm)."

3. Snodgrass (1951) states that Sheldon considered endomorphy, ectomorphy, and mesomorphy primary variables, but he also looked at other variables that he categorized as secondary, tertiary, etc. For instance, the second order variables included dysplasia (or what Sheldon called a "disharmonious mixture" of the three primary components), gynandromorphy (possession of secondary sex characteristics of the opposite sex), a textural variable (or "t-component" as Sheldon called it, which referred to the "fineness" or "coarseness" of the structure of the body), and hirsutism (hairiness of the trunk, arms, and legs). Each of these variables was rated on a 7-point scale, except for hirsutism, which was rated on a 5-point scale.

4. The eugenics movement was popular at the turn of the century in the United States. Eugenicists advocated the forced sterilization of those deemed mentally unfit so as to purify or improve the quality of the population overall. More than 30 states had enacted eugenics laws by 1937. We will address this issue again in Chapter 3 when we examine the relationship between intelligence and crime.

5. Cortes measured temperament by having subjects rate themselves according to sets of traits associated with each of the three personality types. To gauge subjects' need for achievement and desire for power, he used David's McClelland's measure, "Test for Need for Achievement," which the author claims measures individuals' motivation to achieve and seek power.

6. Wilson and Herrnstein (1985) also review the research on body build and crime and report that a muscular body build, while not a *cause* of crime, is nevertheless statistically associated with crime. However, Rowe (1995) reports that muscular body build accounts for only 2–4 percent of the variance in criminality among those studied.

7. In contrast, Christiansen used a large unselected sample. However, given his sample size, it is somewhat surprising that only 5 percent had an official record of any criminal offenses, especially since it has been estimated that the possibility of a juvenile male ever being arrested may be as high as 40 percent.

8. However, Rowe and Gulley (1992) compared 135 pairs of brothers and 142 pairs of sisters. None of the sibling pairs was twins, but all were close in age and in their early teen years. Rowe and Gulley looked at the delinquency rates of the pairs in terms of their concordance or discordance for their friendship groups (i.e., whether they had the same or different friends). They found that the delinquency sibling correlations were about twice as large when the pairs

were concordant for friendship groups. Rowe (1995) cites this research as an example of the effect of shared environmental influences on siblings' behavior.

9. Another chromosomal abnormality that may result is *mosaicism*, a condition in which a different number of sex chromosomes are present in different tissues or parts of the body. For instance, a male may be XYY in some cells of his body, while other cells contain a single X chromosome. This mosaic would be referred to as XO/XYY. For a detailed discussion of these chromosomal abnormalities, see Hoyenga and Hoyenga, 1993.

10. It was later discovered that Richard Speck, who one night brutally murdered nine student nurses in their dormitory rooms, was not, in fact, XYY.

11. For a discussion of this literature, see Renzetti and Curran, 1999.

12. MPAs include fine electric hair, head circumference beyond the normal range, low-seated or asymmetrical ears, adherent ear lobes, high-steepled palate, furrowed tongue, curved fifth finger, and third toe as long or longer than second toe. MPAs cause no serious medical or cosmetic problems for individuals who have them (Fishbein, 2000; Krouse & Kauffman, 1982). Some critics feel, however, that their discussion in the context of criminality is reminiscent of Lombroso.

13. A study of compulsive gamblers also showed that these individuals have low levels of norepinephrine (Goleman, 1989). Since norepinephrine is produced under stressful conditions, such as in situations involving high risk or excitement, it may be that people deficient in this neurotransmitter are compelled to gamble as a way to stimulate the brain to produce more of the chemical.

14. The verdict in the White case generated considerable public controversy that ultimately led to the abolition of the diminished capacity defense in California. This issue is discussed further in Chapter 3.

3 The Criminal Mind: Psychological and Psychiatric Theories of Crime

How many of us, when we hear about a particularly heinous crime, think about the offender and say, "He had to be crazy to do something like that," or "She had to be sick"? Explanations of criminality as a product of mental illness or mental defect date back to ancient Greece and remain popular today.

In this chapter we examine some of the psychological and psychiatric theories that have been applied to criminal behavior. Instead of focusing on abnormalities of the body, these theories emphasize abnormalities of the mind, especially the personality. But readers will be reminded of some of the ideas raised in Chapter 2, since a number of theorists hypothesize that certain mental disorders and defects have biological roots and may even be hereditary.[1] This is perhaps nowhere more obvious than in discussions of intelligence and crime.

Too Dumb to Know Better: The IQ/Crime Controversy

When Charles Goring published his study of *The English Convict* in 1913, he reported that he had found no evidence to support Lombroso's theory of atavism. However, he found that criminals were abnormally low in intelligence and he took this as an indication of hereditary inferiority.

At the time Goring was writing, the idea that criminals were mentally deficient was acquiring a large number of adherents. They argued that those lacking in intelligence were also lacking in morality. "The intelligence controls the emotions and the emotions are controlled in proportion to the degree of intelligence. . . . It follows that if there is little intelligence the emotions will be uncontrolled and whether they be strong or weak will result in actions that are unregulated, uncontrolled and, as experience proves, usually undesirable" (Gould, 1981, pp. 160–161).[2] But how was an individual's level of intelligence to be determined? An answer to this question takes us into the thorny area of intelligence testing.

Early Intelligence Tests and Crime

Attempts to quantitatively measure intelligence began in the late 1800s. However, it was a French psychologist, *Alfred Binet* (1857–1911), who is credited with the development and implementation of the first intelligence test shortly after the turn of the century. Binet was asked by the minister of public education in France to develop a method of identifying children with learning problems so that they could be helped with special education classes. In response, the psychologist assembled a series of tasks involving basic reasoning skills, with each task assigned an age level indicating its difficulty. Quite simply:

> A child began the Binet test with tasks for the youngest age and proceeded in sequence until he [sic] could no longer complete the tasks. The age associated with the last tasks he could perform became his "mental age," and his general intellectual level was calculated by subtracting this mental age from his true chronological age. Children whose mental ages were sufficiently behind their chronological ages could then be identified for special educational programs, thus fulfilling Binet's charge from the ministry. (Gould, 1981, pp. 149–150; see also Lefton, 2000)

Several years later in 1912, a German psychologist named W. Stern revised Binet's method for calculating general intellectual level by *dividing* mental age by chronological age, arguing that this gives a better estimate of degree of deficiency. Division, though, yields a fraction, so Stern multiplied the quotient by 100 to get rid of the decimal point. In so doing, he gave birth to the concept of the **intelligence quotient or IQ**.[3]

Significantly, Binet maintained that an IQ score should be used only as a rough guide for identifying children who need extra help in school, and he stated explicitly that the test "does not permit the measure of intelligence" because intelligence "is not a single, scorable thing like height" (quoted in Gould, 1981, p. 151). Unfortunately, Binet's warning fell on deaf ears in the United States where translators and popularizers of the test took it as a measure of innate intelligence and used the scores to lobby for discriminatory and repressive social policies. For students of criminology, one of the most important proponents of these ideas was *Henry H. Goddard*.

As director of research at the Vineland Training School for Feebleminded Boys and Girls in New Jersey, Goddard used his adaptation of Binet's test to develop a unilinear scale of intelligence. He administered the test to the residents of his institution and to all new admissions and found that none scored above the mental age of twelve (for IQ 75, if one accepts Goddard's assumption that full mental capacity is achieved by chronological age sixteen). Consequently, the mental age thirteen became the cutoff point of normal intelligence. Those who scored between the mental ages of eight and twelve were classified as "feebleminded," "morons," or "high-grade defectives." It was these individuals about whom Goddard expressed greatest concern.

According to Goddard, those with a mental age of thirteen to fifteen had enough intelligence to at least be able to work at semi-skilled jobs, doing the drudgery and thereby making themselves useful to society. Those with a mental age below eight were too enfeebled to do much of anything and, therefore, posed no threat. However, the morons or high-grade defectives were considered potentially dangerous because, even though they could be trained to function in society, their stupidity would very likely get them into trouble. One needed only to test the inmates of U.S. prisons and jails to prove this point; using Goddard's standard, it was found that a median of 70 percent of criminals were feebleminded (Gould, 1981).

Goddard did not stop here. He also attempted to trace the family histories of the residents of his institution in order to demonstrate that feeblemindedness (and hence, the propensity to commit crimes) is hereditary. One of his most famous studies was of the "Kallikaks," a family of morons who lived in the New Jersey pine barrens. Goddard claimed that the 480 Kallikaks that he identified were all descendants of an illicit union between a righteous man and a feebleminded tavern wench. This liaison supposedly gave rise to a whole line of sex perverts, alcoholics, prostitutes, and morons. The same man was also said to have later married a Quaker woman and this union produced a line of intellectually normal and socially upstanding individuals.[4]

From "research" such as this, Goddard concluded that feeblemindedness was hereditary. It followed, then, that the best way to prevent feeblemindedness (and crime) was to prevent the feebleminded from reproducing. The segregation, of the feebleminded in special institutions or "colonies," as well as sterilization, were proposed solutions to the problem. At the same time, Goddard was concerned about the large number of southern and eastern European immigrants who were entering the United States, a high percentage of whom his tests indicated were feebleminded. Even if institutionalization and sterilization lowered the number of "native" morons, he worried that no benefit to society would be realized unless the massive influx of feebleminded immigrants was stopped.

Goddard and his colleagues succeeded in establishing routine IQ testing for a number of groups, including newly landed immigrants and convicted criminals. Of course, there were critics of these ideas and programs, but they were largely ignored until the U.S. army agreed to allow the testing of draftees during World War I. The army tests identified a disturbingly high percentage of feebleminded draftees. In fact, extrapolating from the results, one is led to conclude that, at the time, about half the U.S. population was made up of morons. This shocking (and obviously absurd) finding led a number of observers, including some supporters of the testing program, to question the validity and reliability of the tests (Gould, 1981). Research that ensued not only revealed serious weaknesses in the tests, but also refuted the hypothesized relationship between feeblemindedness and crime. Indeed, several studies showed that incarcerated criminals had higher average IQs than the World War I draftees (see, for example, Sutherland, 1931).

By the 1930s, the idea that most offenders were feebleminded had fallen into disfavor among criminologists. Nevertheless, it would be a mistake to conclude that Goddard and his colleagues' crusade was just an unfortunate episode in the history of science with no practical impact. For one thing, Goddard's claims about the inherited mental deficiency of some immigrant groups figured prominently in the congressional debates that led to the enactment of the Immigration Restriction Act of 1924. For many years, this prevented admission of countless immigrants to the United States, including Jewish refugees seeking to escape the holocaust (Gould, 1981). In addition, a number of states passed laws permitting the forced sterilization of individuals "diagnosed" as feebleminded. In 1927, the U.S. Supreme Court upheld Virginia's compulsory sterilization law in the case of *Buck* v. *Bell*. Within ten years more than thirty states had enacted such laws and it is estimated that at least 60,000 sterilizations were performed (Gallagher, 1999; Gould, 1984).[5] There is perhaps no better illustration of the tragic consequences that can result when bad theory coupled with flawed research are used to inform the development of public policy.

The Resurrection of the IQ/Crime Relationship.   Until the late 1970s, most criminology texts either ignored the IQ issue or discounted its importance. Then, in 1977, two criminologists, *Travis Hirschi* and *Michael Hindelang*, revived the debate in an article that reanalyzed the extant data on IQ and crime. Hirschi and Hindelang examined two kinds of studies: those that relied on official crime statistics and records, and those that utilized self-report questionnaires. In the former, they found a strong negative correlation between IQ and delinquency—that is, as IQ scores increased, delinquent acts decreased. In the latter, they also found a negative relationship, although it was considerably weaker.

Hirschi and Hindelang concluded that low intelligence is a significant factor in crime and delinquency causation, independent of social class and race, although its contribution is indirect. More specifically, children with low intellectual ability are less likely than more intellectually gifted children to be prepared for school, to succeed in school, to receive academic rewards and, consequently, to develop positive attachments to school (see also Chapter 5). One likely outcome of these academic failures is antisocial and delinquent behavior. In other words, the relationship between IQ and crime is mediated by negative school experiences.

Hirschi and Hindelang's argument makes sense, especially in light of the research on education and income that we discussed in Chapter 2. However, additional empirical research indicates that when we look at IQ (as opposed to education) the IQ–crime relationship is more complex than Hirschi and Hindelang made it out to be (Denno, 1985; Menard & Morse, 1984; White et al., 1989). In fact, some researchers have failed to find any significant differences in IQ test scores between delinquents and nondelinquents and among various categories of delinquents, including chronic and violent offenders (see Denno, 1985). Nevertheless, the inconsistency of the findings has not deterred some researches from making inflammatory claims about the role of IQ in the etiology of crime. Robert Gordon (1980, 1987), for instance, points out that the Black/White ratio for delinquency is about 3:1. At the same time, he observes that African Americans score on average 11 to 15 points lower than White Americans on IQ tests. Working under the assumption that an IQ test is a measure of innate intelligence, Gordon concludes from these statistics that the racial difference in delinquency rates is commensurate with the racial difference in IQ scores and that the latter actually explains the former. That is, African Americans commit more crimes than White Americans because they have lower IQs.

More recently, Richard Herrnstein and Charles Murray (1994) published their controversial book, *The Bell Curve*, in which one of the central arguments is that non-White Americans, who make up an increasing percentage of the U.S. population, are intellectually inferior to the rest of the population and that little can be done to improve this situation. Sounding more than a little like Charles Goring (1913), Herrnstein and Murray maintain that women with low IQ scores are reproducing faster than women with high IQ scores, with the result that the national distribution of scores will go down. No educational enrichment or affirmative action program will stem this tide, since the source of the intellectual inferiority is genetics. The inevitable outcome is an even greater split between social classes in the United States, with a small, intellectually and, therefore, economically and socially powerful elite running the country, and a large, intellectually deficient underclass wreaking havoc, which, of course, includes crime (see also Herrnstein, 1988b; Wilson & Herrnstein, 1985).

There are three controversial issues—in addition to the question of how IQ is related to criminality—that are raised in these arguments: (1) that IQ is hereditary; (2) that IQ tests measure general innate intelligence; and (3) that different racial/ethnic groups have different levels of innate intelligence. Although as Herrnstein (1989, p. 13) argues with respect to the first issue "virtually all experts now agree that IQ has a genetic component," experts disagree about the extent to which IQ is heritable. Consider the research on adoptees, for instance. While some researchers have found that adopted children more closely resemble their biological mothers than their adoptive parents in terms of IQ (Eysenck, 1998; Horn, 1983, Plomin et al., 1997), others report that adoptees' IQs are highly malleable to the conditions in which the children are reared (Scarr & Weinberg, 1983; 1994; Schiff et al., 1982). Another way to research the heritability of IQ is to study identical (MZ) twins reared apart, but as we noted in Chapter 2, such cases are few. This research indicates that while there is likely a heritable component to IQ, genetics accounts for far less of the similarities in IQ scores between identical twins—reared apart or together—than has long been assumed. While some researchers have claimed that IQ is 70–80 percent heritable, the recent research with identical twins leads most to conclude that IQ is about 50 percent heritable; in other words, only about half of the observed similarities in the IQ scores of identical twins are likely the result of genetics (Bouchard et al., 1990; Petrill et al., 1998; see also Farber, 1981).

Research on the heritability of IQ raises the more fundamental questions of whether IQ equals general innate intelligence and whether IQ tests measure individuals' native intellectual abilities. Most educators agree that IQ tests are good measures of a child's ability to perform in school, especially with regard to a narrow range of skills, including math and English. At the same time, however, research shows that IQ tests are poor predictors of a child's future financial or employment success. This is because many jobs require broader skills than those measured by IQ tests. For instance, IQ tests reward speed, allowing the test taker from five to fifty seconds to answer each question. On the job, though, or in one's personal life, an individual does not often confront problems that are best solved by snap judgments (Goleman, 1995).

Many psychologists and educators also think that IQ tests are a better indicator of a child's background and learning environment than his or her natural intelligence. As we find in Box 3.1 on pages 72–73, IQ tests are *culturally specific*—they tap a child's

BOX **3.1**   **CONTROVERSY AND DEBATE**
Are IQ Tests Culturally Biased?

Supporters of IQ testing usually concede that the tests measure only a limited range of cognitive activities and reflect particular aspects of test takers' personal backgrounds, including the amount and quality of schooling they have had, how much they have been encouraged or permitted to express themselves verbally, and the availability of books in their homes and the amount of time they have spent reading them (Barrett & Depinet, 1991; Lefton, 2000). Supporters of IQ tests also agree that prior to the 1970s, many IQ tests contained obvious cultural biases. For instance, the following questions were taken from an IQ test administered to Army recruits in 1917:

2. Five hundred is played with:

    rackets   pins   cards   dice

5. The percheron is a kind of:

    goat   horse   cow   sheep

7. Christe Matthewson is famous as a:

    writer   artist   comedian
    baseball player

The correct answers are: cards, horse, and baseball player (Owen, 1985, p. 181). Not surprisingly, when this test was administered to newly arrived European immigrants, most did poorly—not because of innate stupidity, but because of their unfamiliarity with American culture. Moreover, what is considered "general knowledge" varies not only cross-culturally, but also from one historical period to another.

Nevertheless, supporters of IQ testing maintain that since the 1970s, test makers have eliminated cultural biases from the tests. Consequently, while some groups of people do better on the tests than other groups, the tests are not systematically biased against any particular racial or ethnic group. They point out, for example, that differences in siblings' test scores are often as large as differences in test scores across various ethnic groups. In other words, the range in variation in individuals' scores is as large or larger than the range in variation in different ethnic groups' scores (Lefton, 2000; Sattler, 1992). Supporters of the tests are less concerned about cultural biases within the test than with how test results are used. It is in applying the test results, they say, that teachers and employers may inject their own cultural biases.

Critics of IQ testing acknowledge that efforts have been made to reduce the cultural biases in the tests, but believe that many cultural and environmental biases remain. Consider, for instance, the following question:

Recitation is to poet as _____ is to rower.

   a) oar
   b) regatta
   c) water
   d) boat

The correct answer is *regatta*. If you got this question wrong, does it mean you are not as intelligent as someone who got it right? Maybe. An incorrect answer might also mean that you are simply unfamiliar with such things as recitations and regattas. Who is most likely to be unfamiliar with recitations and regattas? Children whose racial or ethnic heritage is not Western European for one, but also children from economically disadvantaged backgrounds, a disproportionate number of whom are racial and ethnic minorities. Yet, this kind of question is commonly used on IQ tests to measure the intelligence or achievements of *all* students, regardless of race, ethnicity, or social class. Not surprisingly, children from wealthy White families do better on such tests than children from non-White and poorer families (Applebome, 1997; Jones, 1994).

Critics of IQ testing cite evidence that people from different ethnic backgrounds display different patterns of cognitive abilities because cultures differ so widely in what they value as knowledge and how they conceptualize time and space (Lefton, 2000). Burg and Belmont (1990), for example, tested 320 Israeli children whose parents had emigrated from diverse areas: Europe, Iraq, North Africa, and Yemen. They found that across each of these four groups, the children showed four different patterns of cognitive abilities. Critics of IQ testing argue, therefore, that any test designed to measure "general knowledge" or "intelligence" or even achievement must be culturally relevant to the test takers. Moreover, many critics believe that the tests need to be able to measure diverse talents and capabilities, not just intellectual ones, and that these talents and capabilities will differ depending on the test taker's background (Geary, 1996; Greenfield, 1997; Sternberg, 1986).

If critics of IQ testing are correct with regard to the cultural biases of the tests, then any observed relationship between IQ and crime may exist because racial and ethnic minorities are disproportionately represented among the disadvantaged and the disadvantaged are disproportionately represented among those who are arrested, convicted, and incarcerated. The relationship between economic disadvantage and crime, as well as race and ethnicity and crime, have long been of interest to criminologists and will be discussed in the remaining chapters of this book.

---

familiarity with White, middle-class language patterns and experiences; but in reality, our society is *culturally diverse*.

> Every group of people develops ways of working with its environment. It develops a set of rules about talking, rules about making tools, or rules about the use of symbols. Makers of standardized IQ tests operate as if there is only one set of rules for all cultural groups. . . . If subjects fail to get a question right, can we be certain that they are unable to perform *the same mental function* if they utilize familiar cultural material? (Hilliard, 1984, pp. 155–156, author's emphasis)

If IQ tests measure familiarity with particular aspects of a given culture, then the differential scores of various racial and ethnic groups is not a reflection of their relative levels of intelligence, but rather of their assimilation of the culture represented by the tests. Consider, for instance, recent research that shows that overall, U.S. IQ scores have risen fifteen points during the last fifty years. Does this mean that Americans as a group are getting smarter or that the gene pool in the United States has improved? Obviously not; instead, the higher scores are most likely the result of the fact that some formerly disadvantaged groups have assimilated White middle-class culture. Polish and Russian Jewish children, for example, scored lower than all other immigrant groups on IQ tests in 1921, but today their descendants' scores are consistently superior to those of most other groups, especially on tests of verbal ability (see Neisser, 1998; Williams & Ceci, 1997). Indeed, as a number of researchers have found, "The more Anglicized a non-Anglo child is, the better he [or she] does on the IQ test" (Mercer, 1972, p. 44). It is hardly surprising, then, that on tests standardized to the cultures of other groups, Whites fare poorly.

Differences in test scores across groups may also be the product of a *self-fulfilling prophecy*—that is, members of different groups get different IQ scores not because of real differences between the groups, but because members of the groups, their teachers, test makers and administrators, and others believe that the differences are real and act accordingly. One researcher found, for example, that test scores were negatively affected by test takers' low self-esteem. Prior to administering a standardized intelligence test, psychologist Claude Steele (1997) told a group of Black test takers that the test showed no differences in scores by race. These students subsequently scored as well as White test takers on the test. However, Black test takers who were told nothing about the test or who were asked to identify their race on the test had lower scores than White test takers.

Where does this leave us with respect to our original concern in this section—the relationship between IQ and crime? Certainly we do not expect our discussion to settle the debate on this issue. In light of the evidence, however, we think it is safe to conclude that while there may well be a negative relationship between IQ and crime—and not all studies have demonstrated even this—it does not mean that low IQs cause crime. As we saw in Chapter 2, we must be careful not to confuse *correlation* with *causation* (see also the Appendix). As Ronald Simons (1978, p. 268) has pointed out, "if one assumes that IQ scores are unstable and subject to social influences, it might reasonably be argued that the causal ordering is of a different sort. The delinquent's negative attitudes toward school or his [sic] teacher's negative attitude toward him may lead to troubles at school and to a lack of motivation to develop the abilities tapped by IQ tests."[6] Moreover, an observed relationship between IQ and crime does not mean that there is a relationship between intelligence and crime if, as the data indicate, IQ tests do not measure innate intelligence. Rather, such a relationship may be a reflection of the racial and social class biases of our society—an issue that is explored further in several other chapters, particularly in Chapter 6.

The Criminal Personality

It has been argued that "defining personality is itself a matter of personality," since psychologists "have yet to settle on any definition of personality that is at once substantive, precise, and generally agreed upon" (Lamiel, 1987, p. 5). Nevertheless, most psychologists would not object to defining personality as "a set of relatively enduring behavioral characteristics (including thoughts) and internal predispositions that describe how a person reacts to the environment" (Lefton, 2000, p. 400).

However, even if most psychologists are willing to accept this definition, disagreements remain over such questions as, "How does personality develop?" and "Is an individual's personality stable over time or can it change in response to certain situations or stimuli?" Moreover, psychologists often talk about personality in different ways. We will see some of these disagreements surface in the pages that follow as we discuss various theories of crime and personality.

Psychoanalytic Views of Crime

There is probably no one among the readers of this text who has not heard of the Austrian psychologist, *Sigmund Freud* (1856–1939). As Martin and his colleagues (1990) point out:

[F]ew views in the social sciences have evoked stronger reactions, theoretically or emotionally, or provided as much controversy as Freud's . . . Over the course of time, Freud and his ideas have been ignored, revered, ostracized, rebelled against, ridiculed, defied, modified, re-modified, discarded, and resurrected. It is inconceivable that any other theory has had greater heuristic impact across the disciplines or has crept deeper into the lay conception of human nature. (p. 83)

Freud did not write specifically about criminality. In fact, Ewen (1988, p. 55) claims that Freud preferred "not to treat such 'worthless' people as juvenile delinquents and criminals." Instead, his is a broad sweeping theory of personality that may be (and has been extensively) applied to the study of crime. In order to understand these applications, then, it is necessary to review some of Freud's central ideas and concepts.

Freud conceived of human personality as having three interrelated parts: the id, the ego, and the superego. The **id** is present at birth. It is entirely *unconscious* and is composed of powerful forces, called *drives* and *instincts*. The two most important drives or instincts are sex (*Eros*) and destruction or aggression (*Thanatos*). The id operates on the *pleasure principle*: It wants immediate gratification so as to relieve the psychic tension produced by its powerful drives (that is, it seeks to maximize pleasure and minimize displeasure). It has no sense of reality, making it not evil, but simply *amoral*.

In contrast, the **ego** operates on the *reality principle*: It tries to satisfy the needs of the id in socially acceptable ways. The ego begins to develop when we are between six and eight months old. It develops from our experiences in our environment as we come to understand that we are separate or distinct from the other people and things around us. The ego is best described as the aspect of the personality that is rational, oriented toward solving problems, and able to delay gratification. As the ego grows, so does the individual's ability to deal with reality.

Finally, the **superego** is typically described as the *conscience*. It develops when we are three to five years old. The superego is the internalization of the values and norms of our society that we are taught initially by our parents or other caregivers and later by other authority figures. It is the superego that produces feelings of *guilt*.

Given the various functions and demands of these different aspects of the personality, the possibility for psychic conflict is obviously great. Usually, though, the three components of the personality work together pretty harmoniously. The ego serves as a kind of leader in this working relationship, helping the individual to achieve pleasure, but also find a safe way to relieve building tensions. The ego of a healthy individual successfully *represses* id impulses or channels them to some acceptable outlet (a process Freud called *sublimation*), while also keeping the superego in check, making certain it does not become too rigid or too perfectionistic. But what if something goes wrong? For example, what if the ego is weak, or the superego is over- or underdeveloped? Criminal behavior is one possible consequence, but to understand why, we need to review more carefully how the personality develops according to Freud.

Freud's Theory of Personality Development.   Freud delineated four stages in personality development: the oral, anal, phallic, and genital stages. During each stage, particular id impulses, primarily sexual in nature, seek satisfaction, and a specific part of the body, called an *erotogenic zone*, is the main source of pleasure. The *oral stage* spans the period from birth to one and a half years of age. As its name implies, the mouth, tongue, and lips are the areas of desire and gratification. At the same time, frustration and conflict arise because food is not always forthcoming when the baby demands it and, eventually, the baby must give up the breast, the bottle, and its thumb in order to comply with societal norms. The *anal stage* is also somewhat self-explanatory. At about one to one and a half years, children become fascinated by excretion and begin to real- ize that they can exercise control over their environment by expelling or retaining feces. Not surprisingly, a major source of frustration during this period is toilet training.

During these first two stages, boys and girls are alike in their behavior and expe- riences. For both, their mother is the chief object of their emotions, since she is their primary caregiver and gratifies most of their needs. During the *phallic stage*, however, from about two to five years of age, children become aware of their genitals and of the fact that the genitals of girls and boys are different. It is during this period that *gender identification* takes place—children begin to adopt the behavior and attributes of their same-sex parent—but this process occurs differently for boys and girls.

For boys, identification is motivated by what Freud called *castration anxiety*. At this age, a boy's love for his mother becomes more sexual, and he now views his father as a rival (the *Oedipus complex*). What quickly cures the boy of this jealousy is a glimpse of the female genitalia. Seeing the clitoris, the boy assumes that all girls have been cas- trated for some reason, and he fears that a similar fate may befall him if he continues to compete with his father. Boys perceive the formidable size and power of their fathers and conclude that their fathers have the ability to castrate competitors. Consequently, instead of competing with his father, the boy emulates him and ends up, in a sense, with the best of both worlds: He gets to keep his penis, but still sexually enjoy his mother vicariously through his father.

In contrast, a girl's identification with her mother is motivated by what Freud called *penis envy*. Penis envy in girls develops upon first sight of the male genitals. See- ing the male's "far superior equipment," as Freud (1933/1983, p. 88) put it, the girl thinks she has been castrated. She becomes overwhelmed by her sense of incomplete- ness, her jealousy of boys, and her disdain for her mother and all women since they share her "deformity." She shifts her love to her father, who does possess the coveted penis, and begins to identify with her mother as a means to win him. Eventually, the girl realizes she can have a penis in two ways: briefly through intercourse, and sym- bolically by giving birth to a baby, especially a baby boy. "The original penis wish is transformed into a wish for a baby, which leads to love and desire for the man as bearer of the penis and provider of the baby" (Frieze et al., 1978, p. 31). However, the female never fully overcomes her feelings of inferiority and envy, which leave indelible marks on her personality. "Shame, which is considered to be a feminine characteristic *par excellence* but is far more a matter of convention than might be supposed, has as its pur- pose, we believe, concealment of genital deficiency. . . . The fact that women must be regarded as having little sense of justice is no doubt related to the predominance of envy in their mental life" (Freud, 1933/1983, pp. 90, 92).

Following the phallic stage is a *latency* period, from five to twelve years of age, during which sexual impulses become somewhat dormant. At around the age of twelve, the *genital stage* begins and continues throughout adulthood. Although conflicts and frustrations continue to arise, they are met maturely. Clearly, for Freud, the most important conflicts occur in early childhood. Indeed, Freud maintained that one's personality is established by the age of six and undergoes little change thereafter. If the psychic tensions of the first three developmental stages are effectively sublimated, one is likely to become a relatively mentally healthy adult. However, if a trauma occurs during one of these stages, or if the child is neglected, abused, or overindulged, personality problems will be manifest in adulthood. Freud maintained that we do nothing by chance; all of our mental and physical activity is determined by prior causes. We are now ready to see how this *psychic determinism* applies to criminal behavior.

Freudian Interpretations of Crime. From the Freudian psychoanalytic perspective, a major cause of crime and delinquency is a malfunctioning ego or superego. For instance, parental neglect may result in an *underdeveloped superego*. A number of psychoanalysts have reported a lack of love and care in the backgrounds of delinquent children and criminal adults (Aichhorn, 1963; Marshall, 1983; Warren, 1979). Such individuals did not adequately internalize societal norms. Their nonconformity, then, is an expression of unregulated id impulses.

Interestingly, however, crime may be caused by an *overdeveloped superego*, which is unusually harsh and rigid. An overdeveloped superego produces constant and intense feelings of guilt in the individual which, in turn, generate a desire for punishment. Consequently, the offender with an overdeveloped superego typically leaves a trail of clues, unconsciously wishing to be caught and punished to allay the guilt feelings (Ewen, 1988).

Crime may also be the result of an immature or *underdeveloped ego*. A lack of physical affection in infancy, overly indulgent parents who give in to their child's every whim, or conversely, parents who persistently frustrate their child, are apt to cause the child to become fixated in a particular psychosexual stage of development. An immature ego cannot satisfactorily resolve the conflicts of that stage. Thus, for example, the female offender is usually fixated in the phallic stage, unable to sublimate her penis envy in a socially acceptable way. Her criminal behavior represents an attempt to be a man: "She is aggressively rebellious, and her drive to accomplishment is the expression of her longing for a penis" (Klein, 1980, p. 88).

Finally, the ego utilizes a number of *defense mechanisms* in dealing with the id. Criminal behavior may be a kind of ego defense against especially threatening id impulses and the intense anxiety they produce. One common defense mechanism is called *displacement*, which "allows some expression to the unacceptable wish, but neutralizes the anxiety or guilt that would otherwise result by substituting for the target or even the form of the act some other target or form that, on an unconscious level, means the same thing to the actor" (Cohen, 1966, pp. 63–64). For instance, a man who had a seductive but rejecting mother may wish to punish her by physically harming her, but this desire is too threatening for him to consciously acknowledge. As a result, he displaces the wish by raping and murdering a woman whom he met at a party but who had spurned his advances. Another type of defense mechanism is called *reaction-formation*. This occurs when an unacceptable or threatening feeling is replaced by its opposite. For example, "a truculent independence and contempt for authority is interpreted as a reaction-formation against secret passive-dependent yearnings" (Cohen, 1966, p. 64; see also Newman et al., 1997; Warren, 1979).

A Critique of the Psychoanalytic Perspective.   Our presentation of the psychoanalytic approach is by necessity simplistic. It is impossible to convey the complexity of Freud's ideas in the limited space available, let alone to summarize here the many revisions and offspring of his theory. Our goal simply has been to provide a general overview of a Freudian psychoanalytic perspective of crime, and the critique that follows is offered in the same spirit.

Perhaps the most serious charge against the psychoanalytic perspective is a methodological one. How does one go about empirically testing the theory? As Ewen (1988, p. 47) notes, "Psychoanalytic theory presents a formidable difficulty: the most important part of the personality, the unconscious, is also the most inaccessible." Consequently, we are left to rely on the psychoanalyst's interpretations of the offender/patient's words and behavior—a highly subjective enterprise indeed. For one thing, the psychoanalyst may be biased by his or her own preconceived notions about criminality, the characteristics of a particular patient/offender, or a whole host of other factors. This may lead him or her to overlook important information that may contradict these beliefs and even to discount the patient/offender's own interpretation of events and actions. It may also cause the psychoanalyst to lead the patient/offender to say things or behave in ways that confirm the psychoanalyst's biases. Such problems plagued Freud himself, as the following example illustrates.

> Disagreement with a psychoanalyst's interpretation is almost always seen as a resistance, rather than as an error by the analyst. When Freud told Dora [one of his patients] that a jewel case in her dream symbolized the female genitals, and she replied with "I knew you would say that," Freud promptly rejected the obvious conclusion (that she knew his theories well enough by then to predict his responses) and regarded her answer as a typical way of resisting the truth of his interpretation. (Ewen, 1988, p. 67; see also Lefton, 2000)

Psychoanalysts often do not agree on what is the "correct" interpretation of a specific patient account. In addition, psychoanalytic interpretations occur after the fact and are based largely on the patient/offender's memories of particular events or actions, especially those that occurred during early childhood. Try now to recall the significant events and interactions that occurred during your third year of life—indeed, try only to remember your third birthday—and you will get some inkling of the dangers of unreliability that plague this method. In short, the psychoanalytic approach does not meet one of the most important criteria for a scientific theory: empirical verifiability. Perhaps this is why attempts to empirically test it have produced highly inconsistent findings (Ewen, 1988; but for an opposing view, see Edelson, 1989).

A second difficulty stems from the Freudian depiction of the personality as established in early childhood and as fixed and stable over time. The theory leaves little room for the possibility of personal or social change (except, of course, for the "adjustments" induced by psychotherapy). However, while it is certainly the case that our personality attributes appear to be quite resilient, it is also true that social learning continues throughout the life cycle and that we may modify our behavior and attitudes as we are exposed to new situations and role models. Freud's emphasis on the biological roots of personality—innate wishes and drives—leads one to ignore the significant impact of social or environmental factors in shaping our desires and motivations. It further implies what some critics see as an overly pessimistic view of humans as naturally (unchangeably) selfish and dissatisfied.

Finally, it is impossible to overlook the antifemale bias in Freudian theory. Females are defined as inadequate; they are inherently jealous, passive, and masochistic according to this perspective. In short, Freudian theory asserts that women are clearly men's inferiors. At best, the perspective simply legitimates gender inequality; at worst, it is misogynistic and harmful to women (Webster, 1995).[7]

Despite these and other damaging criticisms, Freud must be credited with demonstrating the importance of early childhood experiences in influencing our later lives and with alerting us to the potential role that unconscious motivations may play in determining our behavior.

Other Approaches to Crime and Personality

More general than the work of psychoanalysts are attempts by other researchers to differentiate between criminals and noncriminals on the basis of specific personality traits. Typically this is done using one of the various *personality inventories* currently available.

In an early review of more than 110 personality studies, Schuessler and Cressey (1950) found only 40 percent showing personality differences between criminals and noncriminals. Moreover, in studies reporting differences, serious methodological problems may have contaminated the results. Of particular concern was the frequent use of unmatched samples such that differences in the social class and other background characteristics of the subjects could have accounted for the personality differences observed.

Two additional literature reviews, however, present stronger evidence of personality differences between criminals and noncriminals. In both, only studies using matched samples of criminals and noncriminals were examined and, in about 80 percent, personality differences were found (Tennenbaum, 1977; Waldo & Dinitz, 1967). Still, the authors of these reviews caution that the findings do not mean that we can predict criminality on the basis of certain personality traits or types. To understand this caveat better, let's take a closer look at some of the tests and the studies that utilize them.

One of the most popular personality tests is the **Minnesota Multiphasic Personality Inventory-2nd Edition (MMPI-2)**. The MMPI-2 was published in 1989 as a revision of the original MMPI, which was developed in the 1940s.[8] The MMPI-2, like its predecessor the MMPI, is designed as a psychiatric screening device to detect psychological malfunctioning or maladjustment. The test is composed of ten clinical scales that measure such psychological problems as depression, hypochondria, paranoia, and hypomania (excitability, impulsiveness). The test also includes four validity scales to uncover lying, dishonesty, and evasiveness on the part of respondents. In all, the test is made up of 567 true/false statements. The scales were standardized using a pool of 2,600 subjects. Although the original MMPI used only White subjects, the standardization sample for the MMPI-2 was more ethnically diverse with an attempt made to increase the representativeness of the general population (Pope et al., 2000).

Studies comparing the MMPI and MMPI-2 scores of delinquents and criminals with those of nondelinquent and noncriminal samples have shown that the former groups usually score higher on scales 4 (psychopathic deviate), 8 (schizophrenia), and 9 (hypomania) and lower on scales 2 (depression), 5 (masculinity/femininity), and 10 (social introversion) than the latter groups (Arbuthot et al., 1987; Wilson & Herrnstein, 1985). The tests have also been used to distinguish between groups of imprisoned offenders, with the result that the more serious criminals who pose the most difficulties in prison also score higher on scales 4, 8, and 9 compared with less serious offenders (Megargee & Bohn, 1979). These findings have led some observers to conclude that in terms of personality, criminals differ from the normal population in that they have "deficient attachments to others and to social norms, bizarre thinking, and unproductive hyperactivity" (Wilson & Herrnstein, 1985, p. 189).

However, the MMPI and MMPI-2 have been criticized on a number of grounds, not the least of which is the fact that the tests include items that ask about a respondent's past criminal behavior. Consequently, it is not surprising that the tests differentiate between criminals and noncriminals, but this differentiation reveals little about actual personality differences between the two groups (Caspi et al., 1994; Kleinmuntz, 1982).

A second popular test is the **California Psychological Inventory (CPI)**. The CPI was designed to provide personality profiles of the psychologically normal population. However, it correlates highly with the MMPI because half of its 480 true/false statements are from the Minnesota inventory. The CPI consists of eighteen scales that measure such personality traits as dominance, socialization, tolerance, achievement through conformity, achievement through independence, intellectual efficiency, sense of well-being, self-control, and flexibility. Three of the scales are validity scales (Kleinmuntz, 1982). Table 3.1 shows the scales and various items that compose each one.

TABLE 3.1   The California Psychological Inventory: Scales and Sample Items

Scale	Purpose	Sample Item
Dominance (Do)	To identify strong, dominant individuals with leadership abilities	"I think I would enjoy having authority over other people."
Capacity for Status (Cs)	To identify those qualities of ambition & self-assurance that lead to status	"I would like to belong to a singing club."
Sociability (Sy)	To differentiate people with an outgoing, sociable, participative temperament from those who shun involvement and avoid social visibility	"I like to be the center of attention."
Social Presence (Sp)	To assess poise, self-confidence, verve, and spontaneity in social interactions	"I like to go to parties and other affairs where there is lots of loud fun."

TABLE 3.1   Continued

Scale	Purpose	Sample Item
Self-Acceptance (Sa)	To identify individuals who have a strong sense of self-worth and who would be seen as secure and sure of themselves	"I am certainly lacking in self-confidence."
Sense of Well-Being (Wb)	To discriminate individuals feigning neurosis from normals and psychiatric patients responding truthfully	"I am afraid to be alone in the dark."
Responsibility (Re)	To identify people who are conscientious, dependable, articulate about rules and order, and who believe life should be governed by reason	"If I get too much change in a store, I always give it back."
Socialization (So)	To forecast the likelihood that an individual will transgress the norms established by his/her culture	"As a youngster in school I used to give the teachers lots of trouble."
Self-control (Sc)	To assess the adequacy of self-regulation and freedom from impulsivity and self-centeredness	"I would do almost anything on a dare."
Tolerance (To)	To identify permissive, accepting, and nonjudgmental social beliefs and attitudes	"I feel sure there is only one true religion."
Good Impression (Gi)	To identify people who are able to create favorable impressions and who are concerned about how others react to them	"I like to boast about my achievements every now and then."
Communality (Cm)	To detect protocols on which the respondent had not answered in a random fashion	"I can't do anything well."
Achievement via Conformance (Ac)	To measure a strong need for achievement coupled with a deeply internalized appreciation of structure and organization	"I always try to do at least a little better than what is expected of me."
Achievement via Independence (Ai)	To predict achievement in settings where independence of thought, creativity, and self-actualization are rewarded	"I like poetry."
Intellectual Efficiency (Ie)	To provide a set of personality items that will correlate significantly with accepted measures of intelligence	"I seem to be as capable and smart as most others around me."
Psychological Mindedness (Py)	To identify individuals who are psychologically oriented and insightful concerning others	"One of my aims in life is to accomplish something that will make my mother proud of me."
Flexibility (Fx)	To identify people who are flexible, adaptable, and even somewhat changeable in their thinking, behavior, and temperament	"I don't like things to be uncertain and unpredictable."
Femininity (Fe)	To define a continuum of psychological femininity	"I would like to be a nurse."

Source: E. I. Megargee. (1972). *The California Psychological Inventory Handbook.* San Francisco: Jossey-Bass, pp. 39–93. Used with permission.

Of the eighteen CPI scales, only three distinguish between criminal offenders and nonoffenders. On the socialization scale, samples of male and female offenders (including county jail inmates, California prison inmates, and New York training school residents) consistently scored lower than samples of nonoffenders (including high school "best citizens," correctional officers, and nurses).[9] Both male and female offenders also have lower scores on the responsibility and self-control scales (Megargee, 1972). According to Wilson and Herrnstein (1985, p. 184):

> The responsibility scale is often said to measure the understanding of social controls; the socialization scale, the tendency to behave with "rectitude and probity"; and the self-control scale, the approval of social goals. However, since socialization, responsibility and self-control scores are themselves interrelated, it would be a mistake to try to distinguish them too sharply. As a group, the three scales figure prominently in a characteristic described as "conformity," "value orientation," or "social adjustment," the lack of which is apparently part of the typical criminogenic personality.

But before we too quickly jump to the conclusion that the CPI can help us identify criminals or *potential* criminals, it is important to note that the test's usefulness has been questioned. Some critics argue, for instance, that the eighteen CPI scales are redundant and too interdependent to measure distinct personality traits. In other words, items on one scale seem to tap the same thing as items on other scales, even though each scale is supposed to measure a different, discrete personality component (Kleinmuntz, 1982).

Other attempts to distinguish criminals from noncriminals in terms of personality traits have been similarly fraught with problems. For example, Wilson and Herrnstein (1985) argue that criminals are more impulsive than noncriminals and have difficulty delaying gratification. One experimental study they cite to support this claim compared the responses of delinquents and nondelinquents when asked what they would do if they received 25 cents or $2. The delinquents more often than the nondelinquents indicated that they would spend rather than save both sums of money. In a similar study, groups of delinquents and nondelinquents were asked to choose between the immediate reward of a small candy bar and the delayed reward (to be received one week later) of a larger candy bar. The delinquents chose the immediate reward significantly more often than the nondelinquents. Still, Kamin (1986) points out that in such experiments, respondents' choices are influenced by the behavior and characteristics of the experimenter as well as the type of reward offered. In the money experiment, for instance, when the sums were raised to $20 and $200, the delinquents did not differ significantly from the nondelinquents in expressing an intent to save the reward. Kamin (1986, p. 23) interprets this as evidence of greater flexibility and realism on the part of delinquents and concludes that "there is no evidence for (and considerable evidence against) a general personality trait such that some individuals more than others consistently delay gratification in order to obtain larger rewards of all sorts." (This issue will surface once again in Chapter 5.)

It has also been argued that criminals are more extroverted than noncriminals.[10] Wilson and Herrnstein (1985), for example, cite a study in which a personality test was administered to large samples of people in different countries. The Japanese scored considerably higher on the introversion measure than Americans, and Wilson and

Herrnstein suggest that this high introversion may partially account for Japan's significantly lower crime rate relative to that of the United States.[11] However, in a recent study of 100 incarcerated women, Lippen (1989) reports that 62 percent of the respondents had high introversion scores on a test of personality.

In sum, although it has been argued that people who break the law suffer from a personality disorder or have abnormal personalities, the data we have reviewed so far provide only inconsistent evidence to support such a claim. Two recent studies that offer more convincing evidence of personality differences between criminals and non-criminals were conducted by Caspi and his colleagues (1994). Particularly noteworthy in these studies is that the researchers used multiple and independent measures of both personality and delinquent or criminal behavior. One study was conducted in New Zealand and compares males and females; the other study was conducted in the United States and compares White and Black twelve- and thirteen-year-old boys. Personality was measured using the Multidimensional Personality Questionnaire (MPQ) and the California Child Q-sort (CCQ). Delinquency and crime were measured using self-reports, informant reports (parents, teachers), and official records. Although there were some minor variations between males and females (but not between White and Black boys), both studies showed that participation in crime and delinquency was significantly more likely for those respondents who scored high on "negative emotionality" and low on "constraint." In other words, offenders tended to be aggressive, rebellious, and impulsive, and they often took advantage of others. While their findings are strong, Caspi and colleagues (1994) caution that they do not conclusively demonstrate that certain individuals have "crime-prone" personalities, since their research was cross-sectional and, therefore, does not untangle the direction of the personality-crime relationship; longitudinal studies are needed to accomplish this task (see Appendix). Moreover, they emphasize that "crime-proneness" is not a simplistic construct made up by a single trait, such as impulsivity or extroversion, but rather is likely the product of multiple psychological components that have both social (e.g., quality of home environment) and neurobiological (e.g., levels of specific neurotransmitters) origins.

Critics of personality theories of crime believe that these perspectives are faulty because they are premised on a false dichotomy: that an individual *either* is a criminal *or* is not a criminal. However, as we will see in subsequent chapters, criminality may best be understood in terms of a continuum: Few, if any, people are criminal all the time and few, if any, are always law-abiding or conforming. Moreover, most criminals are psychologically normal. Still, we all probably have heard or read about crimes in which the offenders' motives clearly reflect some psychological abnormality. Although these cases represent only a small fraction of all crimes committed, they garner a great deal of public attention. Let's consider, then, the topic of crime and mental illness.

Crime and Mental Illness

The headlines are familiar: "Gunman Kills 6 in Shooting Spree," "So-Called 'Zodiac Killer' Stalks Victims Police Say," and "Woman Who Killed 3 in Mall Shooting Had History of Mental Problems." They report crimes that perhaps inspire the greatest fear—crimes that are violent and apparently random. The offenders in such cases are individuals whom Toch and Adams (1989, p. 2) describe as "both 'mad' and 'bad.'" In other words, such offenders are psychologically disturbed and their mental disorder may manifest itself in extreme anti-social, sometimes violent, behavior.

As Toch and Adams (1989, p. 2) remind us, though, "The headlines do both a service and a disservice. . . . They are helpful in posing a question: How can we protect ourselves from dangerous persons who—some would tell us—belong in hospitals rather than prisons?" However, the headlines may also distort the criminal threat posed by the mentally ill. Some individuals who have been diagnosed as mentally disturbed commit nonserious, nonviolent crimes; many more commit no crimes at all. At the same time, the majority of serious crimes against persons and property are committed by individuals with no diagnosis of mental illness.

Certainly, dramatic headlines confirm the widespread public belief that the mentally ill are dangerous, but how accurate is this perception? An answer to this question is not easy to formulate because available data tend to be contradictory. For example, while one observer has argued that mental illness and criminality are "two sides of the same coin" (Bauer, 1970, quoted in Cocozza et al., 1978, p. 317), most others report no significant relationship, especially with regard to violent crime (see, for example, Cocozza et al., 1978; Heller at al., 1984; Monahan & Steadman, 1984; Teplin, 1985). Let's examine this research more closely.

Studying Mental Illness and Criminality

One way the relationship between mental illness and crime is studied is by comparing the arrest rates of former mental patients with the arrest rates of the general population. Research conducted in this manner from the 1920s through the 1950s showed that former mental patients had lower or equivalent arrest rates relative to the general population. In the 1960s and 1970s, though, studies showed that former mental patients were being arrested more than the general population, especially for violent crimes such as assault, robbery, and rape. Such findings naturally fueled public fear about the consequences of deinstitutionalization—the release of mental patients into the community—that began in the late 1960s. However, according to Joseph Cocozza and his colleagues (1978), the rate of arrest for violent crime by former mental patients during this period is accounted for by one group of patients: those who previously had been arrested.

More specifically, Cocozza and his colleagues found that during the 1960s and 1970s, former patients who had no prior criminal record were less likely than the general population to be arrested for a violent crime. In contrast, former patients with a criminal history of two or more arrests were almost twenty times more likely to be arrested for a violent crime than the general population. "Rather than more mentally ill persons irrationally becoming involved in violent crimes, it appears that there are more persons admitted to state hospitals who continue their patterns of crime after hospitalization, just as would be expected in any offender group." This, in turn, may reflect a growing use of mental hospitals as detention alternatives for individuals who typically would be sent to jails or prisons if these facilities were not overcrowded.

In a careful review of research on mental disorder and crime, Monahan and Steadman (1984) examined two types of studies: (1) "pure" cases that look at the crime rates of those diagnosed as mentally disordered *or* the rates of mental disorder among criminals; and (2) "mixed" cases that sample groups of "mentally disordered offenders," that is, those treated for both mental disorder and criminality. They point out first that it is debatable how many persons legally adjudicated as mentally disordered offenders are suffering from true mental disorder. This raises the question of the accuracy of psychiatric diagnoses, a controversial issue that will be taken up later in this chapter.

Second, Monahan and Steadman (1984) state that while rates of mental hospitalization and imprisonment frequently are thought to be interdependent—as one goes up, the other goes down—their evidence suggests otherwise. In fact, between 1968 and 1978, a period in which the population of state mental hospitals decreased by about 66 percent, the percentage of former mental patients admitted to state prisons increased an average of fewer than three percentage points. Moreover, in half the states studied, the percentage of male prisoners previously hospitalized in state mental facilities actually decreased, indicating that deinstitutionalization was not a major contributing factor in prison overcrowding during this period. However, as Box 3.2 shows, the effect of deinstitutionalization on the crime rate and the number of people imprisoned continues to be debated today, not only in the United States, but in other countries as well.

BOX 3.2 HOW THE WORLD SEES IT
Crime, Mental Illness, and Institutional Treatment

Deinstitutionalization, in which people with mental illnesses are treated in the community rather than in residential psychiatric hospitals, began in the United States in the 1960s and has occurred as well in most other industrialized countries throughout the world. The rationale underlying deinstitutionalization is that community treatment relying primarily on antipsychotic drugs is more humane than hospitalization. At the same time, however, governments saw the opportunity to reduce funding to hospitals and thus save money. Consequently, in the United States, the number of hospitalized mental patients dropped from 559,000 in 1955 to about 69,000 in 1995 (Butterfield, 1998). Comparable declines occurred in other countries. For example, in the state of Victoria in Australia, the proportion of the population residing in mental hospitals declined from 20 per 10,000 people in 1965 to less than 4 per 10,000 people by the mid-1990s (Mullen et al., 2000).

Many of those released from mental hospitals suffer from schizophrenia, a mental disorder discussed in this chapter because it is associated with criminal behavior. Research indicates that people with schizophrenia commit more crimes than those who do not have the disorder (Mullen et al., 2000; Swanson et al., 1990). However, an important question is whether deinstitutionalization increases the likelihood that the mentally ill will engage in crime. Research from other countries as well as our own provides some qualified answers to this question.

One recent Australian study (Mullen et al., 2000) offers convincing evidence that deinstitutionalization per se does not increase crime. The researchers compared the criminal records of three groups: schizophrenic men who had

(continued)

BOX **3.2   Continued**

been hospitalized for the first time in 1975, prior to Australia's move toward deinstitutionalization; schizophrenic men who had first been hospitalized in 1985 when hospitals began closing and community-based services were opened; and a control group of men without a history of mental illness. The researchers found that although both groups of schizophrenic men were more likely than the controls to have a criminal record (24 percent compared to about 7 percent), there were no statistically significant differences in *patterns of offending* from 1975 to 1985 among the three groups. The shift from hospitalization to community-based treatment did not produce any notable change in criminal offending by those diagnosed with mental illness.

Nevertheless, the Australian researchers emphasize that efforts should be made to reduce criminal offending among the mentally ill by improving community-based services (Mullen et al., 2000). In some countries, including the United States, the availability of community-based interventions falls far short of meeting the need for such services. As a result, the mentally ill are increasingly finding themselves in jails and prisons, typically arrested not for serious violent crimes but for minor public nuisance offenses. Some are arrested, but no charges are

filed; the police say they are "mercy arrests" when individuals are behaving "strangely" and might hurt themselves. "In many states, so many public hospitals have closed, or the laws regulating admission to hospitals have been made so tight, that sometimes the only way to get care is to be arrested," especially if one is poor and without health insurance (Butterfield, 1998, p. A26). However, adequate treatment often is unavailable in jails and prisons, and corrections personnel are not trained in how to respond to or care for the mentally ill. Being incarcerated, in fact, can worsen the symptoms of some mentally ill people (Butterfield, 1998).

The U.S. Justice Department has openly recognized what is being called the "criminalization of the mentally ill" and has criticized as unconstitutional the treatment of the mentally ill in many of the nation's jails and prisons (Butterfield, 1998; Rubin & McCampbell, 1995). However, unless the government is willing to spend more money to finance community mental health programs and health insurers loosen restrictions on coverage for such treatment, it is likely that at least in the United States, jails and prisons will increasingly serve as mental hospitals.

Finally, and perhaps most important, Monahan and Steadman (1984) found that:

> The correlates of crime among the mentally disordered appear to be the same as the correlates of crime among any other group: age, gender, race, social class, and prior criminality. Likewise, the correlates of mental disorder among criminal offenders appear to be the same as those in other populations: age, social class, and previous disorder. Populations characterized by the correlates of both crime and mental disorder (e.g., low social class) can be expected to show high rates of both, and they do. (p. 5; see also Cirincione et al., 1991)

In other words, the relationship between mental illness and crime may be spurious. Both appear to be more strongly related to demographic variables, especially social class, than to each other.

A major difficulty with most studies of crime and mental illness conducted prior to the 1990s is that they rely on official statistics, such as arrest rates, incarceration rates, and records of mental hospitalization, or they use only institutionalized samples (Monahan, 1996). Such statistics and samples, though, provide poor estimates of the "true" incidence of a behavior or problem. We know, for example, that many crimes go undetected and that, even if the police are involved, an infraction may not result in an arrest. Only a small proportion of those arrested are convicted, and an even smaller proportion serve any time in prison. Similarly, official statistics on mental hospitalization do not include the many individuals who go undiagnosed or who obtain mental health services from private practices. The National Institute of Mental Health (1985) estimates that during any six-month period, 29 million Americans suffer from one or more classifiable mental disorders, but less than 20 percent use any type of mental health service. Those who obtain private care tend to have a higher socioeconomic status than those in mental hospitals. In general, the lower one's social class, the greater the likelihood of being hospitalized (Goldman, 1998; Hollingshead & Redlich, 1958).

Several recent studies have tried to overcome these methodological difficulties. Teplin (1985), for example, conducted a field study in which more than 1,000 police–citizen encounters were observed in an urban area that included both poor and wealthy residents. Teplin and her associates found that overall, police had few encounters with individuals who exhibited symptoms of mental disorder. When such encounters did occur, the mentally disturbed citizens most often needed assistance. They were not disproportionately suspected of being involved in serious crime. Those who were involved in crime were not more likely to be violent than non-mentally ill suspects. In fact, these two groups did not differ in terms of the types of crime committed (see also Teplin, 1990).

Other researchers have studied the general population as well as formerly hospitalized mental patients. Overall, these studies show that former mental patients are slightly more likely than individuals never hospitalized to engage in violent behavior. However, the research also shows that people with mental illnesses are more likely to be *victims* of violence rather than perpetrators (Monahan, 1996; Swanson et al., 1990). Moreover, Monahan (1996) reports that the relationship between mental disorder and violence has less to do with whether an individual has been diagnosed mentally ill than it does with whether an individual is currently displaying symptoms of mental illness. For example, Link and Stueve (cited in Monahan, 1996) found that regardless of whether an individual had ever been hospitalized for mental illness, those who felt others wished them harm, that their minds were dominated by forces beyond their control, and that others' thoughts were being put into their heads were most likely to get into fights.

It is important to note that most studies of the relationship between crime and mental illness analyze the incidence of mental disorder or the rates of arrest, incarceration, or hospitalization of various *groups* of people rather than those of specific *individuals*. Apart from the aggregate statistics, case studies reveal that there are individuals who are both mentally ill and criminal. These studies also indicate that criminality is associated with particular types of mental disorder. We turn to an examination of these types of disorders now.

Mental Illness Commonly Associated with Crime

One psychiatric diagnosis that is frequently applied to criminals, especially those who have committed bizarre or particularly heinous offenses, is **psychopathy**. (The diagnoses of *sociopathy* and *antisocial personality* typically are considered synonymous with psychopathy, and the terms often are used interchangably.) Psychopaths are described as selfish, callous, unreliable, impulsive, and unable to feel guilt or to learn from experience or punishment (Cleckley, 1976; Hare, 1996; Hart & Dempster, 1997). Cleckley (1976) points out that, on the surface, psychopaths may appear mentally healthy; they may be quite intelligent and even charming. However, this is only a "mask of sanity," as Cleckley puts it, for the psychopath is incapable of loving or becoming emotionally attached to others. This emotional void contributes to the psychopath's dangerousness. Feeling no remorse, the psychopath may embark on a long career of serious and violent crime (Hare, 1996; Hart & Dempster, 1997; Quinsy et al., 1995).

Psychiatrists do not agree on what causes psychopathy. There is some evidence that the illness is the result of brain damage or a defect in the nervous system.[12] There is no evidence that severe emotional trauma during childhood and unstable home environments contribute to psychopathy (Ge et al., 1996; Johnson et al., 1979; McCord & McCord, 1964). Whatever the cause, a number of observers have cautioned that the diagnosis is overused in the criminal justice system and is too readily applied to any offender who has committed a serious or violent crime. As Cleckley (1976) argues, psychopathy and criminality often co-exist, but they are not interdependent. Most psychopaths do not commit serious or violent crimes, and most criminals are not psychopathic.

A second mental disorder frequently diagnosed in criminals is **schizophrenia**. Schizophrenia actually encompasses a range of disorders that includes a deterioration in the ability to think clearly and rationally, impaired memory, a break with reality, and perceptual problems. Schizophrenics—and there are five types of the disorder that have been identified (disorganized, paranoid, catatonic, residual, and undifferentiated)—experience severe distortions of reality, often suffering *delusions* that the world is a hostile place and others are out to get them (delusional persecution) or that they are extremely important people, such as the President of the United States or Jesus Christ (delusional grandeur). *Hallucinations* are also common, especially auditory hallucinations, where the individual hears voices telling him or her what to do. The emotions of the schizophrenic are also disordered; she or he may display inappropriate emotions in certain situations (laughing uncontrollably at a serious accident or crying over something humorous or trivial), or she or he may show no emotion whatsoever, regardless of the circumstances (flat affect). Schizophrenics sometimes also experience **psychosis**, a break with reality so severe that they cannot meet the demands of everyday life.

Schizophrenia is considered one of the most debilitating mental disorders, but its precise cause is unknown. Like psychopathy, there is evidence that it may be brought on by certain social factors, but there is also considerable data that indicate that it is genetically caused. Most recently, schizophrenia has been linked to particular brain

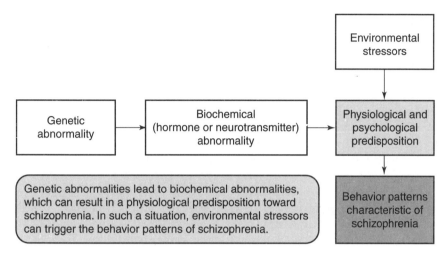

FIGURE 3.1   The Vulnerability–Stress View of Schizophrenia.

Source: Lefton (2000). Used with permission.

abnormalities, including small brain volume and enlarged ventricles (Suddath et al., 1990). According to Lefton (2000), however, most psychiatrists now maintain that people with a genetic predisposition to the disorder become schizophrenic when a particularly stressful life event or environmental condition triggers the onset of the illness. This relationship is illustrated in Figure 3.1.

Criminals diagnosed as schizophrenic have been convicted of a broad range of crimes, including burglary, but also crimes of violence, such as sexual assault and murder (Toch & Adams, 1989). One study, for example, found that individuals with mental illnesses such as schizophrenia showed a significantly higher incidence of violent behavior (11–13 percent) than individuals without mental illnesses (2 percent) (Swanson et al., 1990).

However, schizophrenics constitute a small percentage of offenders, including violent offenders. For example, Heller and his colleagues (1984) found no association between a diagnosis of psychosis and commission of a violent crime. Moreover, very few schizophrenics are ever arrested for the commission of violent crimes. In a study by Phillips et al. (1988), for example, only 0.2 to 2.0 percent of schizophrenic people in the community were arrested for violent crimes. These figures translated into 1.1 to 2.3 percent of all arrests annually for violent crimes (see also Blackburn, 1993; Bonta et al., 1998).

Multiple personality disorder is a psychiatric disturbance distinct from, but frequently confused with, schizophrenia. As the label implies, an individual with multiple personality disorder has a mind that splits or, better put, fractures into a number of different selves. Some of these selves may be of the opposite sex of the patient and of different ages. According to clinicians, multiples (as they often are called) differ from schizophrenics in that each of their personalities is consistent and usually well organized. Whereas schizophrenics are illogical and their behavior is unpredictable, each personality of a multiple behaves the same way whenever it appears, and each personality is unique, with its own attitudes, behaviors, memories, even tone of voice (Steinberg, 1995). It has been argued that this disorder is caused by severe childhood trauma, in particular sadistic child abuse. In order to deal with the abuse, the individual *dissociates* from it by separating into different selves, each of which has its own way of thinking, feeling, and acting. However, psychologists and psychiatrists are in disagreement over whether the illness even exists, and some experts maintain that therapists may actually induce highly suggestive patients to believe they are multiples (Gleaves, 1996; Ondrovik & Hamilton, 1991; Orne et al., 1984).

Multiple personality disorder is very rare, although among the small number of real and suspected cases there have been several very serious offenders (see, for example, "Alter Egos?" 1999; Keyes, 1982). Nevertheless, because it is so rare, this disorder can account for only a minute proportion of crimes.

A Note about the Role of Drugs and Alcohol

In their study of mentally disturbed and violent criminals, Toch and Adams (1989) found that it was not uncommon for such offenders to be under the influence of alcohol or drugs, especially cocaine and PCP, at the time they committed their crimes. Similarly, Swanson and his colleagues (1990) found that the most common diagnosis among individuals in their study who had engaged in violence was substance abuse; 25 percent of violent individuals had abused alcohol, 35 percent had abused drugs. A recent National Institute of Justice study (Mumola, 1999) also found that about 75 percent of all prisoners reported alcohol and drug abuse during the period leading up to their arrest. Certainly, the relationship between substance abuse and crime has long been a concern in U.S. society, and this concern grew during the 1980s and 1990s as an increasing number of reports showed that a significant portion of violent and property crime appeared to be tied to rising rates of substance abuse, especially the use of relatively cheap and highly addictive drugs, such as "crack" cocaine (Golub & Johnson, 1997; Reuter, 1999).

In general, the consumption of alcohol and drugs may encourage or facilitate criminal behavior, especially violence and aggression, because these substances are known to lower inhibitions, impair judgment, and increase recklessness and risk-taking behavior. In addition, it has been argued that drug and alcohol abuse may lead to crime because regular users have difficulty getting and maintaining employment from which they earn legitimate income. However, research on substance abuse indicates that its relationship to crime is considerably more complex than this. Consider, for example, the findings of James Inciardi and his colleagues (1993) who have done extensive research on street-addict lifestyles. They have found that involvement in both drugs and crime seem to begin at around the same time, usually during adolescence. Most adolescents eventually "age-out" of drug use and criminal activity, but for those who continue, escalation of both activities is likely. While increased crime to finance the drug habit and simply to survive is one outcome, Inciardi and his colleagues found that the relationship can also occur in the opposite direction: A lucrative criminal career can make it financially easier to buy drugs, thus increasing drug use. "Over time, any single heroin or cocaine addict experiences many of these drugs/crime interactions leading to a sometimes chaotic existence. Anything that changes one factor—drug use or crime—will have an impact on the other" (Inciardi et al., 1993, p. 112; see also Reuter, 1999).

Other factors that affect the drugs–crime relationship include the type and amount of substance consumed, the background and personality of the user, and the social situation in which the substance is used or in which the user finds himself/herself.[13] For instance, victimization studies show that in as many as three out of every four incidents of spouse abuse, the abuser had been drinking alcohol, using drugs, or both (Brookoff, 1997; Crowell & Burgess, 1996; Greenfeld, 1998). However, rather than *causing* spouse abuse, some researchers report that substance use simply *facilitates* spouse abuse because it is often offered as an *excuse* or *justification* for the violence: "I didn't know what I was doing; I was drunk" (Gelles, 1993).

Most spouse abusers, however, are not alcoholics or drug addicts (Edleson et al., 1985; Gelles, 1993; Herman, 1988). As Greenfeld (1998, p. 1) points out, "most alcohol consumption does not result in crime: the vast majority of those who consume alcohol do not engage in criminal behavior." Many drug users also do not engage in crime apart from the crime of illegal drug use itself. Indeed, looking at Table 3.2 we find that according to victim reports, more than half of all violent offenders were using neither alcohol nor drugs at the time of their offense. Other research that uses tests of samples of arrestees have found that about 68 percent of detained arrestees test positive for one or more drugs and slightly less than 50 percent admit using at least one of ten drugs in the three days prior to their arrest (Taylor & Bennett, 1999). Considerably more research is needed for us to better understand the relationship between substance abuse and criminal behavior (see Greenfeld, 1998; Reuter, 1999).[14]

TABLE 3.2 Offenders Using Alcohol or Drugs at the Time They Committed a Violent Crime

Offender Using:	Percent of all Victims of Violence
Alcohol	28
Drugs	7
Alcohol or drugs	9
Neither alcohol nor drugs	56
	100

Source: Greenfeld, 1998, p. 3.

The Role of Psychiatry in the Criminal Justice System

Psychologists and psychiatrists are sometimes given important roles in the criminal justice system. For example, they may be called on to testify as to whether a defendant is mentally competent to stand trial—that is, whether the defendant has the ability to understand the legal proceedings in which he or she is involved and can consult with a lawyer (Cruise & Rogers, 1998). Psychologists and psychiatrists may be asked to testify, too, about the likely mental state of a defendant at the time the crime was committed, if the defense being mounted is an **insanity defense**: the legal defense that the person was mentally ill at the time he or she committed the crime and therefore is not criminally responsible for his or her actions.

Many Americans view the insanity defense with suspicion if not outright hostility. Although most people are sympathetic toward the mentally ill, they nevertheless want criminals to be held accountable for their offenses. Most public outcries against the insanity defense follow widely publicized trials, such as those of John Hinkley, Jr., who attempted to assassinate former president Ronald Reagan, and Jeffrey Dahmer, who murdered several young men, dismembered their bodies, cooked various body parts and ate them. Both were found not guilty by reason of insanity.[15]

Competency to stand trial and the insanity defense are not the only times in which criminal justice personnel, such as judges and attorneys, use psychiatrists' and psychologists' clinical evaluations. Such assessment may also influence sentencing decisions and rulings regarding the release of an inmate on parole or from a mental hospital. Although each of these issues deserves careful consideration, they are beyond the scope of this book. However, we will briefly discuss critics' concerns about the use of clinical evaluations in criminal justice decision making.

Critics' primary concern is the reliability of psychiatric judgments. Although some researchers have found a high level of agreement among psychiatrists regarding the clinical evaluation of specific patients (see, for example, Phillips et al., 1988), others maintain that the assessment of a given patient frequently varies from psychiatrist to psychiatrist and that diagnoses may be influenced as much by certain innate traits of a patient as by his or her symptoms. For example, studies have repeatedly demonstrated that a patient's sex may influence a psychiatric diagnosis (Gilbert & Scher, 1999; Hansen & Reekie, 1990; Robertson & Fitzgerald, 1990). According to Loring and Powell (1988), the patient's race is also significant; mental health professionals are more likely to judge African Americans than Whites as violent even when the cases they are evaluating are identical in all other respects. Psychiatric diagnoses also change over time as a behavior gains greater acceptance by the general public or as a result of successful lobbying on the part of a particular group. For instance, in its 1980 revision of the *Diagnostic and Statistical Manual for Mental Disorders*—the official psychiatric classification handbook—the American Psychiatric Association voted to delete homosexuality from the listing. Prior to this time, homosexuality was officially considered a mental disorder and was medically "treated" in various ways.[16]

Psychiatrists' judgments of individuals' potential dangerousness or likelihood of engaging in violence have been especially questionable. Most research on this topic has found that mental health professionals' predictions of violence or dangerousness are wrong far more often than they are right (Henzies et al., 1985; 1991). One study, for instance, compared psychiatrists' predictions of potential dangerousness of 257 mental patients with the actual incidence of violent behavior by the patients after their release from hospitalization (Cocozza & Steadman, 1978). The results showed that those who had been judged dangerous were, in reality, no more likely to behave violently than those considered not dangerous. In fact, the psychiatrists' assessments of future dangerousness were so unreliable that the researchers concluded that psychiatric prediction "may be closer to magic than science" (p. 274).

Some observers argue that clinical predictions and evaluations have improved substantially over the past twenty years (e.g., Brizer, 1989; Wexler, 1981). Others point out that the accuracy of predictions improve if they are shared by multiple observers with diverse areas of expertise (e.g., psychiatrists, social workers, nurse practitioners), who can pool their knowledge to get a more holistic evaluation of an individual (Limandri & Sheridan, 1995). Nevertheless, many clinicians do not even agree on what constitutes "dangerousness," and available tools and techniques for distinguishing the mentally ill from the mentally healthy, except in extreme cases, still produce inconsistent and often incorrect results.

Summary and Conclusion

In this chapter we discussed theories of crime causation that focus on psychological and psychiatric abnormalities, especially personality problems, although we also examined the controversy over the relationship between IQ and crime. We found that while there may be an observed correlation between low IQ and criminal involvement as measured by official statistics, this does not mean that low IQ causes crime. It also does not mean that there is any relationship between low intelligence and crime, since it does not appear that IQ tests measure innate intelligence.

Our discussion of the criminal personality began with an examination of Freudian theory, which we found provocative, but also highly problematic. Perhaps its most serious flaw is that it cannot be empirically tested. Other personality theories that focus on differences between offenders and nonoffenders also have testing difficulties. At this point, there is no consistent evidence to support the notion that most criminals have atypical or abnormal personalities.

We discussed several types of mental disorders that are associated with criminal behavior, including psychopathy, schizophrenia, and multiple personality disorder. Fortunately, individuals afflicted with these disorders commit a very small proportion of all crimes. Most crimes are committed by people who have not been diagnosed as mentally ill. In addition, most crimes are committed by individuals who are not intoxicated or on drugs at the time of the offense. In fact, we found that although considerable media attention has been given to the relationship between drug and alcohol use and crime, this relationship appears to be far more complex than it at first appears.

Finally, we reviewed some major concerns about the role of psychiatry in the criminal justice system, especially in terms of the prediction of dangerousness. Although the clinical opinions of psychiatrists and psychologists are often used in criminal justice decision making, theirs appears to be far from a precise or accurate science.

All of the theories we have discussed in this chapter look to the individual offender to find the cause of crime. In the remaining chapters of the text, we will examine theories that look elsewhere, in particular at the offender's environment.

KEY TERMS

California Psychological Inventory (CPI)—a personality test consisting of 480 true/false statements divided among eighteen scales designed to profile the psychologically normal population.

ego—that aspect of the personality identified by Freud as being responsible for the satisfaction of the needs of the id in socially acceptable ways; it operates on the reality principle and begins to develop when we are between six and eight months old.

id—the part of the personality identified by Freud that is entirely unconscious and seeks immediate gratification of its powerful drives and instincts; it is present at birth.

insanity defense—the legal defense that an offender was mentally ill at the time he or she committed the crime and therefore is not criminally responsible for his or her actions.

intelligence quotient (IQ)—a score arrived at by dividing an individual's mental age (as determined by performance on a standardized IQ test) by his or her chronological age multiplied by 100; proponents of IQ testing argue that the score is an indication of an individual's general intellectual level.

Minnesota Multiphasic Personality Inventory 2 (MMP2)—a psychological screening device

composed of ten clinical scales and four validity scales with a total of 567 true/false statements designed to detect psychological abnormalities.

multiple personality disorder—a psychiatric disturbance in which an individual's mind splits or fractures into a number of different selves, each distinct and consistent when it emerges, although each may be of a different age than the patient and some may be of the opposite sex.

personality—a set of relatively enduring behavioral characteristics (including thoughts) and internal predispositions that describe how a person reacts to the environment.

psychopathy—a mental disorder in which those afflicted become impulsive, selfish, irresponsible, callous, and unable to feel guilt or to learn from punishment.

psychosis—a break with reality so severe that an individual cannot meet the demands of everyday life.

schizophrenia—a mental disorder in which the sufferer experiences a deterioration in the ability to think clearly and rationally, impaired memory, a break with reality, and perceptual problems.

superego—that aspect of the personality identified by Freud that is the internalization of societal values and norms; typically referred to as the conscience, it develops when we are three to five years old.

SUGGESTED READINGS

Campbell, J. C. (Ed.). (1995). *Assessing dangerousness: Violence by sex offenders, batterers, and child abusers.* Thousand Oaks, CA: Sage. A collection of articles that reviews various risk markers for differ-

ent types of intimate violence and that critically examines the tools and techniques clinicians use to predict the likelihood that an intimate will become violent or will recidivate.

Gallagher, N. (1999). *Breeding better Vermonters: The eugenics project in the Green Mountain State.* Hanover, NH: University Press of New England. A historical analysis of Vermont's involuntary sterilization program.

Westervelt, S. D. (1998). *Shifting the blame: How victimization became a criminal defense.* New Brunswick, NJ: Rutgers University Press. An analysis of a relatively new criminal defense, diminished responsibility because of the offender's personal history of victimization.

NOTES

1. Although social learning theory is also a psychological perspective, it will be discussed in Chapter 5 along with other theories that emphasize the role of learning processes in the etiology of criminal behavior.

2. Rafter (1992) points out that concern with criminals' low intelligence was especially strong in the United States in the early 1900s and actually grew out of the work of American followers of Lombroso and his school of criminal anthropology.

3. Lefton (2000) notes that one problem with Stern's method of calculating IQ is that young children's scores vary more than older children's or adults' scores, making it difficult to use IQ for predictions or comparisons. As a result, psychologists began using a simpler approach called *deviation IQ*, which is a standardized score with a mean and standard deviation that stays constant across age groups. People who have the same deviation IQ, regardless of their age, fall in the same testing percentile as others their age who have taken the same IQ test.

4. When examining Goddard's volume on the Kallikaks, Gould (1981, p. 171) discovered that Goddard had apparently altered the photographs of the noninstitutionalized Kallikaks to make them look more sinister and depraved.

5. Carrie Buck, the plaintiff in the *Buck* v. *Bell* suit, was sterilized at Lynchburg Hospital in Virginia, where more than 4,000 sterilizations were performed—the last in 1972. Ironically, when psychologists reexamined Ms. Buck in 1980, they judged her to be of "obviously normal intelligence" (Gould, 1984). There is also evidence that some people were sterilized simply because of their racial or ethnic heritage, not because of IQ test results. For example, Native Americans of the Abenaki tribe in Vermont have called for an official inquiry into that state's former sterilization program because they believe that the Abenaki were targeted in what amounts to state-sanctioned genocide. Barry (1999) reports that in other countries, such as Canada and Sweden, which had similar sterilization programs operating into the 1970s, the courts have ordered monetary compensation for those who were sterilized under government orders. It would be comforting to believe that such eugenicist ideas have disappeared, but unfortunately they have not. For instance, in 1999, Californian Barbara Harris, a homemaker, founded the program Children Require a Caring Community (CRACK) with funding from private donations. CRACK pays female addicts $200 if they agree to be sterilized. Harris started the program after her unsuccessful attempt to get the California legislature to declare pregnancy illegal for addicted women. Harris maintains that her program does not target women of any particular racial or ethnic group, but as of August 1999, the vast majority of the sixty-one women who had agreed to Harris's offer were African Americans and Latinas ("Kold Kash in Kalifornia," 1999).

6. Simon's (1978) use of the masculine pronoun is not insignificant since in studies of young women, the traditional IQ-delinquency relationship is not found.

7. For a detailed discussion of the negative impact of Freudian theory on studies of female offenders, see Klein, 1980. Psychoanalysts themselves have critiqued Freud, and some have proposed important revisions to his theory of personality development. For a review of the theories of the major neo-Freudians, see Lefton, 2000.

8. In 1992, another version of the MMPI, the MMPI-A, was developed for use with adolescents. Currently, the MMPI-2 and the MMPI-A are the only versions of the test available, since the copyright holder, the University of Minnesota, decided to discontinue publication and distribution of the original MMPI because of a number of serious problems with the test, including outdated norms, the unrepresentativeness of the sample used for standardization, and

the prejudicial nature of some items (e.g., those questioning a respondent's sexual orientation, Christian beliefs, and religious practices). For a detailed discussion of the MMPI and its successors, the MMPI-2 and the MMPI-A, see Pope et al., 2000.

9. Military officers and psychology graduate students, however, scored only slightly higher than criminal offenders on the socialization scale (Megargee, 1972).

10. The late Hans Jurgen Eysenck was a major proponent of the theory that criminals are highly extroverted. The extrovert, Eysenck argued, is sociable, but impulsive and unreliable, with a high need for excitement. The extrovert is also aggressive and quick to "fly off the handle." Importantly, Eysenck maintained that this personality trait is biologically based; the structure and functioning of the extrovert's nervous system produce intense needs for excitement, thrills, and stimulation. See Eysenck, 1977; and Eysenck & Gudjonsson, 1989.

11. It is interesting to note that in the cross-cultural study discussed by Wilson and Herrnstein (1985), while the Japanese scored higher than Americans on introversion, they also scored higher—in fact, the highest of citizens in all countries tested—on psychoticism. Americans scored among the lowest on psychoticism (Kamin, 1986).

12. See Bartol, 1999, pp. 89–105, for a detailed discussion of the biological/physiological causes of psychopathy.

13. Research shows that alcohol has different effects on different people and even on the same person at different times. In small amounts, alcohol may actually reduce aggression because it tends to induce a feeling of euphoria and cheerfulness. If very large quantities are consumed, aggressive behavior may be impossible because motor coordination usually fails and most people simply pass out. It is at a moderate level of intoxication that aggression and violence are likely because this is when the alcohol usually impairs judgment, lowers frustration tolerance, and induces disinhibition. However, drinks high in ethyl alcohol, such as whiskey, increase intoxication, as does a fast rate of consumption. In addition, the characteristics of the drinker are important. Because females metabolize alcohol differently, they tend to become intoxicated more quickly and from fewer drinks than males even when controlling for differences in body weight. Alcohol also tends to enhance or exaggerate characteristics of the drinker. "Thus, people who become quarrelsome when drunk may also have been somewhat aggressive when sober. . . . People who become melancholic after drinking may have a generally depressive personality" (Buikhuisen et al., 1988, p. 264). Alcohol often does what the drinker expects it to do. "People who think that alcohol cheers one up will experience a certain euphoria; those who think alcohol makes one aggressive will end up in a fighting mood" (Buikhuisen et al., 1988, p. 264). Finally, the social situation of the drinker is significant. For example, aggressive behavior is more likely when the drinker is in the presence of stimuli associated with aggression, such as weapons. The importance of factors such as these is highlighted by recent studies that show that offenders with drug and alcohol problems differ from noncriminal control groups in a variety of ways besides their patterns of alcohol and drug use. For instance, West and Farrington (1977) reported that the juvenile delinquents in their sample not only drank more than nondelinquents, but also had poorer home environments and worse school records—variables that in themselves have been found to be related to delinquency. A similar argument has been made with regard to drugs; that is, "drug use does not directly cause criminal behavior, but the same circumstances that might lead a person to begin committing crimes may also contribute to the development of drug habits" (such as poverty and discrimination) (Innes, 1988, p. 2).

14. Reuter (1999) points out that the research to date indicates that efforts to reduce crime will be most effective if they include drug treatment programs at all stages of the criminal justice process. At the same time, however, the availability of drug treatment programs in federal and state prisons has declined (Butterfield, 1999), while more drug offenders are being sentenced to long, mandatory prison terms even when they have no record of violent crime (Goldberg, 1997).

15. Following Hinkley's acquittal, the U.S. Congress and several states revised their laws on the insanity defense with the goal of making such acquittals less likely. Most analysts believe, however, that much of the public hostility toward the insanity defense is the result of mistaken ideas about how the defense works, how much it is used, how often it is successful, and what hap-

pens to those who use it successfully in their defense. Paswark (1986), for example, found that samples of college students overestimated the number of insanity pleas by a factor of 800, while legislators overestimated the number by a factor of 400 (see also McGinley & Paswark, 1989). Silver and his colleagues (1992) found that the general public's estimate of an insanity plea rate of 37 percent of all cases is 41 times greater than the actual plea rate of 0.9 percent. Silver et al. also found that the public's estimate of the success rate of the insanity plea is about 1.7 times greater than the actual success rate. Those who use the defense successfully tend to be older, well-educated, single women who have a history of hospitalization for severe mental disorders (Callahan et al., 1991). At the same time,

most people believe that those who are acquitted by reason of insanity are either sent to psychiatric facilities, where they spend much less time than if they were sentenced to prison, or are simply set free. The research shows, however, that about 85 percent of insanity acquittees are sent to mental hospitals, where they stay for at least as long—some stay longer—as they would had they been sent to prison (Callahan et al., 1992; Linhorst, 1998; Silver et al., 1992; Steadman et al., 1993).

16. Engaging in homosexual acts such as sodomy, even if the partners are consenting adults acting in the privacy of their own homes, is still illegal in some states as a result of the 1986 U.S. Supreme Court decision in the case of *Bowers* v. *Hardwick*.

4 Sociological Theories of Crime I: Crime and Social Organization

In this chapter and the three chapters that follow, we will examine *sociological theories* of crime. Although each of the theories to be discussed is distinctive in a number of ways, readers will discern some overlap among them. This is because, as sociological theories, they share at least one proposition in common: Specifically, they seek the causes of crime in factors *external* to the individuals involved. Whereas biological/ physiological theorists and psychological/psychiatric theorists see crime as caused largely by individual (internal) pathologies, sociological theorists view criminals and delinquents as essentially normal people whose behavior is influenced in some way by the *environment* in which they live.

In this chapter (and again in Chapters 6 and 7), we examine theories that postu- late that crime is caused by the way particular communities or societies are organized or structured. We begin with a perspective that developed in the United States at the turn of this century and has had considerable influence on subsequent sociological the- ories of crime.

The Chicago School

The University of Chicago is home to the first academic department of sociology in the United States, established in 1892. Until roughly the 1940s, sociologists looked to Chicago as the center of sociological research.

The members of the early sociology faculties at the University of Chicago shared similar social backgrounds. Most, for instance, were born and raised on farms or in small rural communities. Some were the children of ministers, a few ordained minis- ters themselves, and almost all were members of social welfare organizations (Greek, 1992). Given their upbringings, it is not difficult to imagine how these sociologists must have felt when confronted with daily life in turn-of-the century urban America. The cities were the industrial hubs of the nation, and thousands of men and women flocked to them in search of work. Among them were poor Southern Blacks and Euro- pean immigrants whose skin color, language, and "foreign ways" immediately set them outside the "American mainstream." Those who got jobs, despite widespread prejudice and discrimination against them, worked long hours under hazardous conditions for pennies a day. After work, they usually went home to equally unsafe, overcrowded tenement buildings. The Chicago sociologists, who had liberal political leanings, sought to bring about social reform (Turner & Turner, 1990).

The focus of sociological attention came to rest on the problems that beset the lives of city dwellers. A major concern was *social deviance*, which was broadly defined as a violation of society's norms or rules for appropriate behavior. The term *social deviance* came to be used synonymously with the term *social problems*. The goal for these sociologists was to study and explain deviance/social problems so as to devise a practical means for eliminating them. The Chicago sociologists emphasized the *external* sources of social problems—such as the social disorganization of city life—so their solutions rested not in treating individuals, but rather in *social change* (Lindner, 1996).

Robert Park was one of the founding Chicago sociologists. He applied the principles of plant and animal ecology in the task of understanding social deviance and its causes. Consequently, the **Chicago School** is also known as the *Ecological School* or the *School of Human Ecology*. Park, along with his colleagues, including *Ernest Burgess* and *Louis Wirth*, identified several distinct *zones* that expanded out in a pattern of concentric circles from the center of the city. These zones are depicted in Figure 4.1. The out-

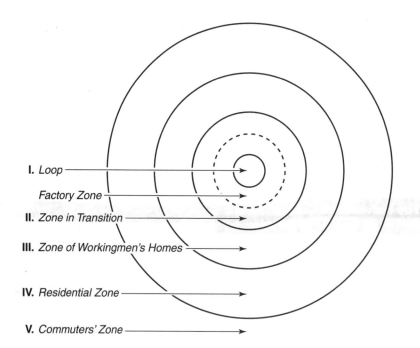

FIGURE 4.1   Burgess's Conception of Urban Development

Source: Burgess, E. W. (1928). "The Growth of the City," in Park, R. E., Burgess, E. W., and McKenzie, R. D. (Eds.), *The City*. Chicago: University of Chicago Press, p. 51. Used with permission.

lying areas (Zones IV and V) were populated predominately by White, middle- and upper-class homeowners who had lived in their communities for many years and who were well-integrated into the dominant culture of the United States. In the area between the center of the city and the outlying districts were the working-class neighborhoods (Zone III), where second- and third-generation immigrant families lived. In contrast, the heart of the city (Zones I and II, areas continually encroached on by the growth of business and industry), had high concentrations of transients and hoboes, Black migrants, and newly arrived immigrants, who occupied street corners and dilapidated housing.

The Chicago sociologists observed that not all urban zones were equally plagued by crime, alcoholism, high rates of mental illness, and other similar problems. Indeed, the further one moved away from the city center, the lower the incidence of social problems. According to the Chicago School, this was the result of the social disorganization that characterized the inner city areas (Park et al., 1967). **Social disorganization**, they argued, was caused by rapid social change that disrupts the normally smooth operation of a social system. In a socially disorganized area, dominant values and norms compete with other, sometimes illegitimate, values and norms. Various cultures conflict, and members of younger generations clash with one another as well as members of older groups. Social cohesion breaks down, and social deviance is one common result.

The Chicago sociologists studied many forms of social deviance. It was, however, primarily *Clifford R. Shaw* and *Henry D. McKay* who undertook an analysis of crime, especially juvenile delinquency, from the perspective of the Chicago School. It is to their work that we turn now.[1]

Crime and Social Disorganization

Shaw and McKay believed that the foundation for an adult criminal career was laid early in life, so the best way to control crime was to prevent juvenile delinquency. To study delinquency, Shaw and McKay used two methods—one quantitative and the other qualitative. The quantitative method was the cornerstone of their neighborhood studies. Using police and court records, they plotted on a series of maps: (1) the houses where juvenile delinquents lived (*spot maps*); (2) the percentage of the total juvenile population in specific census tracts who were involved with the criminal justice system (*rate maps*); and (3) the distribution of delinquency throughout the various parts of the city (*zone maps*). They supplemented these data by conducting extensive interviews with a number of delinquents to obtain their "life histories," including detailed accounts of their social and familial relationships, their school experiences, and other personal data.

Shaw and McKay published their findings in a number of volumes from the 1920s through the 1940s.[2] They concluded that in terms of such characteristics as personality, intelligence, and physical condition, delinquents, for the most part, were no different from nondelinquents. Of equal significance was their finding that crime and delinquency were not consistently dominated by any particular ethnic or racial groups. This could be seen in the fact that while the racial and ethnic composition of certain neighborhoods changed over the years, the rates of delinquency in these neighborhoods remained fairly constant. Thus, what distinguished delinquents from nondelinquents were not individual traits, but rather characteristics of the respective neighborhoods in which they lived.

More specifically, Shaw and McKay reported that the neighborhoods with the worst delinquency problems also had the highest rates of other serious problems, including deteriorated housing, infant mortality, and tuberculosis. The residents of these neighborhoods were the most economically disadvantaged in the city. Not surprisingly, they located these neighborhoods in or next to Zones I and II (see Figure 4.2).

Shaw and McKay did not see these problems as the consequences of economic inequality per se or the exploitation of the areas by commerce and industry. Instead, in the Chicago tradition, they emphasized the impact of social disorganization. These were neighborhoods in transition; they were undergoing the processes of *invasion*, *dominance*, and *succession*. On one hand, the neighborhoods were being invaded by newly arrived immigrant and migrant groups, which resulted in the flight of most of the current residents. These new groups did not have the resources to live in better areas of the city, and they also had to face the difficulty of adjusting to life in a different society. At the same time, business and industry continued to encroach on these areas, allowing conditions to deteriorate further. The instability of these neighborhoods caused traditional social controls to break down and "immoral" values to creep in. As Shaw and McKay (1971) explained it:

> In general, the more subtle differences between types of communities in Chicago may be encompassed within the general proposition that in the areas of low rates of delinquents there is more or less uniformity, consistency, and universality of conventional values and attitudes with respect to child care, conformity to law, and related matters; whereas in the high-rate areas systems of competing and conflicting moral values have developed. Even though in the latter situation conventional traditions and institutions are dominant delinquency has developed as a powerful competing way of life. It derives its compelling force in the boy's [sic] life from the fact that it provides a means of securing economic gain, prestige, and other human satisfactions and is embodied in delinquent groups and criminal organizations, many of which have great influence, power, and prestige . . . [A youth's] attitudes and habits will be formed largely in accordance with the extent to which he participates in and becomes identified with one or the other of these several types of groups. (pp. 87–89)

From this perspective, then, the solution to the crime problem lies not with the treatment of individual offenders, but with programs to shore up traditional social controls in disorganized neighborhoods until they become stable. This was precisely Clifford Shaw's goal in 1932 when he initiated the *Chicago Area Project* (CAP) in three high-delinquency neighborhoods. The CAP was composed of neighborhood councils whose members were local residents committed to bettering their communities from within. As Snodgrass (1976) describes it:

> The CAP stressed the importance of maintaining the autonomy of the community. An effort was made to avoid the imposition of Anglo-Saxon middle-class standards on res-

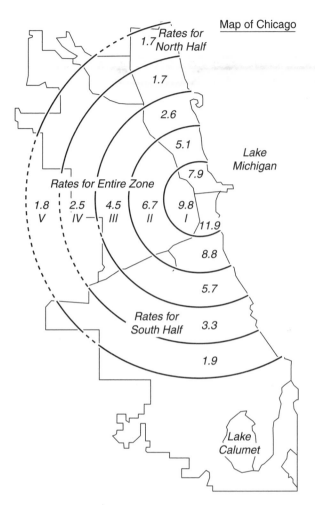

FIGURE 4.2   Zones of Delinquency in Chicago, 1927–1933*

*The Arabic numerals in each zone are the male delinquency rates for the zone.

Source: Shaw, C. R., and McKay, H. D. (1969). *Juvenile Delinquency in Urban Areas.* Chicago: University of Chicago Press, p. 69. Used with permission.

idents. The aim was to "stimulate" community organization without engineering and controlling it and to "spark" the latent potential for community control. Thus, the field worker was to act as a "catalyst," the leadership was to be "indigenous," the council was to be composed of local residents, and management and planning were to be carried out by the residents. There was hope for a wide basis of local democratic participation. (p. 12)

From the outset, the sights of the CAP were turned inward. These were not political action groups struggling for recognition of their rights or a voice in Chicago politics. CAP activities were designed primarily as social programs (including sports and recreation, and summer camps) and for cultural assimilation.

During the twenty-five-year period spanning its start and Shaw's death in 1957, the CAP remained in continuous operation and underwent considerable expansion. The state of Illinois eventually took over the administration of CAP and, although some councils disbanded, a number are still operating. Evaluation research examining the success of programs such as CAP in various U.S. cities has shown a number of positive outcomes: providing youngsters with more prosocial activities, such as sports; giving them the chance to release tension and stress; offering opportunities for learning constructive problem-solving skills; and giving children a structural environment in which they learn to model the behavior of prosocial adults rather than antisocial peers (Miller, 1962; Moffitt, 1997). Nevertheless, the findings with regard to whether such programs reduce crime and delinquency rates are mixed. Simply taking kids off the streets for recreation and other activities does not significantly reduce crime if those children spend the remainder of their time in violent, impoverished homes, schools, and neighborhoods. In fact, the program sites themselves can become sites of crime, especially youth violence. The programs appear to work best if they are one part of a larger crime prevention effort that has as a focal point community development, including job training and job opportunities, study groups and tutoring, improved public housing, and better police–community relations—issues to which we will return shortly (Butterfield, 2000).

Indeed, if the CAP failed in reducing delinquency and crime in transitional areas, many critics believe it was because it did not address the real causes of these problems—specifically, industrial expansion and the powerlessness of impoverished residents to stop it. As Snodgrass (1976) maintains:

> The fact that life resources were held by one class, the fact that landowners allowed their property to deteriorate, the fact that capitalist enterprises and other vaunted institutions invaded and destroyed communities, that this "process" was carried out "legitimately" and without concern for human dislocation and welfare, and that the residents were politically impotent and resourceless (and could offer no resistance) are all "points" unmentioned and apparently unnoticed. By way of contrast, it may be noted that the "Gold Coast" was the only area in the transitional zone preserved from invasion and destruction. It was safeguarded by the power, wealth, and social prominence of its inhabitants . . . the judgment may seem harsh, but the concentration on internal organization and neglect of the political and economic realities of slum residents stems from the fact that there was less concern with rights and welfare than with behavior control, less concern with community prosperity than with community constraint. (pp. 11, 17)

Snodgrass (1976) presents evidence that Shaw and McKay were well aware of the economic and political realities of the transitional areas. It appears that they chose not to take decisive action against the wealthy industrialists because the CAP was, to a large extent, financially dependent on business contributions and philanthropy. Telling in this respect are Henry McKay's comments made in 1935:

> [T]he businessmen who are on the boards [of CAP] want to be told that they are doing something important by their contributions and hours of conferences and that their philanthropy is curing the evil . . . it makes no difference to them that the conditions which they are trying in this trivial manner to correct are largely due to their own every-day behavior. (quoted in Snodgrass, 1976, p. 16)

Shaw and McKay received criticism from their contemporaries on other grounds. Some observers called into question the accuracy of their conclusion that the delinquency rates of various racial and ethnic groups depended on the neighborhoods in which they lived. A number of researchers reported that certain immigrant groups—Asians, in particular—appeared to be especially resilient to criminal and delinquent influences even when they resided in neighborhoods with the highest crime and delinquency rates (see, for example, Hayner, 1933; Jonassen, 1971; McGill, 1938).[3] Shaw and McKay did take note of such findings in *Juvenile Delinquency and Urban Areas* (1942) and, in fairness to them, it should be noted that other researchers have obtained support for their theory of neighborhood succession with regard to some groups, as we will see shortly (see, for instance, Bursik & Webb, 1982).

Shaw and McKay also were criticized on methodological grounds. Despite the fact that they supplemented their quantitative data with qualitative analyses of delinquents' life histories, a number of critics questioned their reliance on police and court statistics for identifying offenders and offense rates. In 1936, for example, Robison discovered that when using data from social welfare agencies as well as the criminal justice system, there was a more even distribution of delinquency among city neighborhoods than Shaw and McKay reported. Her finding was supported by later self-report studies, although such studies themselves are not without methodological weaknesses (see the Appendix, as well as Tittle et al., 1978).

Regardless of these problems, though, Shaw and McKay's work has been described as "a gold mine that continues to enrich criminology today" (Vold & Bernard, 1986, p. 183). You will recognize its influence in the remaining theories to be discussed in this chapter and in the theories we will examine in subsequent chapters. First, let's take a look at some recent offshoots of the ecological approach.

The Chicago School's Descendants

Contemporary research on themes central to the Chicago School takes several forms, but probably the two most popular and widely explored are the geography of crime and the relationship between specific community characteristics and crime. We will discuss each in turn.

The Geography of Crime. The mapping of crime rates and residences of criminals actually predated the Chicago School. In addition to the work of Shaw and McKay, *cartographic criminology*, as it is sometimes called, has its roots in the nineteenth century studies of researchers such as Guerry and Quetelet in France, and Rawson and May-hewe in Great Britain. These men plotted the spatial distribution of offenders and offenses by region of their respective countries and explained the differences they observed in terms of a number of social variables (Dann, 1980). Today, researchers interested in the geography of crime not only utilize more sophisticated techniques, such as computer graphics, but also have broadened the focus of their investigations.[4] There remains some interest in issues such as the effects of population density and cli-mate on crime (see, for instance, Harries & Stadler, 1989), as well as the *journey to crime*—the distances traveled by different types of offenders to commit various crimes (see Nichols, 1980; Phillips, 1980). More recent research, however, has focused increasingly on aspects of the physical environment—for example, how specific spatial designs encourage law-abiding versus criminal behavior, and how certain spatial fea-tures affect inhabitants' perception or fear of crime. This approach is known specifi-cally as **crime prevention through environmental design (CPTED)**.

The role that environmental design plays in precipitating criminal behavior began to receive considerable attention in the early 1970s after Oscar Newman's (1972) book, *Defensible Space*, was published. Newman maintains that crime can be reduced significantly through the utilization of equipment, devices, and even symbolic barriers that "combine to bring an environment under the control of its residents" and defended or protected against intruders (p. 3). A later refinement of the defensible space argument suggests that criminologists look not only at the physical features of a particular building, neighborhood, or other geographic area, but also at how the par-ticular social and cultural features of these places affect residents' victimization and fear of crime (Taylor et al., 1980). To this, Wilson and Kelling (1982) have added the "broken windows" thesis, focusing on how the physical deterioration of a building or neighborhood contributes to crime and disorder. The accumulation of graffiti and trash, along with dilapidated, unrepaired, and abandoned buildings, causes residents to feel vulnerable and to withdraw from participating in maintaining public order. Ini-tially, this lowering of vigilance by residents sends the message to local youth that they can get away with harassment, vandalism, and disorderly conduct, and soon this mes-sage spreads to would-be offenders from outside the area, who take advantage of the neighborhood's vulnerability.

The CPTED approach is based on a neo-classical model of offending in that it assumes that offenders are rational, that they look for unguarded targets in evaluating a crime site. It has had a practical impact on the formulation of various crime preven-tion strategies, such as the Neighborhood or Town Watch programs, and clean-up and beautification projects. However, research indicates that especially with regard to the latter types of programs, most of these efforts do more to improve the confidence and reduce the fear of residents than they do to actually prevent crime (Taylor & Harrell, 1996). Moreover, critics point out that there is little research showing how—or if— most potential offenders perceive and use the physical features of an area to their advantage. In addition, it is unknown whether physical deterioration in an area occurs independently of structural changes in that area or whether it is simply a reflection of those changes. As Taylor and Harrell (1996) point out, for example, physical deterioration may be caused by a decline in the socioeconomic status of residents, which also contributes to an increase in crime. In other words, instead of physical deterioration contributing to crime, it is high unemployment that is causing both increased physical deterioration and a rising crime rate. The answer, then, is not to repair and upgrade housing in the area, but to provide job opportunities to residents. In fact, research indicates *decreasing* deterioration may also send an important message to would-be offenders: A gentrifying neighborhood may signal the presence of lucrative targets (Bottoms & Wiles, 1986; Covington & Taylor, 1989).

Nevertheless, recent research does lend support to the idea that the physical features of a building or neighborhood can affect the crime rate. For instance, Alice Coleman (1989) has studied the effects of particular structural designs on crime rates in British housing estates (the equivalent of U.S. public housing developments). Based on this work, she proposes a *theory of design disadvantagement.* Design disadvantages are simply design defects that encourage criminal behavior in various ways and increase estate residents' vulnerability. Coleman has found that crime rates can be lowered drastically by reducing an estate's design disadvantagement score by making basic changes in housing structure, including dismantling overhead walkways, walling off each estate block to exclude strangers and allow residents to get to know one another, and providing individual gardens for each house or flat. She emphasizes, though, that for crime rates to be lowered, the improvements must be made in the housing *design*, not simply by beefing up police patrols or hiring more management personnel. In addition, research in the United States has shown that something as simple as changing traffic patterns can reduce drug dealing, car theft, and assault in certain neighborhoods, while removing overgrown trees and bushes and installing more lights in public parks can deter drug dealing, vandalism, and assault (Taylor & Harrell, 1996; Weisel et al., 1994).

Other researchers have turned their attention to the concept of "place," not just in terms of spatial position, but rather in the context of the meanings of values that people attach to these positions. David Herbert (1989, p. 3) explains that, "As geographers identify clusters of crime and regard them as 'delinquency areas,' the task is then to understand the ways in which such 'places' have emerged and the characters which they have assumed." This is clearly in the tradition of the Chicago School, but while Shaw and McKay focused on competing value systems in disorganized neighborhoods, many contemporary researchers are examining how public policymaking creates such places. For instance, in their historical study of vice areas in San Francisco, Shumsky and Stringer (1981) found that vice was concentrated in particular areas not because of the values or behavior of area residents, but because of the decisions of city politicians and the actions of police. Similarly, Gill (1977) and others (see Baldwin, 1977; Damer, 1974) have shown that the emergence of "bad" housing estates in Britain is related to a "dumping" policy of local housing authorities who assign families or individuals with criminal records or histories of problems to certain estates. Such studies also raise the issue of stigmatization which, as Herbert (1980, p. 40) points out, is "linked to the theory that reputations, once established, are perpetuated—perhaps undeservedly— because the area is labeled as problematic." We will explore this further in Chapter 5.

Routine Activities Theory.   Another theory premised on the neo-classical principle that offenders are rational social actors is *routine activities theory*, developed by Lawrence Cohen and Marcus Felson in 1979. Like the CPTED approach, routine activities theory holds that offenders evaluate a potential target before committing a crime. Crime, according to this theory, results when three factors converge: (1) there are motivated offenders, (2) there are suitable targets (potential victims), and (3) there is an absence of capable guardians (individuals, including the police, witnesses, and even potential victims themselves, who can act to prevent or foil the crime). The risk of crime increases sharply when you have in the same place at the same time a person or persons with reasons to commit a crime, along with a person or persons who are viable targets, *and* no "guardians" to stop the crime from taking place. Cohen and Felson (1979) believe that changes in people's daily work, school, and leisure activities— their routine activities—have contributed to rising crime rates. More specifically, since World War II, people's routine activities have increasingly taken them away from home and into the public sphere, thus increasing their chances of victimization. For example, more households than ever before contain two adult wage earners, and children spend more time at school and in afterschool activities. There also has been an increase in single-parent families, so that the only adult in these families is likely to be away from home for a large part of the day, leaving the house unguarded and perhaps children unsupervised.

Routine activities theory focuses primarily on victims rather than offenders, assuming simply that motivated offenders always exist. While such an assumption is likely true, critics point out that it is nonetheless important to understand criminal motivation if we are to accurately explain criminal behavior. A number of studies of both property crime and violent crime have found support for routine activities theory (for example, Kennedy & Forde, 1990; Messner & Tardiff, 1985; Sherman et al., 1989). However, critics believe these studies are limited because they typically examine only a part of the theory (usually victims' or potential victims' actual or inferred behavior and/or the presence of guardians), not the complete theory (including the presence of motivated offenders and offenders' actual motivations).

Another important criticism of routine activities theory is its implication that the more a person stays at home, the lower that person's chances are of becoming a crime victim. While this premise appeals to common sense, it is not supported by empirical research on the victimization of women and girls. As we will see in Chapter 7, females are more likely to be victimized by people they know in their own homes than by strangers in public places (Crowell & Burgess, 1996; Renzetti, 1998; Stanko, 1996). Consequently, some criminologists have revised the theory to better take into account gender differences in victimization (see, for example, Schwartz & Pitts, 1994, for a discussion of what they call "feminist routine activities theory"). Regardless of these revisions, however, routine activities theory is less an explanation of criminal behavior than it is a theory of victimization (Kennedy & Baron, 1993).

Communities and Crime.   Contemporary ecological research on communities and crime has redirected attention to Shaw and McKay's theory of invasion, dominance, and succession. This more recent version of social disorganization theory focuses on disadvantaged neighborhoods, as Shaw and McKay did, but expands Shaw and McKay's perspective to include such factors as high poverty, high unemployment, and a high percentage of single-parent families. These factors contribute to crime and delinquency by reducing informal social control (the willingness of residents to monitor their neighborhoods by intervening when they see a potential problem emerging), lowering social integration, and increasing isolation from mainstream social institutions (e.g., employers, schools, and churches) (Bursik & Grasmick, 1993; Sampson & Groves, 1989). Contemporary social disorganization theorists point out that unlike the disadvantaged neighborhoods studied by Shaw and McKay in the 1920s and 1930s, there is actually little residential turnover in many disadvantaged neighborhoods today. Residents of these inner city neighborhoods are increasingly unlikely to experience upward socioeconomic mobility, which allows them to move out to more prosperous or financially stable areas. Instead, today's disadvantaged inner city neighborhoods are areas of residential segregation, largely dominated by chronically unemployed, financially destitute people of color (Rose et al., 1999; Wilson, 1996). The mobility that does occur is coerced; that is, movement out of such neighborhoods is temporary, caused typically by the arrest and incarceration of residents (Rose et al., 1999).

Research that tests contemporary disorganization theory typically measures neighborhood disadvantage and then correlates these rates (e.g., proportion of the population living below the poverty line, unemployment rates, proportion of single-parent households) with the neighborhoods' official crime rates (according to police records) or residents' self-reported involvement in crime. Overall, this research shows a strong relationship between neighborhood disadvantage and crime (see, for example, Bellair, 1997; Peeples & Loeber, 1994; Peterson et al., 1997). However, some researchers report that the relationship between neighborhood disadvantage and crime is indirect, rather than direct (Gottfredson et al., 1991; Sampson & Groves, 1989; Simcha-Fagan & Schwartz, 1986). Specifically, these studies indicate that the effect of neighborhood disadvantage is mediated by other factors, such as friendship networks, feelings of personal attachment to family and school, and organizational participation. Harris (1998) also reports that adolescents' level of religiosity (measured by frequency of participation in religious youth groups, self-reported importance of religion, and frequency of personal prayer) also reduce delinquency, even in disadvantaged neighborhoods.

Finally, Sampson and his colleagues (1998, p. 1) have found that a significant mediator of the effects of neighborhood disadvantage on crime is what they call **collective efficacy**, "mutual trust among neighbors combined with willingness to intervene on behalf of the common good, specifically to supervise children and maintain public order." In other words, collective efficacy is a form of community cohesion or integration that manifests itself as informal social control by neighborhood residents. Sampson et al. (1998) report that in neighborhoods characterized by high collective efficacy, crime rates are significantly lower than in neighborhoods characterized by low collective efficacy. Importantly, when these researchers looked at the effects of poverty and racial composition of a neighborhood on the violent crime rate, they found that the best predictor of the violent crime rate was neither poverty nor race, but rather level of collective efficacy in the neighborhood.

Of course, Sampson and his colleagues recognize efficacy itself can be effected by such factors as concentrated poverty and high ethnic or linguistic diversity in a neighborhood. In fact, they note that "recognizing that collective efficacy matters does not imply that inequalities at the neighborhood level can be neglected" (Sampson et al., 1998, p. 2). Still their research points to the importance of motivating community residents to engage in informal social control. In his study of a White, working- and lower-middle class neighborhood in Chicago, Carr (2000) found that most residents do not want to intervene directly when they see a potential problem in their neighborhood. Rather, they prefer to call the police. Consequently, he reports that informal social control is most effective when it is partnered with the intervention of more formal control agents (e.g., the police, local politicians). Carr refers to this form of social control as the *new parochialism*: "informal social control behaviors engaged in by citizens at the parochial or neighborhood level of control, but that are facilitated by agents from the public sphere" (p. 3). An example that Carr gives is a neighborhood problem-solving group that calls on local politicians to close down a tavern where crime is increasingly taking place. Another example, which has grown largely out of the social disorganization perspective, is community policing, discussed in Box 4.1.

Anomie Theory

There are two explanations of crime that use the title "anomie theory." One was developed in the late nineteenth century by the French sociologist Emile Durkheim; the other was developed in the late 1930s by the American sociologist Robert Merton. Although they are closely related, we will see some important differences between these two perspectives.

Durkheim's Theory of Anomie

Emile Durkheim (1858–1917) was one of the most important social theorists of all time, and his influence in the social sciences is far-reaching. It is difficult to isolate as most important any single contribution of such a prominent writer, but certainly among Durkheim's greatest achievements were the role he played in getting sociology recognized as a legitimate science in the academic world and his specification of the unique concerns of sociologists that set them apart from other scientists. Durkheim demonstrated that much human behavior, including criminal behavior, is caused by *social* factors rather than biological or psychological factors. As such, these behaviors must be understood in sociological, not biological or psychological, terms. Although today we recognize this as the dominant view used to explain crime, it was a fairly radical perspective when Durkheim was writing.

Durkheim began with a particular view of human nature. Humans have innate needs and desires that must be satisfied if they are to be content. However, unlike other animals, most human needs and desires are not physical; they are social and, according to Durkheim, the more one has, the more one wants. In his words, "Human activity

BOX **4.1** **CONTROVERSY AND DEBATE**

Crime Prevention through Community Policing

Traditionally, the police in our society have followed a professional crime-fighting strategy that relies on a disciplined, technically sophisticated, quasi-military force to maintain order, protect citizens, and combat crime. This strategy emphasizes crime control and crime solving at a distance and is largely *reactive*. Underlying this approach is the belief that fair and impartial law enforcement requires minimal interaction between officers and members of the community they serve.

During the 1980s, the professional crime-fighting model was increasingly criticized (Kelling & Moore, 1987). One criticism centered on the reactive nature of the model. Many experts and ordinary citizens felt that the primary role of the police should be to *prevent* crime rather than respond once a crime had already been committed. Second, the emphasis in this model on distancing police officers from the community was criticized for actually hampering the policing effort because it fosters hostility and distrust of the police among citizens. In communities where the police are considered "outsiders" or worse, enemies, residents are unlikely to cooperate with, support, or assist the police.

An alternative model of policing is *community policing*, which in many ways is the opposite of the professional crime-fighting model. Community policing involves building strong relationships between officers and community residents through sustained interaction, such as foot or bicycle patrols instead of mobile patrols. Police are expected to be visible in a nonthreatening way in the communities they serve and to take a *proactive* problem-solving approach to crime. Instead of a military image, the community policing model has a social work orientation (Miller, 1999). One of the goals of community policing is to reduce suspicion and distrust between citizens and police officers so that community satisfaction with the police increases and the quality of community life improves. Residents become partners with the police by both volunteering information about specific crimes and becoming actively involved in crime prevention efforts. Solving crimes also becomes easier for the police because of the increased cooperation of community members and also because officers are more familiar with the neighborhoods in which they are working (Fleissner & Heinzelmann, 1996; Miller, 1999; Skogan, 1990).

There is considerable research evidence that community policing is achieving positive results in many troubled neighborhoods throughout the United States (Fleissner & Heinzelmann, 1996). However, as Miller (1999) found, the success of community policing depends to a large extent on officers' willingness to give up the traditional quasi-military crime-fighting approach and engage in activities that many see as more appropriate for social service agencies than the police. "Administrators and officers need to do far more than just 'talk the talk'; they need to put new goals into practice, to truly 'walk the talk'" (Miller, 1999, pp. 5–6). Future research is needed to determine the extent to which the community policing model has been embraced by officers and the public alike and whether it is successfully improving police–community relations and reducing crime.

---

aspires beyond assignable limits and sets itself unattainable goals" (1897/1951, p. 241). Consequently, human "nature" must be regulated by the "collective order"—society. How this happens depends on the type of society in which one lives. Durkheim distinguished between two types of societies: those characterized by mechanical solidarity and those characterized by organic solidarity.

A society of *mechanical solidarity* is one in which the members are very much alike and there are few individual differences among them. The members of such a society do the same types of work, fulfill the same social roles, have the same world view (a "common consciousness"), and have the same understandings of "right" and "wrong" (a "common conscience"). Durkheim referred to the "totality of social likenesses" as the *collective conscience* (1947/1893, p. 80). It is this collective conscience that binds people together and promotes conformity in the society of mechanical solidarity. However, such a society is not crime-free. Durkheim believed that crime is inevitable; in all societies there will be individuals who violate social norms. Because of the high degree of uniformity in mechanical societies, norm violators meet with a strong social reaction. Durkheim characterized law in such societies as *repressive*: Its goal is punishment and revenge. Despite the negative light in which crime is held, Durkheim also recognized that crime serves some positive functions. For one thing, it highlights and reinforces the moral boundaries of the society. In addition, it enhances social solidarity among conforming members by inducing feelings of moral superiority and righteousness.[5]

Mechanical societies are, by necessity, small and relatively undeveloped technologically. As a society undergoes population growth and technological advancement, social diversity increases and the collective conscience is weakened. Still, social order is preserved because the proliferation of diverse jobs, roles, and ideas actually creates an interdependence among the society's members. Thus, the division of labor largely replaces the collective conscience as the binding force in society.[6] The boundaries of acceptable behavior are widened, and punishment becomes less harsh. Law becomes more civil-administrative, with the primary goal of preserving contracts among the society's members—a kind of law Durkheim called *restitutive*. This is a society characterized by *organic solidarity*.

Crime in organic societies may still serve positive functions, but Durkheim was particularly concerned about such societies because he saw them as being susceptible to conditions that could cause crime and other social problems to become rampant. Durkheim argued that social change in such societies—population growth, industrialization, and urbanization—could occur so quickly that the society would not have adequate time to develop appropriate regulations to govern social interaction. Durkheim called this condition of inadequate or inappropriate social control **anomie**.

Durkheim most fully developed the concept of anomie in his classic work *Le Suicide (Suicide)*, first published in 1897. In analyzing suicide rates, he noticed that suicides not only go up during periods of economic depression, but also during periods of sharp economic growth. While to most this seems paradoxical, Durkheim pointed out that under the latter circumstances, a confusion about social norms frequently prevails. Though some have interpreted anomie to mean "normlessness," it is probably more accurate to describe it as a condition in which traditional norms no longer seem applicable, but new norms have not fully evolved. "It arises when disruption of the collective order allows [people's] aspirations to rise beyond all possibility of their fulfillment—persons aspire to goals which either they cannot attain or find difficult to reach" (Clinard, 1964, p. 7; see also Agnew, 1997). A rise in the suicide rate is one result; a rise in the crime rate is another.[7]

Durkheim's ideas on crime (as well as many other issues) have sparked considerable debate. His analysis of the response to deviation in mechanical societies has received some empirical support, and there is evidence that organic societies provide more room for deviation.[8] However, some researchers maintain that organic societies are not more lenient in terms of criminal punishment and that, while civil-administrative laws do increase in these societies, so does the regulation of morality (Gurr, 1976; Spitzer, 1975). Durkheim's argument that rapid social change in the forms of industrialization and urbanization increases crime and deviance underlies much of the contemporary debate about the impact of economic development on crime, a topic we explore in Box 4.2. Still, Agnew (1997) points out that many of the most interesting and fruitful aspects of Durkheim's anomie theory have been prematurely rejected or simply ignored by contemporary researchers. Agnew notes, for example, that Durkheim's notion that crime results from aspiration toward unrealistic or unattainable goals has been too quickly dismissed with no study even attempting to test it. This, Agnew argues, is unfortunate because the idea has important policy implications: "If goals are unlimited, means to achieve goals are unimportant, and efforts to prevent crime by fostering goal achievement are doomed to failure" (1997, p. 33). Agnew and others (see Passas & Agnew, 1997) are calling on contemporary criminologists to carefully revisit Durkheim's anomie theory.

BOX **4.2**   **HOW THE WORLD SEES IT**

Crime and Economic Development

What effect does economic development have on a society's crime rate? Are capitalist industrialized societies more crime-ridden than agrarian or nonindustrialized societies? The answers to these questions have been debated by criminologists for many years. On one hand, there are those who argue that industrialization "civilizes" a society, eventually causing brutal practices, such as maiming and violent crime to avenge family honor, to disappear. On the other hand, some criminologists contend that industrialization, especially the development of market capitalism, destroys traditional social relations and weakens traditional social control mechanisms. Self-interest replaces concern for the common good, promoting immorality especially in the form of property crime (Rosenfeld & Messner, 1997), although some concede that violent crime may decrease (see, for example, Shelley, 1981).

Trying to decide which argument has the greatest empirical support is difficult because the accuracy and completeness of crime statistics vary widely from society to society. In many economically undeveloped societies, crime statistics are not collected. In developing countries, concerns about other issues mean that the collection of crime statistics is given low priority. However, Rosenfeld and Messner (1997) also point out that both arguments are too simplistic to account for the diversity of societies globally, including variations in culture and social structure that impact on both crime and economic development. They reason that there is nothing inherent in market capitalism that inevitably leads to either increases or decreases in crime. Rosenfeld and Messner hypothesize that the key to the relationship between economic development and crime is what they call the *institutional balance of power*. If the economy is valued over all other institutions in a society so that: (1) noneconomic roles and functions are considered less important than economic ones, (2) noneconomic roles must be accommodated to the requirements of economic roles if the two conflict

(*continued*)

BOX 4.2   Continued

(e.g., family obligations versus work responsibilities), and (3) economic standards become the norm for evaluating noneconomic aspects of life, then an increase in crime is likely.

More specifically, Rosenfeld and Messner (1997) believe that economic dominance in a society contributes to crime by stimulating an *anomic ethic* at the cultural level. That is, economic dominance encourages people to achieve their goals by whatever means necessary: "Persons who pursue goals by any means necessary have no *moral* qualms about using criminal means. The selection of means turns entirely on utilitarian, cost-benefit considerations, which include the perceived probability and severity of the penalties for criminal behavior" (p. 214, authors' emphasis). At the same time, economic dominance contributes to crime by weakening the ability of noneconomic institutions to effectively impose social controls on people. "Feeble institutions do not offer attractive roles to which individuals are likely to become strongly attached. As a consequence, the bonds to such conventional institutions will be tenuous, and

the constraints against crime associated with these bonds will be weak" (p. 216). According to Rosenfeld and Messner, then, the answer to the questions that opened this discussion is that the effect of economic development on the crime rate depends on the level of economic dominance in the society.

Rosenfeld and Messner's hypothesis needs to be carefully tested. They suggest that good places to start would be the former Soviet Union and other previously socialist countries of Eastern Europe, as well as the People's Republic of China. There is already research that suggests that the rush to embrace market capitalism without simultaneously adjusting noneconomic institutions to these critical changes can result in the kinds of institutional imbalance and social dislocation that Rosenfeld and Messner are concerned about (see, for example, Curran, 1998; see also Kick & LaFree, 1985). Additional research will surely refine our understanding of the relationship between economic development and crime and perhaps settle this important criminological debate.

Merton's Theory of Anomie

In an article first published in 1938, and revised and elaborated on at least three times since then, *Robert Merton* revived Durkheim's concept of anomie (Merton, 1975). Whereas Durkheim conceived of anomie as a problematic social condition resulting from sudden and rapid social change, Merton saw it as an endemic feature of the everyday operation of certain types of societies. To understand this better, let's consider how Merton views a society in general.

For the purpose of analysis, Merton divides society into two parts: the cultural structure and the social structure. The *cultural structure* consists of the society's *goals*; in other words, it is what the members of the society value and strive for. The *social structure* is the *institutionalized means* by which the goals are supposed to be achieved. In a well-balanced society, these two structures will be integrated; that is, all members know and accept the goals and have at their disposal the means to achieve them. Not everyone will be uniformly successful in achieving the goals, but in this "ideal" society, people derive satisfaction simply from being in competition with others working toward the same ends.

In some societies, however, an undue emphasis is placed on one of the societal structures. Here Merton turns his attention specifically to the United States where, he says, the most important goal is material success. The culture of U.S. society values money and the accumulation of wealth over all else. [9] This might not be problematic were it not for the fact that, in the United States, the institutionalized means to achieve material success are not equally available to everyone. Despite an ideology of egalitarianism—especially the notion that anyone who is honest and hardworking will be successful—some groups in society find the institutionalized means blocked or closed to them. Indeed, it is the egalitarian ideology that exacerbates the problem of the disjunction between goals and means. The disjunction itself is what Merton calls *anomie*.

Anomie produces strain in those who experience it. Consequently, Merton's anomie theory, as well as the theories that build on it, are called *strain theories*. Merton delineates several different ways that people may respond to this strain. The responses are referred to collectively as the *typology of adaptations* and they are shown in Table 4.1. Three of the adaptations (innovation, retreatism, and rebellion) are considered deviant; the other two generally are not.

Conformity, according to Merton, is the most common adaptation; it makes social order possible. Conformists accept cultural goals and play by the rules to achieve them, no matter how difficult that may be because of a lack of legitimate opportunities. This helps to explain why even in high crime areas, there are many residents who are not criminals.

Ritualism also involves adhering to the rules (institutionalized means), but scaling down the goals so that satisfaction may be obtained through a much lower level of "success." Ritualists "go through the motions" day in and day out, content with modest achievement and thereby avoiding the frustration resulting from being unable to reach loftier aspirations. Merton feels that this adaptation is most common among the lower middle class, largely because of "the strict patterns of socialization in this class, and by the limited opportunities for advancement offered out to its members" (Taylor et al., 1973, p. 97).

TABLE 4.1   Merton's Typology of Individual Adaptations to Anomie

Mode of Adaptation	Cultural Goals	Institutionalized Means
I. Conformity	Accepts (+)	Accepts (+)
II. Innovation	Accepts (+)	Rejects (–)
III. Ritualism	Rejects (–)	Accepts (+)
IV. Retreatism	Rejects (–)	Rejects (–)
V. Rebellion	Rejects, but wishes to replace with new goals (±)	Rejects, but wishes to replace with new means (±)

Source: Adapted from Merton, R. K. (1968). *Social theory and social structure.* Glencoe, IL: Free Press, p. 194.

Among the deviant adaptations, *innovation* traditionally has been considered most important for criminologists. Innovators have bought into the cultural goals but, having found the institutionalized means blocked or closed, they utilize more expedient, though illegitimate means to achieve these ends. Significantly, Merton argues that the tremendous emphasis on material success in U.S. society causes some members of the wealthy and upper middle classes to innovate. As he puts it, "On the top economic levels, the pressure toward innovation not infrequently erases the distinction between business-like strivings this side of the mores and sharp practices beyond the mores" (Merton, 1975, p. 141). Nevertheless, he sees innovation as an adaptation most often employed by those at the bottom of the social class hierarchy. In Merton's view, we should not be surprised that crime rates are highest among the poor, the working class, and minorities, because this type of behavior is "a 'normal' response to a situation where the cultural emphasis upon pecuniary success has been absorbed, but where there is little access to conventional and legitimate means for becoming successful" (Merton, 1975, p. 141).

Merton considers *retreatism* to be the least common adaptation. Retreatists are individuals who have been socialized to accept the cultural goals as well as the institutionalized means to achieve them. However, on failing to succeed through institutionalized means, retreatists do not innovate; instead, they essentially drop out of society. Retreatists include drug addicts, alcoholics, and vagrants.

Finally, *rebellion* is the adaptation of those who reject the current cultural and social structures, but seek to replace them with new ones. Merton is somewhat reluctant to identify rebellion as a deviant adaptation in the same way innovation and retreatism are. Consequently, in a later essay, he refers to rebellion as nonconformity and to innovation and retreatism as aberrant behavior (Merton, 1961).[10]

The value of Merton's work is reflected in a statement made by Marshall Clinard in 1964: "Without any doubt, this body of ideas . . . has been the most influential single formulation in the sociology of deviance in the last twenty-five years, and Merton's paper, in its original and revised versions, is possibly the most frequently quoted single paper in modern sociology" (p. 10). This does not mean, of course, that the theory has not been subject to criticism. Much concern, in fact, has been expressed about the typology of adaptations. As Taylor, Walton, and Young (1973) point out, it is to Merton's credit that he recognized the constraints imposed on people by virtue of the positions they occupy in the social structure. However, they and others feel that the theory may be too rigid in its assessment of which adaptation is most probable among which group.

For example, a number of researchers have questioned Merton's proposition that innovation is concentrated among the lower social classes. There is certainly evidence, as we will see in subsequent chapters, that crime is more widely distributed across social groups. It is true that those most likely to be arrested and processed through the criminal justice system are poor, but this does not necessarily reflect their disproportionate involvement in illegitimate activities. Some observers see this weakness in anomie theory as resulting in part from Merton's failure to closely examine the conformist adaptation. If Merton had paid more careful attention to the conformist adaptation, he would have had to face "the awkward social fact that conforming individuals are few and far between even in those positions in the social structure when, according to his own formulations, structural strain is at a minimum" (Taylor et al., 1973, p. 98). Similarly, Lemert (1964) argues that Merton needs to examine how crime and deviance can be outcomes of social control efforts. Merton, Lemert points out, did not consider the significance of the interactions between social actors and others who react to them. Some people are able to escape being labeled by others as deviant/criminal.

Merton's classification of alcoholics, drug addicts, and other similar groups as prime examples of retreatists also has been questioned. In their study of drug addiction, for example, Lindesmith and Gagnon (1964) discovered several difficulties in applying anomie theory. They point out that failure to succeed is more likely a result of drug addiction than a cause of it. The use of drugs itself may produce anomie. In addition, some drug addicts are materially successful people—physicians, business people, and other professionals. Addiction, moreover, does not usually cause the addict to withdraw from society, but rather to become quite "active" in order to secure drugs. In short, they conclude that "the theory of anomie does not appear to account for the major behavioral aspects of drug use or addiction" (p. 187; see also Inciardi et al., 1993).

Finally, Merton's conceptualization of U.S. culture as monolithic has drawn heavy criticism. In a society as diverse as the United States—indeed, Lemert (1964) maintains, in most societies throughout the world today—it would be difficult, if not impossible, to identify a set of universally shared values. Ours is clearly a pluralistic society, and to argue that all members of this society uniformly hold common values "strains credulity" (p. 66). Still, it is difficult to disagree with Merton's characterization of the *dominant* U.S. culture as highly materialistic.

Agnew (1997) suggests, however, that most researchers who have set out to test anomie theory have failed to appreciate its complexities and have focused almost exclusively on the disjunction between goals and means. There has been a renewed interest in anomie theory in recent years, and criminologists are expanding on Merton's original ideas (Agnew & Passas, 1997). For example, Passas (1997) has explored individuals' differential perceptions of the goals/means discrepancy, emphasizing that one does not have to be objectively deprived, but only to compare oneself negatively to others and, therefore, *feel* deprived for deviance to emerge. The groups that one uses as the basis for comparison are called *reference groups*. A person's reference groups may be made up of people she or he knows well (e.g., friends, relatives, co-workers) or people she or he has never met (e.g., a prospective employer, the rich and famous, television characters). Agnew (1997) argues that we need more research on the role of reference groups in generating anomie and, consequently, crime and deviance. Other researchers are examining how anomie can contribute to white-collar crime and organizational deviance (Rosenfeld & Messner, 1997; Vaughan, 1997).

Such research indicates that anomie theory is "alive and kicking," as Agnew and Passas (1997, p. 22) put it: "That it has a distinctive contribution to make to the explanation of deviance and crime, and that it is worthy of serious consideration." Even before this recent resurgence of interest in anomie theory, numerous criminologists used some of its main ideas—especially the role of *strain*—to develop new perspectives. The remainder of this chapter will look at their efforts.

Subcultural Theories

Merton's argument that criminal behavior is an outgrowth of the strains that people experience because of their particular positions in the social structure is a popular one. A number of theorists have applied this idea to the study of one specific form of criminal behavior, gang delinquency, but others have extended it to adult crime as well. Most of these researchers, however, continue to focus on the poor or lower class. This is especially true of the subcultural theories that we will examine now.

Cohen's Theory of the Delinquent Subculture

Albert Cohen (1955) criticized Merton for making it appear as if individuals' reactions to strain are uninfluenced by their interactions with other people around them.

Cohen also took exception to Merton's depiction of criminal (innovative) behavior as a rational means to a desired end or goal, that is, as utilitarian. While this may be the case for some types of crime, Cohen argued, it does not apply to most of the activities of delinquent gangs that are concentrated in lower-class neighborhoods. In his book *Delinquent Boys*, Cohen (1955) identified five central characteristics of lower-class delinquent gangs. Together these comprise the *delinquent subculture*:

1. *nonutilitarianism*—"We usually assume that when people steal things, they steal because they want them. . . . However, the fact cannot be blinked—and this fact is of crucial importance in defining our problem—that much gang stealing has no such motivation at all. . . . In homelier language, stealing 'for the hell of it' and apart from considerations of gain and profit is a valued activity to which attaches glory, prowess, and profound satisfaction" (pp. 25–26).
2. *maliciousness*—Much delinquent gang activity is "just plain mean." Its purpose is to cause problems for people, to make them unhappy or uncomfortable. Acts of vandalism are good examples: tearing down street signs, putting glue in people's car engines, and so on.
3. *negativism*—Delinquents have a set of values and live by rules that are not just different from those of "respectable" people, they are the "negative polarity" of middle-class norms. "That is, the delinquent subculture takes its norms from the larger culture but turns them upside down" (p. 28).
4. *short-run hedonism*—"There is little interest in long-run goals, in planning activities and budgeting time, or in activities involving knowledge and skills to be acquired only through practice, deliberation and study." Delinquents seek immediate gratification. "They are impatient, impetuous and out for 'fun' with little heed to the remoter gains and costs" (p. 30).[11]
5. *group autonomy*—Delinquent gang members resist any kind of restraint on their behavior except that imposed informally by fellow gang members. They defy or ignore the authority exercised by parents, teachers, and other agents of social control.

Cohen also observed that virtually all delinquent gang members are male; females rarely engage in delinquency and, when they do, it is almost always in the form of sexual deviancy. Cohen wants to know why: How can we account for the development of this delinquent subculture among lower-class males? He believes the answer lies in the strains these boys experience when they are confronted with and judged by middle-class standards.

According to Cohen, the dominant culture of the United States is middle-class culture, which consists of such values as delayed gratification, self-control, ambition, academic and occupational success, good manners, and respect for property. Middle-class parents exert considerable pressure on their children to accept and abide by these values. The socialization of lower-class children, however, is more relaxed. "The child's activities are more likely to be governed by exacting specifications of effort and achievement which are regarded as good in themselves because they are seen as instrumental to some long-range goals" (p. 99). This presents no difficulty for pre-school age children, but once lower-class children enter school, problems arise.

The school is an institution governed by middle-class values, and most teachers are themselves middle class. Not surprisingly, in light of their early socialization, lower-class children do not do well in school. Thus, they do not achieve status through their school performance and, given their parents' limited resources, they do not acquire status from their families. This, according to Cohen, is what produces strain in their lives, or what he called **status frustration**.

Status frustration is a male problem because a primary component of the masculine role is status attainment. "[O]ne measures his manhood by comparing his *performance*, whether it be in stealing, fighting, athletic contests, work, or intellectual achievement, against that of others of his own sex. . . . The delinquent response, however it may be condemned by others on moral grounds, has at least one virtue: it incontestably confirms, in the eyes of all concerned, his essential masculinity" (pp. 139–140). Girls, in contrast, are preoccupied with developing relationships, especially romantic relationships, since marriage is their chief goal and also the best means for improving their status. As Cohen put it, "We do not suggest that girls are in any sense 'naturally' more interested in boys than boys are in girls. We mean that the female's station in society, the admiration, respect and property that she commands, depend to a much greater degree on the kinds of relationships she establishes with members of the opposite sex" (pp. 140–141). Consequently, when girls are delinquent, it is in a feminine way: They are sexually delinquent.

The delinquent subculture, then, is lower-class boys' collective solution to the problem of status frustration: Since they cannot acquire status by conforming to middle-class values, they reject these values. They replace them with a new set of values—the delinquent subculture—against which they can be judged successful, at least by their peers. In the gang, they can prove their masculinity and raise their status, especially if they excel in delinquent activities.

While Cohen's perspective has some appeal, it also has been the subject of extensive criticism. Before we entertain the views of the critics, however, let's review some other subcultural theories. Then we will consider their common strengths and weaknesses.

Other Subcultural Theories

Walter B. Miller.   Several theorists besides Cohen have focused on the proposition that each social class develops its own unique value system reflecting its place in the status hierarchy. One such theorist who, like Cohen, studied delinquent gangs, was *Walter B. Miller.* According to Miller (1958), delinquent gangs form in the lower-class community itself. In Miller's view, Cohen examined lower-class gang delinquency from the perspective of the middle class; that is why he characterized it as nonutilitarian, malicious, and negativistic. In contrast, Miller maintains that such behavior is stable and "essentially ritualized"; it serves to "support and maintain the basic features of the lower class way of life." He argues:

> In areas where these differ from features of middle class culture, action oriented to the achievement and maintenance of the lower class system may violate norms of middle class culture and be perceived as deliberately nonconforming or malicious by an observer strongly cathected to middle class norms. This does not mean, however, that violation of the middle class norm is the dominant component of motivation; it is a by-product of action primarily oriented to the lower class system. The standards of lower class culture cannot be seen merely as a reverse function of middle class culture—as middle class standards "turned upside down"; lower class culture is a distinctive tradition many centuries old with an integrity of its own. (p. 19)

What is the context of the lower-class cultural system? Miller identified six *focal concerns* which, he said, while not restricted to the lower class, are given a distinct priority and weighting by members of this class relative to members of the middle class.[12] These focal concerns, in order of importance, are:

1. *trouble*—This has a variety of meanings: unwelcome involvement with police or other officials; fighting or sexual adventures (for men); sexual activity resulting in unwanted pregnancy (for women). Getting into and staying out of trouble are major preoccupations of all lower-class people.
2. *toughness*—The most important aspects of toughness are physical prowess, "masculinity" (including lack of sentimentality, and the view of women as "sex objects"), and bravery in the face of physical threat.
3. *smartness*—This does not mean good grades in school or mastery of a body of knowledge often called "culture" (art, literature, and so on). Rather, it refers to one's ability to avoid being outwitted, duped, or conned oneself. It is one's "street sense."
4. *excitement*—This involves the search for "thrills," "flirting with danger," and taking risks, often through drinking, fighting, and sexual exploits.
5. *fate*—This is the idea that one's life is determined by forces over which one has no control. It is not a religious notion, but rather has to do with being "lucky" or "unlucky."
6. *autonomy*—Resistance to control of one's life by others and a desire for personal independence are the elements of this concern, although Miller claims that the actual behavior of lower-class people frequently contradicts this. He claims that, "Many lower class people appear to seek out highly restrictive social environments wherein stringent external controls are maintained over their behavior" (including the armed forces, mental hospitals, and prisons). (p. 12)

Miller's central thesis is that illegal behavior is motivated by an attempt to achieve "ends, states, or conditions" that are valued in the lower-class community and to avoid those that are devalued. Sometimes legal means for achieving these goals are available, but illegal means are more expedient. At other times, lower-class culture demands a specific response to a certain situation, and the response itself may be illegal. In other words, "Following cultural practices which comprise essential elements of the total life-pattern of lower class culture automatically violates certain legal norms" (p. 18).

Unlike Cohen, Miller was primarily concerned with the content of lower-class culture, and he took its development as a given. Nevertheless, he did argue that certain social conditions prevalent in lower-class communities combine with lower-class focal concerns to produce a "generating milieu" for gang delinquency. In particular, he cites the high frequency of single-parent, female-headed households in lower-class communities. In such families, adult males are either absent or only sporadically present, having little involvement in child rearing and leaving young boys in the household with no consistent male role models. Thus, "for boys reared in female-based households the corner group provides the first real opportunity to learn essential aspects of the male role in the context of peers facing similar problems of sex-role identification" (Miller, 1958, p. 14).

Marvin Wolfgang and Franco Ferracuti.   In the study of adult crime, *Marvin Wolfgang* and *Franco Ferracuti* (1967) also utilize the concept of subculture. Theirs is an analysis of homicides, in particular, "passion crimes" that are not premeditated and not caused by psychosis or other serious mental disorder. These, they argue, make up the majority of homicide cases and occur predominantly among certain social groups and in certain neighborhoods. Looking at official statistics, they found that most of these homicides are committed by a relatively homogeneous group: young, non-white, lower-class males.[13] "The value system of this group," they contend, "constitutes a subculture of violence" (p. 152).

The subculture of violence is a set of attitudes or social expectations that favors the use of violence in a variety of situations. It includes a willingness to participate in violent activity, to expect violence, and to be ready to retaliate against others. The more integrated an individual is into the subculture of violence, the more likely that person is to resort to violence.

According to Wolfgang and Ferracuti, the direct expression of aggression typically is unacceptable in middle-class households and communities. Middle-class parents, for example, usually do not hit their children to punish them, and a derogatory comment by a neighbor or an associate is likely to be ignored or brushed off as trivial. Among the middle class, violence may be expressed vicariously through films or fantasies, but the high value placed on human life inhibits its overt expression. In contrast, the lower class places less value on life. Physical punishment of children is routine, and "quick resort to physical combat as a measure of daring, courage, or defense of status appears to be a cultural expression, especially for lower class males of both [sic] races" (quoted in Wolfgang & Ferracuti, 1967, p. 153). Among the lower class, Wolfgang and Ferracuti assert, overt expression of violence is rewarded and individuals who shy away from physical confrontation are ridiculed and ostracized.

Thus, in lower-class households and communities, the subculture of violence is passed on from generation to generation and reinforced in everyday interaction. However, Wolfgang and Ferracuti admit that they do not know how the subculture develops in the first place. The best they can do in this regard is to speculate that "the beginning could be a Cohen-like negative reaction that turned into regularized, institutionalized patterns of prescription" (p. 162).

Strengths and Weaknesses of Subcultural Theories

Subcultural theories have been described as seductive (Andersen & Renzetti, 1980). Their appeal lies in the fact that they provide a facilely logical explanation of official statistics that show that delinquency and many other types of crime are committed primarily by members of the lower class. Another strength of these theories is that, as Cohen has argued (1997, p. 53), they do not portray social actors as living "within a box," isolated from the influences of other people. Instead, they take into account the role that social actors' peers, family members, and other reference groups may have in promoting or inhibiting crime and deviance.

An important question, however, is whether subcultural theories receive empirical support. The results of a number of studies call into question the very existence of a distinct lower-class subculture (see Kornhauser, 1978). Most studies indicate that gang members in lower-class neighborhoods both know and accept the norms of the dominant culture (Campbell, 1984; Hirschi, 1969; Short & Strodtbeck, 1965). In fact, research by Hagan and his colleagues (1998) shows that much of what is valued by delinquents is connected rather than opposed to the dominant culture. Moreover, Cao et al. (1997) have found no support for the notion of a Black subculture of violence. In their study using data from the General Social Survey, White males were more likely than Black males to give violent responses when presented with a defensive situation, and there was no racial difference in responses to offensive situations. Interestingly, research examining socialization practices across social classes indicates the opposite of what subcultural theories predict: Middle-class parents appear to allow their children considerable freedom in decision making and encourage curiosity and initiative, whereas lower-class parents more often emphasize conformity to rules and respect for authority (Kohn, 1965; 1976; 1977). Some researchers have identified race differences in socialization practices, with African American parents placing greater importance on children learning to become self-reliant, to take financial responsibility at an early age by earning money for themselves and their families, and to develop racial pride and strategies for responding to and overcoming racism (Hale-Benson, 1986; Poussaint & Comer, 1993).

Kitsuse and Dietrick (1959) were among the early critics of subcultural theories, especially Cohen's approach. They take issue with Cohen's portrayal of most delinquent behavior as nonutilitarian and malicious (that is, annoying, but basically trivial). They argue instead that most delinquents, especially those in gangs, engage in serious, calculated, and utilitarian activities. More recent research supports their position, with most studies showing that gang members engage in more crime than non-gang members from similar social and economic backgrounds, and the crimes of gang members are more serious as well (Brunson & Miller, 2001; Esbensen et al., 1993; Huff, 1998). Nevertheless, most young residents living in disadvantaged neighborhoods do not join gangs. In fact, studies show that less than 25 percent of young people in such neighborhoods are gang members (Bjerregaard & Smith, 1992; Winfree et al., 1992). Moreover, researchers have not consistently found differences in gang members' and non-gang members' perceptions of blocked opportunities (Esbensen et al., 1993; but in support of differences, see Dukes et al., 1997). Vowell and May (2000) report that poverty status increases perceptions of blocked opportunities only among White youth, but not among Black youth.

Finally, subcultural theories, particularly Cohen's and Miller's, portray crime and delinquency as male enterprises. While acknowledging the existence of female offenders, they dismiss female offending as minor, limited to sexual deviance in reaction to the sexual "double standard" (that males have greater sexual freedom). While it is certainly the case that males engage in more crime—and more *serious* crime—than females, and that fewer females than males are gang members, such observations do not justify the exclusion of girls from delinquency and crime research. Feminist criminologists (see Chapter 7) have begun to remedy this oversight in recent years by focusing on gender differences in criminal offending and deviance, including gang membership. Their research shows that female offending, whether committed individually or in gangs, is hardly limited to minor sexual deviance. Moreover, they report that although males and females join gangs for many of the same reasons—the gang provides a sense of belonging and security, excitement and status (Brunson & Miller, 2001; Huff, 1998)—one consistent gender difference is that girls' gang involvement is tied to personal experiences of family violence (Chesney-Lind, 1997; Moore, 1991). For example, Brunson and Miller's (2001) interviews of female gang members revealed that 44 percent had been abused by family members, compared with 22 percent of non-gang members; more than 50 percent had been sexually assaulted, compared with 22 percent of non-gang members. Far fewer male gang members report histories of physical and sexual abuse. As Chesney-Lind (1997, p. 21) points out, subcultural theorists have focused almost exclusively on the relationship between social class and crime—a relationship which, as they have conceived of it, receives little empirical support—but they have almost totally neglected the relationship between gender and crime, which is ironic since gender has been shown to have "a dramatic and consistent effect on delinquency."

Crime and Opportunity

Another response to Merton's anomie theory, as well as to Cohen's theory of the delinquent subculture, was presented by *Richard Cloward* in 1959 and elaborated by Cloward and his colleague *Lloyd Ohlin* in a book, *Delinquency and Opportunity*, published the following year. Their work, known as *opportunity theory*, includes the proposition that delinquency and crime are possible responses to the strain people experience when legitimate means to success are blocked or closed to them. However, they add an important new concept: **differential opportunity**. Let's examine their perspective more carefully, and then look at more recent applications of it.

Differential Opportunity and Delinquent Subcultures

Cloward and Ohlin (1959, 1960) accept much of Merton's argument. They agree that U.S. culture emphasizes material success, but not everyone has equal access to legitimate means to achieve these success goals, despite a dominant ideology of egalitarianism. In response to the frustration induced by this, members of deprived groups may utilize illegitimate means to attain material success. Innovation becomes their adaptation to the lack of legitimate opportunities to be successful by the standards of the dominant middle-class culture. Yet, not everyone who experiences such strain innovates. Why not?

According to Cloward and Ohlin (Cloward, 1959), the key is *differential access to illegitimate opportunities.* It is not enough simply to be motivated to deviate. In addition, the potential deviant must be in an environment conducive to learning deviance and, once trained, must have an opportunity to engage in deviation. And just as anomie theory argues that legitimate means are not equally available to all in the social structure, Cloward and Ohlin (1960) maintain that illegitimate means are not equally accessible either. "Roles, whether conforming or deviant in context, are not necessarily freely available; access to them depends upon a variety of factors, such as one's socio-economic position, age, sex, ethnic affiliation, personality characteristics, and the like. . . . Only those neighborhoods in which crime flourishes as a stable, indigenous institution are fertile criminal learning environments for the young" (Cloward & Ohlin, 1960, pp. 147–148).

Cloward and Ohlin concentrate on the differential opportunity structures of one deprived group: lower-class male youths in large urban centers. There are, they maintain, different types of lower-class neighborhoods, each of which gives rise to a different type of delinquent subculture. For instance, in relatively stable neighborhoods where most community members know one another, youths are socialized into a *criminal subculture* that values material gain through illegitimate means. In this type of neighborhood, adult criminal role models are plentiful and young men may become their apprentices. Through these intimate contacts, lower-class boys learn the techniques for committing crimes and are integrated into a network that includes fences, corrupt police and politicians, and shady lawyers. In contrast, in less stable neighborhoods, a *conflict subculture* is most likely to develop. These are neighborhoods characterized by social disorganization. Most residents live in large housing projects that generate a kind of isolation and anonymity. The illegitimate opportunity structure, then, does not facilitate the pursuit of a long-term criminal career, but instead promotes the use of violence to attain status or a "rep." Finally, there are individuals in all lower-class communities who are unsuccessful in both the legitimate and illegitimate opportunity structures. These "double failures" form a *retreatist subculture*. They withdraw from the lifestyle of their community and turn to drugs, alcohol, or some other "kick." Within this group, a new order of goals and criteria of achievement is created.

"The cat [i.e., retreatist] does not seek to impose this system of values on the world of the squares. Instead, he strives for status and deference within the society of cats by cultivating the kick and the hustle" (Cloward & Ohlin, 1960, p. 27).

Cloward and Ohlin are to be credited for emphasizing the importance of opportunity structures for the commission of crime and other forms of deviant behavior, and for recognizing the role that social learning plays in criminal behavior and careers. In addition, they depict delinquent subcultures as collective responses to strain, rather than as individual adaptations. Nevertheless, by locating crime and delinquency squarely in lower-class communities, they fall into the same trap as other strain theorists. Specifically, they overlook the widespread violation of the law by members of other social classes, especially the upper class. This is unfortunate because, as we show in subsequent chapters, the crimes of the powerful are different in many ways from ordinary street crimes, but clearly they are no less harmful. In addition, these crimes reflect the illegitimate opportunity structure available to dominant groups in our society: the middle class and the wealthy, White people, and men.

Some elements of Cloward and Ohlin's differential opportunity theory have been criticized because they are not supported by empirical data. For example, researchers have been unable to locate the three distinct types of subcultures that Cloward and Ohlin identified. In particular, the retreatist subculture—a gang of lower-class young men organized solely for the purpose of drug use—does not appear to exist at all. Instead, most gang members—and many non-gang members—use drugs, fight, vandalize property, and steal, but no gang or group of young people does these things all the time; most of their time is spent "hanging out" with friends, talking, watching television, listening to music (Brunson & Miller, 2001; Huff, 1998; Short & Strodtbeck, 1965). In addition, Cloward and Ohlin's theory, like Cohen's and Miller's, ignores the role of gender in delinquency and crime. As Chesney-Lind (1997, p. 20) points out, "No mention of female delinquency can be found in their *Delinquency and Opportunity*, except that women are blamed for male delinquency. Here, the familiar notion is that boys, 'engulfed by a feminine world and uncertain of their own identification . . . tend to "protest" against femininity'" (quoting Cloward & Ohlin, 1960, p. 49).

Despite these difficulties, Cloward and Ohlin's differential opportunity theory had a tremendous impact on public policy, a point to which we will return shortly. Moreover, even though Cloward and Ohlin neglected women and girls in their work, other criminologists have applied their ideas to the study of female crime. Let's take a look at some of these applications now.

Women, Crime, and Opportunity

As we have noted in this chapter and elsewhere in the text, historically, criminologists ignored female criminality. The little attention that was given to female offenders usually was limited to three contexts: (1) comparisons that underscored women's lack of involvement in crime relative to men; (2) studies of prostitution; and (3) analyses of the depravity of violent women, the rationale being that since "normal" women are passive, the few women who do commit violent crimes must be "sick" (Edwards, 1986). Most criminologists, as we observed in Chapters 2 and 3, believed simply that it was not in women's nature to be criminal (although they could be quite devious and deceptive). In short, in the minds of criminologists and the general public, "criminal" was clearly equated with "male."

In the mid-1970s, however, this perception began to change largely because of the publication of two books—Freda Adler's *Sisters in Crime* (1975) and Rita J. Simon's *Women and Crime* (1975)—each of which received widespread attention in both the academic and popular presses. The central theme of both books is that women's crime had begun to change in both quantity and quality and that this was due not to an alteration in women's "nature," but rather because of increased criminal opportunities for women.

According to Adler, the United States in the mid-1970s was in the midst of a female crime wave. Although men were still committing a greater absolute number of offenses, the female crime *rate* was increasing more than the male crime rate. For example, Adler cited statistics from the F.B.I. *Uniform Crime Reports* that show that between 1960 and 1972, women's arrest rates for robbery increased 277 percent compared with a 169 percent increase for men. Statistics on juvenile offenders revealed similar changes. What is more, Adler argued that females were not only engaged in greater criminal activity than previously, but their crimes were assuming a more serious and violent character: Women were now committing crimes traditionally committed by men.

Simon's work closely resembles Adler's in many ways. She also argued that women were committing more crimes than ever before and that the increase in the female crime rate was surpassing that of men. Yet, Simon maintained that the increase in female crime was limited primarily to property offenses and that violent crimes by women actually declined. Still, she asserted that women were committing more crimes generally characterized as masculine, particularly white-collar and occupationally related offenses, such as fraud and embezzlement.

Alarming as they are, it was not these claims that caused the greatest stir among criminologists and the public. What received the most attention, especially from the popular media, were Adler's and Simon's explanations of their findings. Specifically, both argued that the changes they uncovered in the rate and character of female crime were logical outcomes of the women's liberation movement. In other words, feminism had opened up illegitimate as well as legitimate opportunities previously closed to women. As Adler (1975) phrased it, "Is it any wonder that once women were armed with male opportunities they should strive for status, criminal as well as civil, through established male hierarchical channels?" (p. 10). Simon's (1975) position was a bit more complex. She argued that the decrease in female violent crime was the result of feminism: "As women feel more liberated physically, emotionally, and legally, and are less subjected to male power, their frustrations and anger decrease . . . [which results] in a decline in their desire to kill the usual objects of their anger or frustration: their husbands, lovers, and other men upon whom they are dependent, but insecure about" (p. 40). The down side, however, was that the feminist movement, by encouraging women's participation in the paid labor force, had also contributed to the rise in female property crime. "As women increase their participation in the labor force, their opportunity to commit certain types of crime [such as white-collar and occupational crimes] also increases" (Simon, 1975, p. 40).

Adler's and Simon's perspective, clearly a form of opportunity theory, is also known as the **emancipation theory** of female crime. Actually, this argument is not totally new; as Chesney-Lind (1997) points out, during the first wave of feminism, criminologists and others warned that the emancipation of women would increase crime and immorality among women and girls. However, the greatest value of Adler's and Simon's work is that it forced a contemporary reassessment of the relationship between gender and participation in criminal activity. In evaluating Adler's and Simon's theory and research, subsequent analyses shed light on the extent to which female crime had readily changed and the degree to which the women's movement may have contributed to such a change by providing women with new *illegitimate* as well as legitimate opportunities.

One problem with both Adler's and Simon's work was their reliance on official crime statistics (see the Appendix). These statistics represent only those crimes known to the police, which, it is estimated, are only about one-third of all crimes committed. A substantial amount of crime goes undetected (see, for example, Inciardi et al., 1993), or is not reported by victims. Even when a crime is reported, the police exercise considerable discretion in deciding which complaints warrant their attention and which should be ignored, so not all crimes are passed along to the F.B.I. A more serious problem stems from the way Adler, in particular, used the UCR data. In comparing male and female rates of increase for specific crimes, she didn't control for the large difference in the absolute base numbers from which the rates of increase were calculated. If one base figure is small, even a slight rise will exaggerate the rate change. Conversely, a sizeable increase in a large base figure is likely to appear as only a minor change (Smart, 1982; Terry, 1978). Take arrests for homicide, for example. Between 1965 and 1970, years included in Adler's analysis, the number of arrests of women for homicide increased almost 79 percent; during the same period, the number of homicide arrests for men increased 73 percent. However, in absolute terms, the number of homicides committed by women rose from 1,293 to 1,645, whereas for men, the figures were 6,533 and 8,858 respectively. If we look only at percent changes without taking into account these major absolute base differences, we end up with a very distorted picture of men's and women's involvement in crime.

A more accurate measure of changes in men's and women's criminal activity is to calculate sex-specific arrest rates, that is, the number of men arrested for the same crime per 100,000 of the male population and the number of women arrested for the same crime per 100,000 of the female population. The sex differential in arrests can then be determined by calculating women's share of all arrests, male and female, for a specific offense. Researchers who have used this method to analyze the sex differential in arrest rates in recent years have found that there has been neither a significant widening nor a significant narrowing of the gender gap in arrests, with the important exception of certain types of property crimes—larceny theft, forgery/counterfeiting, fraud, and embezzlement—and drug offenses (Chesney-Lind, 1997; Simon & Landis, 1991; Steffensmeier, 2001). Are these crimes "traditionally masculine"? Are they occupationally related offenses committed by "liberated" women in the labor force? In short, do empirical data support the emancipation theory of female crime?

Answers to these questions come from two sources. First, studies of female offenders reveal that they are "least likely to respond to ideologies of sex-role equality" (Sarri, 1986, p. 91). Rather, these women tend to be quite traditional in terms of gender (Brunson & Miller, 2001; Campbell, 1984; Chesney-Lind & Rodriguez, 1983). In fact, Adler's (1975) own work indicated that female offenders often expressed a strong dislike of the women's movement and not infrequently considered feminists "kooks."

Second, although women's labor force participation has risen dramatically over the past twenty-five years, women remain segregated in low-prestige, low-paying clerical, sales, and service occupations (Renzetti & Curran, 1999). Simon and Landis (1991, p. 56) argue that the influx of women into these types of jobs affords them greater opportunities to embezzle, defraud, and forge: "They [are] not in a position to steal hundreds of thousands of dollars, but they [are] in a position to pocket smaller amounts." However, it is the low level of financial gain attached to these offenses, as well as characteristics of the offenders themselves, that have led others to maintain that to label them "white-collar" crimes is misleading (Daly, 1989). In fact, in her comparison of male and female offenders, Daly (1989) found that a higher percentage of female offenders had no ties to the paid labor force; they were involved in offenses that were not occupational, but instead included defrauding banks through loans or credit cards, or defrauding the government by obtaining benefits to which they were not legally entitled.

In sum, the claims of emancipation theorists seem overstated at best. With the exception of petty property and drug offenses, women have not made significant gains on male rates of crime, nor do they appear to be engaged in more violent, masculine, or serious offenses. Most female offenders are committing what are considered traditional crimes for women, including shoplifting and check or credit card fraud. But how do we account for the increase in the number of women involved in these crimes and drug offenses? Two other explanations have been offered: (1) the rise in female arrests is simply an artifact of an increased willingness among criminal justice officials to arrest, prosecute, and punish women; and (2) the worsening economic marginalization of some groups of women propels them into crime. We will consider both of these theories in Chapter 7. Now, though, let's turn to a discussion of the public policies that grew out of some of the theories we have reviewed so far in this chapter.

Changing the Opportunity Structure: Public Policy Initiatives

The social disorganization and traditional strain theories had far-reaching effects on the development of various programs to address delinquency, crime, and other social problems. Perhaps none of the criminologists we have discussed in this chapter were more involved in the formation of public policy than Cloward and Ohlin. Just as the Chicago sociologists had established the Chicago Area Projects to combat social disorganization, Cloward and Ohlin, then working at Columbia University's School of

Social Work, put their ideas into practice in the late 1950s at the Henry Street settlement house on the lower east side of Manhattan.

The combined research and community action program they developed, called Mobilization for Youth, received city, state, and federal funding. It was premised on the belief that it is better to prevent delinquency than to treat delinquents. Cloward and Ohlin's method of delinquency prevention mirrored their theoretical perspective: Change the legitimate opportunity structure available to disadvantaged youth. Consequently, Mobilization for Youth, and other programs like it, sought to establish a number of educational and economic reforms in impoverished urban communities. These included pre-school programs, remedial reading classes, programs to increase communication between teachers and their students' parents, inservice training for teachers in the cultural backgrounds of their students, vocational training programs, and job placement (Maris & Rein, 1973).

When the Kennedy Administration took office, Lloyd Ohlin became a consultant for the development of federal policy to prevent delinquency. Many of his ideas were incorporated into Lyndon Johnson's War on Poverty campaign. On a national scale, the Johnson administration initiated a variety of social and economic programs in high-crime, high-poverty areas that were very similar to those of Mobilization for Youth: in education, Foster Parents, Head Start, Upward Bound, and numerous other programs under the Elementary and Secondary Education Act; in employment, Volunteers in Service to America (VISTA), Job Corps, and later the Comprehensive Employment and Training Act (CETA); and still other projects, such as Legal Aid, Model Cities, and Supplementary Security Income (SSI). To what extent were these programs successful in reducing crime?

There are criminologists who argue that this is an unfair question because the War on Poverty programs were so underfunded from the outset that they never had a realistic chance of accomplishing much of what they promised. For instance, the Office of Economic Opportunity (OEO), which was responsible for administering the War on Poverty programs, received a total of less than $6 billion between 1965 and 1968, even though most experts believed that $30–$40 billion was necessary for the OEO to fulfill its mandate (Harrington, 1984; Levitan & Johnson, 1984). Another problem was organization. This problem occurred on at least three levels. Administratively, the OEO bypassed state governments and local welfare bureaucracies, which generated considerable political conflict. Second, while the programs were supposed to encourage maximum participation by those they were designed to help—the poor—no one seemed to know what this meant or how to accomplish it. Consequently, conflicts also emerged among community leaders, politicians, and local welfare officers over who would control decision making and funds. Finally, many of the War on Poverty programs duplicated or overlapped with programs administered by other federal offices, causing confusion and fragmentation of services. However, perhaps the most serious problem of the War on Poverty was that it never directly confronted one of the most important causes of poverty in the United States: income distribution.

Despite these problems, some analysts maintain that the War on Poverty did improve the lives of many poor people. For example, Head Start has been credited with improving the school and test performances of economically disadvantaged students

(Carmody, 1988; Cole, 1985; Haskins, 1989). Moreover, many War on Poverty programs empowered segments of the poverty population to mobilize in community action organizations to demand improved services and to ensure their rights as citizens. Nevertheless, while the War on Poverty was underway, violent crime increased dramatically, especially in urban areas. Some observers believe the increase in crime during this time was actually caused by a major demographic change: There was a surge in the population aged 14 to 24, the age group that accounts for the majority of arrests for conventional street crime. This "demographic overload" was too much for traditional social control mechanisms to handle (Harrington, 1984). Other analysts speculate that the War on Poverty contributed at least indirectly to a rise in crime by raising hopes and expectations, only to leave them unfulfilled.

We may never have a clear picture, though, of how the War on Poverty affected the crime rate because beginning with the Nixon administration, the already meager budgets for these programs were cut. This budget cutting continued during the 1980s when it appeared that then-president Ronald Reagan had abandoned the War on Poverty and instead had undertaken a "war on the poor." As social programs such as CETA and SSI were eliminated or drastically reduced and the economy went into a severe recession, the crime rate climbed. However, despite President Clinton's welfare "reforms" during the second half of the 1990s, which further reduced social and financial supports for the poor, the crime rate dropped steadily, a fact that some observers attribute to a robust economy with the lowest unemployment rate in three decades (Nasar with Mitchell, 1999; see also Chapter 1).

We will explore further the relationship between the economy and crime in Chapter 6. To conclude this chapter, though, let's take a look at one more strain theory.

Agnew's General Strain Theory

A new version of strain theory has been developed by criminologist *Robert Agnew*. Agnew (1992) maintains that earlier versions of strain theory, especially those of Merton, Cohen, and Cloward and Ohlin, fail to receive much empirical support because they are severely limited in their conception of what constitutes strain. Drawing on research from medical sociology, as well as studies of equity/justice and frustration-aggression in psychology, Agnew expands the definition of strain and the types of adaptations individuals may utilize in response to it. In addition, he attempts to specify more precisely than the earlier theories the relationship between strain and delinquency, and he suggests a number of factors that are likely to influence an individual's choice of delinquent versus nondelinquent adaptations to strain.

In expanding the concept of strain, Agnew points out that there are many types of strain besides the traditional criminological formulation of a disjunction between aspirations and actual achievements (see also Hagan & McCarthy, 1997). He categorizes these strains into three major types, all of which may produce anger and frustration in those experiencing them which, in turn, could lead to crime and delinquency. The first major type is strain experienced as a result of *failing to achieve positively valued goals*. Within this first type of strain, Agnew identifies three subtypes. One subtype is the form traditionally discussed by earlier strain theorists: strain that results from a disjunction between aspirations and achievements. However, Agnew notes that "aspirations" are often lofty and idealistic, so that this disjunction may actually produce less strain than the second subtype: strain that results from a disjunction between *expectations* and achievements. One's expectations are likely not as inflated as one's aspirations; they are based on personal experience and realistic comparisons with one's reference groups. Related to this is the third subtype: strain resulting from a disjunction between what an individual perceived as a *fair* outcome and the actual outcome. Thus, while economic deprivation may induce strain, it also may arise from nonfinancial sources and may have more to do with a person's perceptions of equity or fairness than with his or her objective level of disadvantage or deprivation (Agnew & Passas, 1997; Rebellon et al., 1999).

A second major type of strain results from the *denial or removal of previously attained positive achievements*. Such strains are produced by stressful life events. Examples include breaking up with a girlfriend or boyfriend, the illness or death of a close friend or relative, being fired or laid off from a job, even moving to a new neighborhood or school.

The third major type of strain is produced by *exposure to negative or noxious stimuli*. Such strains may include being picked on in school by classmates, experiencing some type of trauma such as an accident, and abuse and neglect. The less power the individual has to control or eliminate the negative stimulus, the more strain that individual will likely experience.

Still, Agnew (1992) does not argue that crime and delinquency are inevitable outcomes of strain. Rather, strain produces *pressure* toward deviance and crime (Agnew & Passas, 1997). Individuals adapt to strain in various ways: for instance, by trying to ignore or minimize it; by taking responsibility for it and thereby blaming themselves; by taking revenge on those they perceive as causing the strain; or taking drugs or drinking alcohol to temporarily escape from the strain. Not all adaptations are criminal or even deviant. Agnew theorizes that whether an individual responds to the strain in his or her life with deviant or criminal behavior depends on a number of internal and external constraints he calls *conditioning factors*. These include: whether the individual has alternative goals/values/identities in which to take refuge; the individual's personal coping resources (such as self-esteem, problem-solving skills, and intelligence); the various forms of social support available to the individual; associations with delinquent peers; and macrolevel or environmental variables, such as money, status, and educational attainment.

Clearly, Agnew's general strain theory is more complex and multifaceted than previous strain theories. Agnew (1992; see also Agnew & Passas, 1997) also suggests methods for testing his propositions. In his own research, he and his colleague Helene Raskin White (1992) obtained qualified support for the theory, with the strain measures they utilized showing a substantial effect on delinquency and drug use. Other researchers have found that exposure to strain increases delinquency (Hoffman & Cerbone, 1999; Hoffman & Miller, 1998; Paternoster & Mazerolle, 1994) and that delinquency allows adolescents to lower the negative emotional consequences of strain (Brezina, 1996). However, researchers have been less successful in garnering empirical support for Agnew's hypothesized role of conditioning factors. Studies indicate that strain increases the likelihood of delinquency regardless of the presence of specific conditioning factors (Hoffman & Miller, 1997; Mazerolle & Piquero, 1997; Paternoster & Mazerolle, 1994). Mazerolle and Maahs (1998), though, believe that this lack of support for conditioning factors may largely be a function of the methodology and data analysis techniques used by the researchers. Using different statistical tests, they found that three specific conditioning factors—exposure to delinquent peers, holding deviant beliefs, and having a disposition toward delinquency—did have an impact on delinquent outcomes when controlling for level of strain.

Because Agnew's general strain theory is new, it needs considerably more empirical testing (see Agnew & Passas, 1997, for suggestions for future research). At the very least, however, it can be said that the theory holds tremendous promise. Unlike earlier strain theories, Agnew recognizes the need to test the theory against the experiences of various social groups, looking, for instance, not only at differences across social classes, but also at racial and ethnic differences (see Rebellon et al., 1999), gender differences (Broidy & Agnew, 1997), and age differences (see Cullen & Wright, 1997; Hagan & McCarthy, 1997; Menard, 1997). Indeed, as we will see in Chapters 6 and 7, many race-based and feminist analyses of crime have roots in strain theory.

Agnew's theory has been instrumental in reviving strain theory within criminology. It also has wide appeal because of its interdisciplinary approach, drawing on literature from sociology, psychology, and other fields, and also because of its ability to incorporate ideas from other popular criminological perspectives, including social learning theories and control theories. These latter theories are the focus of our next chapter.

Summary and Conclusion

In this chapter, we began our examination of sociological theories of crime, which we will continue in the remainder of the book. Sociological theories, we have seen so far, emphasize the role that factors external to individual social actors play in crime causation.

The theories in this chapter largely focused on aspects of community organization. The Chicago School explored the relationship between crime and social disorganization in rapidly changing urban areas and concluded that the instability of these areas was a major contributing factor to the crime problem. Emile Durkheim's theory of anomie also saw crime as one possible outgrowth of sudden and rapid change, but Robert Merton's version of anomie sees crime as a response to a built-in feature of U.S. society: the disparity between cultural goals and the legitimate means available to attain them. Robert Agnew accepts Merton's argument as one form of strain, but adds a number of others as well as an expansion of possible adaptations.

In subcultural and opportunity theories, we began to see a concern with how learning particular ideas or skills may play a part in individuals' likelihood to engage in crime. The theories that we will examine in the next chapter focus our attention more directly on the role of learning processes.

KEY TERMS

anomie—in Durkheim's view, a social condition of inadequate or inappropriate social control caused by sudden and rapid social change; in Merton's view, the disparity between cultural goals and the legitimate means available to attain them—a social condition that he saw as a built-in feature of U.S. society.

Chicago School (Ecological School, School of Human Ecology)—a school of thought developed at the turn of the twentieth century by sociologists at the University of Chicago who believed social problems such as crime were caused by the social disorganization characteristic of inner-city areas.

collective efficacy—mutual trust among neighbors combined with a willingness to intervene on behalf of the common good using informal methods of social control to maintain public order.

crime prevention through environmental design (CPTED)—a crime prevention strategy based on altering spatial designs and patterns in neighborhoods and buildings to discourage crime and lower residents' fear of crime.

differential opportunity—the notion that illegitimate opportunities, like legitimate ones, are not equally open to all individuals in society; members of some groups have greater access to criminal opportunities, just as members of other groups have greater access to legitimate opportunities.

emancipation theory—an opportunity theory of female crime that posits that "women's liberation" has led to an increase in female crime overall and, in particular, an increase in female participation in traditionally masculine crimes.

social disorganization—the instability caused by rapid social change characteristic of inner-city areas in which culturally dominant values and norms compete with other, sometimes illegitimate values and norms. This leads to a breakdown in social cohesion, and crime is one common outcome.

status frustration—a problem of adjustment experienced by lower-class boys when they realize that they cannot achieve material success or status through school or their families.

SUGGESTED READINGS

Bourgois, P. (1995). *In search of respect: Selling crack in el barrio*. New York: Cambridge University Press. One of the best examples of the new urban ethnographies in the tradition of the Chicago School but with the critical added analysis of the intersection of class, race, and gender relations.

Passas, N., & Agnew, R. (Eds.) (1997). *The future of anomie theory*. Boston: Northeastern University Press. A collection of research papers that demonstrate the innovative ways that many contemporary criminologists are revising, expanding, and testing anomie and related strain theories.

NOTES

1. For excellent brief biographies of Shaw and McKay, see Snodgrass, 1976. Lindner (1996) also provides an outstanding overview of Park's life and work and that of other Chicago sociologists.
2. The most widely read of the neighborhood studies is *Juvenile Delinquency and Urban Areas* (Shaw & McKay, 1942, rev. 1969). The published life histories include *The Jackroller* (Shaw, 1930) and *Brothers in Crime* (Shaw, 1938). See also *The Jackroller at 70* (Snodgrass, 1982).
3. Asian American youth continue to have low rates of offending. Asian Americans make up 4.1 percent of the U.S. population under age 18, but they are 2 percent of the population of juvenile detention facilities and constitute 2 percent of juvenile arrestees for violent crimes (U.S. Department of Commerce, Bureau of the Census, 1997; U.S. Department of Justice, Office of Juvenile Justice and Delinquency Prevention, 1997). Some writers attribute Asian Americans' generally lower rates of delinquency and crime to several unique cultural characteristics, including group solidarity, insularity, and strong family ties. See, for instance, Pogrebia and Poole

(1989) for an excellent analysis of these issues with respect to one Asian group, South Korean immigrants. However, other writers are critical of this cultural differences perspective (see Mann, 1993). It is also important to keep in mind that the Asian American population is diverse, comprising at least seventeen different groups who hail from Asia and eight who come from one of the Pacific Islands. Members of these groups differ not only in their cultural background and traditions, but also in terms of their educational achievement and socioeconomic success in this country. Not surprisingly, they also differ in their rates of delinquency and criminal offending (see Mann, 1993).

4. For a review of recent studies by U.S. and British researchers, see Evans and Herbert, 1989, and Taylor and Harrell, 1996.

5. As Taylor, Walton, and Young (1973) point out, Durkheim also recognized that criminals may serve as "functional rebels," advocating for and inducing positive and necessary social change. Durkheim used Socrates as an example of such a "criminal." You can probably think of a number of contemporary examples of Durkheim's functional rebel.

6. It should be pointed out that Durkheim believed this occurs when a "normal" or "natural" division of labor exists in the society (i.e., when jobs are filled by those individuals whose natural talents and skills best fit them for those jobs), as opposed to a "forced" division of labor (i.e., one in which workers are not matched with jobs that reflect their innate aptitude).

7. Interestingly, contemporary researchers report that although suicide rates did rise during the periods Durkheim wrote about, the crime rates did not. See Lodhi and Tilly, 1973, and McDonald, 1982.

8. Erikson's (1966) research, for example, supports Durkheim's theory, although Erikson's analysis is sharply critiqued by Chambliss (1976).

9. We see here that, unlike Durkheim, who saw human goals as being, at least in part, biological (determined by human nature), Merton sees them as *socially* created.

10. Thus, Merton's rebel is similar to Durkheim's functional rebel. Merton also includes ritualism in the category of aberrant behavior. It should be noted, too, that Merton stated that he did not intend his theory and typology as an explanation for all forms of criminal or deviant behavior. Instead, his intent was to focus attention on the problem of anomie.

11. Cohen notes, however, that while short-run hedonism is a main characteristic of delinquent gangs, it is not unique to them. Rather, he maintains, it is characteristic of lower-class people in general. We will see more of this idea shortly when we discuss other subcultural theories.

12. Miller chose to use the term "focal concerns" instead of "values" for three reasons: (1) he argued that focal concerns are more easily identified through direct field observational research; (2) he saw the concept as descriptively neutral, whereas "value" connotes something positive; and (3) he thought the term allows for a more refined analysis of subcultural differences because it represents actual behavior, whereas "value" represents ideas that may or may not be reflected in people's behavior.

13. However, they note that certain groups of females are more violent than certain groups of males. For example, they cite research showing that non-White women commit homicide at a rate two to four times greater than White males. Consequently, they point out that the argument that physical aggression is an expression of masculinity and toughness is not consistently supported by data. In their view, "violent behavior appears more dependent on cultural differences than on sex differences" (Wolfgang & Ferracuti, 1967, p. 154). A more recent review of homicide data, however, shows that Black women in all age groups commit homicide and nonnegligent manslaughter at rates significantly lower than both White and Black men, but significantly higher than White women. For example, in 1997, the homicide/nonnegligent manslaughter offense rate for White males, aged 14 to 17 years, was 15.0 per 100,000 persons in this group; for Black males, it was 112.3; for White females, it was 1.3; and for Black females, it was 4.5. Similarly, among individuals 18 to 24 years old, the rate for White males in 1997 was 28.3 per 100,000; for Black males, it was 246.4; for White females, 2.8; for Black females, 18.1. Finally, among individuals aged 25 or older, the rate for White males was 6.0 per 100,000; for Black males, 46.5; for White females, 0.8; and for Black females, 5.9 (U.S. Department of Justice, Bureau of Justice Statistics, 1998). These data indicate that gender differences may be more important than cultural differences, contrary to Wolfgang and Ferracuti's claim.

5 Sociological Theories of Crime II: Crime and Social Processes

This chapter might well have been titled "Learning to be Criminal," because it focuses on theories of crime that emphasize the role of *social learning* or *socialization* in the development of criminal behavior. Sociologists define **socialization** as the process of social interaction through which a society's culture is taught and learned and human personalities are developed (Renzetti & Curran, 2000). Although we typically associate socialization with early childhood, it is actually an ongoing process that continues throughout an individual's life. The fact that socialization is a process of *social interaction* tells us that it occurs through *communication* with other people; it is not something we do on our own, in isolation. What is taught—that is, the *content* of socialization—varies across societies, communities, and social groups. Those who do the socializing, whom sociologists call **agents of socialization**, also vary. Agents of socialization influence us over the course of our lives: they are individuals, groups, and institutions that have as one of their primary functions the socialization of members of a society by providing explicit instruction in or modeling of social expectations (Renzetti & Curran, 2000).

Criminologists who emphasize the importance of socialization in the etiology of crime study how various agents of socialization—especially the family, the school, the peer group, and, more recently, the media—affect an individual's likelihood of pursuing criminal or noncriminal activities. These theorists maintain that what distinguishes a criminal from a noncriminal is not physiology, genetics, mental disorder, race, sex, or even social class, but rather *socialization experiences*. The first criminologist to forward this argument as a systematic theory of crime was Edwin H. Sutherland. Thus, our exploration of the relationship between crime and social processes begins with his work.

Sutherland's Differential Association Theory

Edwin H. Sutherland (1883–1950) is generally regarded as the leading criminologist of his generation (Martin et al., 1990). Sutherland is best known for his study of white-collar crime (1949), his life-history analysis of a professional thief (1937), and his development of the *theory of differential association*, which is the focus of our discussion here.

Sutherland made his first formal statement of the theory of differential association in 1939 in the third edition of his textbook, *Principles of Criminology*. For the fourth edition, published in 1947, he revised the theory slightly as a result of his own rethinking and in response to the criticisms and suggestions of his colleagues.[1] By this time, however, the theory was "considered to be one of the best known and most systematic and influential of the interpersonal theories" (Martin et al., 1990, p. 155). According to Matsueda (1988), "The theory was instrumental in bringing the perspective of sociology to the forefront of criminology" (p. 277).

Sutherland was critical of biological and psychiatric theories of crime, but he was also dissatisfied with the eclectic and disorganized nature of the prevalent sociological explanations of the time, which took a multi-factor approach to crime causation. In developing his own perspective, Sutherland drew on the work of a variety of scholars. In our examination of differential association theory we will see the influence of *Gabriel Tarde* (1843–1904), whose "*laws of imitation*" included the postulate that people "imitate one another in proportion as they are in close contact" (1912, p. 326). It has been argued, too, that the work of John Dewey was a source of inspiration for Sutherland (Martin et al., 1990).

Clearly, however, Sutherland was most strongly and directly influenced by the writings and research of his friends, colleagues, and associates at the University of Chicago. First, we will recognize in differential association theory the idea of *cultural transmission* (see Chapter 4). Second, we will find that the work of the symbolic interactionists *George Herbert Mead, W. I. Thomas*, and others was influential. As Vold and Bernard (1986) explain, the symbolic interactionists argue that:

> people construct relatively permanent "definitions" of their situation out of the meanings they derive from their experiences. That is, they derive particular meanings from particular experiences but then generalize them so that they become a set way of looking at things. On the basis of those different definitions, two people may act toward similar situations in very different ways. (p. 211)

Although we will discuss symbolic interactionism later in the chapter when we consider labeling theory, suffice it to say here that the interactionists' focus on how individuals construct social reality through communication with one another is also a concern that underlies the theory of differential association.

Finally, the notion of *culture conflict* is a theme in differential association theory. Sociologist *Thorsten Sellin* argued in the late 1930s that crime is an outcome of a clash between cultures. According to Sellin (1938), in a homogeneous society the "conduct norms" that are codified into law represent a consensus of the society's members. But in a heterogeneous society that contains many diverse subcultures, the law represents the conduct norms of the dominant culture only, and members of various subcultures may violate the law when they follow their groups' indigenous conduct norms. From these ideas, Sutherland developed the concepts of *differential social organization* and *differential group organization*. He utilized these concepts to explain variations in crime rates across countries, cities, and groups (Cressey, 1960). Let us turn, now, to the theory of differential association itself.

Sutherland's Nine Propositions

Students usually have little difficulty learning differential association because Sutherland presented it in the form of nine, fairly straightforward propositions, each followed by a brief explanatory statement. These nine propositions are:

1. Criminal behavior is learned.
2. Criminal behavior is learned in interaction with other persons in a process of communication.
3. The principal part of the learning of criminal behavior occurs within intimate personal groups.
4. When criminal behavior is learned, the learning includes (a) techniques of committing the crime, which are sometimes very complicated and sometimes very simple; (b) the specific direction of motives, drives, rationalizations, and attitudes.
5. The specific direction of motives and drives is learned from definitions of legal codes as favorable and unfavorable.
6. A person becomes delinquent because of an excess of definitions favorable to violation of law over definitions unfavorable to violation of law.
7. Differential association may vary in frequency, duration, priority, and intensity.
8. The process of learning criminal behavior by association with criminal and anti-criminal patterns incorporates all the mechanisms that are involved in any other learning.
9. Although criminal behavior is an expression of general needs and values, it is not explained by those general needs and values since noncriminal behavior is an expression of the same needs and values. (Sutherland, 1947, pp. 6–8)

From the outset, Sutherland makes it clear that criminality is not inherited. Rather, it is learned in the same way that any other behavior is learned: through interpersonal communication and social interaction in intimate groups—what sociologists call *primary groups* (including family and friends). What is learned through this process includes particular attitudes and motivations as well as techniques for committing crimes. However, being exposed to criminal attitudes and motivations and even knowing how to commit a crime does not mean that a person will engage in criminal activity. Many people who desperately need money and who know various illegal ways to obtain it nevertheless persevere in solving their financial problems through entirely legal means. Indeed, to become a criminal or a delinquent, one also must learn specific situational meanings or definitions. To quote Sutherland, "A person becomes delinquent because of an excess of definitions favorable to violation of law over definitions unfavorable to violation of law." Sutherland called the process of social interaction by which such definitions are acquired **differential association**.

Sutherland chose the term *differential association* to emphasize that, "In any society, the two kinds of definitions of what is desirable in reference to legal codes exist side by side, and a person might present contradictory definitions to another person at different times and in different situations" (Cressey, 1960, p. 2). All associations are not equal. In fact, Sutherland specified that associations vary in *frequency, duration, priority,* and *intensity*. In other words, associations that occur often (frequency) and are long-lasting (duration) will have a greater impact on an individual than brief, chance encounters. Associations that occur early in a person's life, especially in early childhood, are more important than those that occur later on (priority). And associations with prestigious people or with those one holds in high esteem will be more influential than associations with those for whom one has little regard or who are socially distant in one's life (intensity).

The theory of differential association is an explanation of how individuals become criminal or delinquent. It is important to keep in mind, however, that Sutherland wished to explain not only differences in individuals' participation in criminal activity, but also group and societal variations in crime rates. To go beyond the individual level, Sutherland originally utilized the concepts of *culture conflict* and *social disorganization* (see Chapter 4). In his 1947 statement of the theory, though, he used the terms *differential social organization* and *differential group organization* instead of social disorganization. Sutherland's objective in making this revision was to point out that areas with high crime rates are not unorganized, but rather are composed of various groups with divergent standards of conduct, which increases the probability that members of some groups living there will learn definitions favorable to law violation. As Cressey (1960) explains, "In a multi-group type of social organization . . . there are alternative educational processes in operation, varying with groups, so that a person may be educated in either conventional or criminal means of achieving success" (p. 2). Put somewhat differently, "Sutherland's theory, then, states that in a situation of differential social organization and [culture] conflict, differences in behavior, including criminal behaviors, arise because of differential associations" (Vold & Bernard, 1986, p. 213).[2]

Differential association theory is valuable. It addresses questions that the strain, subcultural, and opportunity theories left unanswered. For instance, how can we account for the fact that individuals who have equal opportunities to commit crimes do not all engage in criminal activity? Why is it that individuals who are equally pressured toward nonconformity by factors such as poverty do not all become nonconformists? And why do some individuals who appear to have all their material needs met—members of the upper- and upper-middle classes—nevertheless embezzle business funds, defraud consumers, and participate in price fixing schemes and insider stock trading, as well as other criminal practices? For Sutherland, the answer was clear: differential association.[3] Other criminologists, however, were less certain, and Sutherland's work became—and to some extent, remains—at the center of controversy.

Strengths and Weaknesses of Differential Association Theory

You will recall from Chapter 1 that one essential criterion for determining the strength of a theory is the extent to which it is supported by empirical testing. Consequently, perhaps the most damaging criticism of differential association theory is that it is untestable (see, for example, Adams, 1974; Glueck, 1956; Hirschi, 1969; Kornhauser, 1978). Sutherland (1947) argued that ideally the propositions of the theory could be "stated in quantitative form and a mathematical ratio [of an individual's exposure to weighted definitions favorable and unfavorable to law violation] be reached" (p. 7). However, he acknowledged that developing such a formula would be extremely difficult.

Matsueda (1980) argues, however, that specific hypotheses, propositions, and empirical implications of the theory are testable, and he as well as others have undertaken such tests. For example, DeFleur and Quinney (1966) used the mathematical model of set theory to determine if empirically verifiable hypotheses can be derived from the theory. They claim that, "Those who have declared Sutherland's theory to be incapable of generating testable hypotheses appear to have underestimated it. In fact, it can generate more hypotheses than could be adequately studied in several lifetimes" (DeFleur & Quinney, 1966, p. 20; see also Orcutt, 1987). The question remains, however, as to how one can measure or observe *an excess of definitions favorable to law violation*. It appears that, despite DeFleur and Quinney's claim, the key variable in the theory is difficult to operationalize. In fact, Cressey considered this to be one of the most serious weaknesses in differential association theory (Akers, 1996).

Still, criminologists have developed various ways to empirically test differential association theory. One popular method is to ask a sample of juveniles or adults not only about their own values and behavior, but also those of their friends (for example, "How many of your friends have been arrested in the past year?" "To what extent do you think your friends approve of [a specific deviant behavior]? "How many of your friends have done any of the following [deviant behaviors] in the past year?"). The underlying assumption of this approach is that an individual will most likely learn delinquency or criminality from friends who approve of delinquent or criminal behavior and who engage in such behavior themselves. This, then, may serve as an *indirect* measure of the acquisition of definitions favorable to law violation. Various measures of the frequency, duration, priority, and intensity of peer associations also are often used in these studies.

Overall, this research lends support to the theory of differential association, showing a strong correlation between individuals' associations with delinquent or criminal peers and their own likelihood of engaging in delinquent or criminal activities (Cheung & Ng, 1988; Matsueda & Heimer, 1987; Orcutt, 1987; Tittle et al., 1986). In fact, "the best predictor of the extent of an adolescent's involvement in delinquent behavior is . . . the number of the youth's delinquent associations" (Johnson et al., 1987). Such findings, however, do not demonstrate the validity of the theory. "In other words, the data indicate a relationship between delinquent [or criminal] behavior and interaction with others, but they do not demonstrate that it is in fact the contact with these certain others that causes the behavior. Causal sequence is not established nor are other potential factors ruled out" (Martin et al., 1990, p. 166; see also Costello & Vowell, 1999). We cannot pinpoint through such research whether delinquent or criminal values were actually transmitted from delinquent or criminal peers. It may also be the case that those who already hold delinquent or criminal values seek out peers like themselves or, as Sheldon and Eleanor Glueck put it, "birds of a feather flock together." The problem of temporal sequence is made worse by the fact that most of these studies rely on cross-sectional data, which do not allow researchers to decipher the temporal sequence of the learning/action process.

One recent study, conducted by Warr and Stafford (1991), addresses the issue of temporal sequence utilizing data from the National Youth Survey, a five-year panel study of a national probability sample of youths who were aged eleven to seventeen in 1976. These researchers uncovered both positive and negative evidence relative to differential association theory. They found, as Sutherland had argued, that "The attitudes of adolescents are influenced by the attitudes . . . of their peers, and those attitudes in turn affect delinquency" (p. 162). They also discovered, however, that the *behavior* of friends has a strong effect on adolescents' behavior independent of attitudes, indicating that Sutherland's theory may be incomplete because of its emphasis on the transmission of *definitions* favorable to law violation. More specifically, Warr and Stafford (1991) found that:

> First, the effect of friends' attitudes and friends' behavior is in fact enhanced when the two are consistent. Friends who behave as well as think in a delinquent fashion produce the most delinquent associates. However, when the attitudes and behavior of peers are inconsistent, the behavior of peers appears to outweigh or override the attitudes of peers. The actions of peers, it seems, speak louder than their attitudes. (pp. 859–860)

Importantly, these findings were obtained when the data were analyzed longitudinally as well as cross-sectionally. Costello and Vowell (1999) also found that friends' delinquent behavior had a greater effect on research subjects' own delinquent behavior than did definitions favorable to law violation.

In another study, Johnson and his associates (1987) examined factors that influence adolescents' use of drugs. They, too, found support for differential association, but at the same time, they identified an intervening variable. Johnson et al. report that parents' use of drugs and parents' prodrug definitions have relatively little impact on adolescents' drug use. "By the time a child reaches adolescence, all of the direct parental influences seem to play only minor roles in determining his or her drug use" (p. 333). Instead, the most significant factor influencing adolescents' drug use is the proportion of the adolescent's best friends who use drugs. This variable itself had a fairly strong effect on friends' prodrug definitions which, in turn, had a moderate influence on drug use. However, regardless of friends' prodrug definitions, friends' actual use of drugs had the strongest effect of all the variables tested.

Johnson et al. (1987) explain this finding by arguing that it is *situation pressures* to use drugs, not peers' prodrug definitions, that play the dominant mediating role in adolescents' drug use. "In other words, most of the impact from friends' drug behavior to personal behavior seems to bypass the definitions or attitudes variable. It is not so much that adolescents use drugs because the drug use of their friends makes drug use seem right or safe; rather, they apparently use drugs *simply because their friends do*" (p. 333, authors' emphasis).

Differential association theory has been criticized for several other reasons as well.[4] One ongoing debate, for instance, centers on the role of the media in crime causation. Sutherland (1947) argued that crime is learned within intimate personal groups and that "impersonal agencies of communication [such as the media], play a relatively unimportant part in the genesis of criminal behavior" (p. 6). Of course, when Sutherland wrote this statement, the media, especially television, were not very influential in adults' and children's everyday lives. However, as we see in Box 5.1, contemporary researchers disagree about the relationship between media consumption and crime, a topic that is widely researched and highly controversial today.

BOX **5.1**   **CONTROVERSY AND DEBATE**
Do We Learn to Behave Violently by Watching Violent Media?

In the 1930s, when Sutherland was about to publish his theory of differential association for the first time, it was argued by some that motion pictures were a major contributing factor to delinquency. During the late 1940s, when Sutherland was revising his theory, a controversy raged over whether comic books contributed to delinquency. In both cases, claims were made that these media graphically depicted crime, violence, and sex in such ways that viewers or readers, especially the impressionable young, could be led into crime or "sexual deviation" by imitating the behavior of their movie or comic strip heroes or heroines. In each case, a multitude of studies was undertaken, and the bulk of the research indicated that there was no empirical evidence supporting a causal relationship between media depictions of crime and violence and people's actual behavior. Even today, however, the media's role in the etiology of crime and antisocial behavior continues to be debated.

In 1993, the Canadian Radio-Television and Telecommunications Commission issued strict rules regulating the broadcast of violent programming. These rules include a ban on the depiction of gratuitous violence, a limitation of the time that adult programming (including ads and promotions) containing violence can be broadcast (between 9 P.M. and 6 A.M.), and a total ban on any violent depictions in children's programs that minimize the effects of violence or that encourage or promote imitation of violence

(Media Report to Women [MRTW], 1993). In contrast, in the United States, little action has been taken to curb media violence. In 1993, the chief executives of the major national networks agreed to air parental advisories before programs the networks considered violent, and in 1997, the networks instituted a six-category ratings system to advise viewers fifteen seconds before the start of a program as to appropriate viewer ages for the program. However, research shows that in the following year, 1998, the number of violent programs increased (Mifflin, 1998).

The debate over the effects of violent viewing is periodically fueled by incidents involving viewers acting out what they have seen in a program or film. In one case, for example, a five-year-old Ohio boy set fire to his family's mobile home after watching the MTV cartoon *Beavis and Butthead*, in which the characters depicted setting fires as fun. The boy's two-year-old sister died in the fire. The films *Natural Born Killers*, *The Program*, *Colors*, and *Taxi Driver* have also been implicated in murders and other violent crimes (Mifflin, 1998). Still, despite literally thousands of studies, we are no closer to definitively answering the question, "Does violent viewing *cause* violent behavior in viewers?" To summarize this voluminous research, it can be said that there is a strong correlation between violent viewing and violent behavior, but a *correlation* between two variables does not necessarily mean that one *causes* the other.

(*continued*)

BOX 5.1   Continued

There are three major explanations of this relationship (Vivian, 1993). One emphasizes the *cathartic effect* of violent viewing, stating that viewing violence can actually reduce the violent drives of viewers because watching allows them to fantasize about violence, thereby releasing tensions that may lead to real-life aggression. It has also been argued that this catharsis may lead viewers to take positive rather than violent action to remedy the problem. For instance, Vivian (1993) reports that following the broadcast of the television movie, *The Burning Bed*, in which a severely abused woman ultimately kills her batterer-husband by setting fire to his bed while he sleeps, domestic violence agency hotlines were flooded with calls from battered women seeking help.

Vivian also notes, however, that *The Burning Bed* may have also inspired some people to take violent action. One man, for instance, set his estranged wife on fire and another severely beat his wife, both claiming they were motivated by the movie. Such acts of direct imitation are at the heart of a second explanation that focuses on the *modeling effect* of violent viewing. Put simply, this explanation maintains that media violence teaches viewers to behave violently through imitation or modeling, a concept that we will discuss in greater detail later in this chapter. Suffice it to say here that despite the sensationalism surrounding individual acts of direct imitation, they are very rare. Moreover, there are several intervening factors that influence whether a specific act will be imitated. These include the model's and the learner's relative age and sex, the model's objective status and her or his status in

the eyes of the learner, and whether the model is rewarded or punished for engaging in the behavior in question.

These and other factors are considered by researchers who propose a third explanation that emphasizes the *catalytic effect* of violent viewing. This position says that if certain conditions are present, viewing violence *may* prompt real-life violence. The emphasis is on *probabilistic causation* rather than direct causation. The violent viewing "primes" the viewer for violent behavior; it increases the risk of violent behavior just like cigarette smoking increases the risk of developing cancer. If the violence is portrayed as realistic or exciting, if the violence succeeds in righting a wrong, if the program or film contains characters or situations that are similar to those the viewer actually knows or has experienced, and if the viewer's media exposure is heavy, the probability of the viewer behaving violently increases (Bok, 1998; Mifflin, 1998; Vivian, 1993).

It is doubtful that the federal government will enact legislation to curb violent programming any time soon. Previous government attempts to regulate broadcast hours in order to prevent children from viewing programs or films with adult themes have been struck down by the courts as a violation of the First Amendment (see, for example, Lewis, 1993). What is more certain, however, is that the majority of U.S. households will continue to fulfill the last condition of the catalytic effect: frequency of viewing. It is estimated that by the time a child leaves elementary school, he or she will have watched 8,000 murders and more than 100,000 violent acts on television (Bok, 1998).

A final criticism of differential association theory comes primarily from those interested in the psychological underpinnings of human behavior. These critics maintain that Sutherland's conception of learning is too simplistic. Although Sutherland said that the process of learning both criminality and law abiding behavior involves all the mechanisms of learning, his propositions only vaguely outline how learning occurs. This criticism is significant not only because it highlights an area that Sutherland neglected, but also because it prompted a number of criminologists to develop new positions that utilize many of the principles of differential association while incorporating more complex work of various learning theorists. Let's examine, then, some of the theoretical offshoots of differential association theory.

Sutherland's Legacy

Akers's Social Learning Theory

First developed in the 1960s by *Robert L. Burgess* and *Ronald L. Akers* (1966) and later elaborated by Akers (1973; 1998), *social learning theory* is a revision of Sutherland's work that utilizes the central concepts and principles of modern *behaviorism*.[5] According to Akers (1994, p. 101), the theory is a "general processual explanation of all criminal and delinquent behavior." Like Sutherland, Akers maintains that criminal behavior is learned. However, the way it is learned, he argues, is through direct *operant conditioning* and *imitation* or *modeling* of others.

The principle of operant conditioning is probably familiar to you; most of us have heard of Pavlov's dogs who were trained or conditioned to salivate when they heard a bell ring. In this kind of conditioning—called *classical conditioning*—the behavioral response is elicited by a prior stimulus. According to Akers, though, the form the behavior takes and its frequency of recurrence depend on *instrumental conditioning*; that is, the behavior is learned or conditioned as a result of the effects, outcomes, or consequences it has on an individual's environment.

> Operants are not automatic responses to eliciting stimuli; instead, they are capable of developing a functional relationship with stimulus events. They are developed, maintained, and strengthened (or conversely are repressed or fail to develop), depending on the feedback received or produced from the environment. (Akers, 1985, p. 42)

There are two major processes involved in instrumental conditioning—*reinforcement* and *punishment*, and each of these may take two forms (see Table 5.1). Behavior is reinforced when the consequences it has or the reactions of others encourage an

TABLE 5.1   Akers's Social Learning Perspective of Deviant Behavior

Stimulus	Behavior increases—reinforcement	Behavior decreases—punishment
+	Positive reinforcement (reward received)	Positive punishment (punisher received)
−	Negative reinforcement (punisher removed or avoided)	Negative punishment (reward removed or lost)

Source: Ronald L. Akers (1985). *Deviant Behavior: A Social Learning Approach* (3rd ed.). Belmont, CA: Wadsworth, p. 45. Reprinted with permission of the author.

individual to do the same thing again when confronted with similar circumstances. In other words, reinforcement causes a behavior to increase in frequency. Sometimes this occurs by rewarding the behavior (*positive reinforcement*). However, a behavior may also be reinforced if engaging in it allows a person to prevent or avoid an unpleasant or painful stimulus (*negative reinforcement*). Punishment also may be positive or negative but, unlike reinforcement, the goal of punishment is to weaken a behavior or to extinguish it altogether. When an unpleasant or painful response (such as a slap) follows a behavior, the punishment is considered *positive punishment*. If a privilege or reward is taken away in response to a behavior, this is *negative punishment*.

Besides direct instrumental conditioning, we noted that behavior may also be developed or extinguished through imitation or modeling. Models may be real or fictitious, and observers may be passive onlookers or active participants in activities with the models but, Akers (1985) cautions, modeling is "a more complicated process than 'monkey see, monkey do'" (p. 46). A number of factors influence the modeling process. For instance, one tends to imitate those one likes, respects, or admires. Imitation is also more likely if the observer sees the model being reinforced, if the model displays pleasure or enjoyment, or if imitating the model in itself is being rewarded. An observer, though, may do the reverse or opposite of what a model does if he or she dislikes the model, sees the model punished, or if imitation of the model is being punished.

According to Akers and his colleagues (1979), "Whether deviant or conforming behavior is acquired and persists depends on past and present rewards or punishments for the behavior and the rewards and punishments attached to alternative behavior" (p. 638). This is the principle of **differential reinforcement**. "Differential reinforcement operates when both acts are similar and both are rewarded, but one is more highly rewarded. But differential learning of this kind is most dramatic and effective when the alternatives are incompatible and one is rewarded while the other is unrewarded" (Akers, 1985, p. 47).

Differential reinforcement is largely a *social* process; it takes place primarily in the context of interaction with others. Here Akers utilizes Sutherland's concept of differential association. Those with whom one has the greatest contact—those who reinforce or punish a person the most—will have the greatest influence over that individual. Typically, these will be a person's family and friends, but may also include media personalities and institutional agents, such as school personnel, employers or co-workers, and government and law enforcement. These sources of differential reinforcement also provide definitions of or give *normative meanings* to behaviors as either right or wrong. "Therefore, deviant behavior can be expected to the extent that it has been differentially reinforced over alternative behavior . . . and is defined as desirable or justified" (Akers et al., 1979, p. 638).

Social learning theory has the advantage that it is more readily testable than differential association theory. In fact, Akers (1998) presents an impressive array of studies that have used field research methods and surveys to test hypotheses derived from the theory. The results of these studies are supportive of social learning theory. For example, Akers and his colleagues (1979) surveyed over 3,000 male and female teenagers from seven communities in the Midwest about a common form of adolescent deviance: the use of alcohol and drugs. They found, as the theory predicts, that the teenagers in their sample used drugs or alcohol to the extent that such behavior was reinforced by their peers (especially those peers they most admired) and was defined by peers as desirable, or at least as justified as abstinence. However, the relationship between the differential reinforcement–differential association variables and alcohol and drug *abuse* were considerably weaker. Similar results were obtained in a longitudinal study of cigarette smoking among adolescents (Spear & Akers, 1988) and a study of drinking among the elderly (Akers et al., 1989).

These findings, however, raise one potential weakness in social learning theory. Specifically, most attempts to test the theory have examined relatively minor forms of deviation and offending. Some criminologists question whether the theory will be supported in studies of serious criminal offending. Boeringer (1992) did test the theory in his study of rape and sexual coercion by male college students and obtained supportive findings (see also Boeringer et al., 1991). Nevertheless, it remains to be seen if the theory can adequately explain other forms of serious criminal offending.

Social learning theory has been praised for its practical implications in the areas of counseling and corrections. For example, many correctional facilities have adopted behavior modification treatment programs based on operant conditioning principles for at least some types of offenders. The difficulty here, however, is that evidence regarding the effectiveness of such "treatments" is contradictory, and some observers have raised serious ethical concerns about a number of these programs.[6]

One final criticism of social learning theory is that it does not address the question of how or where criminal or deviant definitions and labels originate. Akers (1985) admits, "The theory is . . . incapable of accounting for why anyone or anything is socially defined as undesirable. . . . The theory does not say how or why the culture, structure, and social patterning of society sets up and implements certain sets and schedules of reactions to given behavior and characteristics" (p. 43). Although the theory recognizes that some reinforcers exert greater influence on individuals' behavior than others, it nevertheless overlooks the differential access of certain groups to a society's resources and rewards, as well as their differential power to escape punishment, to punish others, and to label others criminal or deviant. This, in fact, is a criticism that may be leveled against a majority of the theories we have discussed so far in this text, and it is an issue that will be raised again in this chapter and especially in Chapter 6. However, it must also be noted that Akers (1994, 1999) is optimistic about the possibility of integrating theories that do address these issues (e.g., social disorganization, anomie, and conflict theories) with social learning theory.

Differential Identification and Differential Anticipation

The notion of **differential identification**, developed by Daniel Glaser (1956; 1973), derives not only from the principle of modeling, but also from *reference group theory*. People belong to and orient themselves toward many different groups. The groups with whom they identify are their *reference groups*, whether they are actually members of these groups or not. One may, for instance, aspire to membership in a group with higher social status than the groups to which one belongs, or identify with the lifestyle of a group portrayed in the media. In any event, individuals tend to judge themselves relative to the norms and values of these groups and try to emulate or model their behavior after those group members whom they most respect or admire. Criminality or deviance, then, results when an individual develops greater identification with members of criminal or deviant groups than with members of conformist groups.

The theory of differential identification is appealing for several reasons. First, it recognizes that people can learn from one another without having direct intimate contact or association. In addition, it concurs with our personal experiences and observations. We know that people generally adopt particular images and incorporate them into their everyday lives. We are likely to recognize, for example, an "executive look" and a "grunge look"; each signifies a set of values and norms for behavior to which the individuals who adopt these models try hard to conform. At the same time, however, the theory is too simplistic in its depiction of identification; to reiterate Akers (1985), modeling is "a more complicated process than 'monkey see, monkey do'" (p. 46). Why are some groups more appealing to certain individuals than other groups? In what ways are one's choice of models limited or constrained? Why do some people who are repeatedly exposed to deviant or criminal images reject crime and deviance in favor of conformity?

To an extent, Glaser (1978) answered at least two of these questions by forwarding a second theory, **differential anticipation theory**. In this approach, Glaser argues as Akers does, that people are likely to engage in behaviors from which they expect to obtain the greatest rewards and the least punishment. These expectations derive from three sources: differential learning, perceived opportunities, and social bonds. *Differential learning* refers to the process by which one develops tastes, skills, and rationalizations about whether he or she can best gratify himself or herself through criminal or noncriminal activities. *Perceived opportunities* reflect an individual's evaluation of his or her circumstances as well as the advantages and risks of engaging in criminal or alternative activities. *Social bonds*, "both anticriminal and procriminal . . . create stakes in conforming to the conduct standards of others so as to please rather than alienate them" (Glaser, 1978, p. 126). According to Glaser (1978), "Differential anticipation theory assumes that a person will try to commit a crime wherever and whenever the expectations of gratifications from it—as a result of social bonds, differential learning, and perceptions of opportunities—exceed the unfavorable anticipations from these sources" (p. 127).

The major weakness in differential anticipation theory is the same one that plagues differential association theory: It is difficult, at best, to test it. More specifically, how does a researcher measure differential anticipation? The theory implies that one can add up an individual's anticipations unfavorable to law violation and subtract them from all the individual's anticipations favorable to law violation and, if the result is positive, a crime will be committed. Needless to say, this is impossible and, consequently, the theory is tautological.

The development of differential anticipation theory was an attempt to integrate the central ideas of a variety of criminological perspectives into one general theory of crime. We recognize in it, for example, aspects of the strain theories that we discussed in Chapter 4, the principles of operant conditioning that we reviewed in this chapter,

and elements of rational choice theory which was presented i̇
sis on social bonds comes from a theory that has enjoyed t̲
criminology: control theory.

Control Theory

Although criminologists historically have been interested in the issue of social control, specific theories of social control became especially popular during the 1940s and again in the 1970s and 1980s. There are, in fact, numerous theories that may be classified as *control theories* (see, for example, Briar & Pilliavin, 1965, Nye; 1958; Reiss, 1951; Toby, 1957).[7]

Virtually all of the theories we have discussed so far in this text focus on answering the question, "Why do some people commit crimes?" In contrast, control theorists adopt a Hobbesian view of human nature; to them, everyone is basically criminal at heart. Everyone is equally motivated to commit crimes because fulfilling one's desires usually can be done most effectively, efficiently, and pleasurably by violating the law. Unlike subcultural and differential association theorists who focus on the problem of culture or normative conflict among diverse groups, control theorists assume that society is characterized by a single, conventional moral order. To the control theorist, then, the question criminologists must answer is "*Why do people obey the rules of their society?*" In answering this question, control theorists argue that it is a person's ties—or, depending on the individual theorist, a person's links, attachments, binds, or bonds—to conventional social institutions, such as family and school, that inhibit him or her from acting on criminal motivations (Liska & Reed, 1985).

Although there are many control theories, the one that undoubtedly has enjoyed the greatest popularity and had the greatest influence is that developed by *Travis Hirschi* in 1969. Consequently, it is to that brand of control theory that we will devote our attention here.

Hirschi's Control Theory

In his book, *Causes of Delinquency*, Travis Hirschi (1969) presented his own version of control theory, along with an analysis of the empirical data he had gathered to test it. Like other control theorists, Hirschi begins with the assumption that "delinquent acts result when an individual's bond to society is weak or broken" (p. 18). Conversely, individuals with strong social bonds are unlikely to engage in delinquency. Hirschi specifies four elements of the social bond: attachment, commitment, involvement, and belief.

The most important element of the bond is *attachment*. Attachment refers to an individual's sensitivity to the feelings of others. "If a person does not care about the wishes and expectations of other people—that is, if he [sic] is insensitive to the opinion of others—then he is to that extent not bound by the norms. He is free to deviate" (p. 18). Thus, attachment to others facilitates the internalization of society's norms and the development of a conscience.

Hirschi refers to the second element of the bond, *commitment*, as the "rational component in conformity." The underlying idea of commitment is that people develop a stake in playing by the rules. They invest their time, energy, money, emotions, and so on in pursuing a specific activity (such as getting an education, building a career, and establishing themselves as respected members of their communities). When considering whether to commit a crime, individuals must factor in what they stand to lose if they get caught. "Most people, simply by the process of living in an organized society, acquire goods, reputations, prospects that they do not want to risk losing. These accumulations are society's insurance that they will abide by the rules" (p. 21).

Involvement is an opportunity element of the bond. The premise underlying involvement is straightforward: If a person is engrossed in conventional activities (such as studying, working, or playing a sport), he or she simply will not have time to participate in deviant or criminal activities. This is a commonly held view and one that provides the rationale for many recreation-oriented delinquency prevention programs, such as the Police Athletic League (PAL).

The final element of the bond identified by Hirschi, *belief*, refers to the extent to which an individual believes he or she should obey the rules of society. As noted previously, control theorists do not recognize variations in normative belief systems among different groups in society. Hirschi, like other control theorists, maintains that all individuals are socialized into a common value system. What Hirschi argues, however, is that there is variation in belief in the moral validity of social rules. The less a person believes a rule should be obeyed—the lower the person's belief in the moral validity of the rule—the greater the likelihood that he or she will violate that rule.[8]

In addition, Hirschi recognized that the four elements of the social bond are interrelated. Thus, an individual who is strongly attached to his or her parents and cares about their feelings will also be likely to express a strong belief in the moral validity of social rules. Likewise, an individual who has a high stake in conformity (that is, a high level of commitment) is also likely to be actively involved in conventional activities. Still, each element of the bond is analytically distinct and "should affect deviance uniquely and additively" (Matsueda, 1989, p. 430). Thus, if we hold three of the elements constant, the remaining element should, by itself, inhibit delinquent or criminal activity.

The majority of *Causes of Delinquency* is devoted to Hirschi's empirical test of his theory. Hirschi surveyed a sample of more than 4,000 junior and senior high school boys in Contra Costa County in the San Francisco Bay area of California. Included in the questionnaire were items that measured the youths' relationships with their parents, teachers, and peers; their attitudes toward school; how frequently they engaged in such activities as working, studying, reading books, and dating; and whether during the past year they had stolen anything worth less than $2, stolen anything worth between $2 and $50, stolen anything worth more than $50, taken a car without the owner's permission, damaged or destroyed another person's property, or had beat up or deliberately hurt someone other than a sibling. These last six items together formed Hirschi's index of delinquency.

Most of Hirschi's findings support his control theory. In particular, he found that youths who had strong attachments to their parents and who cared about their teachers' opinions were less likely to be delinquent than youths without such ties, irrespective of the delinquent activities of their friends. Indeed, Hirschi argued that attachment itself appears to be critical; those boys with strong attachments to their friends were less likely to be delinquent than unattached boys, even if their friends were delinquent. This does not mean that association with delinquent peers would never lead to delinquency, but rather that such associations per se are not sufficient to cause delinquency. Delinquent boys, Hirschi found, have only weak and distant relations with others, including their peers.

Hirschi also found that the more committed a youth was and the stronger his belief in conventional morality and the legitimacy of law, the less likely he was to be delinquent. However, Hirschi's data were equivocal with respect to the relationship between involvement in conventional activities and delinquency. Specifically, Hirschi found that the boys who reported a high frequency of working, dating, reading books, watching television, and playing games were also more likely to be delinquent. According to Hirschi (1969), the data indicate that control theory "overestimated the significance of involvement in conventional activities" and, further, did not take into account how some delinquent activities may contribute to an individual's self-concept or self-esteem, an issue to which we will return later in the chapter (pp. 230–231).

Among Hirschi's most important findings were that there was no relationship between social class and reported delinquency, and there was only slight variation in reported delinquency by race, despite the significant racial disparity in official arrest records. The attachment relationships he discovered held regardless of the boys' race or social class, and he found no evidence of a lower class subculture (see Chapter 4). Instead, he found that academic achievement was related to belief in conventional values: Those boys who did well academically, whatever their objective socioeconomic position, held what Hirschi labeled "middle-class" values, whereas those who performed poorly academically held values that previously were identified as part of a "lower-class subculture." Concluded Hirschi (1969):

> [T]he values in question are available to all members of American society more or less equally; they are accepted or rejected to the extent they are consistent or inconsistent with one's realistic position in that society. They are not, in other words, "class" values in the sense that they are transmitted by class culture.
>
> In short, the data suggest, there are no groups of substantial proportions in American society that positively encourage crime in the sense that those belonging to the groups in question would prefer their children to follow their own rather than a conventional way of life. In fact, on the basis of the data presented here, it appears there are no groups of substantial proportions in American society whose values are neutral with respect to crime. (p. 230)

These findings were good news to criminologists who objected to the class biases and racism of many sociological theories of crime. This is not to say, though, that Hirschi's control theory, as well as his research to test it, were accepted uncritically in the criminological community. As noted earlier, Hirschi's work has drawn more attention, both positive and negative, than any of the other perspectives that fall into the category of control theories. It certainly has been the most extensively tested

(Stitt & Giacopassi, 1992). Let's turn our attention now to some of this empirical research.

Involvement, Belief, and Delinquency.   Recall that Hirschi's hypothesis about the relationship between involvement in conventional activities and delinquency was not supported by his data. The young men in Hirschi's study who reported high levels of involvement also reported high levels of delinquent activity. One recent study undertook a reexamination of the involvement–delinquency relationship by focusing on adolescents' leisure activities (Agnew & Petersen, 1989). Leisure may indirectly influence all four of the bonds identified by Hirschi (that is, participating in enjoyable leisure activities with parents may strengthen adolescents' attachment to their parents). However, it has its most obvious and direct impact on involvement. Adolescents whose free time is consumed by legitimate leisure activities will not have much chance to engage in delinquency.

Recognizing that some leisure activities may be considered more pleasurable than others by adolescents and that some leisure activities, rather than inhibiting delinquency, may actually promote it, Agnew and Petersen considered not only types of leisure activities (that is, sports versus hobbies versus work or chores, and organized versus unsupervised activities), but also with whom the adolescents engaged in each activity (parents or peers) and the extent to which they liked each activity. They also examined the relationship between these variables and serious (stole a car) and minor (stole from a store) delinquency.

Among Agnew and Petersen's (1989) findings were that organized leisure activities, passive entertainment, and noncompetitive sports were *negatively* related to delinquency, whereas "hanging out" with friends and unsupervised social activities with peers were *positively* related to delinquency (the former with total and serious delinquency, the latter with total and minor delinquency). They also found that time spent in most favorite leisure activities with parents was unrelated to delinquency, but time spent in least favorite leisure activities with parents was positively related to delinquency. In general, however, it appeared that the extent to which a leisure activity was liked was unrelated to delinquency.

Agnew and Peterson (1989) report that, "Overall, the leisure variables explain approximately 6 percent of the variance in total and minor delinquency, and 4 percent in serious delinquency" (p. 347). In other words, the leisure variables account for only a small amount of delinquent activity. Although the researchers argue that these figures "are comparable to the effects of variables measuring other institutional spheres, such as family and school . . . [and that] the effect of certain leisure variables . . . is as large or larger than that of many traditional predictors of delinquency" (p. 347), such claims do not necessarily bolster their position. Looking at the glass half empty instead of half full, one might just as aggressively argue that most of the variables traditionally examined—school, family, leisure, or other measures—are all rather poor predictors of delinquency.[9]

Other researchers have concentrated on the belief component of the social bond. What is the empirical relationship between belief in the moral validity of conventional social rules and delinquent activity? Typically, belief is measured by asking a sample of respondents questions about honesty (such as "Is it a good thing to always tell the truth even though it may hurt oneself or others?").

Using such measures, several studies have found support for Hirschi's hypothesis that the stronger one's belief in the moral legitimacy of social norms, the lower one's participation in delinquent or criminal activities (Costello & Vowell, 1999; Krohn & Massey, 1980; Minor, 1984; Wiatrowski et al., 1981). Matsueda (1989) has criticized this research, however, because the samples from which the data were collected were usually small in size, limited to a single geographical area, and drawn from a "captive" population such as the student body of a school. Moreover, the research designs were cross-sectional, looking at attitudes and activities at one point in time; thus, they were unable to specify the causal ordering of any observed relationships. In other words, if the participants in such a study who were highly delinquent were also low on measures of belief, the argument that involvement in delinquency led them to alter their support for conventional rules is at least as plausible as Hirschi's position. In any event, cross-sectional studies cannot demonstrate otherwise.

In his examination of the relationship between moral beliefs and delinquency, Matsueda (1989) developed a complex research design that utilized longitudinal data collected over a period of eight years from a national probability sample of boys who were in the tenth grade in the fall of 1966. Because other studies had shown that control theory explains minor offenses better than it explains serious crimes—a point to which we will return shortly—Matsueda, using questions about honesty as indicators of moral belief, examined the incidence of five nonserious forms of youthful deviation: being suspended or expelled from school; skipping a day of school; running away from home; staying out past curfew; and fighting with parents. As Matsueda (1989) reports, "The results fail to replicate previous research which found support for social control theory's stipulation of the relationship between belief and deviance. Contrary to previous results of cross-sectional studies, the effect of belief on deviance is relatively small and dwarfed by the effect of deviance on belief" (p. 428).[10]

Matsueda believes that participation in deviant activity may affect belief through two social psychological processes: *cognitive dissonance reduction* and *self-perception formation*. First, social psychologists tells us that when we act in a way that goes against an internalized belief, we experience psychological discomfort called *cognitive dissonance*. One way to reduce this discomfort is to change the belief—or our support for the legitimacy of the belief—so that our belief system is consistent with our behavior. In self-perception formation, our behavior provides us with clues about who we are—about the elements of our self-identities, including our individual belief systems. "In short," Matsueda maintains, "belief and deviance should be specified as reciprocally causally related in a dynamic causal model" (p. 434).

Similarly, Agnew (1985) also reports that in his longitudinal research, all of the control variables (involvement, belief, commitment, and attachment measures) together explained only 1 to 2 percent of the variance in future delinquency (see also Agnew, 1991; 1993; Paternoster et al., 1983). He attributes this, at least in part, to the impact that delinquency has on these variables, in particular on involvement, school attachment, and belief. Delinquency did not impact parental attachment, however—a finding supported by additional research, as we will soon see.

School, Family, and Delinquency.   The two remaining elements of the social bond are attachment and commitment. These elements are typically studied in terms of individuals' relationships with family members, teachers, and peers, as well as in terms of attitudes toward education. We will discuss school variables first and then take a look at research incorporating the more complex array of family variables.

It is a well-established fact that failure in school is related to delinquency and crime, but the precise nature of this relationship is not clearly understood (see also Chapter 2). Children who do poorly in school are more likely to engage in delinquency and to be arrested as adults than those who do well in school (Jassim, 1989; Rosenbaum & Lasley, 1990; Thornberry et al., 1985). Moreover, a good deal of crime, including serious violent crime, takes place at school (Applebome, 1996; Chandler et al., 1998; Kozol, 1991; Lively, 1997; Schwartz & DeKeseredy, 1997). Does early exposure to and involvement in delinquency interfere with children's learning activities, thereby lowering their motivation and achievement? Or, do children turn to delinquency and crime when they reap few rewards in the classroom and grow increasingly alienated from school?

In Hirschi's model, children who care about what their teachers think of them and who value their teachers' opinions (indicating high attachment) are less likely to engage in delinquency. In addition, Hirschi (1969) postulates that children who have high educational aspirations, who value good grades, and who say they work hard in school (indicating high commitment) also are unlikely to pursue delinquent activities. While Hirschi himself found support for these hypotheses in his own research, have other criminologists replicated his results?

In a recent study of Japanese youth, Tanioka and Glaser (1991) found fairly strong support for Hirschi's position. Japanese students who stated that they liked school had much lower delinquency rates than students who disliked school. However, the extent to which students cared about what their teachers thought of them was related only to rates of minor status offenses, not more serious crimes, and the relationship was weak. Nevertheless, when Tanioka and Glaser examined all of the school attachment variables simultaneously, they explained 14 percent of the variation in delinquency rates, twice the rate explained by parental attachment variables. Similarly, the school commitment variables showed a strong inverse relationship with delinquency. The higher the students' educational aspirations and scores on an educational "Achievement Index," the lower their rates of self-reported delinquency (see also Tanioka, 1992).

There are, of course, particular features of Japanese society that make it significantly different from the United States. Among these are a stronger educational system, greater government support of education in terms of both regulations and funding, a greater certainty of employment for students once they complete their schooling, a substantially lower poverty rate, and a much higher frequency of extended family households in which not just two adults, but often three or four adults reside with the children (Upham, 1987; White, 1987). Such factors alone or in combination might account for greater attachment and commitment to school *and* low rates of deviation among Japanese youth.

In the United States, where control theory originated, the research findings on school attachment and commitment and delinquency have been somewhat less affirming. For instance, in their analysis of self-report data from 1,508 high school students, Rosenbaum and Lasley (1990) discovered that increases in positive attitudes toward school and educational achievement resulted in significant reductions in delinquent activity *only for the males* in their sample. Although we will examine the issue of sex differences more carefully in the next section, suffice it to say here that in Rosenbaum and Lasley's research, a commitment to success in school had only a minimal impact on female delinquency.

In a study of a school-based delinquency prevention program, Gottfredson (1986) examined the effects of several factors that should have led to increased school attachment and commitment among participating students. The factors included: involvement of school staff, students, and community members in planning and implementing a school improvement initiative; changed disciplinary procedures; an enhanced educational program that included activities designed to raise achievement and create a more positive atmosphere in the school; and special services for high-risk students designed to improve their self-concepts, increase their success experiences, and strengthen their bond to school. The program slightly reduced delinquency and misconduct among the general student body at participating schools, but not among high-risk students. The findings show that high-risk students' commitment to education—as measured by dropout, retention, and graduation rates, as well as by standardized achievement test scores—did increase; however, their rates of delinquency and misconduct simply did not decline.

Liska and Reed's (1985) research may help to explain such anomalous findings. Liska and Reed hypothesized that there is a reciprocal relationship between attachment and delinquency; that is, they argued that delinquency is as likely to affect attachment as attachment is to affect delinquency (see also Matseuda & Anderson, 1998). In fact, their findings showed that most of the negative relationship between school attachment and delinquency that other studies have found is the result of delinquency's effect on school attachment, not vice versa. At the same time, however, their findings did support Hirschi's hypothesized relationship between parental attachment and delinquency: "most of the observed negative relationship between parental attachment and delinquency comes about because of the effect of parental attachment on delinquency" (p. 537).

Liska and Reed explain these findings by noting first that attachment between parents and children is less conditional on the behavior of either party than attachment between teachers/school personnel and students. Moreover, as we have already noted, much juvenile misconduct, including criminal violations, takes place in school or on school grounds. "This leads to reactions by teachers and school administrators, which in turn decrease school attachment" (p. 557). Also, in response to a question we raised at the outset of this section, Liska and Reed argue that "adolescents involved in delinquency simply have less time for school; thus, delinquency, independent of teacher reactions, may decrease school attachment" (p. 557).

Liska and Reed rightly conclude that, "Generally, it is all too clear that the causal structure underlying the relationship between social attachment and delinquency is not as simple as implied in theories of social control" (p. 559). Their findings indicate that it is strong attachment to parents that lowers delinquency, but that delinquency lowers school attachment which, in turn, may weaken parental attachment. Their findings point to parents, not schools, as the major institutional sources of social control. Do other researchers agree with them?

In examining how children's relationships with their parents might affect their delinquency rates, one must also consider a variety of methodological issues. Studies that attempt to measure parental attachments often use adolescents' reports of their parents' behaviors or attitudes. Can we be certain that children correctly perceive, accurately recall, and honestly report their parents' behavior or attitudes (McCord, 1991)? In addition, researchers have operationally defined parental attachments in a wide variety of ways, including questions about "affection and love, interest and concern, support and help, trust, encouragement, lack of rejection, desire for physical closeness, amount of interaction or positive communication, and 'identification,' " as well as with variables measuring direct controls, such as monitoring or supervision and punishment or disciplinary techniques (Rankin & Wells, 1990, p. 142). The question, of course, arises as to whether all of these variables are actually measures of parental attachment. Nevertheless, the correlation between parent–child relationships and crime is one of the most extensively researched in the criminological literature.

Rankin and Wells (1990) have examined the effects of both indirect and direct parental controls on the behavior of male children. Indirect control through parental attachment was measured by two indices: (1) identification, which included questions regarding how much the youth likes his mother and father, how close he feels to each parent, how much he wants to be like each parent, and how much time he spends with his father; and (2) positive communication, which included items about how much influence the youth has in family decisions, how often his parents listen to his side of things in arguments, how often his parents talk over important family matters with him, and how often his parents respond fairly and reasonably to his requests. Direct control of the youth by parents was measured in terms of: supervision (the extent to which parents determined their child's friends and activities—with whom he socializes, where he may go, and what he may do); strictness; contingency of punishment (how often the parents completely ignore instead of punish the child's misbehavior); and strength of punishment (how often parents use yelling, slapping, threats of slapping, and withdrawal of privileges as punishments). Their sample included 1,886 boys who had participated in the Youth in Transition Study, the same data source used in the Liska and Reed (1985) study we discussed earlier.

In general, Rankin and Wells's findings confirm that both direct controls and indirect controls (that is, attachment) are negatively related to delinquency (see also Wiatrowski et al., 1981). However, these researchers found that as parental discipline increases, delinquency does not necessarily decrease. "Punishment that is too strict, frequent, or severe can lead to a greater probability of delinquency *regardless* of parental attachments. That is, a strong parent–child bond will not lessen the adverse impact of punishment that is too harsh" (p. 163). Rankin and Wells (1990) found that while punishment that is consistent is negatively related to delinquency, punishment that is severe is positively related to delinquency. In terms of strictness, there was a curvilinear relationship; medium levels of parental strictness were most effective in lowering delinquency, whereas both low and high levels of parental strictness increased delinquency (see also Straus & Sugarman, 1997).

Similar studies that have focused on child-rearing techniques, monitoring and other forms of direct parental control over children's behavior, and quality of family interaction, have arrived at similar findings. McCord (1991), for instance, reports that mothers judged to be competent (self-confident, affectionate, consistently nonpunitive in their disciplinary style, and providing leadership to their children) seemed to be able to insulate their children against criminogenic influences even in high-crime neighborhoods. Boys who had competent mothers and who grew up in households in which there were high family expectations (children were expected to do well in school) had low rates of juvenile delinquency which, McCord argues, reduces their probability of adult criminality (see also Larzelere & Patterson, 1990; Laub & Sampson, 1988). However, McCord also found that, compared with mothers' influences, fathers' influences are not significant early on, but increase as boys grow older. According to McCord (1991):

> Fathers who interact with their wives in ways exhibiting high mutual esteem, who are not highly aggressive, and who generally get along well with their wives provide models for socialized behavior. Conversely, fathers who undermine their wives, who fight with the family, and who are aggressive provide models of antisocial behavior. Both types of fathers, it seems, teach their sons how to behave when they become adults. (p. 412)

Thus, fathers, unlike mothers, appear to have more of a direct effect on adult criminality than on juvenile delinquency, at least among males. This, McCord maintains, indicates that the causes of crime are not identical across age groups, a point that will be raised again later in this chapter.

Before moving on to other issues accounted for (or overlooked) by control theory, one final dimension of parental attachment deserves our attention: family structure. The "broken home hypothesis" is the notion that children from single-parent homes are more likely to become involved in delinquent activities than children from two-parent homes. The common rationale offered for this hypothesis is that one parent is simply less effective in monitoring children's behavior than two parents. A second rationale, however, derived from the 1965 *Moynihan Report* in which it was argued that delinquency rates are higher among Black youth than among White youth because of "a tangle of pathology" growing out of life in matriarchal (female-headed) households, high rates of births to unwed mothers, high unemployment, and differential socialization. Thus, this perspective attempted to explain "the joint relationships between race, broken homes and delinquency" (Matseuda & Heimer, 1987, p. 826).[11]

In general, it can be said that there is little evidence in support of the broken home hypothesis, although it has managed to repeatedly find its way into public policy debates over the past several decades (see, for example, "OJJDP Model Programs 1990," 1992). Although official statistics show that those youth most likely to be processed through the criminal justice system do come from broken homes, findings from self-report studies indicate little or no relationship between family intactness and delinquency (Johnson, 1996). Given that single-parent, female-headed households are one of the fastest growing types of family structures in the United States, this is a significant finding.

There are, however, several factors that complicate the family structure–delinquency relationship. Van Voorhis and her colleagues (1988), for instance, found that family structure seemed to be related only to incidence of status offenses and was unrelated to overall home quality. Overall home quality, though, regardless of family structure, was a strong predictor of delinquency, but the analysis failed to identify specific aspects of family functioning that contributed most to delinquent activity.

Matsueda and Heimer (1987) have addressed the race–broken homes–delinquency relationship. They found that although broken homes have a greater effect on delinquency rates among Black youth than among White youth, this effect, along with the effects of attachment to parents and peers, were mediated by learning definitions favorable to delinquency. In other words, their work appears to support differential association theory more than control theory. Matsueda and Heimer argue, however, that differences in crime rates by race should be examined in the context of the "historical emergence of social and economic structures that give rise to distinct racial patterns of social organization" and that reflect a history of racial discrimination (p. 837)—a point that we will take up again later in this chapter and in Chapter 6.

It is also important to note that there are different types of intact families as well as different types of single-parent families. Many researchers, for example, have documented negative effects on children when they live in homes where parents are constantly arguing (Barber & Eccles, 1992; Hetherington et al., 1989; Wallerstein & Blakeslee, 1989). In addition, Johnson (1986) found that family structure was unrelated to frequency or seriousness of delinquency, except in mother/stepfather homes where boys had an unusually high involvement in delinquent activity. Johnson, however, found some important sex differences: Although boys, but not girls, in mother/stepfather households reported high levels of delinquency, officials were more likely to respond to the misbehavior of children—especially female children—living in mother-only families. Thus, the myth of the broken home–delinquency relationship appears prevalent among law enforcers, which may account, at least in part, for the higher *official* delinquency rates of both boys and girls from single-parent female-headed households.

Johnson's research highlights the importance of considering sex differences when evaluating any theory of crime. Most tests of control theory have utilized all-male samples, as Hirschi's (1969) study did. In addition to sex, there are several other factors worth considering in our assessment of control theory, such as age and seriousness of offense.

Sex, Age, and Other Factors Affecting Deviation.   As we have already noted, Hirschi (1969) tested his theory by surveying a sample of high school boys, reporting in a footnote that in the analysis, "the girls disappear" (p. 36). Several subsequent tests of social control theory have included females in their samples and, like Johnson (1986) cited previously, these studies reveal significant sex differences in their results. It has been argued by some that control theory actually does a better job of explaining female delinquency than male delinquency (see Jensen, 1990; Krohn & Massey, 1980). Cernkovich and Giordano (1987), though, also report that the extent to which control theory accounts for sex differences in delinquency depends to some degree on how the elements of the social bond are operationalized. For instance, they used a multidimensional measure of attachment and found that "although the total explained variance is similar among males and females, the relative importance of the variables is not" (p. 315). For males, the dimensions that were most strongly associated with delinquency were control and supervision, intimate communication, and instrumental communication, whereas for girls, the most important dimensions were identity support, conflict, instrumental communication, and parental disapproval of peers. According to Cernkovich and Giordano (1987), "This seems to suggest that while family attachment is important in inhibiting delinquency among all adolescents, the various dimensions of this bond operate somewhat differently among males and females" (p. 315).

Researchers have also found that attachment to peers operates differently for males and females. Hirschi (1969) made the controversial argument that attachment to peers, even if peers were delinquent, inhibited delinquency. Others' research has not supported this position. Giordano and her colleagues (1986), for instance, found that boys in peer groups feel considerable pressure from their friends to engage in risk-taking behavior, including delinquency. Girls' groups, in contrast, function differently; girls interact with friends in ways that encourage self-disclosure and foster intimacy. Thus, while boys' attachment to peers may promote delinquency, girls' attachment to peers may inhibit it (see also Fordham, 1996; Gilligan et al., 1995; Matsueda & Anderson, 1998).

Farnworth (1984) has found that among African American youth, problems in school predict delinquency better than family problems for girls; but for boys, family problems seem to be better predictors than school problems. Rosenbaum and Lasley (1990) also examined the school–delinquency relationship and found several significant sex differences. They report, as we noted earlier, that positive attitudes toward school and school achievement inhibit delinquency more for boys than girls. Boys, they argue, appear to have a greater stake in future success predicated on strong school performance than girls do. However, among those girls who did very well in school, "attitudes toward achievement and school seem to have the same insulating effect from delinquency as for males" (p. 510). Rosenbaum and Lasley also found that increased involvement in school activities, as well as positive attitudes toward teachers, inhibited delinquency more for girls than boys. Finally, Rosenbaum and Lasley found social class to be an important intervening variable, with differences in social class producing more significant changes in the school–delinquency relationship for females than for males. They conclude on the basis of this finding that "school conformity will be instilled socially in females and in middle/upper class youths more strongly than in males and in youth from the lower class" (p. 511).

Several researchers have argued that findings such as these, which show differential access to opportunities and rewards on the basis of sex and social class, point to the need to examine power differences between the sexes and classes when attempting to explain crime and delinquency (see Chesney-Lind, 1997). This will be a major theme in Chapters 6 and 7. For now, however, let us conclude our evaluation of control theory by considering two other factors: age and seriousness of offense.

Hirschi concentrated on minor delinquent acts committed by male high school students, and most subsequent tests of his theory have taken a similar approach. A number of criminologists, however, have argued that this focus is too limited. Can control theory account for offending by adults as well as by juveniles? And is control theory, as Matsueda (1989, p. 432) has argued, best at explaining only "trivial impulsive deviant acts, such as status offenses . . . rather than serious event-like offenses, such as crimes against persons"? Whitehead and Boggs (1990) offer an answer to both questions. They studied recidivism among a sample of adult felony probationers in New Jersey, operationalizing attachment by marital status and offender's living arrangements; commitment by years of schooling and percentage of time employed during the two years prior to the current offense; and involvement by whether the offender was either in school or employed at the time of the offense.[12] Whitehead and Boggs report that their "most dramatic finding is the lack of impact of most of the control theory variables. . . . This analysis was hard pressed to find significant effects of control theory variables" (p. 4). Only two control theory variables—those used to measure commitment—were significant in explaining recidivism by the adult felony probationers. Most of the recidivism was accounted for instead by legal variables (previous convictions) and by demographic variables (race and age).

Other studies have obtained support for the applicability of control theory to adults for certain types of offenses, such as white-color crimes, and when the adult offenders were misdemeanants, not felons. Agnew's (1985) research further shows that apart from the age of the offender, control theory appears to apply only to minor forms of delinquency; "the explanatory power of the theory diminishes as we focus on more serious forms of delinquency" (p. 58).

The weaknesses of control theory that we have discussed here and in previous sections are serious, but not fatal. The theory, in fact, may be a very good one, but with limited utility. Certainly, the research conducted thus far has done more to fuel this debate than to settle it. In the meantime, several criminologists, including Hirschi himself, have developed revisions of control theory with wider applicability. Let's look at these theories now.

Tittle's Control Balance Theory

In 1995, *Charles Tittle* published *Control Balance*, in which he offers an important revision of traditional control theory. Tittle accepts Hirschi's proposition that control is the major component of conformity, but he argues that it is not control per se that counts, but rather maintaining a *balance* between the amount of control one is subject to at the hands of others and the amount of control one can exercise over others. This relationship can be expressed as a ratio, where the numerator is the control to which one is subject and the denominator is the control one exercises. If the numerator exceeds the denominator, or vice versa, a *control imbalance* occurs. Control imbalances can result in deviant behavior, including in some cases crime.

Tittle identifies two types of control imbalances. The first type of control imbalance is a *control deficit*, whereby the amount of control to which one is subjected exceeds the amount of control one can exercise over others. A control deficit, Tittle believes, produces **repressive deviance**. There are three forms of repressive deviance, each of which helps individuals escape control deficits and restore balance to their control ratios. The first type of repressive deviance is *predation*, which involves physical violence and is intended to harm others. Predation includes many criminal acts, such as sexual assault and robbery, but also includes many types of property crime, such as theft. The second type of repressive deviance is *defiance*, or deviation that challenges dominant norms but typically does not inflict harm on others. Included in the category of defiance are behaviors such as truancy, having sex with multiple partners simultaneously, and vandalism. The third type of repressive deviance is *submission*, which involves "passive, unthinking, slavish obedience to the expectations, commands, or anticipated desires of others" (Tittle, 1995, p. 139). Tittle includes in this category repressing other people to please someone perceived to be more powerful (e.g., writing racial slurs on the dorm room door of a Latino student to curry favor with members of the all-White, elite fraternity on campus). This category also includes allowing oneself to be physically abused, humiliated, or degraded (e.g., being tied up and whipped for the sexual pleasure of another person).

The second type of control imbalance, which Tittle conceptualizes as a *control surplus*, occurs when the amount of control a person exercises over others exceeds the amount of control others impose on her or him. According to Tittle, a control surplus leads to a different kind of deviance, **autonomous deviance**, which helps the individual further extend control over others and thereby increase her or his control surplus. There are three kinds of autonomous deviance. The first kind is *exploitation*, which is an indirect form of predation that includes such behaviors as hiring someone to injure a rival before a competition. The second kind of autonomous deviance is *plunder*, which is engaged in by individuals or organizations who want to further their own goals while ignoring or trampling the rights and safety of others. For example, plunder occurs when a corporation knowingly sells a faulty product overseas after it was banned for sale in the United States just so it can extend its markets and reap profits. Tittle also includes genocide under the heading plunder. The third type of autonomous deviance is *decadence*, irrational acts engaged in on a whim or the spur of the moment, such as humiliating another person for one's own pleasure.

Clearly, Tittle's control balance theory is designed to cover a wide variety of behaviors, not all of which are criminal. In fact, Tittle is careful to point out that a control imbalance does not inevitably produce deviance of any kind. Tittle draws on a number of theories to specify which conditions are likely to result in deviance when a control imbalance occurs. Whether a control imbalance produces a deviant outcome depends on an individual's predispositional motivations, situational motivations, constraint, and opportunity. Each of these, like control itself, exists along a continuum, varying in form, frequency, and intensity. Tittle conceives of predispositional motivations as natural, the products of one's innate physical and psychological needs and desires, including what he characterizes as the "almost universal" desire for autonomy. Even if one is predisposed to crime or deviance, one must become aware of the control imbalance, and this awareness develops from situational provocations, such as being turned down for a date, fired from a job, or insulted by a friend, relative, or stranger. Although Tittle sees predispositional and situational motivations as being strong precipitators of deviance, he nevertheless believes that deviance still may not occur if the individual faces a high internal or external level of constraint. A quick-tempered person who has just been cut off on the highway by another driver may be motivated to run that fellow driver off the road, but the police car in the rearview mirror constrains him or her. "[C]onstraint refers to the actual probability that potentially controlling reactions will be forthcoming" (Tittle, 1995, p. 167). Of course, even if one is motivated and constraint is low, deviance still may not occur if there is no opportunity to deviate. Realistically, though, Tittle recognizes that the opportunity for some kind of deviation is almost always available.

Tittle's control balance theory gives us much food for thought. One strength of the theory is that, unlike many of the theories we have discussed so far in this text, control balance theory does not concentrate on traditional street crime, but explains as well "hidden offending," such as dating violence, white-collar crimes (e.g., fraud by computer, insider stock trading), and organizational and governmental crimes (e.g., sale of unsafe or banned products, human rights violations). Like all theories, however, control balance theory must be subjected to the test of empirical research to determine its validity, a task made all the more difficult by a fact about which Tittle (1997) himself cautions us: There are no secondary data sets currently available that will allow us to calculate anyone's control ratio. Tests of control balance theory will have to be undertaken "from scratch," with researchers designing appropriate research instruments and systematically collecting and analyzing original data. At least one study has already made an attempt, though limiting itself to a test of two types of repressive deviance (predation and defiance) using a questionnaire administered to a sample of college students (Piquero & Hickman, 1999). In this study, Piquero and Hickman found support for control balance theory, but contrary to Tittle's predictions, both control deficits and control surpluses appeared to lead to predation and defiance. Piquero and Hickman suggest that perhaps control balance theory is incorrect in predicting that one type of imbalance will lead to a specific type of deviation, but correct in predicting that an imbalance can lead to deviation.

A number of criminologists have raised concerns about the basic propositions of control balance theory, ranging from the difficulty in specifying cut-offs for small, medium, and large imbalances, to overlap in the types of deviance specified in the theory, to the theory's neglect of the fact that specific behaviors are evaluated differently by different individuals and groups of people (see Braithwaite, 1997; Jensen, 1999; Savelsberg, 1999; for responses, see Tittle, 1997; 1999). Given the newness of the theory, we hope this debate will motivate criminologists to develop useful strategies for empirically testing the control balance perspective (see, for example, Curry, 1999).

Self-Control and Crime

We have already noted that one of the most consistent findings in the research literature is that relationships between parents and children are strongly associated with delinquent and criminal behavior. Unfortunately, the precise nature of this association remains unclear. Family structure appears to be far less important than emotional ties between members of all types of families. Various child-rearing methods, such as the degree and form of discipline that parents use in responding to their children's misbehavior, also seem to play a prominent role.

In their book, *A General Theory of Crime*, Michael Gottfredson and Travis Hirschi (1990) zero in on ineffective child rearing as the primary cause of all types of deviance, from smoking to victimization to unwanted pregnancy to white-collar crime. Most of the theories we have examined so far in this chapter maintain that crime is learned, but Gottfredson and Hirschi argue that crime is a product of a *lack* of socialization or learning. They accept the classical assumption that "crime is the natural consequence of unrestrained human tendencies to seek pleasure and avoid pain" (p. xiv). Although they state that their theory also incorporates aspects of modern positivism, especially positivistic research on the role of the family in crime causation, Gottfredson and Hirschi place themselves squarely in the tradition of the classical school of criminology and the rational-choice model.

To fully understand Gottfredson and Hirschi's (1990) position, we must consider their definition of crime. Crimes, they tell us, are "acts of force or fraud undertaken in pursuit of self-interest" (p. 15). According to Gottfredson and Hirschi, all crimes share certain common characteristics: They provide easy and immediate gratification of desires; they are exciting, risky, and thrilling; they offer few, if any, long-term benefits; they require little skill, planning, or specialized knowledge; and they often cause pain or discomfort for the victims. What kind of person, then, would engage in such activities? According to Gottfredson and Hirschi, it would be a person with *low self-control*.

People who deviate—whether that deviation is drinking too much or driving recklessly, assaulting someone or embezzling from an employer—lack self-control. Compare Gottfredson and Hirschi's list of the characteristics of crime presented previously with their list of the characteristics of people with low self-control. People lacking self-control: have a concrete "here and now" orientation and have difficulty deferring gratification; tend to lack diligence, tenacity, or persistence in a course of action; are adventuresome, active, and physical; tend to have unstable marriages, friendships, and employment histories, and are uninterested in or unprepared for long-term occupational pursuits; neither possess nor value cognitive or academic skills, nor do they necessarily have good manual skills; tend to be self-centered, and indifferent or insensitive to the needs of others. When individuals low in self-control are presented with opportunities to commit crimes, they more likely than not will commit the crime.

Low self-control, as we have already implied, is a result of ineffective or inadequate socialization. Gottfredson and Hirschi maintain that in order for effective socialization to occur and, consequently, for strong self-control to develop, someone who cares about the child must be responsible for meeting three basic conditions: (1) monitoring the child's behavior; (2) recognizing when the child deviates; and (3) punishing the deviation. Since parents or guardians are typically a child's first socializers, the two theorists lay the blame for inadequate socialization with them. It's not that parents or guardians prefer their children to be unsocialized or to lack self-control; Gottfredson and Hirschi (1990) "rule out in advance the possibility of positive socialization to unsocialized behavior (as cultural or subcultural deviance theories suggest)" (p. 98). Rather, certain factors may inhibit or prevent parents or guardians from sufficiently socializing their children:

> First, the parents may not care for the child (in which case none of the other conditions would be met); second, the parents, even if they care, may not have the time or energy to monitor the child's behavior; third, the parents, even if they care *and* monitor, may not see anything wrong with the child's behavior; finally, even if everything else is in place, the parents may not have the inclination or the means to punish the child. (Gottfredson & Hirschi, 1990, p. 98)

Gottfredson and Hirschi cite in support of their position various studies that show, for example, that parents who are hostile or indifferent toward their children are more likely to have children who become delinquent. They further point out that crime appears to be concentrated in certain families not because of heredity or explicit parental encouragement, but because parents who are themselves criminal—that is, who themselves lack self-control—are not adept at instilling self-control in their children. These parents may not even recognize criminal behavior in their children and tend to be lax in discipline or to use punishments that are "easy, short-term, and insensitive" (Gottfredson & Hirschi, 1990, p. 101).

Ineffective socialization may be especially likely to occur in families with large numbers of children, in single-parent and stepparent families, and in families in which the mother works outside the home. In the first instance, parents often do not have the time or energy to adequately monitor and discipline their children. The single parent shares this problem, but it is compounded by the fact that the single parent has less psychological and social support than co-parents have. The problem in stepfamilies is that stepparents are less likely to have "parental feelings" toward their stepchildren. In households where the mother works outside the home, adequate supervision is again the concern.

Of course, it might be argued that if parents are inadequate socializers, teachers and school personnel can serve as substitutes, especially since the school is a social institution officially charged with socializing children. Unfortunately, according to Gottfredson and Hirschi (1990), "The evidence suggests . . . that in contemporary American society the school has a difficult time teaching self-control" (pp. 105–106). They attribute this not to a lack of adequate educational resources or to poorly paid and often poorly trained teachers, but rather to a lack of cooperation and support from parents who have already failed in their socialization duties. Although the school may have some positive impact on some students, "self-control differences seem primarily attributable to family socialization practices. It is difficult for subsequent institutions to make up for deficiencies, but socialization is a task that, once successfully accomplished, appears to be largely irreversible" (Gottfredson & Hirschi, 1990, p. 107).

Does this mean then that if a child is not adequately socialized by his or her parents, all is lost, that he or she will be deviance-prone and there is nothing anyone can do to prevent or halt the behavior? What are the implications of Gottfredson and Hirschi's position for public policy? First it should be said that Gottfredson and Hirschi do not claim that crime is an *inevitable* outcome of low self-control. While they maintain that criminality is stable over time—that is, there is little or no change among

individuals from high self-control to low self-control—they also point out that socialization is ongoing throughout an individual's life. Consequently, the number of
offenders or deviants declines as a cohort ages. "Even the most active offenders burn
out with time, and the documented number of 'late-comers' to crime, or 'good boys
gone bad,' is sufficiently small to suggest that they may be accounted for in large part
by misidentification or measurement error'" (Gottfredson & Hirschi, 1990, pp. 107–
108). A decrease in the number of crimes committed by people with low self-control
occurs as they get older in large part because of the exigencies of aging and, to a much
lesser extent, because of ongoing socialization.

   In terms of public policy, Gottfredson and Hirschi eschew law enforcement and
crime control programs that involve building more prisons, employing more police, or
enacting gun control laws. Rather they argue that crime prevention efforts should be
targeted at parents and other adults with responsibility for raising children and should
concentrate on teaching them how to be alert to and recognize signs of low self-control
and how to punish children when they display these signs. As Gottfredson and Hirschi
(1990) put it:

> We offer an alternative view, a view in which the state is neither the cause nor the solu-
> tion to crime. In our view, the origins of criminality or low self-control are to be found
> in the first six to eight years of life, during which time the child remains under the con-
> trol and supervision of the family or a familial institution. Apart from the limited ben-
> efits that can be achieved by making specific criminal acts more difficult, policies
> directed toward enhancement of the ability of familial institutions to socialize children
> are the only realistic long-term policies with potential for substantial crime reduction.
> (pp. 272–273)

   Gottfredson and Hirschi's argument is a seductive one in a society such as ours
that places a great deal of faith in the power of socialization to bring about social
change. But to what extent has the theory been empirically verified?

A General Theory of Crime or a Limited One?

Recall that Gottfredson and Hirschi maintain that theirs is a *general* theory of crime,
capable of explaining all forms of deviation, not just criminal offenses. All crimes are
pretty much the same, they tell us; crimes are spontaneous acts that require no specialized knowledge and that yield short-term, simple gratifications. Much of Part III of
their book is devoted to reviewing research that supports their claims (see also Hirschi
& Gottfredson, 2000; LeBlanc & Kaspy, 1998), and this is where much of the criticism
of Gottfredson and Hirschi's argument has centered. The most frequent criticisms of
Gottfredson and Hirschi's work claim that they tailored the facts of crime to fit their
theory and that they selectively overlooked abundant evidence that does not support
their position (Geis, 2000).

   Polk (1991), for instance, takes issue with their characterization of homicide as
being of two basic varieties: (1) those that result from a heated argument that goes too
far, involving two people who know one another and who have argued frequently in
the past; and (2) those that occur during a robbery or, less often, during a miscalculated

burglary in which the victim turns out to be home. According to Polk's own extensive research in this area, however, homicides are far more varied: Many are carefully planned or premeditated; others include "parents starving a child to death in a belief that fasting would cure the child's cold, young girls who cannot face the reality of pregnancy and so the infant dies at birth from neglect," those who kill because "voices" tell them they must, and "criminals who kill a friend because of the possibility that the friend may give vital evidence against them in a forthcoming trial" (Polk, 1991, p. 577). In fact, Polk's research leads him to conclude that there probably is no "typical" homicide. Some homicides are like those characterized as typical by Gottfredson and Hirschi but, as Polk (1991) points out, "Gottfredson and Hirschi do not offer us a general theory of some crime, it is a general theory of crime. If the actual empirical nature of crime is not as Gottfredson and Hirschi describe it, then the theory must collapse" (p. 577).

Similar critiques have been made with respect to Gottfredson and Hirschi's analysis of white-collar crime. The two theorists focus on white-collar crime because they correctly note that positivistic theories have failed to adequately explain it and that many criminologists have come to see it as a unique form of offending that is different from other types of crimes. In contrast, they see white-collar crime as relatively uncommon in occurrence, but as conforming to the same age and race distributions as other crimes, and sharing other crimes' characteristics: spontaneity, quickness, requiring no specialized knowledge, yielding limited profits for offenders. They rely on FBI *Crime Report* data (see Appendix, pp. 243–245) to specify the types and incidence of offenses that constitute the category white-collar crime, and thus focus on embezzlement, fraud, and forgery.

There are several major weaknesses with such an analysis, not the least of which stems from their operationalization of white-collar crime. The crimes they have chosen do readily fit their definition of crime in general, but they hardly encompass the full array of offenses that constitute white-collar crime. In particular, they overlook organizational, corporate, and governmental offending. The UCR data are biased toward minor, low-level offenses, particularly because they reflect arrests; simple offenses are more likely to be detected and result in successful prosecution, whereas more sophisticated crimes are likely to be underrepresented in the UCR. Such crimes include terrorism for political goals, securities fraud, antitrust violations of pollution laws. Numerous studies show that these types of crimes are complex, involve a high level of technical detail, and are difficult to detect and prosecute (Calavita & Pontell, 1983; Geis, 2000; Reed & Yeager, 1996). Reed and Yeager (1996) further point out that a number of sociolegal processes operate in such a way that corporate offenses are screened out of the criminal justice system. These include interagency disagreements and rivalries, but especially the ability of powerful corporations and governments to influence the very definition of lawlessness and compliance.

One may also question Gottfredson and Hirschi's characterization of white-collar crime on at least six other major points, all of which revolve around the inclusion of corporate and business offenses in the definition of this type of crime. First, is white-collar crime really uncommon or as infrequent as these theorists claim? Although it is difficult at best to know for certain how many white-collar offenses are committed each year, given the difficulties with regard to detection raised previously, some researchers argue that such offenses are at least as common, and perhaps more common, than conventional street crime (Reed & Yeager, 1996).

Second, are white-collar offenses quick and spontaneous acts? Again, available evidence indicates that, to the contrary, some corporate offenses are carefully planned and executed over an extended period of time in the interests of continued or future viability of a single business or an entire industry. Long-term price-fixing conspiracies illustrate this point well. These offenses are usually motivated by the rational pursuit of corporate goals rather than by an impulsive pursuit of immediate self-gratification by an undersocialized individual (Reed & Yeager, 1996).

This raises a third issue: Do white-collar crimes typically yield low profits for offenders? If one examines only the offenses Gottfredson and Hirschi consider to be white-collar crimes, the answer is yes. In contrast, if one includes corporate, business, and government offenses, the answer is an unequivocal no. Consider, for example, the savings and loan fraud of the 1980s, which is expected to cost taxpayers between $300 billion and $473 billion by 2021 (Calavita & Pontell, 1993).

Fourth, can anyone, without any specialized knowledge, commit a white-collar offense? The answer, of course, is that it depends. No specialized knowledge is needed to write a bad check or to take money out of a cash register. However, it certainly cannot be claimed that specialized knowledge is not required to commit such crimes as computer fraud or insider stock trading. It seems equally unlikely that such white-collar offenders are interchangeable in this sense with street offenders—that is, that "today's burglar is yesterday's insider trader and tomorrow's rapist." Rather, such white-collar offenders engage almost solely in financial crimes.[13]

Fifth, are the age and race distributions of white-collar offenders the same as the age and race distributions of more conventional street offenders? Polk (1991) points out that if one uses Gottfredson and Hirschi's operational definition of white-collar crime, more Blacks are arrested for such offenses than Whites. However, given the underrepresentation of African Americans and other racial minorities in the upper echelons of corporate America, it is highly unlikely that they are engaged in insider trading, price fixing, military contract fraud, or similar crimes. If newspaper photos may be trusted, such offenders are invariably White. Moreover, given the educational and experiential requirements of their positions, it is also likely that they are older than conventional offenders (Steffensmeier, 1989).

Finally, in light of the characteristics of major white-collar crimes and criminals outlined here, would crime prevention programs aimed at teaching parents and other adults how to spot and punish low self-control in their children be successful? One wonders to what extent such programs would be effective in preventing even most conventional street crime. To support such a claim requires us to discount the roles that factors such as poverty, unemployment, homelessness, and institutional discrimination play in promoting criminal activity. As we will see in Chapter 6, available data do not permit us to make such a quantum leap of faith.

Gottfredson and Hirschi (2000) have responded to some of the criticisms of self-control theory and continue to cite studies that support it. Nevertheless, even in studies that affirm the theory, the findings are modestly supportive at best, explaining just 3-11 percent of the variation in deviance and criminal offending (Longshore, 1998). As Polk (1991) concludes, "too much crime falls outside the boundaries of [Gottfredson and Hirschi's] definition for this general theory to be of much use" (p. 579).

Neutralization Theory

The theories we have discussed so far have highlighted differences between criminals and noncriminals, and delinquents and nondelinquents. A different approach was proposed by *Gresham Sykes* and *David Matza* (1957; Matza, 1964). Sykes and Matza pointed out that if traditional positivist theories of crime are correct, some individuals would be criminal all the time, whereas others would never deviate. They observed, however, that even the most active delinquents spend most of their time in noncriminal pursuits (see also Brunson & Miller, 2001). They were especially critical of the notion of the delinquent subculture which, as we noted earlier, depicts offenders as having a value system at odds with that of the dominant culture. Were this the case, Sykes and Matza argue, delinquents would show no remorse for their behavior and would not view it as wrong. When detected and apprehended, though, delinquents typically exhibit guilt and shame over their behavior. Although some skeptics might see such expressions as an attempt to appease those in authority, Sykes and Matza take these youthful offenders at their word.[14]

Instead of seeing delinquency as a rejection of societal norms, Sykes and Matza view it as the endproduct of a process they call *neutralization*. To understand neutralization, one must also understand the concept of **drift**. According to Sykes and Matza, adolescent behavior runs along a continuum, with total freedom at one end and total constraint at the other. Rather than locate themselves consistently at one pole or the other, adolescents vacillate between these two extremes. "The delinquent *transiently* exists in a limbo between convention and crime, responding in turn to the demands of each, flirting now with one, now the other, but postponing commitment, evading decision. Thus, he [sic] drifts between criminal and conventional action" (Matza, 1964, p. 28, author's emphasis). The drift into delinquency is facilitated by learning justifications or rationalizations that neutralize the constraint of society's norms of behavior and thus legitimate deviation. Sykes and Matza called these justifications or rationalizations **techniques of neutralization**.

Sykes and Matza identified five basic types of techniques of neutralization:

denial of responsibility—The deviant disavows personal responsibility for the offense, claiming that it was not his or her fault. Batterers, for example, frequently deny responsibility for an abusive incident by claiming they were drunk.

denial of injury—The deviant maintains that an offense didn't really occur because no one was harmed by his or her actions. Thus, individuals arrested for illegal gambling will sometimes maintain their innocence on the ground that "nobody gets hurt" from what they do.

denial of victim—By maintaining that their victims deserve what happens to them, offenders may also justify or legitimate their offending. A defense attorney at a recent rape trial, for instance, argued that his client should be acquitted because the woman he raped was dressed provocatively and, therefore, "deserved it."

condemnation of condemners—An offender legitimates his or her behavior by claiming that his or her accusers, judges, or others in authority are corrupt and, therefore, also guilty. For example, a child whose parent catches him or her smoking marijuana may argue, "Why shouldn't I smoke pot? You drink, and everybody knows alcohol is worse for you than marijuana."

appeal to higher loyalties—In this case, the offender disavows personal benefit or gain from his or her behavior, claiming that he or she didn't do it for themselves, but for others. A fraternity member, for instance, was recently apprehended while breaking into a professor's office in whose class he was not even enrolled. During questioning, he admitted that he was planning to steal an exam, but that he was doing this not for his own benefit, but for "his brothers."

In considering these techniques of neutralization, two important points must be made. First, although many of the illustrations offered here are after-the-fact justifications for misbehavior, Sykes and Matza maintain that techniques of neutralization occur *prior* to the commission of a deviant act. They serve to motivate or facilitate deviation by loosening moral constraints on individuals. Second, we can see here a close resemblance between techniques of neutralization and what is defined in law as *mitigating circumstances* (including self-defense, accident, and insanity). This is no coincidence. Because delinquents understand and (usually) adhere to the society's normative value system, they also understand and concur with the law, which allows for extenuating circumstances that negate an offense. Although they agree that people should be held responsible for their actions, they also know that there are conditions under which infractions are excusable and sometimes even permissible. Techniques of neutralization are expansions and distortions of the same conditions that excuse the accused in law (Matza, 1964).

Once the restraints of social norms are temporarily neutralized, individuals are free to drift into delinquency. They may, of course, be diverted, but because they now feel they have no control over their circumstances, that what lies ahead is destiny, they are motivated to act or to make something happen. It is this sense of desperation that provides the will to commit new infractions. "The will to *repeat* old infractions requires nothing very dramatic or forceful. Once the bind of the law has been neutralized and the delinquent put into drift, all that seems necessary to provide the will to repeat old infractions is preparation" (Matza, 1964, p. 184, emphasis added).

Before moving to an assessment of neutralization theory, one final question needs to be addressed. As Sykes and Matza pointed out, "This approach to delinquency centers its attention on how an impetus to engage in delinquent behavior is translated into action. But it leaves unanswered a serious question: What makes delinquency attractive in the first place?" (Matza & Sykes, 1961, p. 712). Their emphasis on the similarity between delinquent values and the values of the dominant culture informs their response. According to Sykes and Matza, coexisting with the explicit or official values of society are a set of *subterranean values*—"values, that is to say, which are in conflict with other deeply held values but which are still recognized and accepted by many" (Matza & Sykes, 1961, p. 716). These are not the conflicting values of two opposing groups, but rather they exist within a single individual. Subterranean values include the element of adventure (displays of daring and the search for excitement and thrills), the desire for a "soft" job where one earns money as quickly and painlessly as possible, the pursuit of conspicuous consumption, and an acceptance of aggression and violence (the ability to "take it and hand it out," to defend one's rights and one's reputation with force, and "to prove one's manhood with hardness and physical courage").

Sykes and Matza maintain, then, that these subterranean values are widely held in U.S. society, but that their manifestations are usually confined to certain circumstances deemed "appropriate" or "proper" (such as sporting events, conventions, or "the big night on the town"). Delinquent youth conform to these values, and frequently accentuate them. Trouble often arises not only because of this accentuation, but also because young people are notoriously poor judges of *appropriate* times and situations.

> In short, we are arguing that the delinquent may not stand as an alien in the body of society, but may represent instead a disturbing reflection or a caricature. His [sic] vocabulary is different to be sure, but kick, big-time spending, and rep have immediate counterparts in the value system of the law-abiding. (Sykes & Matza, 1961, p. 717)

Evaluating Neutralization Theory

The validity of neutralization theory has been challenged by a number of criminologists working from various perspectives. One question that has been raised, for example, is if delinquents and nondelinquents are no different, can variations in delinquency rates among youths be attributable only to some individuals' greater capability to neutralize or to the fact that they just frequently happen to be in situations or with people who promote the will to deviate? How does one explain persistent serious offending and youths who grow up to pursue criminal careers as adults?

Sykes and Matza acknowledge the problem of the "hardcore" delinquent and the persistent offender, but they maintain that their numbers are small and that it may be necessary to explain their behavior in other ways (such as social and personal isolation). Most young people are pretty conventional and most "age out" of delinquency. They come to learn the appropriate times and places to pursue subterranean values and, as they grow older and acquire greater responsibilities and lose a good deal of leisure time, offending is harder to justify. To some critics, though, this response is unsatisfactory since it appears to undermine the theory: The theorists are distinguishing types of delinquents when their goal is to show that there is really no difference between delinquents and nondelinquents (see, for example, Taylor et al., 1973).

Research on the process of neutralization has produced inconsistent findings, although it must also be noted that many of these studies have serious methodological problems, such as the use of small, unrepresentative samples (see, for example, Ball, 1966; Hindeglang, 1970; Minor, 1980, 1981; Regoli & Poole, 1978; see also the Appendix). Hamlin (1988) has persuasively argued that the techniques of neutralization do not precede deviant behavior, but rather follow it. According to Hamlin:

> Motives are utilized and changed in the process of legitimating social action and have very little to do with the actual cause of the action. We generate motive in response to a "question situation" and, through our (read: white, Western, male) perceived progressive linear time, logically put the motive prior to the action. This prior sequencing is a fallacy. Motives are a product of social action. It is not until after a social action, or more precisely, not until action needs to be legitimized, that motives are produced. (p. 431)

Hamlin's critique raises questions not only about the process of neutralization, but also about techniques of neutralization themselves. Some critics point out that one weakness in neutralization theory is the implicit idea that all techniques are equal; they all neutralize the bind of social norms in the same way. Some techniques, however, do not just extend conventional morality, but rather challenge it. An example will make the point clearer: "A homosexual who says he cannot help being a homosexual because he is sick is very different from a homosexual who denies the fact of harm to the victim, who declares 'gay is good' and that his partner agrees" (Taylor et al., 1973, p. 184).

Of course, that various techniques of neutralization may be valued differently by different individuals or social groups at different times and in different circumstances does not negate the importance of Sykes and Matza's work in identifying the existence of these techniques in the first place. There is evidence, in fact, that techniques of neutralization may be more widely used than Sykes and Matza first proposed and that their typology of techniques should be expanded. Coleman (1987), for example, found six techniques of neutralization that are commonly used by white-collar offenders, and he notes that most white-collar employees report that their workplace culture is imbued with a set of expectations that encourage unethical and even criminal business practices. Hagan and his colleagues (1998) believe that these techniques of neutralization grow directly out of the cultural value placed on individualized competition for material success—or what they call *hierarchic self-interest*—that is inherent in market societies. In fact, they hypothesize that societies experiencing rapid economic change to a capitalist market economy are especially likely to feel the effects of hierarchic self-interest expressed through techniques of neutralization that encourage criminal and delinquent behavior. Hagan et al.'s (1998) research in Germany supports this argument. Box 5.2 looks at another possible site for testing their hypothesis.

Box 5.2 is also important because it highlights the gendered nature of crime and deviance. Like most traditional criminological theories, Sykes and Matza's neutralization theory was developed through research that included only males. Few tests of the theory have looked at female offending (for an exception, see Ball, 1977). However, given research indicating that females may use a different vocabulary of motives than males (Gilligan, 1982), studies designed to test the accuracy and pervasiveness of neutralization theory must include women and girls.[15]

BOX **5.2**   **HOW THE WORLD SEES IT**
Sex Tourism

According to children's rights advocates, an increasing number of children in countries such as Brazil, the Philippines, and Cambodia are being kidnapped and forced into prostitution or sold to pimps by their parents, most of whom are desperate for income. The children may be locked in the brothels if they are considered likely to try to escape, but usually such measures are unnecessary; beatings and threats are usually enough to convince the children to stay (Lim, 1998). Accurate estimates of the number of child prostitutes are difficult to come by, with some experts setting the lower limit in the tens of thousands and others saying it is at least one million (Lim, 1998). The children involved, the vast majority of whom are girls, are as young as six and as old as fifteen (the age of consent in most countries is sixteen) (Goering, 1996; Kristof, 1996; Sherry et al., 1995).

Who are the customers of these child prostitutes? Some are local men, neighbors of the children, to whom the children are "rented out" by their parents. Parents often rationalize their behavior by appealing to higher loyalties: Selling their children's bodies provides desperately needed income for the entire family. Even greater financial gains can be had, however, if the children are sold to foreign businessmen and tourists. Some of these men are individual travelers, but others travel on organized sex tours. The tours, which first began in Japan, are now sold in countries such as Great Britain, South Korea, and Taiwan. If a child is a virgin, the fee may be as much as $500, but immediately following the loss of her virginity, a young girl may be hired for anywhere from $2 to $10, depending on her age and experience (Kristof, 1996; Lim, 1998; Sherry et al., 1995).

While the parents' motive for selling their children is arguably understandable on some level, how do most customers rationalize their behavior? One rationalization offered by many customers is that they are helping the children (denial of injury). They argue that they are providing them with much-needed money for their families and preventing them from having to work at even more dangerous or menial occupations. The customers also often rationalize that children from impoverished countries become sexually active at earlier ages anyway.

Another motivation of customers seeking out young children is the belief that child prostitutes are less likely than adult prostitutes to be infected with HIV, the virus that causes AIDS (Sherry et al., 1995). According to international health experts, AIDS is spreading rapidly among prostitutes in many countries, especially in Asia. It is also spreading from country to country because of international trafficking in prostitutes and because of travelers who contract the disease abroad and bring it home with them. Prostitutes report that few of their customers wear condoms, and the younger the prostitute, the more powerless she is to insist that a condom be worn. However, rationalizations for crime and deviance are often not grounded in fact. According to health experts, child prostitutes are at *greatest* risk of contracting HIV because of their age. A child's vagina or anus is more easily torn from intercourse, causing open cuts, sores, and bleeding that facilitate HIV transmission (Lim, 1998). In fact, health experts expect the incidence of AIDS in Asia as well as Latin America to continue to rise, with children making up an increasing percentage of those who become infected and eventually die from the disease.

Self-Esteem and Crime

It is a widely accepted belief that how we behave depends, in large part, on whether we think positively or negatively about ourselves. If we are self-confident and feel capable and in control of our lives—that is, if we have high self-esteem—we will probably behave responsibly and treat others respectfully. Conversely, if we see ourselves as losers or as failures—that is, if we have low self-esteem—we are likely to become withdrawn or to do something to try to pick ourselves up, if only for a short time; we may even engage in some form of self-destructive behavior. Moreover, most of us also know the kinds of experiences that lower self-esteem: "constant failures and a constant bombardment with the message that one does not count as a person or with others" (Smelser, 1989, p. 7).

Given the intuitive appeal of these ideas, it is not surprising that several social scientists have postulated a causal relationship between self-esteem and criminal behavior, and numerous crime prevention and rehabilitation programs are premised on the notion that deviance is a direct outgrowth of the devalued or disvalued self (Pollack, 1998). However, it is *Howard B. Kaplan's* (1975, 1980) formulation that is considered by many criminologists to be the most comprehensive and most widely tested theoretical statement of the *self-esteem model* of crime and delinquency, and so we will concentrate primarily on Kaplan's work in this section.

Kaplan begins with the fundamental sociological observation that we develop our sense of self through interaction with others in the groups to which we belong (our family, our peers). We learn to place a particular value on ourselves as persons and on our behavior through others' reactions to us. Over time, these others need not even be present; we internalize their responses so that our mere imagination of them influences our self-concepts, or "self-attitudes" as Kaplan puts it. According to Kaplan (1975), "persons who in the course of their group experiences have developed relatively negative self-attitudes are significantly more likely to adopt deviant response patterns in a specified future period than persons who in the course of their group experiences have developed relatively positive self-attitudes" (p. 51). For individuals with low self-esteem, crime and delinquency may come to be viewed as self-enhancing opportunities. This is not to say that all individuals with low self-esteem will commit crimes; rather, their low self-esteem predisposes them toward deviant activity. "Whether deviant behavior is adopted and which type is chosen depend on circumstances—what kinds of deviant activity are visible and available, the perceived attractiveness of these opportunities, and so on. Whether the involvement is continued . . . depends in turn on the extent to which deviant activity is in fact felt to be self-enhancing or self-derogating" (Scheff et al., 1989, p. 171).

It is disappointing to report that, despite its widespread intuitive support—indeed, Wells (1989) argues that the idea of a causal link between self-esteem and crime is so well accepted that it seems a "truism"—the empirical support for Kaplan's theory has been weak and often contradictory. Kaplan's (1980) own test of the theory—a longitudinal survey of more than 3,000 seventh-grade male and female students who were questioned each year for three years—initially yielded supportive findings. In this study, those adolescents with initially low levels of self-esteem, as well as those who subsequently experienced increases in self-rejecting attitudes, were more likely than the other adolescents surveyed to later engage in deviant activity. Additional longitudinal tests of other data by other researchers, however, failed to confirm the self-enhancing effects of delinquent behavior and showed negligible or nonexistent direct effects of self-esteem on deviance (see, for example, Bynner et al., 1981; McCarthy & Hoge, 1984; Wells & Rankin, 1983).

In subsequent analyses, Kaplan and colleagues (1986, 1987) respecified some of the variables and elaborated the self-enhancement model to take into account additional factors, such as "early involvement in deviant activities" (reported during the first round of questioning) and "deviant peer associations" (as reported during the second round of questioning). These studies, as well as those of others, have shown that the relationship between self-esteem and deviance may be more complex than Kaplan's theory originally conveyed. In some of the research, low self-esteem had both a positive *and* a negative effect on subsequent deviance. Individuals with pathologically low levels of self-esteem seem to experience self-enhancement through deviant activity. Others, whose self-esteem levels are within the normal range of low-high variation, experience lowered feelings of efficacy as a result of their deviation which, in turn, increases their need to conform and inhibits future deviance. Paradoxically, however, some studies also show that individuals with exceptionally high levels of self-esteem may experience self-enhancement through deviance—a finding that cannot be explained by Kaplan's theory since it says nothing about motivational dynamics at the extreme upper-end of the self-esteem continuum (Evans et al., 1991; Pollack, 1998; Wells, 1989). Pollack (1998), for example, reports that female inmates whom she interviewed explained their offending in terms of high self-esteem. As one woman told the interviewer, "I *love* myself, that's why I did this. I wanted money, that's why I did this" (quoted in Pollack, 1998, p. 5, author's emphasis).

Pollack (1998) points out another serious weakness in self-esteem theory: Focusing on low self-esteem as the cause of crime individualizes the crime problem and decontextualizes offenders from the social, political, and economic constraints they face in their everyday lives. Offending becomes a psychological problem, while oppression in the form of classism, racism, and sexism are ignored as contributing factors. "[T]he problem, *and the solution* to the problem, lie within the individual" (Pollack, 1998, p. 3).

We will return to the question of how oppression contributes to crime in the next chapter. Now, however, we will take another look at the relationship between low self-esteem and crime. Individuals may engage in a deviant act for any number of reasons, but if their deviance is detected and elicits a negative reaction, they may internalize the stigma, develop a negative self-concept, and engage in future deviation because they have come to see themselves as deviants. This idea is one of the central tenets of the final theoretical perspective we will discuss in this chapter, labeling theory.

Crime and Stigma: The Labeling Perspective

Labeling theory, or *social reaction theory* as it is sometimes called, was developed in rebellion against the dominance of the positivist paradigm in criminology. At the same time, however, although one of its goals was to assert the rational element of deviation, it also would be inappropriate to consider it a descendant of the classical school. Labeling theory does not fall within the boundaries of the Marxist paradigm either, but it is perhaps best to characterize it, as some observers have, as a bridge or link to the radical criminological theories we will examine in the next chapter (Martin et al., 1990).[16]

Labeling theory constituted a bold new approach to explaining crime. It gained popularity understandably during a period of sweeping social change—the 1960s and 1970s—when questioning authority and the status quo was widespread (see Chapter 1). Whereas most criminological theories focused on criminal behavior, labeling theorists struck out in a new direction; their emphasis was on how certain behaviors come to be defined as criminal and the consequences of these definitions for individuals found to be engaging in such activities. To understand their approach more clearly, let's begin with a discussion of labeling theorists' views of crime itself.

The Relativity of Crime

Up to this point, the theories we have discussed have held an *absolutist* view of crime; that is, crime is behavior that violates a law, an agreed-upon rule. From this perspective, there are some behaviors whose characteristics inherently make them criminal; rape and homicide are two frequently cited examples. If one accepts this position, then the logical course of action is to identify those who break the law and try to discover what it is about them (biological and psychological theories) or about their environments, life conditions, or circumstances (sociological theories) that would lead them to commit crimes.

In contrast, labeling theorists see crime from a *relativist* point of view. An act becomes criminal or deviant only when it is defined as such by a group of observers. As Howard Becker (1973) put it in a much-quoted passage from his book, *Outsiders*:

> [S]ocial groups create deviance by making the rules whose infraction constitutes deviance, and by applying those rules to particular people and labeling them as outsiders. From this point of view, deviance is not a quality of the act the person commits, but rather a consequence of the application by others of rules or sanctions to an "offender." The deviant is one to whom that label has been successfully applied; deviant behavior is behavior that people so label. (p. 9; author's emphasis)

There are several aspects of this view of crime that deserve to be highlighted. First, labeling theorists are pointing out that what is defined as criminal or deviant depends on a number of factors, including the situational and historical contexts in which the behavior occurs, the characteristics of the individual engaged in the behavior, and the characteristics of the definers. Say, for example, someone sees your lips moving as if you are having a conversation, but there is no one visibly present to whom you could be speaking. The observer asks you what you are doing, and you reply that you are talking to God. If you are in a church, synagogue, or other official place of worship, such a response probably would not be considered deviant. If, however, you are at the neighborhood deli eating lunch, it might be viewed at least as unusual or odd. Similarly, many behaviors formerly against the law are now legal and vice versa. In the nineteenth century, for instance, there were state and local laws that prohibited women from phoning men for dates, undressing in front of a photograph of a man, and appearing on a public highway wearing a bathing suit (unless they were accompanied by at least two officers or armed with clubs). Surely, today we would consider these laws, not the behaviors they prohibit, deviant.

The characteristics of the actors and definers are also significant. Labeling theorists are quick to point to the preoccupation among criminologists and law enforcement agents with street crimes, while overlooking or downplaying most forms of high-level white-collar crime, including corporate and governmental deviance. There are, of course, significant differences, including racial and social class differences, between street offenders and corporate rulebreakers. The relative powerlessness of the former makes it highly likely that they will be apprehended and processed through the criminal justice system, while the status of the latter allows them to escape being identified and labeled criminal (Becker, 1970). Some groups—what Becker (1973) refers to as *moral entrepreneurs*—are also better able to get their interests represented in law, thus ensuring that certain behaviors (read: not their own) get defined as criminal, while others do not.

This brings us to a second major point of labeling theory's view of crime: It sees crime as the product of social *interaction*. What is crucial is not that an individual violates a rule or a law, but rather that others respond to that individual's behavior, labeling him or her a criminal or deviant. This may be done informally, but of greater significance to labeling theorists is when this process takes place in what they refer to as public *status degradation ceremonies*, such as court hearings or trials (Garfinkel, 1965). With the label attached, the individual undergoes a fundamental change in identity. Indeed, the labels *criminal* and *deviant* constitute a **master status**—a status that takes precedence over all other statuses or characteristics of the individual. Others, who have deeply ingrained, proconceived ideas of what a criminal is like—untrustworthy, unpredictable, sinister—begin to structure their interactions with the labeled individual on the basis of these stereotypes (for example, they stop doing business or socializing with him or her). They may even redefine past behavior on the part of this individual so that it conforms to stereotypes attached to the deviant label (for example, the routine hug upon greeting an old friend is seen in a new light after the friend comes out as gay or lesbian).

If we imagine for a moment what such experiences may be like for the labeled person, it is not difficult to understand that eventually he or she may come to accept the label and begin to alter his or her behavior to conform to it (Crocker et al., 1998). What occurs is a **self-fulfilling prophecy**: expectations about how the individual will behave are fulfilled, not so much because the person is truly "bad" or "abnormal," but because both the person and others have come to believe he or she is "bad" or "abnormal" and they act accordingly.[16]

In short, labeling theorists see social reaction as the key element in crime and deviance causation. As Edwin Lemert (1967), whose work is part of the foundation of labeling theory, put it:

> This is a large turn away from older sociology which tended to rest heavily upon the
> idea that deviance leads to social control. I have come to believe that the reverse idea,

i.e., that social control leads to deviance, is equally tenable and the potentially richer premise for studying deviance in modern society. (p. v)

Lemert's controversial statements raise the issue of the consequences of social reaction for the labeled individual, a point that we have already touched upon, but which warrants closer consideration.

Social Reaction and Commitment to a Deviant Career

A useful way of understanding labeling theory's view of the impact of social reaction on the labeled individual is to consider Lemert's (1951) distinction between primary deviation and secondary deviation. **Primary deviation** is simply rule breaking. An individual may engage in primary deviation for any number of reasons that may be social, economic, or political. He or she may be acting on a hedonistic impulse or out of desperate need for money to buy food or to satisfy a drug habit. Whatever the specific causal factors that give rise to it, primary deviation is of little concern to labeling theorists *unless* it is detected and elicits a reaction.

Secondary deviation is deviation that results from societal reaction. As we noted previously, when an individual's deviation elicits, in particular, a formal, public reaction, the reaction process can lead to a total reorientation of the individual's self-perceptions. As Cohen (1966) wrote:

> The label—the name of the role—does more than signify one who has committed such-and-such a deviant act. Each label evokes a characteristic imagery. It suggests someone who is *normally* or *habitually* given to certain kinds of deviance; who may be expected to behave in this way; who is literally a bundle of odious or sinister qualities. It activates sentiments and calls out responses in others: rejection, contempt, suspicion, withdrawal, fear, hatred. (p. 24, author's emphasis)

In other words, others' reactions may close off legitimate or nondeviant opportunities and interactions for the labeled individual. The alcoholic, for example, may not be invited to parties or to friends' homes anymore, thus adding to his or her isolation. The ex-convict may face tremendous difficulty in getting a good-paying job.

This closing off of legitimate opportunities and interactions, coupled with the destruction of one's public image and character, may leave the labeled individual with little choice but to seek out deviant associations and to pursue deviant or criminal opportunities. The reaction process, then, may cause the *resocialization* of the labeled individual toward acceptance of and conformity to the role attached to the deviant label. That is, the labeled individual becomes committed to a deviant identity and embarks on a deviant career. This secondary deviation is essentially a defensive and adaptive strategy on the part of the labeled individual; it is an effort to survive and "a means of sustaining a 'social self' in the face of exclusion and stigmatization" (Taylor et al., 1973, p. 151; see also Lemert, 1951).

The relationship between primary and secondary deviation is represented schematically in Figure 5.1. Notice here that typically primary deviation goes undetected

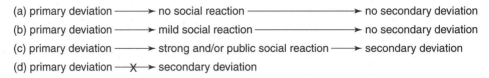

(a) primary deviation ——————→ no social reaction ————————————→ no secondary deviation

(b) primary deviation ——————→ mild social reaction ——————————→ no secondary deviation

(c) primary deviation ——————→ strong and/or public social reaction ——→ secondary deviation

(d) primary deviation ——✗——→ secondary deviation

FIGURE 5.1   The Relationship between Primary Deviation and Secondary Deviation

(a). Even if it is detected, the response may be mild or rather limited, leading to no further deviation (b). The more dramatic the response, though, the more likely that secondary deviation will be the outcome (c). However, *there can be no secondary deviation without social reaction* (d).

It is not difficult to see why the labeling perspective ignited a fierce debate among criminologists and policymakers alike. Let's examine first some of the empirical research that has attempted to test the basic tenets of the theory, and then move on to consider the policy implications of this perspective.

The Empirical Validity of Labeling Theory

The majority of the research on labeling theory has focused on the phenomenon of secondary deviation and the extent to which the social reaction process affects or alters the labeled individual's self-concept and behavior. Much of the early criticism of the perspective focused on its determinism. As Akers (1962) expressed it, "One sometimes gets the impression from reading this literature that people go about minding their own business, and then—'wham'—bad society comes along and slaps them with a stigmatized label" (p. 465). To such a critique, Becker (1973) has replied:

> [T]he act of labelling [sic], as carried out by moral entrepreneurs, while important, cannot possibly be conceived as the sole explanation of what alleged deviants actually do. It would be foolish to propose that stick-up men stick people up simply because someone has labelled them stick-up men, or that everything a homosexual does results from someone having called him [sic] homosexual. Nevertheless, one of the most important contributions of this approach has been to focus attention on the way labelling places the actor in circumstances which make it harder for him to continue the normal routines of everyday life and thus provoke him [sic] to "abnormal" actions . . . The degree to which labelling has such effects is, however, an empirical one, to be settled by research into specific cases rather than by theoretical fiat. (p. 179)

The question remains, then, has the notion of secondary deviation been empirically verified?

The answer to this question is largely no. For one thing, many studies have failed to show that being labeled criminal or delinquent leads to a negative self-image on the part of those so labeled (Evans et al., 1991; Martin, 1985; Shoemaker, 1984). At best, researchers have found only weak support for a relationship between labels and secondary deviance (Gold, 1970; Gold & Williams, 1969; McEachern, 1968, Smith & Paternoster, 1990). A number of researchers have even reported that informal labels, imposed early in one's life, especially by parents, have a far greater impact on individuals' self-concepts than formal public "degradation ceremonies" that may not occur until adolescence (Paternoster & Triplett, 1988).

A second difficulty with this perspective highlighted by the research is that labeling theorists depict individuals as being rather passive during the labeling process, when, in fact, the imposition of a deviant label is often strenuously resisted by those being labeled. Moreover, there is evidence that deviant labels are not indelible. Individuals can, and often do, overcome stigma (Prus, 1975; Rogers & Buffalo, 1974).

Third, in some cases, the deviant label is valued and even sought after. Akers (1968) uses the example of gang members whose deviant identity is formed before they are ever officially labeled. We might also consider political terrorists and rebels, who adopt a deviant identity to set themselves apart from the authorities they challenge. The process of officially being labeled deviant by these authorities is often to them a symbol of accomplishment. Mankoff (1971), in particular, has argued that one of the most significant weaknesses of labeling theory is its failure to recognize that individuals may choose to embark on a criminal or deviant career without ever having experienced social reaction to their behavior.

Among the other criticisms that have been leveled against labeling theory are those that have to do with its position on who is most likely to get labeled deviant or criminal. Siegel (1992), for example, argues that while labeling theory leads us to believe that it is the poor and powerless who are most likely to get (unfairly) labeled deviant or criminal, the justice system is not consistently unfair and biased against the poor or in favor of the rich. However, Taylor, Walton, and Young (1973) are critical of labeling theory because of its failure to more fully examine "the way in which deviance and criminality are shaped by society's larger structure of power and institutions" (p. 169).

This disagreement forms the core of a debate that we will take up again in Chapter 6. To conclude the present chapter, however, we will examine the policy implications of the labeling perspective. It is in this area that some of the strongest criticisms of the theory have been centered.

What Is to Be Done?

Labeling theorists' response to the question that serves as the title of this section would undoubtedly be "nothing," or at most, "very little." Keeping in mind that labeling theory sees deviance as being amplified and promoted by labeling and that processing through the criminal justice system, as one of the strongest and most public social reactions, generates secondary or career deviance, it is no wonder that labeling theorists argue, as Wright (1991) puts it, that less is best when it comes to punishing offenders. Labeling theorists favor, for example, the legalization of "victimless crimes," such as prostitution and drug offenses, pointing out that such laws are incredibly difficult to enforce and, rather than reducing crime, simply engender greater deviation (including bribery and police corruption; public disrespect for the law, given widespread demand for particular illegal goods and services; and secondary offending, such as when a drug addict takes to stealing to support his or her habit) (see, for example, Schur, 1965).

However, the most hotly debated policy recommendation of the labeling theorists is *nonintervention*. This position was promoted most strongly by *Edwin Schur* (1973) in his discussion of the treatment of juvenile offenders. He argued that the state should legalize many acts currently considered delinquent and ignore most others. Only the most serious infractions should reach the attention of the courts, but in any event, even these offenders should not be committed to correctional facilities. Indeed, Schur advocates abolishing juvenile correctional institutions and replacing them with noninstitutional programs that are largely voluntary. In Schur's (1973) own words, the tenet that should guide policymakers and those working in the juvenile justice system is *"leave kids alone wherever possible"* (p. 155).

We have already reviewed a considerable amount of research that shows that support for the proposition that labeling causes secondary deviation is rather weak and inconsistent. In addition, there is a body of evidence that indicates that offenders who are formally processed through the criminal justice system are actually *less* likely to recidivate than those who are treated informally or who are simply ignored (Wright, 1991).

Wright (1991) also makes the point that social reaction in the form of official processing serves two important crime-reduction purposes: (1) incapacitation—if offenders are incarcerated in correctional facilities they cannot engage in secondary deviant activities; and (2) general deterrence—although some offenders may be "hardened" by labeling and incarceration, others in the society at large may see through their example that "crime doesn't pay" and be inhibited from offending. Although there is ample data that call into question the effectiveness of both the incapacitation and deterrence functions of imprisonment, Wright's critical assessment of nonintervention policies that have been implemented gives one reason to pause and carefully reconsider the wisdom and long-term efficacy of such an approach. Thus, even if social reaction produces some secondary deviation, the question arises as to whether it may actually reduce crime more than it creates it.

More recently, some researchers have tried to identify those conditions under which social reaction may be beneficial to offenders. Australian criminologist *John Braithwaite* (1989) argues, for example, that the key to beneficial social reaction lies in the process of shaming. Braithwaite (1989) defines *shaming* as social disapproval with the "intention or effect of invoking remorse in the person being shamed and/or condemnation by others who become aware of the shaming" (p. 100). According to Braithwaite, "Societies with low crime rates are those that shame potently and judiously" (p. 1). What about labeling theorists' contentions that shaming—or, as they would put it, stigmatization—pushes offenders into criminal or deviant subcultures and launches them on a criminal or deviant career? In response, Braithwaite makes a distinction between disintegrative and reintegrative shaming.

Disintegrative shaming is counterproductive and may lead to further criminality because it separates offenders from the community and treats them as outcasts. In such cases, "punishment erects barriers between the offender and the punisher through transforming the relationship into one of power assertion and injury" (Braithwaite,

1989, p. 73). It should come as no surprise, therefore, that offenders who experience disintegrative shaming are highly likely to recidivate and to become members of criminal or deviant subcultures, since within these groups they at least receive some social support and self-validation.

In contrast, *reintegrative shaming* is first of all an expression of disappointment in the individual who has done wrong. Rather than treating the offender as a "bad person," reintegrative shaming actually reaffirms the offender's morality; the disappointment stems from the fact that a "good person" would do something wrong. "Reintegrative shaming means that expressions of community disapproval, which may range from mild rebuke to degradation ceremonies, are followed by gestures of reacceptance into the community of law-abiding citizens" (Braithwaite, 1989, p. 55). Importantly, the offender is encouraged to assume the role of repentant.

Braithwaite maintains that reintegrative shaming is most likely to be found in societies characterized by a strong sense of community and a high level of interdependency among its members. Braithwaite believes that contemporary Japanese society fits this description, although he recognizes that Japanese culture and traditions cannot simply be transposed onto other societies. However, among Braithwaite's policy recommendations for all societies are an increased use of informal institutions of social control that can best employ techniques of reintegrative shaming; the integration of the repentant role (similar to that used at Alcoholics Anonymous and other twelve-step programs) into rehabilitation programs; and more media coverage not only of wrongdoing by individuals and corporations, but also of corporate and individual offenders who can be held up as models of reform following their wrongdoing.

Braithwaite's idea of reintegrative shaming understandably has drawn considerable attention from criminologists (see, for example, Hay, 1998; see also Chapter 6). Undoubtedly, it will be the subject of debate and the focus of extensive research in the years to come, much the same way labeling theory was during the 1960s and 1970s.

Summary and Conclusion

The focus of this chapter has been on theories that emphasize the role of learning or socialization in the etiology of crime. Using only the length of the chapter as a gauge, it is easy to perceive the popularity of this approach Nevertheless, we have seen that there is tremendous diversity among the many perspectives that may be considered learning theories of crime.

The commonalities of the theories, and the intuitive appeal of many of them, have led some criminologists to develop *integrative perspectives* that combine elements of two or more of the theories, such as differential association and social control, or social control and labeling (see, for example, Elliott et al., 1985; Triplett, 1990). Other criminologists, however, maintain that despite their promise of providing a truly social analysis of crime causation, these theories fall far short of that mark by ultimately drawing one's attention back to characteristics of individual offenders and their social psychological development. Such a focus is inevitable as long as one operates within a positivist framework, as many social learning theorists do. From the point of view of critical criminologists, then, social theories of crime must be developed within a completely different framework and, for many of them, this framework is the Marxist paradigm. We take up their work in the next chapter of this text.

KEY TERMS

agents of socialization—individuals, groups, and institutions that have as one of their primary functions the socialization of members of a society by providing explicit instruction in or modeling of social expectations.

autonomous deviance—deviance produced by a control surplus, which helps an individual further extend control over others and thereby increase his or her control surplus.

differential anticipation theory—the view that people are likely to engage in behaviors from which they expect to obtain the greatest rewards and the least punishment.

differential association—the process of social interaction by which individuals acquire definitions favorable and unfavorable to law violation.

differential identification—the process by which criminality develops because of an individual's greater identification with members of criminal or deviant groups as opposed to members of conformist groups.

differential reinforcement—the process by which deviant or conforming behavior is acquired and internalized through past and present rewards and punishments attached to one form of behav-

ior relative to those attached to the alternative behavior.

drift—the process of vacillation along the behavioral continuum of total freedom versus total constraint.

master status—a status that takes precedence over all other characteristics or statuses of an individual.

primary deviation—rule breaking, which may be caused by any number of individual, social, economic, or political factors.

repressive deviance—deviance produced by a control deficit as an individual attempts to escape the deficit and restore balance to his or her control ratios.

secondary deviation—deviation that results from the process of being labeled.

self-fulfilling prophecy—expectations that are fulfilled not because of true causes, but because people believe them to be true and act accordingly.

socialization—the process of social interaction through which a society's culture is taught and learned and human personalities are developed.

techniques of neutralization—a priori justifications or rationalizations that legitimate and, therefore, facilitate deviation.

SUGGESTED READINGS

Akers, R. L. (1998). *Social learning and social structure: A general theory of crime and deviance*. Boston: Northeastern University Press. Akers's most recent, and most extensive, discussion of his social learning theory.

Braithwaite, J. (1989). *Crime, shame, and reintegration*. Cambridge: Cambridge University Press. Braithwaite introduces his idea of reintegrative shaming and examines contemporary Japanese society in support of his position.

Ermann, M. D., & Lundman, R. J. (Eds.). (1996). *Corporate and governmental deviance*. New York: Oxford University Press. A collection of articles

that examines various forms of business and political crime, from the *Challenger* disaster to police use of force in the Rodney King case. Read it and decide for yourself how well these data support some of the theories discussed in this chapter.

Meier, R. F., & Geis, G. (1997). *Victimless crime?* Los Angeles: Roxbury. An analysis of four topics (prostitution, drugs, homosexuality, and abortion) that have been hotly debated with regard to whether the behaviors associated with them should be considered criminal and how the legal system should deal with them, if at all.

NOTES

1. Sutherland's *Principles of Criminology* was first published in 1924. After Sutherland's death in 1950, his close friend and leading proponent, *Donald Cressey*, who also became a prominent criminologist, took the textbook through six subsequent editions; the tenth was published in 1978. In these editions and other publications, Cressey offered what he considered clarifications, not revisions of the theory. Following Cressey's death, David Luckenbill revised the text, but not the theory, for an eleventh edition of *Principles of Criminology*, published in 1992.

2. Vold and Bernard (1986) actually use the term *normative conflict* instead of culture conflict because after Sutherland's death, Cressey made this substitution. Cressey made the change, he said, to bring greater clarity and specificity to the theory. "Culture" is a broad term that encompasses not only a group's or society's norms, but also many other things, material (objects) and nonmaterial (beliefs). Norms, on the other hand, are simply rules of behavior. Normative conflict occurs when various groups in a social setting hold divergent views about what is "correct" or appropriate behavior in a given situation. According to Cressey, the term *normative conflict* more accurately conveys the meaning of Sutherland's position.

3. Sutherland was highly critical of those theorists who associated the causes of crime with such factors as poverty and "broken homes." He argued that criminal behavior is found among all social classes; only its forms vary across class groups. He frequently cited his study of white-collar crime (1949) to support this position.

4. Some criminologists argue that many of these criticisms are based on misinterpretations of the theory and misreadings of Sutherland's and others' work. See, for example, the exchanges between Akers (1996) and Hirschi (1996), and between Matsueda (1997) and Costello (1998). When the theory was first published, it also received extensive acclaim and criticism. For a detailed discussion of these early critiques as well as a careful response to them, see Cressey, 1960.

5. For a more detailed discussion of behaviorism, see Akers, 1998; Bandura, 1977; Lefton, 2000; and Skinner, 1953. Akers's social learning theory was originally called *differential association-reinforcement theory*, an indication of its strong affiliation with Sutherland's differential association theory.

6. For instance, the use of particular behavioral modification techniques in corrections and counseling has been challenged in the courts. See *Mackey* v. *Procunier* (1973) and *Kamowitz* v. *Michigan Department of Mental Health* (1973).

7. Walter Reckless's (1961) *containment theory* is also a form of control theory. In addition, some theorists consider Sykes and Matza's (1957) *drift theory*, to be discussed later in this chapter, a form of control theory.

8. Some observers have likened Hirschi's beliefs element of the social bond to Sutherland's notion of definitions favorable or unfavorable to law violation. However, Costello and Vowell (1999) make an important distinction between the two ideas by pointing out that Hirschi and Sutherland specified different learning processes. Sutherland maintained that definitions regarding law violation were learned through interaction with others, indicating that the individual is integrated into the social group. In contrast, Hirschi's control theory makes the claim that "tolerant attitudes toward law violation are more reflective of a lack of social integration than the result of learning definitions through integration into deviant groups" (Costello & Vowell, 1999, p. 834).

9. One might also take issue with Agnew and Petersen's (1989) distinction between serious and minor delinquency. Although it is obvious that using a knife or gun to get something should be weighted more in terms of seriousness than stealing an expensive car part, the difference between hurting someone badly (weighted four in terms of seriousness) and serious fighting (weighted two) is less clear. Moreover, "hit mother," "hit father," and "hit instructor or supervisor" are all weighted two without taking into account the degree of harm done. Can we assume that adolescents who completed the self-report delinquency scale on which these items appeared would report such hitting as "hurt someone badly" if injury had occurred during the incident?

10. However, Costello and Vowell (1999, p. 834) argue that "because most studies of delinquency are conducted with respondents old enough to have already established attachments, commitments, involvements, and beliefs, it is unlikely

that even longitudinal studies can untangle the true temporal priority of each dimension of the bond. Thus, it makes sense to conceptualize these dimensions as contemporaneous rather than try to specify one element as a cause of another."

11. Importantly, Hirschi (1969) hypothesized that single-parent households have rates of delinquency comparable to two-parent households because, all things being equal, one parent can as effectively socialize children as two parents can. However, as Matsueda and Heimer (1987) point out, all things are rarely, if ever, equal in single-parent households, especially those headed by women, relative to two-parent households. This does not mean, however, that the absence of one of two parents from the home *causes* delinquency or that delinquency is an inevitable outcome of growing up in a single-parent family (see also Demo & Acock, 1992). For a discussion of the difficulties faced by single-parent families, particularly those headed by women, see Renzetti and Curran, 1999.

12. Whitehead and Boggs (1990) decided not to measure the belief element of the social bond in their study because their sample was composed of people who had already violated the law: known felony offenders.

13. Several researchers point out that even "ordinary" street offenders often specialize in particular types of crimes. See, for example, Benson and Moore, 1992, and Wright et al., 1995.

14. Matza, in particular, is committed to a methodological approach he calls *naturalism*, which he defines as remaining true to that which one is studying. Matza believes that most researchers'

explanations of deviance distort or contradict the explanations deviants themselves would give of their behavior. Researchers, Matza says, should let deviants speak for themselves. See Matza (1964) for a fuller treatment of naturalism. See Taylor et al. (1973) for a sympathetic critique of this approach.

15. Hagan and his colleagues (1998) suggest that their concept of hierarchic self-interest may be helpful in explaining gender differences in offending. They hypothesize that males are more susceptible to hierarchic self-interest than females. Their research in Germany offers strong support for this hypothesis and will hopefully encourage additional research on this topic.

16. Many of those who are identified as labeling theorists resist reference to labeling as a theory, preferring instead to call it "a way of looking at a general area of human activity; a perspective whose value will appear, if at all, in increased understanding of things formerly obscure" (Becker, 1973, p. 181). Becker, who is one of the founders of labeling, has also argued that he prefers to call it an interactionist theory of deviance, but conventionally it continues to be referred to as *labeling theory* or *social reaction theory*.

17. For one classic analysis of the self-fulfilling prophecy in education, see Rosenthal and Jacobson (1968). However, the application of the self-fulfilling prophecy to crime and deviance is not a unique contribution of contemporary labeling theorists. It was actually raised in the 1930s by Frank Tannenbaum (1938), who warned against the negative consequences of what he called "the dramatization of evil."

6 Crime and Power: Radical Criminologies

The term *radical* is defined in *The American Heritage Dictionary* as "favoring or effecting revolutionary changes" (Morris, 1981, p. 1076). In this chapter, we discuss criminological theories that may be considered radical in at least two ways. First, when taken together, these theories represent a dramatic break with the paradigmatic frameworks of the theories discussed in Chapters 2 through 5. Indeed, they are openly critical of and pose direct challenges to both the classical and positivist conceptions of crime and law. Second, these theories advocate fundamental changes in our society's social structure, in particular in our mode of producing and distributing resources, in order to substantially reduce or eliminate crime.

The theories to which we are referring are at times identified collectively as "Marxist criminology" and "critical criminology" (1982). As Bohm (1982) has pointed out, however, each of these titles actually names a branch or offshoot of what we will call simply **radical criminology**.[1] Despite the important differences among the various forms of radical criminology, they share a common heritage and a set of core propositions and focal concerns that allow them to be considered jointly. Before we examine the substance of radical criminology, then, let's begin with a look at its theoretical and historical roots.

Origins and Antecedents

Radical criminologists maintain that there is no such thing as an inherently criminal act. In other words, in order for behavior to be criminal, it must be defined as such by some members of the society. If you have already read Chapter 5, this proposition should be familiar to you. It is a basic principle of labeling theory and, without doubt, radical criminology owes a debt of gratitude to the labeling perspective. As we pointed out in Chapter 5, labeling theory is often seen as a bridge or link from the traditional schools of thought to contemporary radical theories.

Radical criminology has also been informed by the propositions of another contemporary perspective, *conflict theory*. Pioneered in the late 1950s and 1960s largely by *Ralf Dahrendorf* (1959) in sociology and *George Vold* (1958) in criminology, conflict theory depicts society as a battleground of competing interest groups. As its name indicates, this perspective sees societies as characterized by conflict, which grows out of the struggle between heterogeneous groups to have their interests represented in law. Of course, in a stratified society such as our own, not all groups will have sufficient resources to be equally successful in this struggle. Consequently, some groups will be able to dominate others, although according to Dahrendorf (1959) and other conflict theorists, the same groups will not consistently dominate all segments of society, and those that dominate one segment will conflict with those that dominate others. Vold, whose work was developed independently of Dahrendorf's, argued that:

> A great deal of criminal behavior results from the conflict among groups struggling over control of power in the political organization of the state. . . . Such political conflicts often involve a great deal of what would otherwise be called ordinary criminal behavior. . . . On the surface these offenses seem to be ordinary crimes, but on closer examination they are revealed as the acts of good soldiers fighting for a cause against the threat of enemy encroachment. The age-old psychological principle of group conflict comes to the fore—the end (i.e., the defense of group position) justifies the means. (Vold & Bernard, 1986, p. 275)

Vold was especially concerned with explaining crime and deviance generated by conditions of inequality, most of which other criminologists historically had ignored (including violence arising from acts of political protest against discrimination).

We will see the influence of conflict theory in radical criminologists' concern with the struggle between the haves and have nots in capitalist society, their emphasis on the role of inequality in generating crime, and their focus on behavior that traditionally has not been defined as criminal either by the legal system or by criminologists. There are, however, significant differences between conflict theory and radical criminology. One of the most important differences centers on the issue of *pluralism*. We have seen that conflict theory emphasizes interaction among conflicting interest groups and suggests that power is diffused among these groups rather than consistently concentrated in the hands of one or a few. This relates, too, to a criticism of labeling theory raised in Chapter 5, where we noted that some criminologists maintain that the theory does not go far enough in analyzing how society's power structures shape both law and crime. "Radicals, on the other hand, emphasize structured inequalities as they relate to the distribution of wealth and power in capitalist society, and hence define power in terms of class affiliation rather than diffuse interest groups or segments" (Lynch & Groves, 1986, p. 40; see also Bohm, 1982, pp. 566–568).[2]

A second significant difference between conflict theory and radical criminology has to do with the applicability of the theories and what is studied by criminologists. There are actually two dimensions to this difference, and both pertain to labeling theory as well. Critics of both labeling and conflict theory point to their limited scope in explaining crime. Labeling, we noted in Chapter 5, is especially applicable to the study of "victimless" crimes, and Vold himself argued that conflict theory "is strictly limited to those kinds of situations in which the individual criminal acts flow from the collision of groups whose members are loyally upholding the in-group position" (Vold & Bernard, 1986, p. 276). In short, neither perspective fares well in explaining the etiology of behaviors we most often think of as crime, nor do they adequately address many types of seemingly irrational and impulsive crimes. In contrast, radical criminologists maintain that virtually all crime can be explained by examining the patterns of economic organization in a society. As one radical criminologist put it, "Criminal and other socially harmful behaviors emerge for the most part as individuals attempt to create meaningful lives as defined by their view of the world and the real and perceived alternatives for action that exist in a given economic, political, and social context" (Michalowski, 1985, p. 17).

This is a central theme of radical criminology that will occupy our attention throughout much of this chapter. For now, however, let us consider another dimension of the difference between how labeling, conflict, and radical criminologists view crime. This dimension of difference centers on the issue of relativism. At the outset of this section we noted that radical criminologists basically agree with labeling theorists' proposition that no behavior is inherently criminal—it must be defined as such by some members of the society. Conflict theorists also concur in this position (Turk, 1980). We identified this approach to crime in Chapter 5, as a *relativist* one as opposed to an *absolutist* one. However, while radical criminologists share this relativism to a considerable extent, they do maintain that there is an objective reality to crime. More specifically, they argue that crime is "behavior which needlessly alienates people from their full humanity" (Young, 1985, p. 3). "A radical perspective defines crime as a violation of politically-defined human rights" (Platt, 1975, p. 103). Thus, radical criminologists maintain that what gets *officially* defined as crime is relative to the economic, political, and social structural conditions in which behavior takes place. That, though, is an issue separate from the objective harm or damage done by specific behavior, whether or not it is officially labeled criminal. This, too, is a point to which we shall return shortly.

You may have begun to see in this discussion of the differences between radical criminology and both labeling and conflict theory another source of inspiration for the radical position. As Bohm (1982) notes, radical criminology has sometimes been referred to as "the new criminology," but many of its propositions are hardly new at all, having their roots in the work of Karl Marx and Frederick Engels.[3] We discussed at length the Marxist paradigm in Chapter 1, so we will not repeat Marx and Engels's views on crime and law here. However, it is worth reiterating that Marx and Engels said very little explicitly about crime and law, and that it has become the task of their later followers to extrapolate from their general writings a Marxist theory of crime and law. Much of this work has been done only recently and will be presented in this chapter. However, contemporary Marxist (radical) criminologists have often relied heavily on the writings of a Dutch criminologist, *Willem Bonger* (1876–1940), which were published during the first half of this century.

The Criminology of Willem Bonger

Writing in the late nineteenth and early twentieth centuries, Bonger observed increases in crime rates in Europe and sought to explain these in terms of the effects of the development of the capitalist economic system. In what is perhaps his most frequently cited work, *Criminality and Economic Conditions* (1916), Bonger compared life in pre-capitalist—what he called "primitive communist"—societies with life in the European capitalist societies of the late nineteenth and early twentieth centuries. He described primitive communist societies as being characterized by *altruism*, which grew out of the way production in these societies was organized. More specifically, production was for immediate consumption; what was produced was not exchanged for money or to accumulate a surplus or to make a profit. Production was also preindustrial and, therefore, people were subject to the whims of nature; they experienced prosperity or poverty collectively, depending on natural conditions. The universality of experience in this type of society caused people to develop a sense of community. They shared similar interests and a similar goal—to survive—and this led them to "not only abstain from acts harmful to their companions, but [also to] come to their aid whenever they can" (quoted in Taylor et al., 1973, p. 225).[4]

In contrast, the capitalist mode of production generated *egoism*. Bonger "identified the advent of capitalism with the break in the process of civilizing social relationships" (Taylor et al., 1973, p. 225). The capitalist mode of production, with its emphasis on production for exchange and accumulation of wealth, demoralizes and dehumanizes those who live under it. Capitalism makes people greedy, ambitious, and competitive. Rather than thinking of others and ensuring that they have what they need, people think only of themselves and how they can get wealthier regardless of their needs. Indeed, capitalism created "unnatural" needs by producing enormous quantities of goods and enticing the public to buy them. In Bonger's view, then, it is the egoism produced by capitalism that causes crime.

Bonger applies his theory to an analysis of a wide variety of crimes, including sex offenses, economic crimes, crimes of vengeance, and "pathological crimes." Importantly, his discussion is not limited to crimes committed by the poor and the working class; rather, Bonger argues that egoism also leads to crime among the middle and upper classes. Members of these strata may commit crimes out of economic necessity, too—for example, to prevent their business from failing—but they are frequently motivated by sheer greed; they wish to grow richer and richer. "In either case, Bonger's case is contingent on the moral climate engendered by the economic system" (Taylor et al., 1973, p. 228). However, it is not the middle and upper classes who will feel the force of the law despite their deviations, for as Bonger notes, "In every society which is divided into a ruling class and a class ruled, penal law has been principally constituted according to the will of the former" (quoted in Taylor et al., 1973, pp. 229–230).

The obvious solution to the crime problem for Bonger was the transformation of capitalism to socialism. Bonger maintained that under socialism, egoism would be replaced by altruism. He argued, in fact, that among those workers who had already joined socialist organizations, one could see a gradual "civilizing effect" and a growth in their concern for others.

Bonger's work has been rightly and extensively criticized on a number of grounds.[5] However, for criminologists in the late 1960s and 1970s who were searching for an alternative to the classical and positivist paradigms dominant at that time, Bonger's writings proved invaluable. It was one of the only studies of crime and deviance available that had been written by a self-identified Marxist (Taylor et al., 1973).

The questioning of the classical and positivist paradigms was brought about by political events and widespread social changes occurring at that time. As we noted in Chapter 1, a *paradigm revolution* is likely when a dominant paradigm is unable to explain new problems and changing conditions without compromising its basic organizing principles in some fundamental way. The Vietnam War, the Watergate scandal, the civil rights movement, and the feminist movement all raised questions about power and inequality in society and created an atmosphere in which criticism of "the establishment" was not only permissible, but encouraged. Within universities, both in the United States and abroad, academics began to reassess traditional models of research that claimed to be value-neutral and found them instead to be conservative "defenders of the status quo": pro-government, pro-industry, racist, sexist, legitimators of oppression (see, for example, Krisberg, 1975; Quinney, 1973). Rather than accepting societal consensus with respect to law and crime as given, these criminologists began to question the legitimacy of the legal system itself. Far from assuming the posture of value-neutral scientists, they asked, "Science for what?" and "Whose side are we on?" (Becker, 1967).

For criminology, the center of this ferment in the United States was the University of California at Berkeley. Some of the most noted Marxist criminologists in the country worked there—Anthony Platt, Julia and Herman Schwendinger, and Paul Takagi—and it was there that the first radical journal of criminology, *Crime and Social Justice*, was published.[6] But while Berkeley may have been, as Lynch and Groves (1986) phrase it, "a hotbed of radical thought," the popularity of radical criminology was far-reaching (p. 3). Let's now turn our attention to some of the work that grew out of this critical reappraisal of the discipline.

Early Radical Criminology

Much of the early work generated by radical criminologists can be characterized as **instrumental Marxism**. From this perspective, law, law enforcement agencies, and government itself are instruments of the ruling class to maintain their advantageous position in society and to control those who pose a threat to that position. This view is perhaps best exemplified in the writings of *Barry Krisberg* and *Richard Quinney*. To understand it better, then, let's take a closer look at the work of these two criminologists.

Crime and Privilege

Writing in the mid-1970s, radical criminologist Barry Krisberg (1975) argued that crime must be studied within "the broader quest for social justice" which, in turn, requires that one understand the relationship between crime and privilege. He defines privilege as "the possession of that which is valued by a particular social group in a given historical period"; it includes money and property, but also such intangibles as "life, liberty, and the pursuit of happiness" (p. 20). Krisberg asserts that:

> The dynamics of crime can be understood within the context of the structures of injustice that are created by the powerful to further their domination. The concept of crime, as usually presented serves to deflect attention from the violence and social damage that those with power inflict upon the mass of people in order to keep them subordinate and oppressed. (p. 20)

There often are a number of privilege systems operating simultaneously in a stratified society such as ours; there is, for instance, a class privilege system, a race privilege system, and a sex privilege system, among others. If we examine the operation of the criminal justice system, we can see each of these privilege systems at work. Krisberg discusses research that shows that from the moment of contact with the police to conviction and sentencing in the courts, class, race, and sex variables influence outcomes. The poor and racial minorities are more likely than the middle class, the wealthy, and White people to be arrested, charged with an offense, and held over for trial. They are also more likely to be convicted and to receive harsher sentences. Although women are less often involved in the criminal justice system, those who are involved are often subjected to harsher conditions than men—a point to which we will return in the next chapter.

In Krisberg's analysis, then, the poor, racial minorities, women, and other "underprivileged" or deprived groups do not necessarily commit more crimes than middle- and upper-class White men, but they are more likely to be subject to the control and degradation of the criminal justice system. Krisberg, in fact, gives considerable attention to the "criminality of the privileged," but points out that much of this behavior is not officially considered crime at all, but rather standard business practice. The legal system, although portrayed as impartial, is, in reality, an active partner in preserving the privilege of the elites. "Criminality is used as a cultural device to mask the inequities of the social structure" (Krisberg, 1975, p. 64).

Before we evaluate this position, let's examine it further with a discussion of Richard Quinney's work.

Crime and Oppression

In a series of important publications, *Richard Quinney* developed a criminological theory that grew increasingly more Marxist and more radical in its orientation. In one of his first books, *The Social Reality of Crime*, Quinney (1970) delineated six propositions that today could best be characterized as constituting a conflict approach. Although he focused on interests and power, his perspective was more pluralist than materialist. According to Martin and his colleagues (1990), however, by the time *The Social Reality of Crime* appeared in print, Quinney's views had already evolved to the point where he identified the interests that control society as materialistic interests, and power as capitalist corporate power.[7]

In his next book, *Critique of the Legal Order*, Quinney (1973) challenged criminologists to develop a "critical imagination" in analyzing crime and crime control in contemporary capitalist society. He saw criminology in its traditional form as having served a single purpose: "legitimation of the existing social order," which he called "Scholarship in the Service of Social Control" (Quinney, 1973, p. 26). Traditionally, criminologists have provided "the kinds of information that governing elites use to manipulate and control those who threaten the system" (p. 27). Criminologists must instead *demystify* crime and the legal order, getting to "the deeper meaning of the American experience." Criminologists who utilize a critical legal philosophy will "begin to recognize that the legal order (that which supposedly makes for civilization) is actually a construction of the capitalist ruling class and the state that serves it. . . . [L]aw and the state in America exist for the promotion of the capitalist system" (pp. v–vi).

Quinney's analysis of crime and the legal system in *Critique of the Legal Order* was explicitly Marxist. He argued that American society could best be understood in terms of its class structure. "[L]ife in the United States is determined by the capitalist mode of production. And here as in any capitalist society, a class division exists between those who rule and those who are ruled" (Quinney, 1973, p. 53). The majority of the population constitutes a subordinate class. The ruling class, in contrast, is composed of those who own and control the means of production: "a small, cohesive group of persons related to one another in their power, wealth, and corporate connections. . . . This is the class that makes the decisions affecting the lives of those who are subordinate to it. It is according to the interests of the ruling class that American society is governed" (pp. 53–54). Quinney subsequently asked, "What, then, is the economic and political nature of criminal policy-making in America?" His answer was that "the ruling class formulates criminal policy for the preservation of domestic order, an order that assures the social and economic hegemony of the capitalist system" (p. 59).

Quinney examined the composition of various criminal policymaking bodies in the United States, including special commissions and advisory groups, and legislative bodies and crime control bureaucracies, and documented their overwhelming domination by members of the financial and political elite. Moreover, he analyzed the government's "war on crime" during the mid-1960s, showing how criminal justice agencies, such as the FBI, turned to spying on U.S. citizens in order to suppress any actions that might pose a threat to the status quo. He argued that the most violent and repressive actions of the government against political protesters were officially deemed legitimate and necessary, while the expressions of political dissent by these protesters were labeled crime. According to Quinney (1973), "When the existing order is in crisis, the emphasis on crime is escalated" (p. 149). He maintained that this was done by the ruling class to insure that public opinion about crime and crime control conformed to official ideology and policy. Of course, it was the crimes of the powerless, not those of the powerful, on which government policy, public opinion, and media propaganda focused.

What is to be done about all this, Quinney finally asked? The alternative he advocated was democratic socialism. In this type of society, private ownership of capital is abolished and everyone has equal access to material and cultural resources. This allows individuals to participate in the decisions that affect their lives. It also frees them from the alienating effects of "acquisitive individualism." Members of a democratic socialist society cooperate with one another and share an egalitarian sense of unity. At the same time, though, they respect diversity and protect individuals' rights regardless of their differences. In short, according to Quinney (1973), "The socialist vision is one of human liberation" (p. 189).

In such a society, there is no need for the state or for state law. "Law as we know it today will be relegated to the history of a former age" (Quinney, 1973, p. 190). In place of law, community custom will be used for the "patterning of our daily lives," and breaches of custom will be resolved by the popular tribunal. Rather than being punitively sanctioned, those who breach custom will be re-educated within the community.

Moving to a socialist society, Quinney recognized, would not be easy, particularly since the ruling class and its arm, the state, would attempt to subvert any revolutionary activity with counterrevolution. Nevertheless, Quinney (1973) remained optimistic: "This new radical movement is spreading" (p. 196).

We have devoted considerable attention to Quinney's ideas because, as Martin and his colleagues (1990) note:

> For the past twenty years there is no other individual who has had as much influence in helping to propel the discipline forward. While many have rejected Quinney's work they have been forced to make note of his criticisms and reconsider their positions and policies. For those who have embraced his thinking it has helped them formulate policy to reflect a better system. (pp. 388–389)

As we will see later in this chapter, Quinney's theorizing continues to have a substantial impact on the field of criminology. For now, however, let's turn our attention to an evaluation of instrumental Marxism.

The Strengths and Weaknesses of Instrumental Marxism

According to the instrumentalist position, the mode of production of a society shapes the institutions and social relations of that society. A capitalist society is a class-stratified society, divided between the haves (the ruling class) and the have-nots (the subordinate class or deprived groups). The institutions of the society, including the legal system, will further reflect this stratification. As a tool of ruling class domination, the legal system will define as criminal the behaviors most frequently engaged in by members of the subordinate class or deprived groups, while actions of the ruling class, although often more harmful and damaging, will escape the criminal label. The legal system, therefore, effectively functions to preserve the privileged position of the ruling class and to suppress any threat to ruling class hegemony posed by the subordinate class or deprived groups. Because this system is a direct outgrowth of the capitalist mode of production, reform of existing institutions will do little to fundamentally change it. Real change can only come about by replacing the capitalist system with a new mode of production, specifically a democratic socialist one.

The first major difficulty we confront in evaluating this position is one of methodology. Early radical criminologists, we noted, were highly critical of positivistic methods of research. Consequently, they tended to rely heavily on qualitative evidence, historical analyses, and secondary sources for data in support of their theories. Thus, they cited statistics on wealth distribution, memberships on corporate boards of directors, and, as Quinney did, compositions of various commissions and legislative bodies, as evidence of the existence of a ruling class: an interlocking directorate of economic, political, and social power elites. While such data do clearly document the existence of a small, somewhat cohesive upper class, they do not demonstrate that members of this class consciously and directly manipulate and control the legal system to further their own class interests. To the contrary, a number of critics of the instrumentalist position have pointed out that not all laws favor the interests of the ruling class. Health and safety laws, antitrust laws, child labor laws, antidiscrimination laws, and similar forms of legislation are all examples of the legal system acting for the benefit of the subordinate class or deprived groups (see, for example, Curran, 1993). In addition, even very powerful people are sometimes arrested, prosecuted, and punished for criminal wrongdoing. Consider, for example, that Charles Keating, mastermind of the national savings and loan fraud of the 1980s, and other banking executives involved in the scandal were sentenced to prison. In the 1990s, Republican Senator Bob Packwood of Oregon was charged with sexual harassment and Democratic Representative Dan Rostenkowski of Illinois was indicted on 17 counts of fraud and corruption. Moreover, critics argue that instrumentalists exaggerate the cohesiveness of the ruling class and overlook the substantial conflicts that occur among capitalists themselves (Chambliss & Seidman, 1982; Chambliss & Zatz, 1994; Spitzer, 1983). As Lynch and Groves (1986) point out, "An instrumental perspective on law comes close to a conspiracy theory" (p. 22).

Other critics of early radical criminology have argued that it is ahistorical and that its claim that capitalism is the "root of all evil" is not testable theory, but rather political dogma that begs the question of crime causation (Klockars, 1979). A number of critics are also skeptical of the merits of socialism and point to the persistence of crime in socialist societies as evidence of weakness and political naiveté in early radical criminology (Kennedy, 1976; Klockars, 1979; Shumann, 1976). And still other critics object to radical criminologists' attempts to expand the definition of crime to include sexism, racism, imperialism, and human rights violations, seeing this expansion as overly broad, vague, highly subjective, and unscientific (Toby, 1979; Turk, 1975).

Early radical criminologists were also accused of failing to conduct sound empirical research (Sparks, 1980), but there is one dimension of early radical criminological theory that has been subject to extensive empirical testing: the proposition that the criminal justice system is biased against the poor, women, racial minorities, and other minority groups. In Box 6.1 on pages 192–193, we consider the issue of racism in the criminal justice system. In Chapter 7, we will examine the issue of sexism in the criminal justice system. Here, however, let's briefly review the research on class bias in the criminal justice system, keeping in mind that these various forms of inequality are interrelated and that they frequently intersect, thereby amplifying their impact.

Is the Criminal Justice System Biased against the Poor?

The research findings with regard to class bias in the criminal justice system are inconsistent, but are heavily weighted in favor of the view that one's economic resources, which, of course, are a function of one's social class, impact one's chances of being arrested and convicted of an offense and also influence criminal sentencing. A number of early studies, for example, found that in police contacts with youths, those from the lower class were more likely to be arrested than those from the middle and upper

BOX **6.1**   CONTROVERSY AND DEBATE
Is the Criminal Justice System Racist?

A quick look at criminal justice statistics shows quite clearly that people of color are overrepresented at every stage of criminal case processing. This means that there are more people of color processed through the criminal justice system than we would expect given their proportion in the general population. African Americans, in particular, face a high risk of arrest, detention, and incarceration. In New York, for example, it was found that Black citizens were six times more likely and Hispanic citizens four times more likely than White citizens to be stopped and frisked by city police officers, often without adequate legal justification (Report, 1999). In Florida, a study of the processing of "habitual" offenders (i.e., individuals with two prior felony convictions or one prior violent felony conviction) showed that Black male and female defendants wee significantly more likely than White defendants to receive "enhanced" sentences, meaning they would have to serve at least 75 percent of their sentence before being eligible for parole compared with the state average of 40 percent (Crawford, 2000; Crawford et al., 1998). A recent analysis by researchers at the U.S. Department of Justice showed racial differences to be present in the juvenile justice system as well (Snyder & Sickmund, 1999). In this study, Black juveniles were significantly more likely than White juveniles to be arrested, more than twice as likely to be referred to court, and almost twice as likely to be detained. If arrested on a drug charge, Black juveniles were almost four times more likely to be detained than White juveniles (see also Fletcher, 2000).

These statistics are probably not unfamiliar to most readers, but the point of contention among criminologists is *why*. Are people of color overrepresented in the criminal justice system because the police and courts discriminate against them? Or are they overrepresented because they are involved in more criminal activity? After all, overrepresentation is not necessarily caused by discrimination. There may be behavioral rea-

sons (e.g., non-Whites commit more crimes) or legal factors (e.g., their crimes are more serious, they have a longer criminal record) (see Covington, 1999; Wilbanks, 1987).

What happens, then, when researchers control for such factors as offense seriousness and prior record? Do racial differences in criminal case processing disappear or at least narrow? Unfortunately, the majority of studies that have examined these questions show that even after major legal factors have been taken into account, a significant race effect remains. In other words, apart from factors such as offense seriousness and number of criminal convictions, the race of the offender has an impact on whether he or she is arrested, detained, held over for trial, and incarcerated. It also affects the length of incarceration (Crawford, 2000; Crawford et al., 1998; Snyder & Sickmund, 1999). Race also interacts with other non-legal factors, including age, social class, and employment status, to affect criminal justice outcomes. For instance, Spohn and Holleran (2000) found that young, unemployed Black and Hispanic male offenders are significantly more likely than middle-aged, employed White male offenders to be incarcerated (see also Steffensmeier et al., 1998).

According to Snyder and Sickmund (1999), racial disparity in treatment is most pronounced at the earliest stages of criminal justice processing. This is most likely because it is at this point that criminal justice decision makers exercise the greatest discretion. The initial decisions of whom to arrest and which charges will be filed with the prosecutor rest with the police. Some criminologists believe that the police are more suspicious of people of color. It is not uncommon for young African American men, regardless of their social class, occupation, or style of dress, to report being stopped by police for simply walking or driving through a predominantly White neighborhood. If they are driving an expensive or late-model car, they are suspected of having stolen it or of having gotten the money to buy it illegally (Feagin, 1991; Lee, 1997).

Aggregate statistics on arrests and other criminal justice decisions do show substantial variation in terms of racial and ethnic differences, partly because these data are gathered from local jurisdictions, so inconsistencies across

regions and time periods are to be expected (Snyder & Sickmund, 1999). Nevertheless, the everyday experiences of people of color provide powerful testimony that racism is alive and well in many of our police departments, courts, and correctional facilities, as well as in the larger society.

---

classes, even when offense was controlled (Chambliss, 1973; Gold, 1966; Thornberry, 1973). Similarly, the poor are more likely than members of the middle and upper classes to be held in pretrial detention, a situation that is a direct outgrowth of one's economic resources: The poor are less likely to be able to post bail. As Lynch and Groves (1986) report, "Several researchers have demonstrated that the inability to post bail biases the administration of justice against the poor and minorities by causing them to await trial in jail, in effect suffering 'punishment' in the form of restricted freedom without ever having been convicted" (p. 87; see also Box, 1981; Farrell & Swigert, 1978; Michalowski, 1985).

A lack of economic resources also impacts on the quantity and quality of legal representation afforded the poor. Poor people are typically represented in court by public defenders who work under the stress of enormous caseloads, which impinges on the amount of time these attorneys can spend preparing their "clients' " cases (Smith & DeFrances, 1996). Although the services of the public defender are free, this does not mean that these services will be adequate. Individuals with the economic resources to hire private attorneys receive more and better quality legal services and, not surprisingly, fare better in court (Barak, 1980).

Finally, there is considerable research that indicates a class bias in sentencing. Reiman (1995) and others (for example, Hagan & Bumiller, 1983; Lizotte, 1978) report that, controlling for offense committed and the race of the defendant, lower-class defendants receive longer sentences than middle- and upper-class defendants. Additional research documents the use of administrative and regulatory agencies rather than the criminal courts to process and sanction white-collar and corporate offenders. Studies show the rather weak sanctions imposed on white-collar and corporate offenders by these bodies—including warnings, injunctions, and relatively small fines. Indeed, the sanctions are usually so mild that it appears inappropriate to refer to them as punishments (Curran, 1993; Hagan, 1989; Lynch & Stretesky, 1999).

In short, although some researchers have found no evidence of class bias in the criminal justice system (see, for instance, Chiricos & Waldo, 1975), the majority of the data appear to support the position of radical criminologists on this point. It is also important to note that many of the criticisms leveled against early radical theories of crime have been subsequently addressed by criminologists working within the radical perspective. Thus, as Lynch and Groves (1986) maintain, while the criticisms we have previously outlined may have been legitimate in the mid-1970s, they no longer apply to radical criminology today. Let us turn now, then, to an examination of several recent developments in radical criminological theory.

Structural Criminology

A number of radical criminologists responded negatively to what they saw as the inflexibility and utopianism of the instrumental Marxists. From this critical introspection emerged several more sophisticated and empirically sound radical theories of law and crime. Among the most important of these are structural Marxism and, more recently, what is simply referred to as *structural criminology*. We will consider each of these in turn, and then look at other contemporary or emerging radical perspectives.

The position of **structural Marxism** with regard to law and the legal system is presented well by such criminologists as *William Chambliss, Robert Seidman, Michael Lynch*, and *Raymond Michalowski*. According to Chambliss and Seidman (1982), law is an attempt to resolve a crisis precipitated by the inherent contradictions of capitalism. What is at stake during such a crisis are not the interests of individual capitalists nor the collective interests of a cohesive ruling class, but rather the preservation of the capitalist system as a whole. Like instrumentalists, structural Marxists contextualize their analysis of law in terms of the larger economic system. However, rather than being simply a tool of the ruling class, law serves to preserve the long-term interests of capital. According to Chambliss and Seidman (1982), "A great deal of state action concerns not the enhancement of profit for a particular faction of the ruling class, but the maintenance of relations of production that make capitalism possible" (p. 313). Thus, the state may enact a health and safety law to protect workers that costs capitalists money and exposes them to the possibility of fines and other sanctions for violation of the law. By averting, temporarily at least, a large-scale crisis generated by conditions endemic to the capitalist production process, the capitalist system as a whole is protected, while the personal interests of individual capitalists are overridden (Curran, 1993).

The structural Marxist position with respect to law leads to two additional propositions. One proposition focuses on the disparity between the written law and the law "in action." More specifically, structural Marxists observe that simply because a law is "on the books," it does not mean that it will be effectively implemented and enforced. There are, in other words, biases in law enforcement. Second, social class remains a central variable in the structural Marxist explanation of crime causation. One's position on the social class hierarchy largely determines one's life chances and opportunities. Crime may occur as individuals respond and adapt to—that is, give meaning to—their experiences and perceived as well as real opportunities (Michalowski, 1985). Both of these propositions have important implications that deserve further attention.

The structural Marxist proposition regarding the disparity between the written law and the law "in action" helps us make sense of the research findings we have discussed that highlight race and class biases within the criminal justice system. It also provides a response to the criticism of early radical criminology, which stated that, contrary to the radical position, the law, through constitutional guarantees and other legislated rights, often serves to redistribute power from the privileged to the deprived. Such rights are empowering only to the extent that one has the resources to exercise them; otherwise, they constitute little more than rights on paper. Moreover, while it may be granted that "People are more powerful with the right to a jury trial than without it" (Klockars, 1979, p. 497), the extent of that empowerment is called into question by widespread manifestations of inequality in the criminal justice system, such as when all-White juries sit in judgment of African American defendants.

The structural Marxist proposition with respect to crime causation is also enlightening. By drawing connections among the economy, stratification, and crime, structural Marxists help us better understand a large body of data that shows relationships between various social factors and crime, while also allowing us to explain crime across social classes.

> In practical terms this means that radical criminologists attempt to make sense of causation by placing micro causal explanations in a wider sociopolitical context. By broadening the scope of criminological inquiry to include significant social, political, and economic institutions, radical criminologists simultaneously expanded the arena in which we search for causes. The goal of radical inquiry is to expand and integrate causal levels, to try to see how micro level variables such as broken homes or defective educational institutions are "shaped by larger social structures." (Lynch & Groves, 1986, p. 48)

In other words, these criminologists are not satisfied with the assertions that a society's economic structure or the presence of inequality alone cause crime. Although these macro level variables remain central to their thesis, they also examine the "immediate origins" of crime—micro level variables—and analyze how the "wider arena of political economy will condition more immediate social milieus, [so] that these two levels together cause crime" (Lynch & Groves, 1986, p. 49).

Consider, for example, the relationship between poverty and crime. The notion that poverty causes crime is so widely accepted that it has become a truism. As Michalowski (1985) points out, however, such a postulate confuses poverty with inequality.

> Poverty is the condition of having little. Inequality is the condition of having less than others, and it is this condition more than poverty itself that serves to stimulate crime. As we have seen, throughout history there have been many societies and social groups that have been materially poor by contemporary standards, yet their "poverty" was not a fertile seedbed for criminality. Quite to the contrary, many of these societies suffered relatively little crime compared with contemporary industrial nations. Even today we can find societies substantially poorer than our own and pockets of poverty in our own society both of which are comparatively low in crime. It is the objective condition of being unequal, and the subjective consequences of that experience, rather than poverty itself, that serves as a stimulus for crime among the victims of inequality. (p. 407)

Blau and Blau's (1982) research lends support to this position. They report that as socioeconomic inequality increases, so does the rate of violent crime (see also Blair, 2000; Currie, 1998). Inequality, they argue, promotes alienation and animosity, while simultaneously destroying social cohesiveness, by highlighting differences among racial and ethnic groups as well as between social classes. Such conditions lead to high levels of social disorganization which, in turn, breeds crime.[8] This position is also reinforced by available data on hate crimes, both in the United States and abroad (Goleman, 1990; Whitney, 1992).

John Hagan, whose position is self-identified as structural criminology has explored these issues as well. Let's briefly review Hagan's ideas.

Crime and Power Relations

In his award-winning book, *Structural Criminology*, John Hagan (1989) argues that the distinguishing features of **structural criminology** are "its attention to power relations and . . . the priority it assigns them in undertaking research on crime" (p. 2). The word *relations* in the phrase "power relations" should be given as much emphasis as its modifier *power*. We tend to think of power as linear or additive, whereas Hagan's point is that it is *relational*; it exists vis-à-vis other social actors and is connected to different crimes in different ways. Power relationships may be *instrumental*, "as in the use of rights of ownership to manipulate corporate resources in the commission of white-collar crimes," or *symbolic*, "as in the relational assignment of victim and villain statuses to users and dealers of drugs" (Hagan, 1989, p. 2). Typically, these two elements of power relations will complement one another. "That is, power usually brings preferential symbolism, as when corporate criminals are seen as more reputable and credible than street criminals. In any case . . . what makes structural criminology unique is its insistence that crime be understood and therefore studied in terms of power relations" (Hagan, 1989, p. 2).

Hagan tests his argument by examining the empirical connections between one type of power relations, social class relations, and crime. Hagan is critical of research on social class that operationalizes the concept in terms of gradational variables, such as respect or status, which simply locate individuals above or below one another on a scale. Rather, in keeping with the requirements of a structural criminology, Hagan defines social class in terms of relations of ownership and authority, locating social actors in relation to one another in the social organization of work. This permits him to examine, for instance, "how owners of businesses and persons with occupational authority are located in positions of power that allow use of organizational (usually corporate) resources to commit larger crimes than persons located in employee positions without authority" (Hagan, 1989, p. 4).[9] In addition, it allows him to clarify the connection between social class and criminal sentencing disparities. Researchers who have found no relationship between class and criminal sentencing (for example, Chiricos & Waldo, 1975) operationalized class in terms of status. In contrast, relational measures of social class illuminate more clearly the ways that this variable may influence sentencing.

> For example, relational measures of class highlight positions of persons who are unemployed members of the surplus population. It may be the fact of unemployment, more directly than low status, that leads to punitive sentencing decisions. . . . It may be a

position of powerlessness, rather than a relative deprivation of status, that better accounts for punitive sentencing decisions. Indeed, what is potentially most interesting is that the law scarcely bothers to deny this. (Hagen, 1989, p. 7)

Hagen's own research on this issue, as well as that of others, supports this proposition (see Hagan, 1989, especially Chapters 2 and 4). It also illuminates how those in positions of authority within a work organization can use the power and resources of the corporation to distance themselves from criminal prosecution, while successfully pursuing the convictions of individuals against whom they initiate criminal prosecutions.

One important application of Hagan's structural criminology lies in his analysis of gender differences in juvenile delinquency. We will review this work in the context of recent feminist theories of crime in Chapter 7. Now, however, let's continue our discussion of recent developments in radical criminology.

Other Recent Developments in Radical Criminology

Structural Marxism and structural criminology are just two of the perspectives developed by radical criminologists who are dissatisfied with the instrumental Marxist position on crime and law. There are many others, but unfortunately, time and space constraints prevent us from reviewing all of them. Instead, we will look at three additional radical approaches that we think have generated the most discussion within the discipline: left realism, peacemaking criminology, and postmodern theory.[10]

Left Realism

Beginning in the 1980s, the political climate in the United States and Great Britain underwent a decidedly conservative shift. Politicians seized on the general public's disillusionment with correctional "treatment" plans that failed to rehabilitate, calling for a tougher approach to crime and criminals. Among the results has been the enactment of such laws as "three strikes and you're out" (see Chapter 1) and unprecedented funding for building more prisons, including the harshly punitive "boot camp" facilities (Butterfield, 1997). In some jurisdictions, chain gangs have been reinstituted and prison "amenities" such as exercise equipment, cable television, and even hot meals have been eliminated (Kilborn, 1997). Criminologists, especially radical criminologists, have also been the target of the conservative backlash, being accused of excusing offenders for their wrongdoing, absolving them of responsibility for their crimes (DeKeseredy & Schwartz, 1996).

Interestingly, at least one group of radical criminologists share the view that in its zeal to highlight the crimes of the powerful, radical criminology has historically romanticized crimes committed by the poor and working class as crimes of the downtrodden struggling for survival. These criminologists call themselves *left realists*; their theoretical perspective is **left realism**. While clearly distancing themselves from right-wing conservatives, left realist criminologists are also critical of many radical criminologists whom they consider *left idealists*.[11] Most crime, left realists argue, is not a mode of rebellion against the oppression of capitalism, nor is the criminal "the champion of the underprivileged" whose goal is to redistribute private property (Matthews, 1987, p. 373). Most offenders, though often poor, are not motivated to commit crimes to secure the necessities of life. Instead, "they crave luxuries" (Burney, 1990, p. 63). They are, as DeKeseredy and Schwartz (1996, p. 250) put it, "the ultimate capitalists. These are people who watch the same TV ads as everyone else and who are hustling to obtain products and status symbols such as color TVs, fancy cars, and expensive gold jewelry." These offenders victimize other people like themselves. For example, while the poor (individuals with annual incomes less than $15,000) have the highest arrest rates, they also have the highest rates of criminal victimization. Similarly, 84 percent of White homicide victims are murdered by White offenders; 93 percent of Black homicide victims are murdered by Black offenders (U.S. Department of Justice, Bureau of Justice Statistics, 1998). Thus, while left idealists are correct that the wealthy do commit crimes and that their crimes are often more costly and more injurious than street crime, left realists point out that the poor and working class, as well as people of color, are more likely to be victimized not only by crimes of the powerful, but also by street crime. And street crime is harmful:

> [It] has a negative effect upon the cohesion and the quality of life of communities—urban communities in particular. . . . Crime tends to extend the fragmentation of urban life, mimic individualistic and acquisitive values, limit public space and social and political participation. (Matthews, 1987, p. 373; see also Lea & Young, 1984; Young, 1987)

In short, left realists want radical criminologists to undertake a careful analysis of the causes and consequences of street crime, returning to local communities to identify rates of victimization and the specific fears and concerns of residents (MacLean, 1992).[12]

Left realists also part company with both left idealists and right realists on the most effective ways to address street crime. Left realists are critical of left idealists who maintain that intervention will only make things worse or there is nothing that can be done about crime short of replacing capitalism with socialism. As they correctly point out, those who are victimized by crime certainly want something done about it (Council of State Governments/Eastern Regional Conference, 1999; Jones et al., 1987). At the same time, however, left realists do not think the solution to the crime problem lies in the get-tough methods of conservatives. They do not support investing more funds in building new prisons or developing more repressive social control technologies, such as stun belts (Kilborn, 1997). In fact, left realists are concerned with the cost of the criminal justice process, for it is the working class and the poor who invariably bear a disproportionate burden of financing our massively expensive and inefficient legal system, either through taxes or funding cuts to social programs (Matthews, 1987, p. 377).

What, then, works from a left realist perspective? First, left realists emphasize the importance of participatory democracy and accountability in the development of effective crime control policy. Actual and potential victims of crime must mobilize to voice their concerns and their needs with respect to strategies for controlling crime. According to one left realist, "the majority of people who suffer most from crime are critical of existing penal policy and are relatively progressive on the issue" (Young, 1987, p. 355), perhaps because they are also the ones most likely to know someone caught up in the system or to get caught up in the system themselves (but see also Council on State Governments/Eastern Regional Conference, 1999). At the same time, left realists advocate what they call **preemptive deterrence**, that is, criminologists and other social activists working within specific neighborhoods to prevent crime rather than relying on increased police surveillance. They also suggest programs to bring about **demarginalization** or, more specifically, programs that reintegrate into the community members, especially jobless young men, who have come to see themselves as "outsiders" with nothing to lose and much to gain through crime (Lea & Young, 1984).

A major strength of left realism is its recognition of the severely negative impact of crime on the lives of the disadvantaged and its demand that radical criminologists not only take this situation seriously, but also work to develop effective but nonoppressive crime control policies. Nevertheless, left realism has also been criticized for a number of reasons. For instance, some observers point out that although left realists are sensitive to class and race issues, they have neglected gender issues, particularly violence against women, a topic we will take up in Chapter 7. In addition, critics argue that left realists have too simplistic a view of communities, overlooking the fact that there are often racist and sexist divisions within neighborhoods that put groups in conflict over "community concerns and priorities." These problems could be worsened through "community control" of decision making (DeKeseredy & Schwartz, 1996; see also Schwartz, 1991, for additional criticisms). And while the left realist perspective is provocative, there are few tests of its empirical validity (but see Lea & Young, 1986). Left realists, though, are committed to this enterprise:

> The world is full of surprises. The social reality of crime is inevitably far more complex than available theories. Thus there is a need to engage in detailed empirical investigation of the object in every case rather than dogmatically reiterate abstract beliefs. (Matthews, 1987, p. 377)

Peacemaking Criminology

Another group of radical criminologists who are concerned about the increasing harshness of the criminal justice system has developed a perspective called **peacemaking criminology**. Among those at the forefront of developing this position are *Hal Pepinsky* and *Richard Quinney* (1991), whose work on crime and oppression we discussed earlier in this chapter.

Peacemaking criminologists see crime as one of many forms of violence perpetrated in our society and others. Moreover, violence only begets more violence, so if we respond to crime with harsh, punitive social control measures, we are not likely to see a reduction in crime, but rather the opposite: more crime. Indeed, peacemaking criminologists describe our current criminal justice system as a system of warmaking. It is no coincidence that our country's crime control strategies are collectively referred to as the "war on crime" and that specific programs are depicted as campaigns to fight and wipe out certain types of offenses. In contrast, peacemaking criminologists theorize that crime as violence is suffering, so to end crime we must end suffering, not impose more suffering through legal penalties. How do we end suffering? Like other radical criminologists, peacemaking criminologists see this as coming about only with a fundamental transformation in our social structure that allows for an equitable distribution of resources, including a balance of power among social groups.

Most readers are probably thinking this goal is worthy, but hardly realistic. Peacemaking criminologists are not so naive as to think that this goal can be achieved quickly or easily. Nevertheless, they believe that each individual criminologist who is committed to peacemaking instead of warmaking can help bring about change. As Pepinsky (1999) explains, peacemaking on a macro level first requires self-transformation:

> Given that meaningful changes in the culture sufficient enough to make judges, offenders, journalists, police officers, victims, attorneys, and the like, more reliable overall will take generations, the change *we* create by doing what it takes to make peace with anyone, anywhere, anytime is a logical starting place for all of us. In any interaction, we gain control by looking past the difficulties of the moment confronting us, tempering our urges to lash out or to say the polite and proper thing with conscious self-awareness of what tenor of response we can anticipate. (p. 67)

Besides the efforts of individual criminologists and others to make peace, peacemaking criminologists also advocate for specific immediate changes in the practice of criminal justice. For example, they encourage programs that bring offenders and victims together for mediation, conflict resolution, and reconciliation rather than processing through the adversarial system of our courts. In addition, they favor nonpunitive responses to offenders, especially those who have committed minor crimes or who are first-time offenders. These responses include having the offender apologize to the victim, make restitution by paying the victim back and/or paying the community back through service, and requiring the offender to make charitable donations.

Peacemaking criminologist Hal Pepinsky (1999, p. 57) states that peacemakers must be willing to listen "most carefully to [their] harshest or most immediate critics," and certainly peacemaking criminology has been subject to critical evaluation. A major concern is that the nonpunitive crime control strategies recommended by peacemaking criminologists should be implemented cautiously. DeKeseredy and Schwartz (1996) note that some of these ideas have been successfully put into practice in Canada and on a smaller scale in the United States and other countries. Box 6.2 discusses one of the ways this is being done in Australia and elsewhere. However, DeKeseredy and Schwartz (1996) along with others (e.g., Selva & Bohm, 1987) point out that the nonpunitive nature of these programs could easily be transformed into more severe sanctions. For example, judges who wish to impose harsh sentences to "teach offenders a lesson" can, if they choose, require restitution *and* community service *and* charitable donations—a sentence that may actually impose greater hardship on indigent defendants than a year on probation or thirty days detention. In addition, some criminologists are concerned that the crime control strategies of peacemaking criminology could, in practice, have a "net-widening" impact for the criminal justice system by encouraging police to arrest, prosecutors to charge, and judges to sentence more individuals whom they might have previously decided to simply warn and give a second

B O X 6.2 HOW THE WORLD SEES IT

Nonpunitive Intervention: The Family Group Conference Model

The Family Group Conference model is based on a conflict resolution process first used by the Maori people of New Zealand. In 1989, it was incorporated into New Zealand's legal system. In 1991, it was introduced in Australia and, largely through the efforts of David Moore and John McDonald (2000), it has been applied in noncriminal justice settings to resolve conflicts such as workplace disputes. The growing popularity of the Family Group Conference model lies largely with the fact that it can successfully address problems such as juvenile offending without the punitive, bureaucratic, and costly intervention of the courts and correctional system, which many advocates feel often make matters worse. To understand this position, let's compare the traditional model of intervention with the Family Group Conference model when a juvenile is arrested for an offense.*

In Australia, when a juvenile is arrested and admits to having committed an offense, the police decide how to respond: Either the youth is warned and released, or he or she is brought before a court. In most cases, when the youth has committed what we in the United States would label a status offense (e.g., drinking), the police issue an official warning (or *caution*, as it is called in Australia). However, if the offense is more serious, such as a burglary or an assault, the police usually bring the offender before a court. One criticism of using the courts is that those closest to the offender are typically excluded from the judicial process. A parent, other relatives, and friends may be present in court, but they are not allowed to participate in the proceedings. A second criticism of using the courts is that their focus is solely on determin-

ing the guilt or innocence of the offender, not with making amends between the offender and the victim. In a criminal case, the victim is part of the process only as a witness. The courts also typically overlook the fact that in addition to the victim, there are many others affected by the crime, including the victim's family and friends, neighbors, employer, and co-workers. In court, the effects of the crime on these people is rarely considered; the court evaluates the evidence to determine the guilt of the offender and, if found guilty, imposes a sentence (i.e., a punishment).

This is the system of judicial intervention most familiar to people in Australia as well as the United States. The Family Group Conference works much differently. When a juvenile is arrested and admits to an offense, the police have another option: They can call in professionals trained in the conferencing method to organize a group conference. The conference facilitators first invite anyone legitimately connected with the offense to participate in a meeting at a convenient, comfortable, and nonthreatening location. Those invited would include the victim, the victim's family and friends, the offender, and the offender's family and friends. At the meeting, a facilitator begins by asking the offender to describe what he or she did and how it has affected other people. Then the victim is asked to speak: to describe what happened and how the crime has affected his or her life. The victim's family and friends are invited to share their feelings, and following them, the offender's family and friends are asked to state how the crime has impacted them. Once everyone assembled who wishes to speak has had the opportunity, the victim is asked to offer his or her ideas about what can be done to make amends; that is, how can the harm caused by the offender's actions be repaired? The group discusses the victim's ideas, contributing some of their own, with the role of the facilitator being

*We are grateful to John McDonald and David Moore of Transformative Justice Australia (Sydney) for generously sharing with us the philosophy and practice of the Family Group Conferencing model as well as their experiences as conference facilitators.

(continued)

BOX **6.2**   Continued

to negotiate an agreement between the victim and the offender about how the offender will make amends. The agreement is negotiated within the context of the group because the model recognizes that both the offender and the victim need the support of those who care about them to not only work out the terms of the agreement, but also to make sure the terms are fulfilled. It may require more than one meeting to reach an agreement, but once the terms have been worked out, those involved sign a document stating their willingness to carry out the agreement. The group approach ensures that the offender receives support from his or her family and friends for repairing the harm done, and the victim and his or her family and friends are assured that others will help the offender make amends.

This description of the Family Group Conference shows clearly that the goal is not determining an offender's guilt or innocence, but rather figuring out who has been wronged by whom and how the wrong can be righted. The model recognizes that when a crime is committed, it is committed in the context of a community and many more people than just the offender and the victim are affected. The model strives to build connections among community members, including the offender's and victim's family and friends. The offender is not shamed and then isolated from the community to serve out a jail or prison sentence while the victim is left to cope with the physical, emotional, and financial consequences of victimization. Instead, the offender is shamed, but reintegrated into the community, the victim is compensated in some way, and both the offender and victim receive the support of those who care about them.

Although the Family Group Conference model is currently being used on a very limited basis even in New Zealand and Australia, it is gaining attention throughout the world, including in the United States, Canada, and Great Britain.

chance. "People who would not be 'under the net' of the criminal justice system might now be drawn into it" under the pretense of doing them and society some "good" (DeKeseredy & Schwartz, 1996, p. 272).

Peacemaking criminology is clearly one of the newest theoretical perspectives in the discipline. Although it, too, will need to withstand empirical testing, it is already provoking considerable debate and is even leading some criminologists to reconsider their personal responses to conflicts in everyday life (Pepinsky, 1999).

Postmodern Criminology

Throughout this text, we have emphasized the need to empirically test each theory we have discussed. Underlying this position are the assumptions that theory can be evaluated using scientific methods and that the data we collect using these methods allow us to determine which theory is *true*. Indeed, the discipline of criminology, like the other social *sciences*, has been built on the belief that truth is knowable. There is, however, a group of radical criminologists who dispute these claims. Their perspective is called **postmodern criminology**.

Postmodern theory has its origins in Europe, primarily France and Germany, where intellectuals developed it as a critique of philosophy and modernity. It began to gain a sizeable following in the United States during the 1980s and 1990s, especially among faculty who specialize in literary criticism in university English departments. These academics focused on how language, whether written, spoken, or even acted out, helps to construct reality (Wonders, 1999). You may well be asking yourself how a perspective popular with English professors migrated to criminology. To answer your question, let's consider some of the central ideas of postmodernism.

First, postmodernists reject the notion of objectivity and question whether it is possible to discover truth using the scientific method or any other method for that matter. They see "truth" as a social construction; it is, as Wonders (1999, p. 116) puts it, "just one possible story about reality." What is accepted as truth changes over time, and across places, and from one "storyteller" to another. This does not mean that truth doesn't exist, but rather that "there is no way to test whether one story is closer to the truth than any other" (Flax, 1992, p. 454). In short, truth is *contingent* on many factors, including history and present circumstances, both personal and social, a fact that makes truth not absolute, but instead partial and fluid. One of the research goals of the postmodernist, then, is to learn how truth is constructed through everyday social interaction, a goal best accomplished using qualitative research methods (e.g., unstructured interviews, observations) rather than the quantitative methods more common in criminological studies (see Appendix).

While truth is socially constructed and, therefore, variable, so too is one's ability to participate in the social construction of truth and to get others to accept one's truth. In other words, some individuals and groups—the more powerful segments of our society—are better able than others to construct and disseminate "truth." One of the truths they construct has to do with *difference*, which is typically constructed as a dichotomy, and the two groups formed by the dichotomy of difference are imbued with unequal value; one is privileged over the other. The construction of dichotomous differences affects individual and group identities. Identity is the endproduct of a particular type of social construction postmodernists called **positionality**, "the ongoing process by which we attribute meaning to things, and then the things take on the meaning we have given them" (Wonders, 1999, p. 118). The example Wonders (1999) uses nicely illustrates how positionality works:

> [I]f the state claims young people who use drugs are criminal (rather than "ill," as is done in many other industrialized countries), then the state has played an active role in shaping the identities of teenagers and others who use drugs—it has changed who they are. But positionality goes further by arguing that through this discursive process—through the use of language and words—the word *criminal* comes to be associated with who it is applied to. (p. 118)

In the United States, the word *criminal* is most often associated with young Black men, so that in the mind's eye of many members of the general public, criminal = young Black man.

We have seen that radical criminologists are fundamentally concerned with power differences in our society and how these affect what is defined as crime, who is labeled criminal, and how the criminal justice system operates. Postmodern criminologists are no exception. However, they look not only at the power that institutions and groups wield through coercion or force, but also at how power is exercised in everyday social interactions between ordinary individuals and through cultural symbols, such as language (e.g., how a situation is described, explained, or understood) and objects (e.g., what meaning is attached to a pair of Nike Air Jordans, a particular make of car, the American flag) (Wonders, 1999). Postmodernists look at the convergence of macro- and micro-level sources and expressions of power. Henry and Milovanovic (1996), for example, see the meaning of crime as being co-produced by individuals who engage in it, who attempt to control it, and who study it. One of the goals of postmodern criminologists is to *deconstruct* the meanings and social processes we attach to crime and justice. Such efforts show how power operates through language, symbols, and everyday interactions to often produce harmful outcomes. This work calls into question what we have come to take for granted—as criminologists, criminal justice personnel, members of the general public—as the "reality" of crime (see Arrigo, 1995; Henry & Milovanovic, 1996; Michalowski, 1993).

Postmodern criminologists have been criticized for being apolitical or for adopting a stance of political neutrality rather than offering useful suggestions for public policy and social activism (Dews, 1987; Schwartz & Friedrichs, 1994). This criticism, however, is only partially justifiable. Given the postmodern emphasis on social constructions and their strongly relativist stance, it is not surprising that postmodernists do not believe in universal solutions to any social problem nor that any one group or individual can speak on behalf of others, since what might be helpful or just for one may not be helpful or just for others. Nevertheless, this "does not mean that they believe that we can afford to ignore our responsibility to make the best decisions we can, for the moment. In fact, once we understand that we shape the world and can change it, we have perhaps a greater responsibility to make choices that construct the world in ways that we can live with and feel good about" (Wonders, 1999, p. 122). Like peacemaking criminologists, postmodernists believe that the social construction of justice rather than injustice takes place not only on an institutional level, but also in one's daily life as we make decisions about how we treat others. Each time we choose to reduce harm rather than inflict it, we are helping to shape a more just world. Through deconstruction, we can also actively resist the negative, harmful, and hierarchical group identities that have been constructed by the powerful for the oppressed (Grant, 1993). At the same time, however, postmodernists caution that we must be careful not to assume that we know what is "best" for oppressed groups. "[L]ocal people everywhere need to develop their own definitions of their experiences and to work out their own methods of resistance to oppression" (DeKeseredy & Schwartz, 1996, p. 274). There are, of course, many criminologists who find these postmodernist strategies unsatisfying or insufficient.

Although we have presented postmodern criminology as a single perspective, it is important to keep in mind that there are many variations of postmodernism (Rosenau, 1992). No doubt, many criminologists who call themselves postmodernists will object to our characterization of it here. It is also the case that some postmodern theorists are working to blend the ideas of postmodernism with other theoretical perspectives. As we will see in Chapter 7, one of the more successful of these efforts has produced postmodern feminism.

Summary and Conclusion

In this chapter, we examined a variety of theories that collectively may be categorized as radical criminology. This discussion encompassed instrumental Marxism, structural Marxism, structural criminology, left realism, peacemaking criminology, and postmodern criminology. We considered the strengths and weaknesses of each perspective, but noted that the most recent developments in radical criminology are already playing a major part in shaping the direction of future research and theorizing in the discipline.

Of course, it is always risky to make predictions about the future. Attempts by colleagues in the past have too often proved wrong. Consider, for example, Richard Sparks's (1980) assessment that radical criminology would never have a great effect on criminological thought. As we have seen in this chapter, however, radical criminology has enjoyed increased interest and has experienced substantial growth, stemming largely from the critically introspective debate waged by radical criminologists themselves. One prediction we would be willing to offer at this point is that the future of criminological theory will be heavily influenced by the work of feminist criminologists, who in the past two and half decades have arguably done nothing less than revolutionize our field. We will conclude the book, therefore, with a discussion of feminist criminology.

KEY TERMS

demarginalization—a crime reduction strategy advocated by left realist criminologists that involves developing programs that reintegrate into the community members, especially jobless young men, who have come to see themselves as outsiders with nothing to lose and much to gain through crime.

instrumental Marxism—the theoretical perspective that sees law, law enforcement agencies, and government itself as tools or instruments of the ruling class to maintain their advantageous position in society and to control those who pose a threat to that position.

left realism—a branch of radical criminology that includes an examination of crimes by the wealthy, but also emphasizes the importance of taking street crime seriously as a problem committed primarily by the poor against the poor.

peacemaking criminology—a branch of radical criminology that sees crime as one of many forms of violence that can be most successfully addressed through nonviolent, harm-reduction measures rather than through harsh, punitive social control techniques.

positionality—the ongoing process, studied by postmodern criminologists, by which we attribute meaning to things and then the things take on the meaning we have given them.

postmodern criminology—a branch of radical criminology that questions our ability to know truth since truth is socially constructed through everyday interactions and language, and that sees as a major goal of the field the deconstruction of the meanings and processes we attach to crime and criminal justice.

preemptive deterrence—a crime reduction strategy advocated by left realist criminologists that involves criminologists and other social activists working within specific neighborhoods to prevent crime rather than neighborhoods relying on increased police surveillance and other repressive control techniques.

radical criminology—a body of diverse theories that nonetheless collectively emphasize the role of inequality in crime causation and criminal justice processes as well as the necessity for fundamental social structural change in order to reduce crime and oppression.

structural criminology—a theoretical perspective that gives primacy to the role of power relations in understanding and undertaking research on crime.

structural Marxism—the theoretical perspective that sees law as an attempt to resolve societal crises precipitated by the inherent contradictions of capitalism.

SUGGESTED READINGS

Arrigo, B. A. (Ed.). (1999). *Social justice, criminal justice*. Belmont, CA: Wadsworth. A collection of essays by leading theorists in radical criminology who explore the major principles of some of the newest theoretical developments in the field, including those we have discussed in this chapter and others, such as chaos theory.

Kauzlarich, D., & Kramer, R. C. (1998). *Crimes of the American nuclear state: At home and abroad*. Boston: Northeastern University Press. A thorough—and often frightening—study by two well-known radical criminologists who apply Marxist theory in their analysis of governmental deviance perpetrated in the name of "national security."

Mann, C. R., & Zatz, M. S. (Eds.). (1998). *Images of color, images of crime*. Los Angeles: Roxbury. A collection of essays that examine racial discrimination in the criminal justice system as well as effects on people of color of racial stereotyping by politicians and the media.

Pepinsky, H., & Quinney, R. (Eds.). (1991). *Criminology as peacemaking*. Bloomington, IN: Indiana University Press. The primer on peacemaking criminology edited by two of its founding theorists.

NOTES

1. Bohm (1982) provides an excellent analysis of the differences between these various theoretical branches, pointing out that what critics typically refer to as radical criminology is a false, monolithic conception that fails to consider the significant philosophical, theoretical, and practical differences among those who work within this framework. Bohm identifies other branches as well, including "dialectical" criminology, "materialist" criminology, and "socialist" criminology. Some criminologists also include feminist criminology in their discussions of radical criminology. However, we think feminist criminology has unique features that set it apart from other radical theories in addition to having a unique impact on the field as a whole. Consequently, we discuss feminist criminology separately in Chapter 7.

2. This point is underlined by Lynch and Groves (1986) in the title they chose for the chapter in which this quote appears: "Incipient Radicalism: Conflict and Labeling Approaches."

3. Readers are encouraged to consult both Bohm (1982) and Lynch and Groves (1986) for a more detailed discussion of the differences among these three perspectives. It should also be noted that a number of early radical writers identified their position as conflict theory, but because of the differences between their approaches and that of theorists such as Vold and Dahrendorf, it became necessary to distinguish the former as Marxist conflict theory. One of the reasons we chose to use the term *radical criminology* to refer to the theories in this chapter was to avoid the confusion that might arise from discussing theories with the same names, but differing points of view.

4. Our discussion of Bonger's work relies heavily on Taylor et al.'s (1973) excellent critical analysis of his work.

5. Again, readers are directed to Taylor et al. (1973) for an insightful and thorough critique of Bonger's perspective. In addition, *Criminality and Economic Conditions* was reissued by Indiana University Press in 1969. Although an abridged version of the original, the book contains a valuable introduction by criminologist Austin Turk. For a provocative contemporary account of how inequalities of wealth generate humiliation which, in turn, produces crime, see Braithwaite (1991).

6. Conflict between radical criminologists and traditional criminologists was common and sometimes cost people their jobs. Herman Schwendinger, for instance, was denied tenure at Berkeley, a decision many considered a punishment for his radical views and activism. Shortly thereafter, the entire school of criminology at Berkeley was closed in what many observers also saw as a political move by the University's administration to quash the radical movement (Lynch & Groves, 1986).

7. Martin et al. (1990) provide a fascinating biography of Quinney in addition to their analysis of his research and theorizing. It should also be pointed out that Quinney has continued to develop and revise his positions on crime, law, and society as a whole, combining his interpretation of Marxism with other philosophies, including Buddhism, Christian socialism, and

liberation theology. We will discuss some of these recent developments later in this chapter when we look at peacemaking criminology. Readers should also consult some of Quinney's recent books, including *Providence* (1980), *Journey to a Far Place: Autobiographical Reflections* (1991), and *For the Time Being* (1998), for insight into the ideas and lived experiences of this remarkable criminologist.

8. Readers may recognize in this argument elements of the theories discussed in Chapter 4. Lynch and Groves (1986), in fact, devote considerable attention to the compatibility between radical criminology and various other criminological perspectives, including strain theory and control theory.

9. By larger crimes, Hagan means crimes that exact a greater toll in terms of monetary losses, physical damage, injuries, and death than ordinary street crimes.

10. Of course, we understand that some of our colleagues may disagree with our choices and our rationale for them. Some might prefer a discussion of anarchist criminology, for example, or chaos theory. We suggest readers consult Arrigo (1999) for an excellent review of these perspectives and other radical theories.

11. In adopting the label *left* realist, left realist criminologists are distinguishing their brand of realism from that of conservative criminologists, such as James Q. Wilson and Ernest Van den Haag, who reacted against liberal and radical positions in criminology and argued that the discipline needed to become more "practical" or "realistic." These conservatives, therefore, are often referred to as *right realists*. For a more detailed discussion of the differences between right and left realism, see Matthews, 1987.

12. You probably recognize in left realism aspects of other theories we have discussed in earlier chapters (for example, social disorganization theory and strain theory). Left realism, in fact, has been praised for "synthesizing prior theories to extract what value they have and placing these ideas in new frameworks" (DeKeseredy & Schwartz, 1996, p. 257).

7 Gender, Crime, and Justice: Feminist Criminologies

As we saw in Chapter 6, the late 1960s and early 1970s were tumultuous years in the United States, and academic disciplines did not escape—nor hide from—the upheaval. Some academics, including some criminologists, became socially active, protesting against the War in Vietnam, calling for the resignation and prosecution of corrupt politicians following the Watergate scandal, and participating in civil rights demonstrations to win equal rights for African Americans. They questioned the traditional focus of criminological theory on street crime and the contention that crime is concentrated in the lower classes. They also questioned the legitimacy and purported value neutrality of the legal system, identifying its class and race biases. It was during this social and political (re)awakening in criminology that contemporary radical criminological theories were born, drawing in particular on the work of Karl Marx and Willem Bonger.

Nevertheless, while these radical theories offered a sweeping critique of what were considered mainstream criminological perspectives, especially those in the positivist tradition, and reframed the theoretical and methodological questions with which criminologists should occupy themselves, something was missing. There was at least one way in which these radical theories were no different from the theories of which they were so critical: They continued to overlook the *gendered* nature of criminal offending, criminal victimization, and criminal justice processing. They remained preoccupied with male offenders and crimes committed mostly by men and boys—with the exception of men's violence against women—and neglected female offenders and the crimes they were most likely to commit. This was hardly surprising, given that the discipline—like our society—was unquestionably male-dominated. But the civil rights and anti-war movements were not the only social movements influencing criminologists at the time. Another social movement that had—and continues to have—a significant impact on criminology, as well as on society as a whole, is *feminism*.

Before we look at feminist criminology, let's first discuss feminism in general, since many people today know little about its origins, principles, and goals and are informed only by stereotyped images, such as those portrayed in popular media.

What Is Feminism?

Feminism is not a single, unified theory, but rather a group of related theories (Delmar, 1986). However, there are several ideas that virtually all feminist-identified perspectives share.

At the core of feminism is the recognition of *gender* as a central organizing component of social life. **Gender** is made up of *socially generated* expectations about the attitudes and behaviors of women and men that are typically organized dichotomously as femininity and masculinity respectively, and that are reproduced and transmitted through social learning. This is not to say that biology plays no part in the development of gender. However, feminists stress that it is virtually impossible to separate the precise influences of biology because the process of learning about gender begins immediately after birth. The feminist perspective acknowledges the complex interaction between biology and culture, but assumes that gender is essentially socially created, not innately determined.

The social construction of gender as dichotomous also implies exclusivity: A person is *either* masculine *or* feminine. However, masculinity and femininity are not valued equally in either our society or many others. Thus, a second core principle of feminism is that our society, both on a macro- (structural/institutional) level and a micro- (interpersonal) level is characterized by **sexism**, the differential valuing of one gender over the other. In our society, this sexism takes place within the context of a social system known as a **patriarchy**, in which men dominate women, and what is considered masculine is more highly valued or labeled as more important than what is considered feminine.

The sexism characteristic of our patriarchal society has meant that within the academic disciplines, women have been systematically excluded from many fields not considered "feminine," including criminology. In addition, women have been systematically excluded from the studies conducted by members of male-dominated fields under the assumption that what women do, think, or say is unimportant or uninteresting (Lorber, 1993). Consequently, another core principle of feminism is the inclusion of female experiences and perspectives in all research. This is not to be accomplished by excluding male experiences and perspectives, but feminists deliberately seek to make female voices heard where previously they have been silenced or ignored. For feminists, a major goal of research is to uncover similarities and differences in women's and men's behaviors, attitudes, and experiences to gain a *holistic* understanding of how women and men, because of their different locations in (and imposed valuing by) the social structure, encounter different opportunities and constraints and respond to or resist their relative circumstances (Hess & Ferree, 1987; Offen, 1988).

This last point is important because many people think of feminism as applicable only to so-called "women's issues." While feminists' primary concern is to study women, they view feminism as relevant to the experiences of both sexes. Feminists, as we shall see shortly, have not left the social construction of masculinity unanalyzed. In fact, in studying men's lives, feminists have found that although virtually all men benefit from patriarchy, not all men are equally privileged. "It is thus not women alone who are disadvantaged by the organization of U.S. society but poor people, people of color, and sexual minorities as well" (Bem, 1993, p. 3). Another core principle of feminism, therefore, is recognition that the consequences of sexism are not identical for all groups of women and men. Instead, the effects of gender inequality are made worse by other types of discrimination. Consider, for example, the likely dissimilarities in the lives of a White, middle-class, middle-aged, gay man and a poor, Latina teenager who is pregnant and unmarried. Both may think of themselves as oppressed, but their objective circumstances are very different. Feminists try to account for the gender-based experiences of many diverse groups of women and men in our society. They analyze the inextricable links among *multiple* oppressions: sexism as well as racism, classism, ageism, heterosexism, abilism, and other inequalities (Crenshaw, 1994; King, 1988).

Finally, feminism is not just a theoretical framework; as noted at the outset of this chapter, feminism is a *social movement*, composed of people who act collectively to eliminate sexism and promote gender equity in all areas of social life. The feminist social movement is not new; documents dating to the Middle Ages offer historical evidence of women's protests against patriarchal oppression (Lerner, 1993). However, the first feminist movement in the United States dates from the 1830s to the 1920s. It grew largely out of the movement to abolish slavery, but after the Civil War—and even to the present—it came to be associated with activism to win women the right to vote. Following ratification of the Nineteenth Amendment in 1920, the feminist movement did not disappear, but it did not enjoy the level of activism that it had since the 1830s (Cott, 1987; Taylor, 1990). It was not until the 1960s that feminism experienced a broad-based resurgence.

The impetus for the resurgence of feminism in the 1960s came from a variety of sources. Some trace it to the appointment in 1961 by then-President John F. Kennedy of a federal commission to study the problem of sex discrimination. Others credit the publication in 1963 of Betty Friedan's book, *The Feminine Mystique*, which voiced the unhappiness and boredom of White, educated, middle-class housewives, isolated in what Friedan called "comfortable concentration camps" (their suburban homes). And certainly some women came to feminism from the political left, disillusioned by male dominance within the civil rights and anti–Vietnam War movements. These women were struck by the contradiction between the ideology of equality and freedom espoused by radical men and the men's sexist treatment of women, often relegating women to traditional female roles as cooks, typists, and sexual partners (Evans, 1979; Shulman, 1980).

In short, **feminism** is a school of thought that explains gender in terms of the social structure in which it is constructed and emphasizes the importance of taking collective action to end sexism. Not surprisingly, the diverse sources that gave birth to the second feminist movement also produced diverse branches of feminist theory, each with variations on the core principles we have presented and the strategies for achieving feminist goals. Some observers have identified four types of feminism (liberal, radical, Marxist, and socialist), while others have identified several additional types (e.g., lesbian feminism, psychoanalytic feminism, standpoint feminism, postmodern feminism) (see Beirne & Messerschmidt, 1995; Lorber, 1998). This diversity has found its way into feminist criminological theory as well. According to Jurik (1999, p. 34),

"Beginning in the mid-1970s, feminist-inspired analyses drew attention to the neglect of women and the bias in male-centered theories of crime and criminal justice." As we noted in Chapter 4, some of the first feminist studies of crime focused on changes in female offending as a result of the women's liberation movement. These studies, by Adler (1975) and Simon (1975), were written from a *liberal feminist* perspective. Other, more radical analyses of gender, crime, and victimization were developed from the perspectives of radical feminism and socialist feminism. More perspectives are still emerging, including postmodern feminist criminology. Let's begin our examination of feminist criminologies, then, by looking at the liberal feminist approach. Then we'll discuss radical and socialist feminist theories along with some newly emerging perspectives, keeping in mind that these theories, despite their diversity, do not represent the full range of feminist criminologies.

Liberal Feminism and Criminology

Liberal feminism focuses on securing the same legal rights for women that men enjoy. Liberal feminists believe that one cause of gender inequality is blocked opportunities, so a goal of their social activism is the removal of any obstacles women face in the paid labor force, education, government, and other social institutions. The main strategy for accomplishing this goal is legal change: abolishing gender discriminatory laws and enacting laws that prohibit gender discrimination. However, legal change is not enough, since liberal feminists also believe that gender inequality derives from the way males and females are socialized in our society. Males are socialized to be aggressive, independent, and competitive, whereas females are socialized to be passive, dependent, and nurturing. Thus, a second goal of liberal feminists is to revise gender socialization practices so that males and females learn to be more alike.

In Chapter 4, we discussed the emancipation theory of female crime developed independently by Freda Adler (1975) and Rita James Simon (1975). Since we examined Adler's and Simon's ideas and research extensively in that chapter, we will only quickly review the basic premise of the theory here. Emancipation theory says that female offending is an outgrowth of the women's liberation movement. This movement has opened more opportunities to women to participate in legitimate activities, such as working in the paid labor force, and has also encouraged women to be more assertive, independent, and competitive (that is, more like men). As women gain more legitimate opportunities, they also have more occasions to participate in illegitimate activities. Their new-found assertiveness, independence, and competitiveness will further empower them to pursue both types of activities. Adler and Simon used this idea to explain what they saw as a rising crime rate among women and the increasing "masculinization" of women's criminality.

It is easy to see that emancipation theory is the application of liberal feminist ideas to traditional opportunity theory. In Chapter 4, we offered an extensive critique of emancipation theory as well as Adler's and Simon's analyses of the data on changing crime rates. Readers may wish to review that discussion before continuing this chapter. Here, however, we will reexamine what can be called the "gender gap" in crime, since many feminist theories have been developed specifically to explain women's lower rates of offending and differences in the types of crimes women and men commit. We will then consider another liberal feminist theory of crime, Hagan's power-control theory.

The Gender Gap in Crime

You will recall from Chapter 4 that although Adler (1975) and Simon (1975) argued that women's rate of offending was increasing more rapidly than that of men, subsequent analyses did not support this claim. Looking at Table 7.1 on page 214, in fact, we see that while the arrest of women has increased substantially in recent years, women's arrest rates are still dramatically lower than men's for all types of crimes except prostitution and commercialized vice. As Table 7.1 shows, crime remains, to a large extent, a male enterprise. Over 79 percent of those arrested in the United States in 1996 were males; males accounted for 84.9 percent of individuals arrested for violent crimes and 71.9 percent of individuals arrested for proporty crimes. Moreover, researchers have found that, for the most part, there has been neither a significant widening nor a significant narrowing of the gender gap in arrests over the past several decades (Chesney-Lind, 1997). However, there are important exceptions to this general pattern. Specifically, the increase in arrests of women is accounted for almost entirely by just five types of crimes: larceny theft, forgery/counterfeiting, fraud, embezzlement, and drug offenses.

As we stated in Chapter 4, the property crimes that have shown increases in women's arrest rates—larceny theft, forgery/counterfeiting, fraud, and embezzlement—are not high-stakes white-collar crimes committed by "liberated" women. These crimes result in low-level financial gains for female offenders. In addition, research indicates that the typical female offender is young, non-White, poor, a high school dropout, and a single mother (Arnold, 1990; Chesney-Lind, 1997; Gilfus, 1992). "These women rather than being recipients of expanded rights and opportunities gained by the women's movement, are, instead, witnessing declining survival options" (Crites, 1976, p. 37).

How, then, can we explain increases in women's arrest rates for these property crimes and for drug offenses? Box 7.1 on pages 215–216 discusses one explanation, which calls into question what is known as the **chivalry** or **paternalism hypothesis**: the position that because females are generally law-abiding and, when they do offend, their crimes are relatively minor, they are treated more leniently than male offenders by the criminal justice system. Another explanation, however, has been offered by criminologist John Hagan, whose power-control theory we will examine next.

Power-Control Theory

Some criminologists classify John Hagan's *power-control theory* as a type of control theory, like Hirschi's (1969), which we discussed in Chapter 5. However, unlike Hirschi and other control theorists, Hagan's theory is a direct attempt to explain gender differences in criminal offending, specifically delinquency. Moreover, we discuss

TABLE 7.1   Total Arrest Trends by Sex, 1987–1996

Offense Charged	Males			Female		
	1987	1996	% Change	1987	1996	% Change
Murder and nonnegligent manslaughter	12,247	12,062	−1.5	1,719	1,384	−19.5
Forcible rape	24,551	21,505	−12.4	299	247	−17.4
Robbery	93,885	101,998	+8.6	8,431	11,091	+31.6
Aggravated assault	209,782	284,004	+35.4	31,716	61,640	+94.3
Burglary	264,041	209,076	−20.8	24,442	27,190	+11.2
Larceny-theft	663,264	655,775	−1.1	297,624	337,434	+13.4
Motor vehicle theft	106,604	104,562	−1.9	11,454	16,427	+43.4
Arson	10,144	10,431	+2.8	1,603	1,860	+16.0
Crime Index total*	1,384,518	1,399,413	+1.1	377,288	457,273	+21.2
Other assaults	454,944	695,386	+52.9	81,583	177,644	+117.7
Forgery and counterfeiting	39,931	51,372	+28.7	21,056	28,105	+33.5
Fraud	127,472	168,385	+32.1	98,537	116,746	+18.5
Embezzlement	5,355	5,633	+5.2	3,329	4,619	+38.8
Stolen property: buying, receiving, possessing	86,771	84,867	−2.2	11,419	14,435	+26.4
Vandalism	160,482	182,709	+13.9	19,222	29,336	+52.6
Weapons: carrying, possessing	123,403	135,565	+9.9	10,177	11,637	+26.4
Prostitution and commercialized vice	29,335	30,657	+4.5	56,253	46,097	−18.1
Sex offenses (except forcible rape and prostitution)	62,263	59,062	−5.1	5,026	5,324	+5.9
Drug abuse violations	554,554	857,057	+54.5	99,872	173,831	+74.1
Gambling	16,811	13,834	−17.7	2,747	2,206	−19.7
Offenses against family and children	30,037	61,308	+104.1	6,493	19,263	+196.7
Driving under the influence	983,915	756,935	−23.1	127,476	130,246	+2.2
Liquor laws	320,504	352,456	+10.0	69,066	83,737	+21.2
Drunkenness	547,595	422,6055	−22.8	54,833	57,656	+5.1
Disorderly conduct	389,340	437,824	+12.5	90,856	116,257	+28.0
Vagrancy	27,324	16,168	−40.8	3,439	4,135	+20.2
All other offenses (except traffic)	1,624,731	2,039,086	+25.5	297,922	465,210	+56.2
Total arrests	7,061,872	7,918,554	+12.1	1,512,860	2,056,390	+35.9

*The Index Crimes are the eight crimes considered most serious by the F.B.I.

Source: Federal Bureau of Investigation, 1997, p. 219.

BOX 7.1   CONTROVERSY AND DEBATE

Is Chivalry Dead in the Criminal Justice System?
Was It Ever Alive?

One version of liberal feminist emancipation theory explains increases in female arrest and conviction rates in terms of the end of chivalry in the criminal justice system. It is argued that as a result of the women's movement, police, prosecutors, and judges no longer treat women as leniently as they once did. They are more willing to arrest, prosecute, convict, and send women to prison in the name of "gender equality." Some observers, however, question whether women were ever treated leniently or "chivalrously" by the criminal justice system. And others believe that the "get tough, lock 'em up" approach to crime, which now characterizes criminal justice policy in the United States, has negatively affected both female and male offenders. What do the data show? A thorough analysis of all phases of criminal justice processing is beyond the scope of this book. Our brief discussion will focus only on sentencing.

Early studies of sentencing disparities between male and female offenders showed that women were given preferential treatment by the courts and were less likely than men to receive prison sentences for their crimes (Faine & Bohlander, 1976; Nagel & Weitzman, 1972). A weakness in this early research, however, is that it did not control for the less serious nature of most women's crimes (Chesney-Lind, 1997). One recent study that took into account such factors as type of offense and prior convictions showed that offense severity and prior record have the largest effects on sentencing for both male and female offenders, and that when men and women appear in court under similar circumstances—that is, charged with similar crimes and coming from similar backgrounds—they are treated alike (Steffensmeier et al., 1993). Other researchers argue that an offender's background often has the greatest influence on sentencing outcomes. For example, studies show that the perceived *respectability* (in terms of conformity to traditional gender norms) of the offender, male or female, influences sentencing. Married, employed men with no prior criminal record—that is, men who conform to the gender prescription of "respectable" masculinity—are sentenced more leniently than single, unemployed men with previous arrests or convictions. This is especially true for Black men; single Black men are sentenced more harshly than single White men (Daly, 1994; Miethe & Moore, 1986; Myers & Talarico, 1986; see also Chapter 6).

Similarly, women who conform to a traditional model of femininity—for instance, economic dependence on a man, no evidence of drug or alcohol use, no evidence of sexual deviance—may receive lighter sentences than women deemed less "respectable" by the courts (Daly, 1994). However, judges are not inclined to give female drug offenders a "break" because they see them as being as likely as male drug offenders to get in trouble again (Steffensmeier et al., 1993). Not surprisingly, then, most incarcerated women are young, poor, Black single mothers, who have committed petty property crimes or drug offenses, usually drug possession rather than drug trafficking (Bush-Baskette, 1998; Chesney-Lind, 1997).

One way that the "get tough, lock 'em up" approach to crime control has manifested itself in recent years has been in the imposition of longer sentences. Again, race and sex intersect to produce differential outcomes. Researchers report that not only are women of color more likely to be sentenced to prison, but the actual time they serve is longer than the time served by White women. Mann (1989) found, for example, that although the White women in her study who were convicted of crimes against the person received sentences twice as long as those of the African American women convicted of the same crimes, the African American women actually stayed in prison longer than the White women (see also

(continued)

BOX 7.1   Continued

Bush-Baskette, 1998; Mann, 1995; Mauer & Hauling, 1995; and Chapter 6).

Finally, the "get tough" approach to crime control, emphasizing punishment over rehabilitation, also appears to have resulted in a greater willingness to sentence offenders, including women, to death. In 1998, the ratio of men to women on death row was 70:1, but there were strong indications that states were increasingly willing to execute women. Within the first three months of 1998, two women were executed; prior to that time, only one woman had been executed in the United States since the death penalty was reinstated in 1977. The dominant attitude expressed by the general public has been that an offender's sex should have no bearing on whether she or he is executed (Verhovek, 1998; see also Chapter 1).

The data reviewed here indicate that the criminal justice system has not been especially chivalrous in the past; leniency has been shown toward women *and* men who adhere most closely to traditional gender norms for their sex. In recent years, the "get tough" approach to crime control has resulted in harsher treatment of both women and men, especially non-White women and men. However, because women commit fewer and less serious crimes than men overall, this conservative shift in criminal justice policy has had a greater negative impact on them, resulting in what Chesney-Lind (1997, p. 151) refers to as "equality with a vengeance when it comes to the punishment of crime." And it is women of color who are bearing the brunt of this growing punitiveness.

power-control theory in this section because we think it falls squarely within the framework of liberal feminism.

Hagan (1989; Hagan et al., 1987) begins with the observation that males and females in our society are socialized differently, and certainly there is ample evidence that documents this differential gender socialization. Many studies show that parents impose more restrictions on daughters than on sons, particularly during adolescence. But, Hagan observes, a number of researchers have also found that social class is a mediating factor in gender socialization. They report that lower-class parents are more rigid in socializing their children according to traditional gender norms, while middle- and upper-class parents tend to give their children more freedom, at least during childhood and early adolescence.

Hagan contends that differences in male and female delinquency rates reflect these differential socialization experiences. He grounds his theory, however, on the premise that the socialization that takes place in the family depends in large part on parents' experiences in the workplace. Power relations within the family are derived from power relations within the workplace. For Hagan, therein lies the relationship between class relations and delinquency:

> The particular form of structural criminology that we propose here, power-control theory, argues that to understand the effects of class position in the workplace on crime and delinquency, it is important to trace the way that work relations structure female relations, particularly relations between fathers and mothers and, in turn, relations between parents and their children, especially mothers and their daughters. (Hagan, 1989, p. 13)

In short, Hagan proposes that the gendered division of power in the home is a reproduction of the power and other resources that fathers and mothers have at work.

Hagan identifies three types of two-parent families: matriarchal, patriarchal, and egalitarian or balanced (McCarthy et al., 1999). In matriarchal families, the wife/mother who works outside the home enjoys a higher workplace class position than her spouse. The greater resources she accrues at work afford her greater power at home, such as a greater say in decision making. However, Hagan and his colleagues (McCarthy et al., 1999) report that matriarchal families are rare; in their research, they were unable to find enough matriarchal families to include in the analysis (less than 7 percent of their sample). More common are patriarchal and egaliatrian or balanced families.

In the traditional patriarchal family, the gendered division of labor places the husband/father in the paid labor force; he is the family breadwinner. The wife/mother remains at home to care for the household and to socialize the children. Even in patriarchal families where both spouses work, the husband/father enjoys greater resources at work and this transfers to male dominance in the home. The wife/mother accepts this gendered division of power at home. Indeed, she reproduces it through her socialization practices by imposing tighter controls over her daughters than her sons. Consequently, daughters socialized in patriarchal families become like their mothers: domestic, controlled, unlikely to take risks, and, therefore, unlikely to become involved in delinquency. Sons, on the other hand, are subject to less maternal control, are freer to take risks (and to see risk-taking as pleasurable), so they are more likely to engage in delinquent behavior. Hagan contends that this type of family is common among the working class.

In the egalitarian or balanced family, both spouses/parents are likely to work outside the home and to enjoy similar access to power and resources in their workplaces. In these families, mothers exercise less direct control over both their daughters and their sons. The relatively equal dominance of the spouses/parents in the workplace and at home results in daughters and sons being treated more alike. Daughters' behavior in these families is parallel to that of sons; daughters and sons share similar attitudes toward risk-taking and, therefore, delinquency. This type of family is more prevalent, Hagan believes, among the middle class.

In both patriarchal and egaliatarian/balanced families, males are more likely than females to engage in delinquency. However, Hagan predicts that the gap will be narrower in egalitarian/balanced families because girls in these families are more open to risk-taking. In a recent revision of power-control theory, Hagan and his colleagues (McCarthy et al., 1999) argue that a further factor reducing the gender gap in delinquency in egalitarian/balanced families is that mothers in these families *increase* their direct control over sons, while also teaching their sons to reject traditional masculine gender norms that encourage risk-taking and delinquency.

Although Hagan and his colleagues have obtained some support for power-control theory in both its original and slightly revised forms, most other researchers have failed to confirm the theory, and comparison of the studies reveals conflicting results (Chesney-Lind & Sheldon, 1992). For instance, in one study using a national sample, sex differences in delinquency were found regardless of family type, patriarchal or egalitarian/balanced (Morash & Chesney-Lind, 1991). In this study, quality of relationship between mother and child showed a strong negative relationship with delinquency, but this was especially true for boys. In contrast, Heimer and DeCoster (1999), who also used a national sample, found that for boys, violent delinquency is inhibited most by direct parental controls (coercive discipline), while for girls, violent delinquency is inhibited most by indirect parental controls (emotional bonds with the family). In Morash and Chesney-Lind's research, negative sanctions—a factor not studied by Hagan—were related to delinquency for both girls and boys. In addition, they found that a family's social class—apart from family type—showed a strong negative relationship to delinquency for both girls and boys. Heimer and DeCoster (1999) also report that economic disadvantage and marginalization increase the likelihood of violent offending for both girls and boys, although adherence to traditional gender norms lowers this likelihood for girls, but not boys.

Apart from the lack of empirical support, another significant weakness in power-control theory is its limited definition of patriarchal control. In power-control theory, patriarchal control is reduced to parental supervision. It is this narrow conceptualization of patriarchal control that leads Hagan to argue that mothers who work outside the home increase their daughters' likelihood of risk-taking and delinquent behavior. Here we see that power-control theory is essentially a variation of the liberal feminist emancipation theory: Mother's liberation (i.e., employment outside the home and balanced power within the home) contributes to daughters' delinquency (Chesney-Lind, 1997).

One further weakness in power-control theory is that although it claims to establish the relationship between social class and delinquency by examining the reproduction of class relations in the family, it overlooks important class differences among types of family structures. Hagan focuses on two-parent families, but the number of single-parent families has been growing dramatically since the 1970s, increasing from 13 percent of families with dependent children in 1970 to 29 percent of families with dependent children in 1993 (U.S. Department of Commerce, Bureau of the Census, 1997). Most single-parent families (86 percent) are headed by women, and single-parent female-headed families are disproportionately represented among the poor. For instance, consider the data in Table 7.2 Here we see that the median family income of married couple families with both spouses/parents in the paid labor force is nearly three times greater than the median income of single-parent female-headed households. The median income of single-parent male-headed households is almost $10,000 higher than the median income of single-parent female-headed households. We also see in Table 7.2 that these income differences are even greater when race is taken into account; non-White families have significantly lower median incomes than White families regardless of family type, but non-White families headed by women have the lowest median incomes of all. Certainly, the objective life conditions of young women from two-parent families in which both parents work are considerably different from those of young women from single-parent families headed by their mothers, whether the mothers work or not. These differences in objective life conditions may play a significant part in motivations for risk-taking and delinquency apart from mothers' supervision (Chesney-Lind & Sheldon, 1992). Yet, even in their revised version of

TABLE 7.2   Median Family Income by Type of Family and Race/Ethnicity, 1994

	Median Income ($)			
Type of Family	All Families	White	Black	Hispanic
Married couple families	44,959	45,474	40,432	29,621
Wife in paid labor force	53,309	53,977	47,235	38,559
Wife not in paid labor force	31,176	31,747	25,396	20,676
Male householder, wife absent	27,751	29,460	20,977	21,787
Female householder, husband absent	18,236	20,795	13,943	12,117

Source: U.S. Department of Commerce, Bureau of the Census, 1997, p. 471.

power-control theory, Hagan and his colleagues dismiss the importance of considering these differences, noting that they assume single-parent female-headed households are "typically more matriarchal in their structure" and that, in any event, most single mothers involve other adults in their families, including male partners (McCarthy et al., 1999, p. 767).

Just because a single-parent family is headed by a woman does not mean that the family is matriarchal as Hagan and his colleagues have defined the term—that is, having enhanced access to resources in the workplace, which translates into control in the home with implied freedom from male dominance. Given the statistics we have reviewed regarding the economic status of single-parent female-headed households, it hardly appears that they have "enhanced access to resources in the workplace." Moreover, even if a male adult partner is not present in their homes, they are not necessarily free from male dominance, especially since many must rely on the "benevolence" of the male-dominated state—which is not only sexist, but also racist and class-biased—for assistance (see, for example, Edin & Lein, 1997; Fineman, 1996).

One feminist theory that emphasizes the role of the state and, in particular, law in preserving male privilege and female subordination is radical feminism, which we will discuss next.

Radical Feminist Criminology

Radical feminism is a theoretical perspective that sees gender inequality or sexism as the most fundamental form of oppression. According to radical feminists, women historically were the first oppressed social group, and today, women continue to be the most oppressed social group in the world. Indeed, according to radical feminists, the subordination of women cuts across all racial and ethnic groups and all social classes. The primary way that men maintain their privilege and dominance is through control of women's sexuality. In patriarchal society, male power and female subordination are preserved through compulsory heterosexuality and the threat or actual use of violence

(MacKinnon, 1989; Walby, 1990). Pornography, rape, sexual harassment, battering, and other types of physical, psychological, and sexual abuse all serve to keep men in power and women powerless (MacKinnon, 1989; Stanko, 1985). For radical feminists, then, eliminating sexism will require much more than the enactment of laws prohibiting sex discrimination. Indeed, since the legal system, like all social institutions in our society, is male dominated and reflects men's interests, it cannot be trusted to bring about meaningful social change on women's behalf (MacKinnon, 1989; Radford, 1987). However, even as dramatic a change as the replacement of class-based society with a classless one will not suffice from the radical feminist perspective, since sexism can be found in socialist and capitalist societies alike. Instead, what needs to be overthrown are patriarchal relations, not class relations (Daly & Chesney-Lind, 1988).

Not surprisingly, radical feminist criminologists have largely focused their research not on women as offenders, but rather on women as crime victims and how the legal system has failed to protect women from men's violence. It is difficult to argue with their evidence on the pervasiveness of male violence against women. Consider, for example, that according to the F.B.I.'s "crime clock," one forcible rape is committed every six minutes in the United States (Federal Bureau of Investigation, 1997). Only about 6 percent of rape victims are males (U.S. Department of Justice, 1997). Moreover, at least 55 percent of rapes are *acquaintance rapes*, that is, the victim is familiar with or knows her assailant (Koss et al., 1987; Schwartz & DeKeseredy, 1997; U.S. Department of Justice, 1994). The younger the victim, the more likely she is to know her assailant; acquaintance rapes account for 90 percent of reported rapes involving victims under the age of twelve (Greenfeld, 1996). Ironically, we tell girls not to talk to strangers, but they are more likely to be harmed by someone they know. Women are three times more likely to experience violent victimization at the hands of an acquaintance or friend, a relative, or an intimate than a stranger, whereas for men, the chances of being violently victimized by a stranger are nearly the same as the chances of being violent victimized by someone they know (Craven, 1996).

This latter point is underscored by the data on intimate partner abuse. By conservative estimates, about 12 percent of women are abused by their husbands each year (Straus, 1993). Many of these women incur serious injuries, and about 1,200 are killed. In fact, women are more likely to be killed by male intimates than men are to be killed by female intimates. About one-third of female homicide victims are killed by husbands, ex-husbands, boyfriends, or ex-boyfriends, whereas only about 3 percent of male homicide victims are killed by wives, ex-wives, girlfriends, or ex-girlfriends (Crowell & Burgess, 1996; Greenfeld, 1998).

As radical feminist criminologists point out, in spite of these data, the police, the courts, and criminologists have been preoccupied with male street crime. The legal system, for example, has been overwhelmingly ineffective in regulating the manufacture and sale of pornography, even pornography that depicts the torture, mutilation, or death of women and girls (MacKinnon, 1986; Russell, 1993). When women are raped, they often think that it is they, not the rapist, who must prove their innocence by showing that they conform to traditional standards of respectable femininity and that they did nothing to precipitate the rape: They were not drinking or using drugs at the time of the rape, they were not walking alone at night, they did not willingly go home with the assailant or invite him into their own home, they did not go to a bar unescorted, they were not dressed nor did they behave "seductively" (see, for example, Estrich, 1987; as well as "Lawmaker's Rape View," 1995; "Nature of Clothing," 1990; "New Zealand Judge," 1996). Similarly, while services for battered women have improved significantly in the past three decades, many battered women still find the police and courts' responses to their calls for help inadequate and ineffective. Consider, for instance, a 1994 case in which a Maryland judge sentenced a defendant, a man who had killed his wife after he found her in bed with another man, to just eighteen months probation, stating that most men would have felt compelled to "punish" their partners under such circumstances ("Punishment Is 18 Months," 1994).

This judge's statement quite clearly illustrates the radical feminist argument that the legal system acts to uphold male authority over women: Women are rightfully subject to male control; if they step "out of bounds," they deserve to be punished. Certainly, one of the strengths of radical feminist criminology has been its unrelenting effort to spotlight men's violence against women and the dangerous unresponsiveness of the criminal justice system to female victims of crime perpetrated almost exclusively by men (see Box 7.2 on page 222). DeKeseredy and Schwartz (1996) also point out that radical feminism was the first theoretical perspective to emphasize the intersection of gender, patriarchy, and sexuality to understanding crime and law.

Critics have identified several weaknesses in radical feminist criminology. First, critics object to radical feminist criminologists' characterization of *all* men as oppressors—as equally likely to harass, rape, or batter women. There are pro-feminist men, men who work to end violence, including violence against women (DeKeseredy & Schwartz, 1996). And there are nonviolent, rape-free societies in the world (Reiss, 1986; Sanday, 1981; Sutlive, 1991). Research in the United States also shows that while women of all races and ethnicities as well as all social classes may be victims of male violence, some groups of women, especially poor women, are at greater risk of victimization than other groups of women (Moore, 1997; Schwartz, 1988). Intimate violence, in fact, is the leading cause of death for young, African American women (Stark, 1990). Related to this criticism, then, is a second one: that in elevating gender oppression as *the* primary oppression, radical feminists overlook the importance of other inequalities, particularly social class inequality and racism, which exacerbate the negative effects of sexism in women's—and men's—lives (Walby, 1990).

Finally, radical feminist criminology has been criticized for much the same reason instrumental Marxism was criticized (see Chapter 6): for portraying the legal system too simplistically, in this case not as an instrument of ruling class domination, but as an instrument of male domination (Messerschmidt, 1993; Ursel, 1991; Walby, 1990). While the police and the courts have undoubtedly shown themselves to be male-dominated and male-biased, important changes in recent years, brought about largely through feminist activism, have led to improvements in police and court responses to female victims of male violence. Passage of the Violence Against Women Act in 1994 is one example. This legislation includes increased federal funding for battered women's shelters, a mandate for harsher penalties for batterers, and a provision that makes crossing state lines in pursuit of a fleeing partner a federal offense. Although the benefits for women of such legislation and other state actions continue to be

BOX **7.2**   **HOW THE WORLD SEES IT**

*Should Violence against Women Be Considered
a Human Rights Issue?*

Radical feminists, we have said, have been at the forefront of work to increase awareness of the frequency and seriousness of violence against women, not only in the United States, but throughout the world. Historically, the physical and psychological abuse of women, though widespread in many societies, has not been considered a human rights problem. Indeed, there has been a high level of official and social tolerance of violence against women, with most governments and official agencies labeling it a private, individual matter or simply a "natural" consequence of being female (Chapman, 1990). For example, when nineteen teenage girls were killed and seventy-one others were raped by male classmates during a protest over fees at a boarding school in Kenya in 1991, school officials told reporters that the rapes of female students by men on campus were not unusual at their school or others. The deaths were accidental, they said; as the deputy principal explained, "The boys never meant any harm against the girls. They just wanted to rape" (quoted in Perlez, 1991, p. A7). However, officials have not only excused or ignored violence against women, they have also directly perpetrated it. The rape and sexual abuse of female political prisoners while in official custody has been documented by human rights advocates (Amnesty International, 1991; Chapman, 1990; Sontag, 1993).

The idea of treating violence against women as a human rights issue began to gain greater support in 1993, when media in the United States and Europe began to report on the systematic rape, sexual enslavement, torture, and murder of Bosnian Muslim women and children by Serbian military forces in the former Yugoslavia. It is estimated that 20,000 Muslim women were raped by Serb soldiers (Riding, 1993). Investigators found that rape was used as a weapon of war, serving as a central element in the Serbian "ethnic cleansing" campaign. Bos-

nian men were killed, while the women were raped with the goal of impregnating them to produce offspring with "desirable" genetic material. At the same time, the rapes were intended to demoralize and terrorize the Bosnian communities and to drive residents from their home regions. According to a European Community investigative report, the rapes were carried out in especially sadistic ways to inflict the greatest humiliation on victims (Nikolic-Ristanovic, 1999; Riding, 1993).

Using rape and sexual abuse as weapons of war is not unique to the former Yugoslavia, however (see, for example, Brownmiller, 1975). During World War II, for instance, the Japanese government enslaved an estimated 100,000 to 300,000 women from South Korea, Indonesia, China, Taiwan, the Philippines, and the Netherlands to sexually service Imperial Army soldiers. The women forced into prostitution were euphemistically referred to as "comfort women" (McGregor & Lawnham, 1993). More recently, attorneys assisting refugees seeking asylum in the United States and Canada have documented extensive state-supported violence against women, such as gang rape by police and military personnel, in many countries, including Haiti, Honduras, El Salvador, and Iran (Sontag, 1993). As a result, the United Nations High Commission on Refugees has issued special guidelines for government agencies to follow when evaluating women's applications for asylum so as to accurately identify when these women are being persecuted because of their sex.

The United Nations has also issued a Convention on the Elimination of All Forms of Discrimination against Women which, although it does not include a specific provision on violence, does include a number of provisions that in their effect impose sanctions for violence against women. To date, at least 101 countries have ratified the Convention, but unfortunately the United States is not among them. The United States did not address violence against women as a human rights abuse until 1994, when, for the first time, it included violence against women in its annual human rights report (U.S. Department of State, 1994). Radical feminists and others see this as a positive step, but continue to work for recognition of violence against women as a human rights issue throughout the world.

debated from various feminist perspectives (see, for instance, Renzetti, 1998; Ursel, 1991), many feminists are more optimistic than radical feminists that legal change can help turn the tables on men who historically have been afforded more protection than the women they victimize.

Socialist Feminist Criminology

We noted that one of the criticisms of radical feminism is that it prioritizes sexism over social class inequality as a form of oppression. In contrast, some feminist criminologists argue that class inequality in capitalist society is the primary oppression, with all other oppressions growing largely out of unequal economic conditions and class struggles. *Marxist feminists*, such as Julia and Herman Schwendinger (1983), for example, argue that violent crimes against women are not prevalent in all societies or throughout all historical periods. Instead, modern capitalist societies have dramatically high rape rates because the male dominance that breeds male violence is a product of the exploitative class relations inherent in capitalism. If capitalism is overthrown and replaced with an egalitarian mode of production, other forms of inequality, including gender inequality, will also be eliminated.

Not all feminist criminologists share the view that social class inequality takes precedence over gender inequality *or* vice versa. Some feminist criminologists argue that we must examine how class inequality and gender inequality operate *in tandem* to affect both the crimes women commit and the crimes committed against them. Their perspective is known as *socialist feminism*.

Socialist feminists analyze the gendered division of labor in both the workplace and the home. Prior to the emergence of industrial capitalism, most work took place in the home and all family members participated if they were able. As work increasingly moved from the home into factories and offices, women were increasingly excluded from paid labor. The unpaid labor they perform at home nevertheless reproduces the paid labor force in several ways: literally, through reproduction, new workers are born; current workers and children are nurtured and cared for; and men, freed from household responsibilities, can devote themselves to paid production. Even when women work outside the home, their salaries are significantly lower than those of men. In 1998, for example, women, on average, earned 76 percent of what men earned. In other words, for every dollar a man made, a woman made 76 cents (Love, 1998).[1] Socialist feminists argue that this gendered division of productive and reproductive labor is maintained through an ideology of male dominance as well as through legal regulations, such as marriage laws and abortion laws. Other social institutions reinforce men's control of women, too, and the threat of male violence is constant (Jurik, 1999). But law and the criminal justice system are also reflective of class interests, so in studying crime and criminal justice, socialist feminists examine how gender and class shape criminal opportunities, victimization experiences, and responses by the criminal justice system to both offenders and victims.

These ideas are seen clearly in the work of James Messerschmidt (1986) who offered what is considered to be one of the most important contributions to the development of socialist feminist criminology (DeKeseredy & Schwartz, 1996). Messerschmidt looks at the intersection of gender and class to explain why men and women commit different crimes. He proposes that it is the gendered and class-based division of labor coupled with gender and workplace socialization experiences that account for differences in the frequency, seriousness, and motivations for offending between men and women in different social classes.

Messerschmidt observes that wealthy men who hold powerful positions in government and the economy are best situated to commit some of the most serious crimes in terms of harm and losses incurred. These crimes include insider stock trading, the sale of products known to be hazardous, illegal disposal of toxic waste, and human rights violations. Very few women are found in the sorts of jobs that afford these types of criminal opportunities. Moreover, the "old boys" network for recruiting new employees for these kinds of jobs assures that women will continue to be largely excluded. The workplace socialization that takes place at this elite level teaches new recruits that sometimes ethics and morality must be sidestepped for the greater good of the corporation or government. Increasing or maintaining profits, remaining competitive in the marketplace, or preserving national security may all mean that one must occasionally "wink at the law." In contrast, working class and poor men do not have the opportunities to commit corporate and political crimes, but they do have ample opportunities to commit traditional street crimes, including larceny theft, drug dealing, assault, and robbery. Their crimes, however, like those of elite men, reflect both their social class position and their socialized conceptions of masculinity (Messerschmidt, 1993).

What about women? Messerschmidt (1993) actually focuses on masculinity as central to understanding crime because males of all social classes commit significantly more crimes than females, a point that underlines the fact that feminist criminological theory is relevant to men's as well as women's experiences. He argues that women are subject to greater controls in society; they are more closely supervised by parents and also by husbands and boyfriends. And, as we noted previously, they are underrepresented in positions of economic and political power. Both of these factors limit women's opportunities for white-collar, political, and street crime (Messerschmidt, 1986). The crimes they do commit—larceny theft, minor fraud and embezzlement, and drug offenses—reflect their economic marginalization. We observed earlier that the typical female offender is young, non-White, poor, a high school dropout, and an unmarried mother (Arnold, 1990; Chesney-Lind, 1997; Gilfus, 1992). Although the economy has been booming in recent years, not all groups of women have benefited. Economic discrimination has its greatest impact on the same groups of women who most frequently commit crimes, and recent welfare "reforms" make the financial circumstances of many of these women worse instead of better (Edin & Lein, 1997; McCrate & Smith, 1998). Thus, from a socialist feminist perspective, a rise in recent years in women's petty property crime and drug offenses is a product of the "feminization of poverty," the increasingly difficult struggle for survival for particular groups of women.

Socialist feminist criminologists have also challenged the traditional criminological conception of offenders and victims as two distinct or dichotomous groups (Jurik, 1999). With regard to women and girls, in particular, socialist feminist criminologists have uncovered links between victimization and offending. Chesney-Lind (1997), for example, has shown through her research that many young women charged as runaways within the juvenile justice system are actually attempting to escape from physically and sexually abusive homes. Studies of young people entering the juvenile justice system show that girls are more likely than boys to have been abused. Similarly, Davis (1993) reports that homeless women and girls, who engage in petty theft and street hustling to survive, are frequently victimized by men and boys on the streets as well as by the police who often harass them. Their abject poverty and fear of victimization may force them back to homes where they were abused. As Chesney-Lind (1997) found, because the juvenile courts are committed to preserving parental authority, they often force these girls to return to their abusers, routinely ignoring the girls' complaints about abuse. Ironically, "statutes that were originally placed in law to 'protect' young people have, in the case of some girls, criminalized their survival strategies" (Chesney-Lind, 1997, p. 28). Socialist feminist analyses such as those by Chesney-Lind and Davis, then, also challenge the traditional dichotomization of home as "safe haven" and the public world as "dangerous" as well as notions of the legal system as a "protector" of women (Jurik, 1999; see also Osthoff, 2001; Richie, 1996).

To summarize, the strengths of socialist feminist criminology are its analysis of the dual importance and interactive effects of gender and class inequalities in shaping women's and men's offending and victimization experiences, and its challenges to traditional criminological depictions of victims and offenders as distinct groups, the home as safe and the public world as dangerous, and the legal system as a value-neutral protector that acts in females' "best interests." Nevertheless, some criminologists are critical of the socialist feminist perspective. Some, for instance, maintain that despite socialist feminists' best efforts to equalize gender and class in their analyses, in most cases, they fall short and end up giving primacy to one or the other, usually class (Smart, 1987). Others point out that socialist feminists (as well as other feminists) have overlooked the importance of race and ethnicity in their analyses, treating women as a homogenous group or as distinguished only by social class. Rice (1990), for example, points out that both criminal offending and criminal victimization experiences, along with the responses of the criminal justice system, are different for Black women and White women, and that it is race as well as social class that accounts for these differences (see also Richie, 1996). It is only very recently that socialist feminist criminologists have begun to examine the intersections of gender, class, and race as well as other social locating factors such as sexual orientation and age. A related concern arises because of socialist feminists' call for the elimination of both patriarchy and capitalism to achieve justice. Some critics respond that what is just for some social groups may not be just for others and, therefore, eliminating patriarchy and capitalism will not inevitably result in an egalitarian or just society; other oppressions, particularly racial and ethnic discrimination, may remain in place. Consequently, work toward a just society must begin with the formation of alliances among diverse oppressed groups who participate in the struggle on an equal footing.

Jurik (1999) discusses other criticisms of socialist feminist criminology. To conclude this chapter, then, let's briefly consider some other recent developments in feminist criminologies.

Feminism and the Future of Criminology

Critiques of liberal feminism, radical feminism, and socialist feminism have prompted many feminist criminologists to undertake the daunting task of developing alternative theoretical perspectives. For example, postmodern feminist criminologists are critical of socialist feminists' and others' assumption that truth is knowable through social science research. Recall our discussion of postmodern criminology in Chapter 6. How is postmodern *feminist* criminology different from postmodern criminology?[2] Postmodern feminist criminologists share the basic principles of postmodern criminologists: a rejection of objectivity and the idea that truth is knowable; the importance of positionality in the construction of identity and truth claims, particularly the construction of difference; the need to deconstruct identities and truth claims, to unpack the power relations that underlie their construction; and a recognition that power is not only exercised on a macro level, but also on a micro level in everyday interactions through symbols, objects, and especially language. Feminist postmodernists are particularly interested in how differences and hierarchies are constructed through discourses on gender, race, social class, sexual orientation, and age. We noted in Chapter 6, however, that postmodernists are sometimes accused of being apolitical. As Wonders (1999) points out, this is a charge rarely leveled at feminists. Consequently, postmodern feminist criminology "offers a deeper sense of the political and has developed strategies for social change that do not reproduce oppression but transform it" (Wonders, 1999, p. 121).

Other emerging perspectives include materialist feminism and multiracial/multicultural feminism. As Jurik (1999) explains, these labels refer to:

> a variety of feminist works that examine the relationships and contradictions among consciousness, ideology, production-reproduction of material life, and human conformity-resistance. These factors are viewed as equally important and mutually determining. (p. 46)

These perspectives examine how criminal offending, criminal victimization, and criminal justice have varied historically and by gender, race and ethnicity, social class, age, sexual orientation, and nation or culture, thus extending the analysis beyond the United States or even Western societies to include developing and economically undeveloped societies (see also Lorber, 1998).

As we noted at the outset of this chapter, however, our discussion of feminist criminologies is hardly exhaustive. Just as feminism is not a unified theoretical perspective, nor are the individual theories we have discussed single, unitary approaches to the study of crime. Theorists working within each perspective often inject nuances that take the theory in a slightly new direction or deepen its scope. But even many criminologists who do not consider themselves feminists and do not use feminist theories to inform their work have been alerted to the importance of at least considering the possible effects of gender in their research. While criminology largely ignored gender—and, more specifically, women and girls—for more than two centuries, we are grateful to feminist criminologists that as we embark on the twenty-first century our discipline is no longer gender-blind.

Summary and Conclusion

In this chapter, we discussed feminist theories of criminology, a diverse group of theories that share in common the assumption that gender is socially constructed and serves as a central organizing factor of social life. While feminist criminologists apply their theories to the experiences of women *and* men, they deliberately seek to make female voices heard because the discipline has traditionally ignored them. However, feminist criminology is more than just a theoretical framework, it is also a social movement: In addition to explaining gendered differences in crime, victimization, and criminal justice, feminist criminologists explore strategies for brining about social change toward a more just society.

In this chapter, we discussed several feminist theories: liberal feminism, radical feminism, and socialist feminism. As we have done throughout this book, we considered some of the strengths and weaknesses of each theory. Regardless of their weaknesses, however, we believe feminist theories have made the especially important contribution of raising awareness within the discipline of the significance of gender, as well as race and ethnicity and social class, in understanding crime, victimization, and criminal justice. They are a welcome addition to the family of criminological theories.

KEY TERMS

chivalry hypothesis—the position that because females are generally law-abiding and, when they do offend, their crimes are relatively minor, they are treated more leniently than male offenders by the criminal justice system.

feminism—a school of thought that explains gender in terms of the social structure in which it is constructed and emphasizes the importance of taking collective action to end sexism.

gender—the socially generated expectations about the attitudes and behaviors of women and men that

are typically organized dichotomously as femininity and masculinity respectively, and that are produced and transmitted through social learning.

paternalism hypothesis—see *chivalry hypothesis*.

patriarchy—a social system in which men dominate women, and what is considered masculine is more highly valued or labeled as more important than what is considered feminine.

sexism—the differential valuing of one gender over the other.

SUGGESTED READINGS

Chesney-Lind, M. (1997). *The female offender*. Thousand Oaks, CA: Sage. A feminist exploration of offending by women and girls that makes the fundamental link between female crime and female victimization.

DeKeseredy, W. S. (2000). *Women, crime and the Canadian criminal justice system*. Cincinnati, OH: Anderson Publishing Co. A feminist analysis of female crime and victimization as well as criminal justice responses that focuses primarily on Canadian women, including Aboriginal women, but also provides some helpful comparisons with diverse groups of women in the United States.

Miller, S. L. (Ed.) (1998). *Crime control and women*. Thousand Oaks, CA: Sage. A collection of essays that looks at sexism in criminal justice and how crime control policies that appear value neutral or even beneficial to women can actually harm them.

Renzetti, C. M., Edleson, J. L., & Bergen, R. K. (Eds.). (2001). *Sourcebook on violence against women*. Thousand Oaks, CA: Sage. A collection of readings that examines various aspects of violence against women, including sexual assault, sexual harassment, sex tourism, and violence against women as a human rights issue.

NOTES

1. The wage gap persists regardless of workers' levels of education and race or ethnicity. For example, in 1993, female workers who had not graduated from high school earned on average $621 per month compared with male workers with the same educational attainment who earned $1,211 per month. Female college graduates had mean monthly earnings of $1,809 compared with male college graduates' mean monthly earnings of $3,430. In fact, female college graduates earned on average $3 less per month than male high school graduates. The wage gap is narrowest for individuals holding Ph.D's: $4,020 for women and $4,421 for men (U.S. Department of Commerce, Bureau of the Census, 1996). The wage gap is also narrower for women and men of color. While the female/male wage gap for White workers in 1997 was 74.6 percent, it was 86.8 percent for African American workers and 85.7 percent for Hispanic American workers (U.S. Department of Labor, 1998).

2. Our answer to this question relies heavily on Nancy Wonders's (1999) insightful and thorough comparison. Readers should consult Wonders's chapter in Arrigo (1999) for a far more detailed discussion of postmodern feminist criminology than we can provide here.

APPENDIX

Methods of Criminological Research

As we state in Chapter 1, one of the major criteria for evaluating a theory is its accuracy as determined by empirical research. Research itself, however, varies in kind and quality. Consequently, this appendix is intended as a primer in the basic methodological concepts and techniques frequently used by criminologists. It is by no means a substitute for a course in research methods or data analysis, but students who have not had such courses should find it helpful in deciphering and assessing the many criminological studies discussed throughout the text. Students with a background in research methods may wish to skip this section altogether or to use it as a resource as needed. Other, more detailed and thorough resources are listed at the end of the appendix. Our objective here is simply to enhance students' understanding of the theoretical and empirical material presented in the text.

The Research Process

The research process may best be thought of as a spiral. One begins with a problem or idea to be investigated. Often the formulation of this problem or idea has been informed by the propositions of a particular theory, but theory may also be derived from research. In some cases, the researcher begins from her or his own experience or observations. In any event, once the research problem has been identified, the researcher must decide how it will be studied—that is, the research project must be designed. This includes identifying units of analysis or research subjects and developing research instruments and measures. The data are then collected and analyzed, and the findings are reported and discussed. This allows the researcher to draw conclusions about the validity of a particular theory—certainly, if the job has been well done, the researcher knows more than he or she did before the project began—but also typically new questions or problems are raised for subsequent investigation. Thus, the process begins again.

Shortly, we will examine the elements of the research process in greater detail, defining some key terms along the way and elaborating on major methods of recruiting research participants and collecting and analyzing data. First, however, it is necessary to point out that there exist different philosophies or models of inquiry, each of which fills in our outline of the research process in dramatically different ways.

In the traditional or *positivist* model of inquiry, the researcher is an objective scientist who sets out to uncover social facts. Values and biases have no place in the research process; the researcher is to remain detached from those he or she studies from the outset of the project to its completion, including the uses to which the research is put. In this model, the researcher may offer "expert" advice or opinions based on the research findings, but he or she is not a political or social advocate. The researcher must remain impartial.

In contrast, *radical* and *feminist* models of inquiry view value neutrality in the research process as both impossible and undesirable.[1] Researchers select problems to be studied at least in part on the basis of their personal values. Moreover, researchers should adopt an ethic of care with respect to those they study and to society at large; that is, their values should inform the uses to which they allow their research to be put. Research should bring to light problems confronting oppressed and powerless groups, and the findings should be used to whatever extent possible to empower members of these groups. As such, the researcher should not be detached or separated from the researched; rather, both should participate in the research process as teachers and learners. Research should be a collaborative enterprise between the researcher and the researched, one that contributes to both personal and social transformation.

It is not difficult to see how each of these models influences the researcher to adopt particular methods of data collection and analysis. Let's turn now to a discussion of various research strategies and techniques, highlighting those that tend to fall within each of the models of inquiry we have just outlined.

Formulating the Research Problem

Ideas for research projects come from many sources: personal observations and experiences, a book or article one has read, or suggestions of mentors. Often, research problems begin as rather vague ideas that must be reshaped into answerable questions. The formulation of a research problem always benefits from an examination of existing research on one's topic, a process called a **literature review**. By scouring the available literature, one "refines that which is to be examined and relates it to current and past inquiries, thus preventing the reinvention of the wheel or rediscovery of a dead end" (Hagan, 1993, p. 19).

This is an important stage of the research process, too, because the problem chosen for investigation suggests the methods that should be used to investigate it. In other words, a researcher does not decide to write a questionnaire and subsequently determine the topic on which the questionnaire will focus. Rather, the researcher selects a problem to study and it, in turn, raises feasible research strategies, while simultaneously ruling out others. As we will see shortly, no single research method is inherently superior to another; each has its advantages and disadvantages. What is most important is that the method used should logically generate the kind of data needed to answer the question posed. This point will become clearer as we examine more fully other stages of the research process.

Research Design

Once the research problem has been formulated, the researcher must undertake the task of designing the research project. Effective research design involves at least three things: clarifying the goals of the project (determining what the researcher wants to accomplish through this project), identifying what will be studied, and specifying how it will be studied.

Considering the goals of the project first, the researcher may wish to test a theory or specific propositions within a theory, or he or she may wish to describe a certain situation or to "give voice" to the experiences of people whose perspectives have been muted or previously unheard. In either case, the researcher usually also wants to explain what factors caused a particular phenomenon or a specific set of circumstances to occur.

The clarification of the project's goals leads the researcher to an identification of the kinds of information that are sought: Will the researcher need to discern people's attitudes or feelings; gauge the incidence of specific behaviors; or calculate changes in behavior, policies, or practices over time? If the researcher is interested in studying changes in people's attitudes and behavior over time, a longitudinal design is appropriate. A **longitudinal study** involves selecting a group of people to be studied and questioning them and/or observing their behavior at various points over a specific period of time. In contrast, a **cross-sectional study** involves selecting a group of people to be studied and questioning them and/or observing their behavior at one point in time only.

Apart from whether the research will be longitudinal or cross-sectional, the researcher must also consider the issue of identifying *data sources*. Will the researcher generate original raw data, gathered purposely for the project at hand, or will he or she mine existing data (such as arrest records, parole reports, diaries of prisoners, or newspaper stories) generated by others for other purposes? Again, the source of the data to be analyzed depends to a considerable extent on the research problem, but it is also influenced by the researcher's philosophy of inquiry as we discussed earlier, by the amount of time and financial resources available, by the researcher's skills and training, and by sheer availability (that is, the data ideal to study a particular problem simply may not exist or it may not be possible, feasible, or ethical to generate it).

In identifying data sources, the researcher is identifying who (or what) he or she will actually study. Another way to put this is to say that the researcher is specifying his or her **units of analysis**. Often, the unit of analysis in criminological research is the individual person, although it may be, more specifically, individual persons who have used drugs in the last twelve months, college students, young men and women between the ages of ten and eighteen, or some other subgroup. Not infrequently, however, the units of analysis in criminological research are police departments, prisons, families, corporations, towns, movies or television programs, "or anything else that has some social relevance and can be observed. We might, for example, observe a large number of rock music videos, noting the genders of the performers and measuring the degree of violence or hostility portrayed. We could then determine whether the two variables were related" (Babbie, 1998).

In this example, rock music videos are the units of analysis, but the example is significant for other reasons as well. In particular, it raises several additional issues that researchers must take into account in designing their research projects: sampling, conceptualization, operationalization, and measurement. These have to do with the who (or what) and how of the research project. Let's consider each in turn.

Sampling

Regardless of the units of analysis selected, a researcher cannot expect to study every case. In the example we cited, the researcher would observe *a large number* of rock music videos, not every single rock music video that has been made. The latter task would be impossible. Similarly, a researcher who selects U.S. youths between the ages of ten and eighteen as the units of analysis could not be expected to question or observe every young man or woman aged ten to eighteen in the country. Instead, from the array or **population** of cases that could potentially be studied, the researcher selects a **sample** or subset of cases to participate in the research. Once the data are gathered and analyzed, the researcher typically wishes to *generalize* the findings to the larger population. The extent to which **generalization** is possible depends on the degree of **representativeness** of the sample, or, the degree to which the sample and the population are similar. "A sample of individuals from a population, if it is to provide useful descriptions of the total population, must contain essentially the same variations that exist in the population" (Babbie, 1998, p. 294). There are several ways a sample can be drawn, but all of these techniques fall into one of two basic categories: probability and nonprobability sampling. We will examine each of these sampling strategies more carefully.

Probability Sampling.   **Probability sampling** is considered by most methodologists to be the preferred sampling strategy because it allows us to study a relatively small number of people, but nevertheless get a fairly accurate picture of the attitudes, opinions, and behaviors of the entire population of interest. In addition, with a probability sample, the researcher can calculate an estimate of the accuracy or representativeness of the sample; this is called the *sampling error*. Probability sampling is based on the **equal probability of selection method** or **EPSEM**. More specifically, in probability sampling, all members of the population have an equal chance of being selected in the sample. Of course, this requires that the entire population be known to the researcher. This is not to say that the researcher must personally know each and every member of the population of interest, but rather that the researcher can specify the members of the population so as to generate or locate a *sampling frame*: a list of all the elements (such as people, television programs, or prisons) in the study population.

> In practice, existing sampling frames often define the study population rather than the other way around. We often begin with a population in mind for our study; then we search for possible sampling frames. The frames available for our use are examined and evaluated, and we decide which frame presents a study population most appropriate to our needs. (Babbie, 1998, p. 199)

Some examples of sampling frames include telephone directories, class rosters, census blocks, police department arrest records, and lists of registered voters. Obviously, some sampling frames are better (more complete) than others. The sampling frame the researcher develops or utilizes has a tremendous impact on the study, since a poorly constructed and incomplete sampling frame may seriously lower the representativeness of the study sample and subsequently limit the generalizability of the research findings.

It is from the sampling frame that the sample is drawn, but there are a number of different ways of drawing a probability sample. Let's consider some of those most frequently used.

The most basic type of probability sampling is *simple random sampling*. Suppose you had ten tickets to a concert, but you have fifty friends who want to go with you. You want to be fair and give each of your friends an equal chance of being selected to go, not showing favoritism toward any of them. So you bring them together in a room, write each one's name down on separate pieces of paper of equal size, put all the pieces of paper into a big hat, shake the hat, close your eyes, and draw from the hat nine of the fifty papers (assuming you want to save a ticket for yourself); the nine selected get to go with you to the concert. Simple random sampling works basically the same way. Each element in the sampling frame is assigned a single unique number in order and then the researcher selects elements from the sampling frame until he or she has achieved the desired sample size. The process may be done by computer if the sampling frame is in machine-readable form.

Another type of probability sampling is *systematic sampling*. To draw a systematic sample, the researcher must first number the elements in the sampling frame as he or she would do in simple random sampling. Next, the researcher must specify the desired sample size and calculate the *sampling interval*. In systematic sampling, every kth element in the sampling frame is systematically selected for inclusion in the sample; k is the sampling interval. To calculate the sampling interval, the researcher simply divides the population total by the sample total; thus, if the population is composed of 1,000 elements and the researcher wants a sample of 100, he or she would have to select every tenth element in the sampling frame. According to many methodologists, systematic sampling is a simpler and, in some cases, more accurate sampling strategy than simple random sampling, but one must be certain that the elements in the sampling frame are not arranged in a cyclical pattern that corresponds to the sampling interval; this could result in a biased, nonrepresentative sample.

Stratified random sampling is a type of probability sampling that takes into account the distribution of particular characteristics (such as race, sex, or criminal record) in the population that may be central to the research so as to increase the representativeness of the sample. Let's say, for instance, that one is interested in whether support for the death penalty varies across racial/ethnic groups. The sampling frame for the study contains 1,000 people: 600 are White, 200 are African American, 100 are Hispanic American, 75 are Asian American, and 25 are Native American. The desired sample size is 100. Conceivably, if one drew a simple random sample from this sampling frame, all of the people chosen could be White; obviously, such a sample would not allow the researcher to gauge differences in support of the death penalty across racial/ethnic groups. In drawing the sample, therefore, the researcher would need to employ a strategy that would allow him or her to ensure that members of all the racial groups in the sampling frame would be included in the sample. Stratified sampling would be an appropriate sampling strategy to use in such a case.

There are two types of stratified random samples. In both types, the researcher first divides the sampling frame into subgroups or *strata*, based on the characteristic in question; in our example, there would be five racial/ethnic subgroups. In *proportionate stratified random sampling*, elements are selected for the sample in proportion to their representation in the population. Thus, in our example, since Whites constitute 60 percent of the population, they would constitute 60 percent of the sample; 60 of the 600 Whites in the population would be randomly selected for inclusion in the sample. Similarly, 20 African Americans would be selected, 10 Hispanic Americans, 7 Asian Americans, and 3 Native Americans. The question arises, however, as to whether the opinions of 7 Asian Americans or 3 Native Americans would be sufficient to allow us to draw comparisons with White Americans. To draw comparisons, the researcher needs groups fairly comparable in size. An alternative sampling strategy, therefore, would be *disproportionate stratified random sampling*, in which very small groups are oversampled to increase their representation. In our example, the researcher could randomly select 20 people from each of the subgroups; subsequently, the researcher could *weight* the responses of the oversampled groups to adjust for their actual representation in the population. Note that once the population is stratified and the decision is made with regard to proportionate versus disproportionate sampling, the sample may be drawn using the simple random or systematic technique.

Finally, *cluster sampling* is a probability sampling strategy that is especially useful if the population is dispersed over a wide geographic area. In this sampling method, the population is first divided into clusters (such as census tracts, counties, or voting districts), and a random sample of the clusters is chosen. Once the clusters have been sampled, probability samples (simple random, systematic, or stratified) of the desired size may be drawn from each cluster. Cluster sampling involves a number of sampling stages that actually incorporate the various sampling techniques we have already discussed.

Nonprobability Sampling.   As we have noted, a fundamental assumption of probability sampling is that the population is known and that a sampling frame is available to or can be constructed by the researcher. Frequently, however, criminologists study topics that are highly sensitive and that examine the behavior of hidden or stigmatized groups. In such cases, it is usually not possible to even accurately estimate the size of the population, let alone enumerate a sampling frame for the purposes of drawing a probability sample. Consequently, a different sampling strategy, **nonprobability sampling**, must be used, and there are several nonprobability sampling techniques. Nonprobability samples may yield very valuable data, but because we cannot estimate the sampling error when using them, we must be especially cautious in generalizing the findings obtained from such samples to study populations.

Quota sampling, one type of nonprobability sampling, requires the researcher to have some knowledge of the population and the distribution of particular characteristics of interest within the population. The researcher then constructs a matrix, or *quota frame*, with each cell showing the proportion of the sample that must have the specific characteristics of interest. The researcher then goes out and questions or observes the specified number of individuals in each cell. A familiar example of quota sampling is the "shopping mall survey," in which interviewers are instructed to stop and attempt to interview a certain number of people with particular characteristics. Although quota sampling tries to approximate the conditions of probability sampling, it is not a probability method, and the quality of the sample drawn is highly dependent on the accuracy of the quota frame.

Accidental sampling involves relying on whomever is available to the researcher. The classic example is the "person on the street" survey in which anyone the researcher can stop and ask some questions of is included in the study. The representativeness of such a sample is clearly doubtful, yet this technique is not infrequently used. A more common example is when researchers who are also faculty members at a college or university use the "captive audiences" of students in their classes as study samples. While such samples may have limited utility in certain cases, it is unlikely that students enrolled in a criminology course at a particular university during any given semester are representative of all people their age or even of all college students.

Despite the likely unrepresentativeness of accidental samples, sometimes researchers simply have no choice but to rely on those individuals who are available to them in their studies. Researchers have utilized an ingenious array of techniques to sample hidden, rare, deviant, and stigmatized populations. These include advertising for study volunteers (for example, Renzetti, 1992), as well as hanging out at locales where population members are likely to congregate and approaching potential study participants to ask for their cooperation (for example, Sudman & Kalton, 1986; Sudman et al., 1988). Another common strategy is to use *network* or *snowball sampling*. Network or snowball sampling involves recruiting an initial study participant or group of participants and subsequently asking them to recommend additional participants, either by leading the researcher to these potential participants or by asking associates to contact the researcher (see Martin & Dean, 1993). The generalizability of findings obtained from such a study is questionable at best, but in studies involving some form of hidden or deviant behavior (such as undetected criminal activity), network or snowball sampling may be the most feasible sampling strategy.

While network or snowball sampling does not allow the researcher to determine precisely the degree to which the sample is representative, representativeness may be improved if the researcher has developed extensive knowledge about the population. Samples that are chosen on the basis of the researcher's knowledge of or professional judgments about the study population are called *purposive* or *judgmental samples*. These are especially useful to researchers who can identify a particular subset of a population, such as an urban street gang, but it is not possible for the researcher to enumerate and sample all gangs in a given urban area. Based on his or her knowledge of gangs in the city in question and of street gangs in general, the researcher can get a sense of the representativeness of the gang he or she is studying. However, it is important to keep in mind that this gauge of representativeness is still little more than an educated guess, and caution must still be exercised in generalizing the research findings.

Returning to the issue of models of inquiry raised earlier, it should be noted that neither probability nor nonprobability sampling is exclusive to either model we outlined. At the same time, however, it may be said that probability sampling is most favored by those working within a positivist model of inquiry, while radical, critical, participatory, and feminist researchers (although they do not denounce probability sampling) frequently choose research problems and methods that make probability sampling impossible or infeasible. Consequently, it is safe to say that they utilize nonprobability sampling techniques more often than positivists do. The major differences between these two models of inquiry, however, arise in terms of the data collection methods typically employed. Before we explore this topic, though, let's consider the other research design issues of conceptualization, operationalization, and measurement.

Conceptualization, Operationalization, and Measurement

In the example we cited previously, we said that a possible research project could involve observing a large number of rock videos, recording the sex of the performers, and *measuring* the degree of violence or hostility portrayed. Our goal is to see if there is a relationship between two *variables*: sex of video performers and violence in rock music videos. If we asked you what you would be looking for when you record the sex of the performers, you would probably have little trouble answering; the obvious response is that you would record whether each performer was a male or a female. Suppose, however, that we asked you what you would be looking for when you record the degree of violence or hostility portrayed in the videos. Chances are that responses would vary among our readers. No doubt each of us has an idea or mental image of what violence and hostility are, but we cannot assume that our individual ideas and mental images correspond; in all likelihood they do not. Consequently, it is important that we define what we mean by the term *violence*. In doing so, we are engaged in the process of **conceptualization**. Conceptualization is a process of specification; when we conceptualize a term, we state precisely what we mean by it. As a result, even if others disagree with our definition, they will at least know exactly what we mean by the terms we are using. In our example, we may conceptualize violence as any act in which the intent to do harm is conveyed or in which harm is actually portrayed as being inflicted on another.

Conceptualizing the terms that are central to our research leads us to ways of identifying the presence or absence of the particular phenomenon we are interested in. In other words, the process of conceptualization suggests to the researcher specific *indicators* of the phenomenon in question. In our example, we could think of a multitude of indicators of violence as we have conceptualized it: hitting, damaging other people's property, yelling insults, stabbing or shooting someone, and so on. Clearly, there are various *dimensions* of the concept *violence*. Specifying these various dimensions is important because it refines and adds complexity to our research problem. We may find, for instance, that female performers engage in as many portrayals of violence as male performers, but because we have delineated the various dimensions of violence, we may further observe that male performers engage in more portrayals of what we consider *severe violence* compared with female performers. At the same time, by using only indicators of *physical violence*, we have ruled out of the study the use of indicators of other types of violence, such as *psychological violence*.

Despite our greater level of specificity here, we still do not know exactly how we will measure our concepts. The process by which we specify precisely how we will measure our concepts is called **operationalization**. The end product of operationalization is a clear statement of the *operations* that will be utilized to measure a concept in our study. In reaching this point, however, a number of issues must be addressed and decisions made. We will consider some of these now.

Reliability and Validity.   Researchers obviously are concerned that the measures they develop for their study be of good quality, but what makes for a high quality measure? In answering this question, we tackle the issues of reliability and validity. **Reliability** concerns whether a measure produces the same results when used repeatedly. If, for example, you step onto a scale several times to be weighed and each time the scale registers a different weight, you can be reasonably certain that the scale is an unreliable measure. This, though, is a separate issue from validity. **Validity** concerns the *accuracy* of a measure. If you step onto a scale several times to be weighed and each time the scale registers 120 pounds, the consistency of the results indicates that the scale is a reliable measure. But suppose you actually weigh 150 pounds? The scale, while reliable, is not accurate; it does not produce valid results.

Ideally, researchers strive to develop measures that are both reliable and valid, but if the researcher must trade one of these off against another, validity becomes the chief goal. A wide variety of factors may affect validity. For instance, if people know they are being studied for a specific reason, they may not be truthful in their answers because they are embarrassed to admit the truth, they know their true answer is a socially undesirable one, or they wish to please the researcher by giving the answer they think he or she wants to hear.[2]

Variables and Levels of Measurement.   We have used the term *variable* repeatedly throughout our discussion so far, but many students are not clear about exactly what a variable is. A **variable** is composed of *attributes* or *qualities* that describe something; the distribution of these attributes or qualities *varies* among the population that possesses them. In our earlier example, then, we identified one of the variables we are interested in as the *sex* of the performers in rock music videos; the variable *sex* is composed of the attributes *male* and *female*. Moreover, in this example, *sex* is the **independent variable** in the study, while *hostility* or *violence* are the **dependent variables**. Perhaps the easiest way to understand this is to think in terms of the language of causation. In a cause and effect relationship, the independent variable is the cause and the dependent variable is the effect. Typically, what a researcher wishes to discover is whether a change in the independent variable produces a change in the dependent variable. In other words, the researcher is looking to see if there is a *relationship* between the independent variable and the dependent variable.

In operationalization, the researcher must specify precisely how he or she will measure the independent and dependent variables in the study. One might operationalize sex, for instance, with the question:

What is the sex of the performer in the video you are watching?
a. male
b. female

In most cases, however, variables are not so easily operationalized, and the researcher has an array of choices to make in developing the measures to be used. One important question has to do with the *range of variation* appropriate to the project. How fine must the distinctions be between the attributes that compose each of the variables in your study? If you are interested in religion, for example, will it be enough for you to ask the question, "What is your religion?" and supply only the response categories, "Christian" and "Nonchristian"? For purposes of your study, does it matter if a respondent is Protestant, Catholic, Jewish, Muslim, or another religion? Must you get even more specific?

The level of detail tapped by your measures must be informed by the purposes of your project. This discussion of detail, however, raises the point that there are different *levels* of measurement. Specifically, there are four levels of measurement: nominal, ordinal, interval, and ratio.

Nominal measures are variables whose attributes are simply *exhaustive* and *mutually exclusive*. A variable is exhaustive if every observation the researcher makes can be classified in terms of one of the attributes composing the variable. It is mutually exclusive when the researcher can classify each observation he or she makes in terms of one and *only one* attribute of the variable. The variable *sex*, composed of the attributes *male* and *female*, is again a useful example.

Every variable must meet the minimal standards of exhaustiveness and mutual exclusiveness. However, while nominal measures do this and thus allow us to name or label research participants in terms of the presence of particular characteristics, they can provide us with no other useful information. *Ordinal measures*, in contrast, are variables whose attributes may be logically rank-ordered. If we think of social class in terms of lower class, middle class, and upper class, we have an example of an ordinal variable. Ordinal measures allow us to state that some research participants have more or less of something, but they do not permit us to say how much more or less. We know, for instance, that middle-class people are wealthier than lower-class people, and upper-class people are the most wealthy, but without more precise information, we cannot say in this case how much wealthier either the middle or the upper class is relative to the lower class.

Interval measures are variables for which there are standard meaningful intervals between each of the attributes, thus allowing us to make statements about how much more or less of something research participants possess relative to one another. However, interval measures are characterized by an arbitrary zero point; that is, a score of zero does not mean the complete absence of the quality or attribute in question. The most frequently cited example of an interval measure is IQ. A score of 90 is ten points lower than a score of 100, and a score of 110 is ten points higher than a score of 100. However, a person who scores 0 on an IQ test could not be said to be totally without intelligence; nor could it be said that someone who scores 100 is twice as intelligent as someone who scores 50.

Ratio measures permit us to make these more precise kinds of statements because they have a true zero point in addition to all of the characteristics of the three previous types of variables. Thus, if we ask the respondents to a questionnaire to write in a space provided how many times they have been the victim of a crime, and one respondent writes 0, we can say that that person has never been victimized. At the same time, we may say that the respondent who writes "ten times" has been victimized twice as much as one who writes "five times."

The types of measures or variables used in a study are important not only because different levels of measurement yield different kinds of information, but also because particular data analysis techniques require the use of variables at a specific level of measurement. Unfortunately, a discussion of the statistical tools of data analysis is far too complex an undertaking in an appendix intended only as a methods primer. However, a review of some of the issues involved in operationalization does raise questions with regard to the process of data collection, the topic to which we will turn next.

Gathering Data

The actual collection of data may be accomplished using a wide variety of methods. In the sections that follow, we will review some of the methods used most frequently by criminologists. Each method has particular advantages and disadvantages that must be weighed in terms of the purposes of the study as well as other factors, such as finances, time, skills and training of the researcher, and ethical considerations.

Survey Research

Survey research is undoubtedly one of the most popular research methods used not only by criminologists, but by all social scientists. There are a number of ways surveys may be done; the two most common involve either the *self-administered questionnaire* or the *in-person interview*.

Most readers are probably familiar with self-administered questionnaires; many have likely completed more than one of these. The popularity of questionnaires stems from the fact that they permit the researcher to collect extensive information from large numbers of people in a relatively quick and inexpensive manner. All respondents are asked the same questions in the same way, and usually they select their answers from a given set of response categories (such as strongly agree or strongly disagree), thus providing data that are standardized. These standardized data can then be computer-analyzed using a variety of statistical tests. The fact that questionnaires also often provide respondents with anonymity makes them especially useful for researching some of the sensitive topics (such as undetected deviant or criminal acts) that criminologists frequently study. Individuals who may be embarrassed to admit having engaged in a particular behavior may feel less inhibited if they know the person to whom they are reporting their actions cannot identify them.

However, the strengths of self-administered questionnaires also constitute their major weaknesses. The high level of standardization characteristic of most questionnaires gives them the disadvantage of being inflexible in that they allow respondents little if any opportunity to explain their answers or to put them into context. Many of us know the frustration of reading the response choices for a question on a questionnaire and feeling that none of them adequately expresses our opinion or that each of them does under various circumstances. Moreover, in the interest of quantifying people's attitudes and behaviors, questionnaires overlook the richness of diversity in most individuals' opinions and actions. Finally, despite the anonymity provided by self-administered questionnaires, we still cannot be certain that what people report on them is true. We know well that what people say they believe or what they say they do is sometimes not reflected in actual behavior. People may lie, or they may, for a number of reasons, unintentionally misrepresent their true feelings or behavior. Questionnaires, then, suffer from the problem of artificiality. Regardless of their disadvantages, however, the standardization of questionnaires, the quantifiable nature of questionnaire data, and the distance questionnaires place between researcher and researched make them particularly popular with positivist criminologists.

Many of the disadvantages of self-administered questionnaires can be overcome with in-person interviews. Like the self-administered questionnaire, the in-person interview is designed to ask respondents questions on specific topics, but instead of having respondents put pen to paper, the researcher or a trained assistant meets with each respondent and asks the questions face-to-face. Interviews range from highly structured to completely unstructured. The *structured interview* is most similar to the questionnaire in that the interviewer asks each respondent the same questions in exactly the same way and may even offer them response categories. In contrast, in the *unstructured interview*, the interviewer lets the respondent lead the way. Apart from a few initial questions to encourage a respondent to talk and questions or *probes* to clarify particular points or get respondents to elaborate, the interviewer plays a rather passive role in the unstructured interview. Many interviews, however, fall somewhere in between these two extremes and may be considered *semi-structured*. In the semi-structured interview, the respondent has specific questions he or she wishes to ask, but also allows respondents considerable freedom to raise topics or issues they want to discuss.

Researchers planning to conduct in-person interviews have traditionally been advised to know the questions they wish to ask well enough so that they can maintain a conversational tone and style to the interview, rather than having it seem like an interrogation or a test. An important goal is to establish rapport with respondents so that they will feel comfortable talking to you, especially about sensitive topics. Positivists have favored the highly structured interview for most of the same reasons they prefer self-administered questionnaires; they warn interviewers against establishing so much rapport that they lose "scientific detachment" and engaging in self-disclosure for fear of influencing respondents' answers. Radical and feminist researchers, on the other hand, are highly critical of this approach to interviewing. They favor unstructured and semi-structured interviews in which respondents have greater control over the interview situation. Moreover, they advocate self-disclosure and reciprocity in the interview situation. Interviewers, they maintain, owe it to their respondents to freely answer any questions the respondents have about the research or about them as researchers or individuals. Indeed, interviewers should encourage respondents to "talk back" to them regarding the research. Rather than biasing data in a negative sense, these researchers see self-disclosure and reciprocity as essential to the success of a project.

Regardless of the approach one takes to interviewing, however, it too has some drawbacks. It is a more time-consuming data collection technique than the self-administered questionnaire, and it is more expensive. Logistical problems mean that one usually must rely on a smaller sample with a narrower geographic reach if conducting interviews rather than sending self-administered questionnaires. Moreover, even if one highly values reciprocity and self-disclosure, characteristics of the interviewer relative to respondents may inhibit some respondents from answering fully or truthfully, depending on what is being asked. Female respondents, for example, may feel uncomfortable speaking with male interviewers about certain topics; White interviewers may have difficulty establishing rapport with African American and other minority respondents (see Edwards, 1993). And finally, as with self-administered questionnaires, while in-person interviews afford the interviewer limited opportunity to make observations, they still suffer from artificiality in that they depend on respondents' self-reports of their attitudes and behavior.

Field Observation

A data collection method that overcomes the artificiality problem of survey research is field observation. In **field observation**, the researcher watches the social phenomenon he or she is studying unfold in its natural setting. For instance, if one wishes to understand street prostitution, a fruitful strategy might be to hang around areas known for street prostitution and watch what transpires.

There are basically two types of observational research: *participant observation* and *nonparticipant observation*. As the terms suggest, in participant observation, the researcher becomes actively involved in what he or she is studying, while in nonparticipant observation, the researcher simply watches the social interaction taking place, but makes no attempt to become personally involved in it. As with any method, each of these has both advantages and disadvantages. As a participant observer, the researcher experiences firsthand what he or she is studying, thus obtaining a level of understanding of the phenomenon not possible with other methods. However, by participating directly in the interaction, the researcher runs the risk of changing it or affecting it in some significant way—an unavoidable disadvantage of participant observation. Ethical and legal problems may also arise if the behavior in which one is participating is illegal. In addition, there is the danger that the participant observer may become so personally involved in what he or she is studying that the important element of objectivity in the analysis of the findings will be diminished or lost. Nonparticipant observers are less likely to encounter these problems, but at the same time, they are also less likely to develop a complete sense of what is being studied.

In any event, both participant and nonparticipant observers must decide if they will make their identities as researchers known to those they are studying. On the one hand, it may be argued that by concealing one's identity as a researcher and trying to "pass" as a member of the group being studied, the researcher is likely to get more valid data. As we noted earlier, if individuals know they are being studied, they may behave less naturally, or they may try to conceal or change aspects of their behavior. On the other hand, concealing one's true identity is a form of deception, which raises ethical issues for the researcher. It also poses particular risks for the researcher. A researcher who attempts to pass as a member of a group must be extraordinarily knowledgeable about the group. Depending on the group being studied, a group member discovered to be an impostor could be in danger at the hands of other group members.

Regardless of the type of field research undertaken, the field researcher must carefully record his or her field observations in a *field journal*. This is far more difficult than it may at first seem, especially if one's identity as a researcher is unknown to those being studied. High-quality field journals, however, are essential to the success of observational research projects because they contain the data to be analyzed. These data are rarely amenable to quantification and typically must be analyzed using qualitative techniques in which patterns of behavior and their underlying meanings are discerned. Not surprisingly, the qualitative nature of field research, as well as the other characteristics of the method we identified earlier, make it largely unfavored by positivists, but it is frequently used by radical and feminist researchers.

Unobtrusive Methods

We have already noted that researchers frequently run the risk of altering the subject area they are studying simply by virtue of studying it, because their methods are often quite intrusive. There are, however, a number of research methods that preclude the possibility of the researcher impacting what he or she is studying. These are referred to as *unobtrusive methods*, and we will discuss two of these: content analysis and analysis of existing statistics.

Content Analysis.   **Content analysis** involves analyzing the content of some form of communication. Our hypothetical study of the relationship between sex of performer and portrayals of hostility or violence in rock music videos is an example of a project that would use content analysis. Content analysis is especially useful, however, when researchers wish to study events, attitudes, practices, or a previous historical period. Unless, of course, the phenomena of interest are relatively recent, it is virtually impossible for the researcher to interview or administer questionnaires to individuals with firsthand experience. Instead, criminologists conducting *historical research* typically must depend on archives and surviving documents—such as historical records and registries, diaries, letters, speeches, and newspaper articles—to discern what was happening during the period of interest.

Content analysis is a highly subjective method that requires the researcher to develop criteria for selecting representative material from the communications available, identifying indicators of the variables of interest in the study, and inferring patterns and relationships from what are often piecemeal data. Babbie (1998) warns of at least two serious difficulties in conducting content analysis for historical research. One is that the researcher cannot trust the accuracy of historical records and accounts on face value regardless of whether they are official or unofficial, first hand or secondary; a "fact" may be seen or interpreted differently by different people. He suggests that the best way to handle this problem is through *corroboration*: "If several sources point to the same set of 'facts' your confidence in them might reasonably increase" (p. 329). Second, he urges researchers to be aware of the possible biases of their data sources. For example, "The diaries of well-to-do gentry of the Middle Ages may not give you an accurate view of life in general during those times" (p. 329). Consequently, whenever possible, researchers should collect their data from sources that provide a variety of viewpoints.

Analysis of Existing Statistics. Instead of generating their own data through questionnaires or interviews, researchers may locate a data set that was collected previously (and often for a purpose different from their own), but that provides information about their topic of interest. Sometimes these data were collected by another researcher and the researcher in the present study wishes to reanalyze them (for example, the National Youth Survey discussed in Chapter 5); this is called *secondary analysis*. Not infrequently, however, these data are official statistics collected by government and nongovernment agencies; in such cases the researcher is undertaking an **analysis of existing statistics**.

The quality of these analyses depends heavily on the quality of the statistics themselves. In general, an analysis of existing statistics raises serious questions of reliability and validity including: Are they accurate records of what they claim to report? and Do they in fact measure what it is you wish to measure in your study?

Despite reliability and validity concerns, the analysis of existing statistics is a popular method in criminological research. Consequently, to conclude this appendix, we will take a brief look at two of the most commonly used sources of official statistics in criminological research and evaluate their strengths and weaknesses.

The Uniform Crime Reports (UCR). The *Uniform Crime Reports* (UCR) is the major source of official data on crime in the United States. Begun in 1930 by the U.S. Justice Department, the UCR is a compilation of crimes reported to the Federal Bureau of Investigation by law enforcement agencies throughout the country. Despite the fact that participation is voluntary, law enforcement agencies submitting crime data to the UCR represent about 95 percent of the total U.S. population. Over the years, the comprehensiveness of the reports have steadily improved, and participating departments receive instructions to ensure that their reports are standardized so as to facilitate nationwide comparisons of the data.

The UCR is divided into two parts. Part I tends to get the most attention in the media and contains what are called the *index crimes*: the eight offenses of murder and non-negligent manslaughter, forcible rape, robbery, aggravated assault (which collectively are referred to as *violent crimes against the person*); and burglary, larceny-theft, motor vehicle theft, and arson (which are collectively known as *crimes against property*). The index crimes are singled out because of their seriousness, frequency of occurrence, and likelihood of being reported to the police. Part II of the UCR contains data on twenty-one other crimes, including simple assault, fraud, vandalism, prostitution and vice offenses, drunkenness, and disorderly conduct.

For each crime and each crime category, the UCR provides a wealth of information, including not only the number of specific crimes that have occurred, but also the crime rate. The *crime rate* is the number of crimes per segment of the population, usually per 100,000 people in the population. The UCR also provides breakdowns of the number of crimes and the crime rates for particular population groups (by sex, race, and age), population areas (cities, suburbs, or rural areas), and geographic region (such as northeastern United States or western United States).

Despite the large amount of data contained in the UCR, however, it is as important for methodological reasons to mention what it does not provide as what it does provide. There have been extensive critiques of the UCR on various grounds, but we will raise here only the three main criticisms that have traditionally been leveled. First, the UCR does not include a number of offenses that have a serious impact on society, particularly corporate, white-collar, and organized crime.

It may be argued, then, that the UCR does not represent all crime committed in the United States, but primarily street crimes. This, however, raises a second criticism, for the UCR contain only *crimes known to the police* and many crimes, including many street crimes, go either undetected by anyone or unreported to authorities. Indeed, as we will see shortly, surveys of crime victims indicate that there are significantly more crimes committed than those that are reported to the police. Moreover, this characteristic of the UCR means that the yearly changes in the crime rates contained in it may be an artifact of the public's increased or decreased willingness to report crimes to the police.

The final criticism of the UCR involves the possible biases that may affect the recording of crimes. There are many sources of bias. One is *official discretion*; police often use discretion in deciding to which citizen-initiated complaints they will respond and which complaints warrant official submission to the UCR. Sometimes politics becomes a factor. For instance, Chambliss (1988) found significant changes in police recording of crime in Washington, D.C., when Richard Nixon began using Washington as the model city to prove how effective his "War on Crime" had been:

> During this period, the police in Washington were under pressure to reduce the crime rate. The most common form of "serious" crime reported to the FBI by local police departments is felonious larceny (theft). For larceny to be considered "serious" it must be of property worth more than $50.00. To create the impression that the "war on crime" was effective, the Washington, DC, police began reporting most of the larcenies known to them as larceny involving property valued at $49.99, which kept them from being reported as felonies and, thus, kept the serious crime rate down. (p. 30)

At other times, police are pressured to curb certain criminal activities, which results in an arrest increase for that particular offense category.

Taken together, these criticisms bring to light the serious shortcomings of the UCR. This is not to say that the UCR is useless, but rather that researchers need to be aware of the limits of the data and to be cautious in generalizing from them. At the end of the 1980s, the U.S. Department of Justice began implementing major revisions in the UCR system, converting it to what is called the *National Incident-Based Reporting System* (NIBRS). The NIBRS has major advantages over the traditional UCR, including an expanded list of offense categories and greater specificity in the data (Hagan, 1993). It is expected that the NIBRS will significantly improve analyses of official crime statistics, but because the NIBRS still represents only crimes known to the police, many of the criticisms leveled against the UCR pertain to it as well.

The National Crime Victimization Survey.   Initiated by the U.S. Department of Justice in 1967 to learn more about the crimes that are not reported to the police and about the victims of crime in general, the *National Crime Victimization Survey* (NCVS) has become the major source of official data on victimization in the United States. The NCVS provides extensive information on characteristics of offenders and victims, as well as data about specific criminal acts. It has been especially helpful in highlighting the gap between the official UCR figures on crime and the volume of crime reported by victims, along with the fact that the probability that crimes will be brought to the attention of the police is quite low. For example, although there is a great variation across offenses, NCVS data nevertheless indicate that when self-reported victimizations are compared to the UCR statistics, only about 41 percent of all violent personal crimes (excluding murder) and only 34 percent of all household (property) crimes are reported to law enforcement authorities (U.S. Department of Justice, Bureau of Justice Statistics, 1998).

 The NCVS also provides data on: the reasons people give for not contacting the police when they have been victimized; victims' relationships to offenders, if known; victims' perceptions of drug and alcohol use by violent offenders; protective actions taken by victims and bystanders when a crime is being committed; and victims' perceptions of the responses of police and other criminal justice authorities to reported crime.

 There has been considerable debate regarding the comparability of the UCR and NCVS (see, for example, Blumstein et al., 1991, 1992; McDowall & Loftin, 1992; Menard, 1992). With respect to the NCVS itself, it does appear to enlighten us about many areas of criminal behavior and the processing of crime. However, like the UCR, it falls short of telling the whole story because of its limited scope. Researchers who use this official data source must be clear on the purposes of their project and must exercise caution in generalizing their findings.

Summary and Conclusion

In this appendix, we have attempted to provide readers who have had limited exposure to research methods with a brief overview of major methodological concepts and central issues in the research process. We have highlighted two of the major models of inquiry as well as the basic steps of the research process, from developing the research problem to collecting the data. Techniques for analyzing the data collected, however, have not been reviewed here, and readers are urged to consult the resources listed in the Suggested Readings section that follows for detailed presentations of specific analytic techniques as well as in-depth discussions of the topics raised here.

KEY TERMS

analysis of existing statistics—a research method in which the researcher analyzes a data set collected previously (usually by government and nongovernment agencies for purposes other than research).

conceptualization—the process of specifying what a term means.

content analysis—a research method through which the researcher analyzes the content of some form of communication.

cross-sectional study—a research method that involves questioning a group of people and/or observing their behavior at one point in time only.

dependent variable—the variable that is affected or changed by a change in another (independent) variable.

equal probability of selection method (EPSEM)—all members of a population have an equal chance of being selected for a sample.

field observation—a research method in which the researcher, either as participant or nonparticipant, watches the phenomenon he or she is studying unfold in its natural setting.

generalization—the process by which a population's characteristics are inferred from the characteristics of a sample.

independent variable—the variable that induces a change or effect in another (dependent) variable.

literature review—an examination of the available literature on a research topic to help refine the topic and relate it to current and past inquiries.

longitudinal study—a research method that involves questioning a group of people and/or observing their behavior at various points over a specific period of time.

nonprobability sampling—a nonrandom sampling strategy in which the degree of error cannot be calculated.

operationalization—the process of specifying how one will measure particular concepts.

population—the entire array of cases that could potentially be studied in a research project.

probability sampling—a sampling strategy involving random selection and guided by a calculable degree of error.

reliability—the consistency of a measure.

representativeness—the degree to which the sample and the population are similar.

sample—a subset of cases selected from a population for participation in a research project.

survey research—a research method in which the researcher asks a sample of respondents questions using a questionnaire or by interviewing them.

unit of analysis—who or what the researcher will actually study.

validity—the accuracy of a measure.

variable—a logical set of attributes or qualities.

SUGGESTED READINGS

Babbie, E. (1998). *The practice of social research*. Belmont, CA: Wadsworth. One of the leading research methods textbooks. Readers who need exposure to or review of the basics of social research, including an overview of various methodologies, will find this book helpful.

Dowdall, G., Logio, K., Babbie, E., & Halley, F. (1999). *Adventures in criminal justice research*. Thousand Oaks, CA: Pine Forge. An introduction to data analysis techniques as well as some useful data sets for criminal justice researchers. The book comes with a disk containing SPSSx, Student Version, as well as several data sets.

Ferrell, J., & Hamm, M. A. (Eds.). (1998). *Ethnography at the edge: Crime, deviance and field research*. Boston: Northeastern University Press. A collection of essays that relates the field experiences of sociologists and criminologists who have conducted their research by immersing themselves in the everyday lives of pimps, phone sex workers, and terrorists. Readers get a firsthand account of the challenges of observational research.

Renzetti, C. M., & Lee, R. M. (Eds.). (1993). *Researching sensitive topics*. Newbury Park, CA: Sage. A collection of essays in which researchers discuss some of the methodological difficulties—and solutions—to studying such topics as HIV/AIDS, policing in Northern Ireland, and the underground economy.

The *Journal of Criminal Justice Education* also recently devoted a special issue to teaching research methods and statistics in criminal justice: Byers, B. (Ed.). (1999). Special issue. *Journal of Criminal Justice Education, 10* (2).

NOTES

1. Although these perspectives may be collectively distinguished from the positivist model of inquiry because of their shared criticisms of that model, there are important differences among them. For a discussion of these differences, see Maguire, 1987.

2. An extensive discussion of factors impinging on reliability and validity and ways of minimizing the effects of these factors is beyond the scope of this brief appendix. Most of the resources listed in the Suggested Readings at the end of the appendix treat these issues at length.

REFERENCES

Adams, L. R. (1974). The adequacy of differential association theory. *Journal of Research in Crime and Delinquency, 11*, 1–8.

Adler, F. (1975). *Sisters in crime*. New York: McGraw-Hill.

Agnew, R. (1985). A revised strain theory of delinquency. *Social Forces, 64*, 151–167.

Agnew, R. (1991). A longitudinal test of social control theory and delinquency. *Journal of Research in Crime and Delinquency, 28*, 126–156.

Agnew, R. (1992). Foundation for a general strain theory of crime and delinquency. *Criminology, 30*, 47–87.

Agnew, R. (1993). Why do they do it? An examination of the intervening mechanisms between "social control" variables and delinquency. *Journal of Research in Crime and Delinquency, 30*, 245–266.

Agnew, R. (1997). The nature and determinants of strain: Another look at Durkheim and Merton. In N. Passas & R. Agnew (Eds.), *The future of anomie theory* (pp. 27–51). Boston: Northeastern University Press.

Agnew, R., & Passas, N. (1997). Introduction. In N. Passas & R. Agnew (Eds.), *The future of anomie theory* (pp. 1–26). Boston: Northeastern University Press.

Agnew, R., & Petersen, D. M. (1989). Leisure and delinquency. *Social Problems, 36*, 332–350.

Agnew, R., & White, H. R. (1992). An empirical test of general strain theory. *Criminology, 30*, 475–499.

Aichhorn, A. (1963). *Wayward youth*. New York: Viking.

Akers, R. L. (1968). Problems in the sociology of deviance: Social definitions and behavior. *Social Forces, 46*, 455–465.

Akers, R. L. (1973). *Deviant behavior: A social learning approach* (1st ed.). Belmont, CA: Wadsworth.

Akers, R. L. (1985). *Deviant behavior: A social learning approach* (3rd ed.). Belmont, CA: Wadsworth.

Akers, R. L. (1994). *Criminological theories: Introduction and evaluation*. Los Angeles: Roxbury.

Akers, R. L. (1996). Is differential association/social learning cultural deviance theory? *Criminology, 34*, 229–247.

Akers, R. L. (1998). *Social learning and social structure: A general theory of crime and deviance*. Boston: Northeastern University Press.

Akers, R. L. (1999). Social learning and social structure: Reply to Sampson, Morash, and Krohn. *Theoretical Criminology, 3*, 477–493.

Akers, R. L., Krohn, M. D., Lanza-Kaduce, L., & Radosevich, M. (1979). Social learning and deviant behavior: A specific test of a general theory. *American Sociological Review, 44*, 635–655.

Akers, R. L., LaGreca, A. J., Cochran, J., & Sellers, C. (1989). Social learning theory and alcohol behavior among the elderly. *Sociological Quarterly, 30*, 625–638.

Alter Egos? (1999, July 5). *Dateline NBC*. Transcript produced by Burrell's Information Services, Livingston, NJ.

Amnesty International. (1989). *When the state kills: . . . The death penalty as a human rights issue*. London: Author.

Amnesty International. (1991). *Women on the front lines*. New York: Author.

Amnesty International. (1999). Executions by state. Available online: http://www.icom.ca/aiusa/abolish/dpus.html

Andersen, M. L., & Renzetti, C. M. (1980). Rape crisis counseling and the culture of individualism. *Contemporary Crises, 4*, 323–339.

Applebome, P. (1996, March 3). Shootings at schools prompt new concerns about violence. *New York Times*, p. 12.

Applebome, P. (1997, May 4). Tests, too, have their failings. *New York Times*, p. E4.

Arbuthot, J., Gordon, D. A., & Jurkovic, G. J. (1987). Personality. In H. C. Quay (Ed.), *Handbook of juvenile delinquency* (pp. 139–183). New York: John Wiley & Sons.

Arnold, R. A. (1990). Processes of victimization and criminalization of Black women. *Social Justice, 17*, 153–165.

Arrigo, B. A. (1995). The peripheral core of law and criminology: On postmodern social theory and conceptual integration. *Justice Quarterly, 12*, 447–472.

Arrigo, B. A. (Ed.). (1999). *Social justice, criminal justice*. Belmont, CA: Wadworth.

Babbie, E. (1998). *Methods of sociological research*. Belmont, CA: Wadsworth.

Bachman, R., Paternoster, R., & Ward, S. (1992). The rationality of sexual offending: Testing a deterrence/rational choice conception of sexual assault. *Law and Society Review, 26*, 343–372.

Bailey, W. C. (1998). Deterrence, brutalization, and the death penalty: Another examination of Oklahoma's return to capital punishment. *Criminology, 36*, 711–733.

Baker, S. W. (1980). Biological influences on human sex and gender. *Signs, 6*, 80–96.

Baldwin, J. (1977). Urban criminality and the problem estate. *Local Government Studies, 1*, 12–20.

Ball, R. A. (1966). An empirical exploration of neutralization theory. *Criminologica, 4*, 22–32.

Ball, R. A. (1977). Emergent delinquency in an urban area. In T. N. Ferdinand (Ed.), *Juvenile delinquency: Little brother grows up* (pp. 101–120). Beverly Hills, CA: Sage.

Bandura, A. (1977). *Social learning theory.* Englewood Cliffs, NJ: Prentice-Hall.

Barak, G. (1980). *In defense of whom? A critique of criminal justice reform.* Cincinnati: Anderson.

Barber, B. L., & Eccles, J. S. (1992). Long-term influence of divorce and single parenting on adolescent family- and work-related values, behaviors, and aspirations. *Psychological Bulletin, 111*, 108–126.

Barrett, G. V., & Depinet, R. L. (1991). A reconsideration of testing for competence rather than intelligence. *American Psychologists, 46*, 1012–1024.

Barry, E. (1999, August 15). Eugenics victims are heard at last. *Boston Globe*, p. B1.

Bartol, C. R. (1999). *Criminal behavior: A psychosocial approach.* Englewood Cliffs, NJ: Prentice-Hall.

Bauer, W. (1970). The other side of the coin. *Illinois Medical Journal, 137*, 158–161.

Beccaria, C. (1963/1764). *On crimes and punishments.* Indianapolis: Bobbs-Merrill.

Becker, G. S. (1968). Crime and punishment: An economic approach. *Journal of Political Economy, 76*, 169–217.

Becker, H. S. (1967). Whose side are we on? *Social Problems, 14*, 239–247.

Becker, H. S. (1970). *Sociological work.* Chicago: Aldine.

Becker, H. S. (1973). *Outsiders.* New York: Free Press.

Becker, P. (1994, November). *Controversy over meanings: The debate between Cesare Lombroso and his critics about the signs and the habit of criminals.* Paper presented at the Annual Meeting of the American Society of Criminology, Miami, FL.

Beirne, P. (1987). Adolphe Quetelet and the origins of positivist criminology. *American Journal of Sociology, 92*, 1140–1169.

Beirne, P. (1991). Inventing criminology: The "science of man" in Cesare Beccaria's *Dei delitti e delle pene* (1764). *Criminology, 29*, 777–820.

Beirne, P. (1993). *Inventing criminology: Essays on the rise of* Homo Criminalis. Albany: State University of New York Press.

Beirne, P., & Messerschmidt, J. (1995). *Criminology.* San Diego: Harcout Brace Jovanovich.

Bellair, P. E. (1997). Social interaction and community crime: Examining the importance of neighborhood networks. *Criminology, 35*, 677–703.

Bem, S. L. (1993). *The lenses of gender: Transforming the debate on sexual inequality.* New Haven: Yale University Press.

Benson, M. L., & Moore, E. (1992). Are white-collar and common offenders the same? An empirical and theoretical critique of a recently proposed general theory of crime. *Journal of Research in Crime and Delinquency, 29*, 251–272.

Beres, L. S., & Griffith, T. D. (1998). Did "three strikes" cause the recent drop in California crime? An analysis of the California Attorney General's Report. *Loyola of Los Angeles Law Review, 32*, 101–132.

Bjerregaard, B., & Smith, C. (1993). Gender differences in gang participation, delinquency, and substance use. *Journal of Quantitative Criminology, 4*, 329–355.

Blackburn, R. (1993). *The psychology of criminal conduct: Theory, research and practice.* Chichester, England: Wiley.

Blair, J. (2000, March 13). In side effect of economic prosperity, white-collar crime flourishes. *New York Times*, pp. B1, B4.

Blau, J., & Blau, P. (1982). The cost of inequality: Metropolitan structure and violent crime. *American Sociological Review, 47*, 114–129.

Blum, D. (1997). *Sex on the brain.* New York: Viking.

Blumstein, A., Cohen, J., & Rosenfeld, R. (1991). Trend and deviation in crime rates: A comparison of UCR and NCS data for burglary and robbery. *Criminology, 29*, 237–263.

Blumstein, A., Cohen, J., & Rosenfeld, R. (1992). The UCR-NCS relationship revisited: A reply to Menard. *Criminology, 30*, 115–124.

Boeringer, S. (1992). *Sexual coercion among college males: Assessing three theoretical models of coercive sexual behavior.* Unpublished Ph.D. dissertation, University of Florida.

Boerginer, S., Shehan, C. L., & Akers, R. L. (1991). Social contexts and social learning in sexual coercion and aggression: Assessing the contribution of fraternity membership. *Family Relations, 40*, 558–564.

Bohm, R. M. (1982). Radical criminology: An explication. *Criminology, 19*, 565–589.

Bok, S. (1998). *Mayhem: Violence as public entertainment.* Reading, MA: Addison-Wesley.

Bonger, W. (1916). *Criminality and economic conditions.* Boston: Little, Brown.

Bonta, J., Law, M., & Hanson, K. (1998). The prediction of criminal and violent recidivism among mentally disordered offenders: A meta-analysis. *Pyschological Bulletin, 123,* 124–142.

Booth, A., Shelley, G., Mazur, A., Tharp, G., & Kittock, R. (1989). Testosterone and winning and losing in human competition. *Hormones and Behavior, 23,* 556–571.

Bottoms, A. E., & Wiles, P. (1986). Housing tenure and residential community crime careers in Britain. In A. J. Reiss, Jr. & M. Tonry (Eds.), *Crime and justice: A review of research, Communities and crime* (pp. 101–162). Chicago: University of Chicago Press.

Bouchard Jr., J. T., Lykken, D. T., McGue, M., Degal, N., L., & Tellegen, A. (1990). Sources of human psychological differences: The Minnesota study of twins reared apart. *Science, 250,* 223–228.

Bourgeois, P. (1995). *In search of respect: Selling crack in el barrio.* New York: Cambridge University Press.

Box, S. (1981). *Deviance, reality and society.* New York: Holt, Rinehart and Winston.

Boyd, S. C. (1999). *Mothers and illicit drugs: Transcending the myths.* Toronto: University of Toronto Press.

Braithwaite, J. (1989). *Crime, shame and reintegration.* New York: Cambridge University Press.

Braithwaite, J. (1991). Poverty, power, white-collar crime and the paradoxes of criminological theory. *Australian and New Zealand Journal of Criminology, 24,* 40–58.

Braithwaite, J. (1997). Charles Tittle's *Control Balance* and criminological theory. *Theoretical Criminology, 1,* 77–98.

Bremner, J. D., Randall, P., & Vermetten, E. (1997). Magnetic resonance imaging-based measurement of hippocampal volume in posttraumatic stress disorder related to childhood physical and sexual abuse—A preliminary report. *Biological Psychiatry, 41,* 23–32.

Brezina, T. (1996). Adapting to strain: An examination of delinquent coping responses. *Criminology, 34,* 39–60.

Briar, S., & Piliavin, I. (1965). Delinquency, situational inducements, and commitment to conformity. *Social Problems, 12,* 35–45.

Brizer, D. A. (1989). Introduction: Overview of current approaches to the prediction of violence. In D. A. Brizer & M. Crowner (Eds.), *Current approaches to the prediction of violence* (pp. xi–xxx). Washington, DC: American Psychiatric Press.

Broidy, L., & Agnew, R. (1997). Gender and crime: A general strain theory perspective. *Journal of Research in Crime and Delinquency, 34,* 275–306.

Brookoff, D. (1997). *Drugs, alcohol, and domestic violence in Memphis.* Washington, DC: National Institute of Justice.

Brownmiller, S. (1975). *Against our will.* New York: Simon and Schuster.

Brunson, R. K., & Miller, J. (2000). Girls and gangs. In C. M. Renzetti & L. I Goodstein (Eds.), *Gender, crime and criminal justice* (pp. 44–59). Los Angeles: Roxbury.

Buikhuisen, W. (1987). Cerebral dysfunctions and persistent juvenile delinquency. In S. A. Mednick, T. E. Moffitt, & S. A. Stack (Eds.), *The causes of crime: New biological approaches* (pp. 168–184). New York: Cambridge University Press.

Buikhuisen, W., Van Der Plas-Kornehoff, C., & Bontekoe, E. H. M. (1988). Alcohol and violence. In T. E. Moffitt & S. A. Mednick (Eds.), *Biological contributions to crime causation* (pp. 261–276). Dordrecht: Martinus Nijhoff.

Burg, B., & Belmont, I. (1990). Mental abilities of children from different cultural backgrounds in Israel. *Journal of Cross-Cultural Psychology, 21,* 90–108.

Burgess, R. L., & Akers, R. L. (1966). A differential association-reinforcement theory of criminal behavior. *Social Problems, 14,* 128–147.

Burney, E. (1990). *Putting crime in its place.* London: Centre for Inner City Studies, Goldsmith College, University of London.

Bursik, R. J., & Grasmick, H. G. (1993). *Neighborhoods and crime: The dimensions of effective community control.* New York: Lexington Books.

Bursik, R. J., & Webb, J. (1982). Community change and patterns of delinquency. *American Journal of Sociology, 88,* 24–42.

Bush-Baskette, S. R. (1998). The war on drugs as a war against Black women. In S. L. Miller (Ed.), *Crime control and women* (pp. 113–129). Thousand Oaks, CA: Sage.

Butterfield, F. (1992, January 31). Studies find a family link to criminality. *New York Times,* pp. A1, A16.

Butterfield, F. (1997, September 28). Crime keeps on falling, but prisons keep on filling. *New York Times,* Section 4, pp. 1, 4.

Butterfield, F. (1998, March 5). Prisons replace hospitals for the nation's mentally ill. *New York Times,* pp. A1, A26.

Butterfield, F. (1999, Janaury 6). Drug treatment in prisons dips as use rises, study finds. *New York Times,* p. A14.

Butterfield, F. (2000, March 4). Cities reduce crime and conflict without New York-style hardball. *New York Times,* pp. A1, B4.

Byers, B. (Ed.) (1999). Special issue. *Journal of Criminal Justice Education*, *10* (2).

Bynner, J. M., O'Malley, P. M., & Bachman, J. G. (1981). Self-esteem and delinquency revisited. *Journal of Youth and Adolescence*, *10*, 407–444.

Cadoret, R. J. (1978). Psychopathology in adopted-away offspring of biologic parents with antisocial behavior. *Archives of General Psychiatry*, *35*, 176–184.

Cain, M. (1982). The main themes of Marx' and Engels' sociology of law. In P. Beirne & R. Quinney (Eds.), *Marxism and law* (pp. 63–73). New York: John Wiley.

Cain, M., & Hunt, A. (1979). *Marx and Engels on law.* London: Academic Press.

Calavita, K., & Pontell, H. N. (1993). Savings and loan fraud as organized crime: Toward a conceptual typology of corporate illegality. *Criminology*, *31*, 519–548.

Callahan, L. A., McGreevy, M. A., Cirincione, C., & Steadman, H. J. (1992). Measuring the effects of the guilty but mentally ill (GBMI) verdict. *Law and Human Behavior*, *16*, 447–462.

Callahan, L. A., Steadman, H. J., McGreevy, M. A., & Robbins, P. C. (1991). The volume and characteristics of insanity defense pleas: An eight-state study. *Bulletin of Psychiatry and the Law*, *19*, 331–338.

Campbell, A. (1984). *The girls in the gang.* New York: Basil Blackwell.

Cao, L., Adams, A., & Jensen, V. J. (1997). A test of the Black subculture of violence thesis: A research note. *Criminology*, *35*, 367–379.

Carmody, D. (1988, September 21). Head Start gets credit for rise in scores. *New York Times*, p. B9.

Carr, P. J. (2000). *The new parochialism: The implications of the Beltway case for arguments concerning informal social control.* Unpublished manuscript, St. Joseph's University, Philadelphia, PA.

Caspi, A., Moffitt, T. E., Silva, P. A., Stouthamer-Loeber, M., Krueger, R. F., & Schmutte, P. S. (1994). Are some people crime-prone? Replications of the personality-crime relationship across countries, genders, races, and methods. *Criminology*, *32*, 163–195.

Center on Crime, Communities and Culture. (1997). *Education as crime prevention.* New York: Author.

Cernkovich, S. A., & Giordano, P. C. (1987). Family relationships and delinquency. *Criminology*, *25*, 295–321.

Chambliss, W. J. (1973). The Saints and the Roughnecks. *Society*, *2*, 24–31.

Chambliss, W. J. (1976). Functional and conflict theories of crime. In W. J. Chambliss & M. Mankoff (Eds.), *Whose law, what order?* (pp. 1–28). New York: John Wiley.

Chambliss, W. J. (1988). *Explaining crime.* New York: Macmillan.

Chambliss, W. J., & Seidman, R. (1982). *Law, order, and power.* Reading, MA: Addison-Wesley.

Chambliss, W. J., & Zatz, M. (1994). *Making law: Law, state and structural contradiction.* Bloomington: Indiana University Press.

Chandler, K. A., Chapman, C. D., Rand, M. R., & Taylor, B. M. (1998). *Students' reports of school crime, 1989 and 1995.* Washington, DC: U.S. Department of Education and U.S. Department of Justice.

Chapman, J. R. (1990). Violence against women as a violation of human rights. *Social Justice*, *17*, 54–70.

Chasnoff, I. J. (1991). Cocaine and pregnancy: Clinical and methodological issues. *Clinics in Perinatology*, *18*, 113–123.

Chesney-Lind, M. (1997). *The female offender.* Thousand Oaks, CA: Sage.

Chesney-Lind, M., & Rodriguez, N. (1983). Women under lock and key. *The Prison Journal*, *63*, 47–65.

Chesney-Lind, M., & Sheldon, R. G. (1992). *Girls' delinquency and juvenile justice.* Pacific Grove, CA: Brooks/Cole.

Cheung, Y., & Ng, A. M. C. (1988). Social factors in adolescent deviant behavior in Hong Kong: An integrated theoretical approach. *International Journal of Comparative and Applied Criminal Justice,* *12*, 27–45.

Chiricos, T., & Waldo, G. (1975). Socioeconomic status and criminal sentencing: An empirical assessment of a conflict proposition. *American Sociological Review*, *40*, 753–772.

Chrisler, J. C. (1991). The effect of premenstrual symptoms on creative thinking. In D. L. Taylor & N. F. Woods (Eds.), *Menstruation, health and illness* (pp. 73–83). New York: Hemisphere.

Christiansen, K. O. (1974). Seriousness of criminality and concordance among Danish twins. In R. Hood (Ed.), *Crime, criminology and public policy* (pp. 63–77). New York: Free Press.

Christie, N. (1997). Four blocks against insight: Notes on the oversocialization of criminologists. *Theoretical Criminology*, *1*, 13–23.

Cirincione, C., Steadman, H. J., Robbins, P. C., & Monahan, J. (1991, November). *Mental illness as a factor in criminality: A study of prisoners and mental patients.* Paper presented at the Annual Meeting of the American Society of Criminology, San Francisco, CA.

Clark, J., Austin, J., & Henry, D. A. (1997). *"Three strikes and you're out": A review of state legislation.* Washington, DC: National Institute of Justice.

Clarke, R., & Cornish, D. (1985). Modeling offenders' decisions: A framework for research and policy. In M. Tonry & N. Morris (Eds.), *Crime and justice: An annual review of research, Vol. 6* (pp. 147–185). Chicago: University of Chicago Press.

Cleckley, H. (1976). *The mask of sanity.* St. Louis, MO: Mosby.

Clinard, M. B. (1964). The theoretical implications of anomie and deviant behavior. In M. B. Clinard (Ed.), *Anomie and deviant behavior* (pp. 1–56). New York: Free Press.

Cloward, R. A. (1959). Illegitimate means, anomie and deviant behavior. *American Sociological Review, 24,* 164–176.

Cloward, R. A., & Ohlin, L. E. (1960). *Delinquency and opportunity: A theory of delinquent gangs.* New York: Free Press of Glencoe.

Coccaro, E. F. (1992). Impulsive aggression and central serotonergic system function in humans: An example of a dimensional brain-behavior relationship. *International Clinical Psychopharmacology, 7,* 3–12.

Cochran, J. K., Chamlin, M. B., & Seth, M. (1994). Deterrence or brutalization? An impact assessment of Oklahoma's return to capital punishment. *Criminology, 32,* 107–134.

Cocozza, J. J., Melick, M. E., & Steadman, H. J. (1978). Trends in violent crime among ex-mental patients. *Criminology, 16,* 317–334.

Cocozza, J. J., & Steadman, H. J. (1978). Prediction in psychiatry: An example of misplaced cadence in experts. *Social Problems, 25,* 265–276.

Cohen, A. K. (1955). *Delinquent boys.* New York: Free Press of Glencoe.

Cohen, A. K. (1966). *Deviance and control.* Englewood Cliffs, NJ: Prentice-Hall.

Cohen, A. K. (1997). An elaboration of anomie theory. In N. Passas & R. Agnew (Eds.), *The future of anomie theory* (pp. 52–61). Boston: Northeastern University Press.

Cohen, L. E., & Felson, M. (1979). Social change and crime rate trends: A routine activities approach. *American Sociological Review, 44,* 588–608.

Cole, B. P. (1985). The state of education for Black Americans. In F. Schultz (Ed.), *Annual editions: Education 85/86* (pp. 148–151). Guilford, CT: Duskin Publishing Group.

Coleman, A. (1989). Disposition and situation: Two sides of the same crime. In D. J. Evans & D. T. Herbert (Eds.), *The geography of crime* (pp. 108–134). London: Routledge.

Coleman, J. (1987). Towards an integrated theory of white-collar crime. *American Journal of Sociology, 93,* 406–439.

Collins, R., & Makowsky, M. (1989). *The discovery of society.* New York: Random House.

Conrad, L. T. (1989, February 26). Battling post-partum depression. *Philadelphia Inquirer,* pp. J1, J6.

Cornish, D., & Clarke, R. (1986). Introduction. In D. Cornish & R. Clarke (Eds.), *The reasoning criminal* (pp. 1–16). New York: Springer-Verlag.

Cortes, J. B. (1972). *Delinquency and crime.* New York: Seminar Press.

Coser, L. A. (1977). *Masters of sociological thought.* New York: Harcourt Brace Jovanovich.

Costello, B. J. (1998). The remarkable persistence of a flawed term: A rejoinder to Matseuda. *Theoretical Criminology, 2,* 85–92.

Costello, B. J., & Vowell, P. R. (1999). Testing control theory and differential association: A reanalysis of the Richmond Youth Project data. *Criminology, 37,* 815–842.

Cott, N. F. (1987). *The grounding of modern feminism.* New Haven: Yale University Press.

Council of State Governments/Eastern Regional Conference. (1999). *What do we want (and what are we getting) from the criminal justice system? Comparing the general public's expectations and perceptions with crime victims' experiences.* New York: Author.

Covington, J. (1999). African-American communities and violent crime: The construction of race differences. *Sociological Focus, 32,* 7–24.

Covington, J., & Taylor, R. B. (1989). Gentrification and crime: Robbery and larceny changes in appreciating Baltimore neighborhoods in the 1970's. *Urban Affairs Quarterly, 25,* 142–172.

Craven, D. (1996). *Female victims of violent crime.* Washington, DC: U.S. Department of Justice.

Crawford, C. (2000). Gender, race, and habitual offender sentencing in Florida. *Criminology, 38,* 263–280.

Crawford, C., Chiricos, T., & Kleck, G. (1998). Race, racial threat, and sentencing of habitual offenders. *Criminology, 36,* 481–511.

Crenshaw, K. W. (1994). Mapping the margins: Intersectionality, identity politics, and violence against women of color. In M. A. Fineman & R. Myktiuk (Eds.), *The public nature of private violence* (pp. 93–119). New York: Routledge.

Cressey, D. R. (1960). The theory of differential association: An introduction. *Social Problems, 8,* 2–6.

Crist, G. (1997, December 8). Cunning lawyers slick up their clients for jurors. *Fort Worth Star-Telegram,* Metro section, p. 1.

Crites, L. (Ed.). (1976). *The female offender.* Lexington, MA: Lexington Books.

Crocker, J., Major, B., & Steele, C. (1998). Social stigma. In D. T. Gilbert, S. T. Fiske, & G. Lindsey (Eds.), *Handbook of social psychology* (pp. 504–553). New York: Random House.

Cronkhite, C. (1996, November). *Biochemistry, cloning and DNA engineering: An answer for curbing future criminal behavior*. Paper presented at the Annual Meeting of the American Society of Criminology, Chicago, IL.

Crowe, R. R. (1972). The adopted offspring of women criminal offenders. *Archives of General Psychiatry, 27,* 600–603.

Crowe, R. R. (1975). An adoptive study of psychopathy: Preliminary results from arrest records and psychiatric hospital records. In R. R. Fieve, D. Rosenthal, & H. Brill (Eds.), *Genetic research in psychiatry* (pp. 95–103). Baltimore: Johns Hopkins University Press.

Crowell, N. A., & Burgess, A. W. (1996). *Understanding violence against women*. Washington, DC: National Academy Press.

Cruise, K. R., & Rogers, R. (1998). An analysis of competency to stand trial: An integration of case law and clinical knowledge. *Behavioral Sciences and the Law, 16,* 35–50.

Cullen, F. T., & Wright, J. P. (1997). Liberating the anomie-strain paradigm: Implications from social-support theory. In N. Passas & R. Agnew (Eds.), *The future of anomie theory* (pp. 187–206). Boston: Northeastern University Press.

Curran, D. J. (1993). *Dead laws for dead men: The politics of federal coal mine health and safety legislation*. Pittsburgh: University of Pittsburgh Press.

Curran, D. J. (1998). Economic reform, the floating population, and crime: The transformation of social control in China. *Journal of Contemporary Criminal Justice, 14,* 262–280.

Currie, E. (1998). Crime and market society: Lessons from the United States. In P. Walton & J. Young (Eds.), *The new criminology revisited* (pp. 130–142). New York: St. Martin's Press.

Curry, T. R. (1999, November). *Framing control balance theory: Causal processes with situational control ratios*. Paper presented at the Annual Meeting of the American Society of Criminology, Toronto, Canada.

Dahrendorf, R. (1959). *Class and class conflict in industrial society*. Palo Alto, CA: Stanford University Press.

Dalgaard, S. O., & Kringlen, E. (1976). A Norwegian twin study of criminality. *British Journal of Criminology, 16,* 213–232.

Daly, K. (1989). Gender varieties in white-collar crime. *Criminology, 27,* 769–793.

Daly, K. (1994). *Gender, crime and punishment*. New Haven, CT: Yale University Press.

Daly, K., & Chesney-Lind, M. (1988). Feminism and criminology. *Justice Quarterly, 5,* 497–538.

Damer, S. (1974). Wine Alley: The sociology of a dreadful enclosure. *Sociological Review, 22,* 221–248.

Dann, C. S. (1980). Crime area research. In D. E. Georges-Abeyie & K. D. Harries (Eds.), *Crime: A spatial perspective* (pp. 5–25). New York: Columbia University Press.

Davis, N. J. (1993, Summer). Female youth homelessness—systematic gender control. *Socio-Legal Bulletin,* pp. 22–31.

DeFleur, M. L., & Quinney, R. (1966). A reformulation of Sutherland's differential association theory and a strategy for empirical verification. *Journal of Research in Crime and Delinquency, 3,* 1–22.

DeFeudis, F. V., & Schauss, A. G. (1987). The role of brain monoamine metabolite concentrations in arsonists and habitually violent offenders: Abnormalities of criminals or social isolation effects? *International Journal of Biosocial Research, 9,* 27–30.

DeKeseredy, W. S. (2000). *Women, crime and the Canadian criminal justice system*. Cincinnati, OH: Anderson Publishing Co.

DeKeseredy, W. S., & Schwartz, M. D. (1996). *Contemporary criminology*. Belmont, CA: Wadsworth.

Delmar, R. (1986). What is feminism? In J. Mitchell & A. Oakley (Eds.), *What is feminism? A re-examination* (pp. 8–33). New York: Pantheon.

Demo, D. H., & Acock, A. C. (1992, August). *Family structure and adolescent behavior*. Paper presented at the Annual Meeting of the American Sociological Association, Pittsburgh, PA.

Denno, D. W. (1985). Sociological and human development explanations of crime: Conflict or consensus? *Criminology, 23,* 711–742.

Dews, P. (1987). *Logic of disintegration: Poststructuralist thought and the claims of critical thought*. New York: Verso.

Dirks-Linhorst, A., & Laster, J. D. (1998, November). *Chemical castration: An alternative for sex offenders*. Paper presented at the Annual Meeting of the American Society of Criminology, Washington, DC.

Dowdall, G., Logio, K., Babbie, E., & Halley, F. (1999). *Adventures in criminal justice research*. Thousand Oaks, CA: Sage.

Dukes, R. L., Martinez, R. O., & Stein, J. A. (1997). Precursors and consequences of membership in youth gangs. *Youth and Society, 29,* 139–165.

Durkheim, E. (1893/1947). *The division of labor*. New York: Free Press.

Durkheim, E. (1897/1951). *Suicide*. New York: Free Press.

Easteal, P. W. (1991). Women and crime: Premenstrual issues. *Trends and issues in crime and criminal justice, No. 31*. Canberra, Australia: Australian Institute of Criminology.

Edin, K., & Lein, L. (1997). *Making ends meet*. New York: Russell Sage Foundation.

Edleson, J. L., Eisikovits, Z., & Guttmann, E. (1985). Men who batter. *Journal of Family Issues, 6*, 229–247.

Edelson, M. (1989). *Psychoanalysis*. Chicago: University of Chicago Press.

Edwards, R. (1993). An education in interviewing. In C. M. Renzetti & R. M. Lee (Eds.), *Researching sensitive topics* (pp. 181–196). Newbury Park, CA: Sage.

Edwards, S. S. M. (1986). Neither bad nor mad: The female violent offender reassessed. *Women's Studies International Forum, 9*, 79–87.

Elliott, D., Huizinga, D., & Ageton, S. (1985). *Explaining delinquency and drug use*. Beverly Hills, CA: Sage.

Ellis, H. (1915). *The criminal*. New York: Scribner.

Ellis, L. (1982). Genetics and criminal behavior. *Criminology, 20*, 43–66.

Engels, F. (1845). *The condition of the working class in England*. New York: International Publishers.

Erikson, K. T. (1966). *Wayward puritans*. New York: John Wiley.

Ermann, M. D., & Lundman, R. J. (Eds.). (1996). *Corporate and governmental deviance*. New York: Oxford University Press.

Esbensen, F., Huizinga, D., & Weiher, A. W. (1993). Gang and non-gang youth: Differences in explanatory factors. *Journal of Contemporary Criminal Justice, 9*, 94–116.

Estrich, S. (1987). *Real rape*. Cambridge: Harvard University Press.

Evans, D. J., & Herbert, D. T. (Eds.). (1989). *The geography of crime*. London: Routledge.

Evans, R. C., Corpus. G., Hodgkinson, P., & Sullenberger, T. (1991, November). *A cross-cultural comparison of the self-concepts of confined youthful offenders by country, residence, and race*. Paper presented at the Annual Meeting of the American Society of Criminology, San Francisco, CA.

Evans, S. M. (1979). *Personal politics*. New York: Knopf.

Ewen, R. B. (1988). *An introduction to theories of personality*. Hillsdale, NJ: Lawrence Erlbaum Associates.

Eysenck, H. J. (1977). *Crime and personality*. London: Routledge and Kegan Paul.

Eysenck, H. J. (1998). *A new look at intelligence*. London: Transaction.

Eysenck, H. J., & Gudjonsson, G. H. (1989). *The causes and cures of criminality*. New York: Plenum.

Fagan, J., & Freeman, R. B. (1999). Crime and work. In M. Tonry (Ed.), *Crime and justice: A review of research* (pp. 113–178). Chicago: University of Chicago Press.

Faine, J. R., & Bohlander, E. (1976, November). *Sentencing the female offender: The impact of legal and extra-legal considerations*. Paper presented at the Annual Meeting of the American Society of Criminology, Tucson, AZ.

Farber, S. L. (1981). *Identical twins reared apart: A reanalysis*. New York: Basic Books.

Farnworth, M. (1984). Male-female differences in delinquency in a minority group sample. *Journal of Research in Crime and Delinquency, 21*, 191–212.

Farrell, R., & Swigert, V. (1978). Prior offense record as a self-fulfilling prophecy. *Law and Society Review, 12*, 437–453.

Feagin, J. R. (1991). The continuing significance of race: Anti-Black discrimination in public places. *American Sociological Review, 56*, 101–116.

Federal Bureau of Investigation. (1997). *Crime in America*. Washington, DC: U.S. Government Printing Office.

Ferrell, J., & Hamm, M. S. (Eds.). (1998). *Ethnography on the edge: Crime, deviance and field research*. Boston: Northeastern University Press.

Fineman, M. A. (1996). The nature of dependencies and welfare "reform." *Santa Clara Law Review, 36*, 1401–1425.

Fink, A. E. (1938). *The causes of crime: Biological theories in the United States, 1800–1915*. Philadelphia: University of Pennsylvania Press.

Fishbein, D. H. (2000). How can neurobiological research inform prevention strategies? In D. H. Fishbein (Ed.), *The science, treatment and prevention of antisocial behaviors* (pp. 25–30). Kingston, NJ: Civic Research Institute.

Fishbein, D. H., & Pease, S. (1988, June). The effects of diet on behavior: Implications for criminology and corrections. *Research in Corrections, 1*, 1–44.

Fiske, E. B. (1989, September 27). Can money spent on schools save money that would be spent on prisons? *New York Times*, p. B8.

Flax, J. (1992). The end of innocence. In J. Butler & J. W. Scott (Eds.), *Feminists theorize the political* (pp. 445–463). New York: Routledge.

Fleissner, D., & Heinzelmann, F. (1996). *Crime prevention through environmental design and community policing*. Washington, DC: National Institute of Justice.

Fletcher, M. A. (2000, February 3). Calif. minority youth treated more harshly, study says. *Washington Post*, p. A16.

Fordham, S. (1996). *Blacked out: Dilemmas of race, identity, and success at Capital High.* Chicago: University of Chicago Press.

Forero, J. (2000, March 4). Reading, writing and rehabilitation. *New York Times*, pp. B1, B3.

Foucault, M. (1977). *Discipline and punish.* New York: Pantheon.

Freud, S. (1983/1933). Femininity. In M. W. Zak & P. A. Motts (Eds.), *Women and the politics of culture* (pp. 80–92). New York: Longman.

Friedan, B. (1963). *The feminine mystique.* New York: W. W. Norton.

Friedman, R. C., Hurt, S. W., Aronoff, M. S., & Clarkin, J. (1980). Behavior and the menstrual cycle. *Signs, 5,* 719–738.

Frieze, I. H., Parsons, J. E., Johnson, P. B., Ruble, D. N., & Zellman, G. L. (1978). *Women and sex roles.* New York: W. W. Norton.

Gallagher, N. (1999). *Breeding better Vermonters: The Eugenics Project in the Green Mountain State.* Hanover, NH: University Press of New England.

Garfinkel, H. (1965). Conditions of successful degradation ceremonies. *American Journal of Sociology, 61,* 420–424.

Ge, X., Conger, R. D., Cadoret, R. J., Neiderhiser, J. M., Yates, W., Troughton, E., et al. (1996). The developmental interface between nature and nurture: A mutual influence model of child antisocial behavior and parent behavior. *Developmental Psychology, 32,* 574–589.

Geary, D. C. (1996). Biology, culture, and cross-national differences in mathematical ability. In R. J. Sternberg & T. Ben-Zeev (Eds.), *The nature of mathematical thinking* (pp. 145–171). Mahwah, NJ: Lawrence Erlbaum Associates.

Geis, G. (1955). Pioneers in criminology VII: Jeremy Bentham (1748–1832). *Journal of Criminal Law, Criminology and Police Science, 46,* 159–171.

Geis, G. (2000). On the absence of self-control as the basis for a general theory of crime: A critique. *Theoretical Criminology, 4,* 35–54.

Gelles, R. J. (1993). Alcohol and drugs are associated with violence—They are not its cause. In R. J. Gelles & D. R. Loseke (Eds.), *Current controversies on domestic violence* (pp. 182–196). Newbury Park, CA: Sage.

Gemignami, R. J. (1994). *Juvenile correctional education: A time for change.* Washington, DC: Office of Juvenile Justice and Delinquency Prevention.

Gibbons, D. C. (1970). *Delinquent behavior.* Englewood Cliffs, NJ: Prentice-Hall.

Gibson, C. L., & Tibbetts, S. G. (1998). Interaction between maternal cigarette smoking and Apgar scores in predicting offending behavior. *Psychological Reports, 83,* 579–586.

Gilbert, L. A., & Scher, M. (1999). *Gender and sex in counseling and psychotherapy.* Boston: Allyn and Bacon.

Gilfus, M. (1992). From victims to survivors to offenders: Women's routes of entry into street crime. *Women and Criminal Justice, 4,* 63–89.

Gill, O. (1977). *Lake Street.* London: Macmillan.

Gilligan, C. (1982). *In a different voice: Psychological theory and women's development.* Cambridge: Harvard University Press.

Gilligan, C., Taylor, J. M., & Sullivan, A. (1995). *Between voice and silence: Women and girls, race and relationship.* Cambridge: Harvard University Press.

Giordano, P., Cernkovich, S., & Pugh, M. (1986). Friendships and delinquency. *American Journal of Sociology, 91,* 1170–1202.

Giovannini, M. J. (1992). The relevance of gender in postpartum emotional disorders. In T. L. Whitehead & B. V. Reid (Eds.), *Gender constructs and social issues* (pp. 209–231). Urbana: University of Illinois Press.

Gitlin, M. J., & Passnau, R. O. (1990). Psychiatric symptoms linked to reproductive function in women: A review of current knowledge. *American Journal of Psychiatry, 146,* 1413–1422.

Gjerdingen, D. K., Froberg, D. G., & Fontaine, P. (1990). A causal model describing the relationship of women's postpartum health to social support, length of leave and complications of childbirth. *Women and Health, 16,* 71–87.

Glaser, D. (1956). Criminality theory and behavioral images. *American Journal of Sociology, 61,* 433–444.

Glaser, D. (1973). Role models and differential association. In E. Rubington & M. S. Weinberg (Eds.), *Deviance: The interactionist perspective* (pp. 369–373). New York: Macmillan.

Glaser, D. (1978). *Crime in our changing society.* New York: Holt, Rinehart and Winston.

Glass, R. (1982, January 24). Some fear abuses in premenstrual tension decisions. *Philadelphia Inquirer,* p. 8C.

Gleaves, D. H. (1996). The socioeconomic model of dissociative identity disorder: A reexamination of the evidence. *Psychological Bulletin, 120,* 42–59.

Glueck, S. (1956). Theory and fact in criminology: A criticism of differential association. *British Journal of Criminology, 7,* 92–109.

Glueck, S., & Glueck, E. (1950). *Unraveling juvenile delinquency.* Cambridge, MA: Harvard University Press.

Glueck, S., & Glueck, E. (1956). *Physique and delinquency.* New York: Harper.

Goering, L. (1996, May 21). Fighting lucrative sex trade a losing battle. *Chicago Tribune*, p. 4.

Gold, M. (1966). Undetected delinquent behavior. *Journal of Research in Crime and Delinquency, 3*, 27–46.

Gold, M. (1970). *Delinquent behavior in an American city*. Belmont, CA: Brooks/Cole.

Gold, M., & Williams, J. (1969). National study of the aftermath of apprehension. *Prospectus, 3*, 3.

Goldberg, C. (1997, November 25). Study casts doubt on wisdom of mandatory terms of drugs. *New York Times*, p. A14.

Goldman, E. L. (1998, September). Typical psychiatric patient rates "fairly severe." *Clinical Psychiatry News, 26*, 32.

Goleman, D. (1989, October 3). Biology of brain may hold key for gamblers. *New York Times*, pp. C1, C11.

Goleman, D. (1990, May 29). As bias crime seems to rise, scientists study roots of racism. *New York Times*, pp. C1, C15.

Goleman, D. (1995). *Emotional intelligence*. New York: Bantam.

Golub, A. L., & Johnson, B. D. (1997). *Crack's decline: Some surprises across U.S. cities*. Washington, DC: National Institute of Justice.

Golub, S. (1992). *Periods: From menarche to menopause*. Newbury Park, CA: Sage.

Gordon, R. A. (1980). Research on IQ, race, and delinquency: Taboo or not taboo? In E. Sagarin (Ed.), *Taboos in criminology* (pp. 37–66). Beverly Hills, CA: Sage.

Gordon, R. A. (1987). SES versus IQ in the race-IQ delinquency model. *International Journal of Sociology and Social Policy, 7*, 30–96.

Goring, C. (1913). *The English convict: A statistical study*. London: His Majesty's Stationary Office.

Gorio, A., Germani, E., Mantegazza, P., Di Guilio, A. M., & Bertelli, A. (1992). Perinatal exposure to ethanol affects postnatal degeneration and regeneration of serotonergic pathways in the spinal cord. *Drugs Experimental and Clinical Research, 18*, 461–464.

Gottfredson, D. C. (1986). An empirical test of school-based environmental and individual interventions to reduce the risk of delinquent behavior. *Criminology, 24*, 705–731.

Gottfredson, D. C., McNeill III, R. J., & Gottfredson, G. D. (1991). Social area influences on delinquency: A multilevel analysis. *Journal of Research in Crime and Delinquency, 28*, 197–226.

Gottfredson, M. R., & Hirschi, T. (1990). *A general theory of crime*. Stanford, CA: Stanford University Press.

Gould, S. J. (1981). *The mismeasure of man*. New York: W. W. Norton.

Gould, S. J. (1984, July). Carrie Buck's daughter. *Natural History*, pp. 14–18.

Grant, J. (1993). *Fundamental feminism: Contesting the core concepts of feminist theory*. New York: Routledge.

Gray, G. E. (1986). Diet, crime and delinquency: A critique. *Nutrition Reviews, 44*, 89–94.

Greek, C. E. (1992). *Religious roots of American sociology*. New York: Garland.

Greene, R. (1986, September). What's your destiny? *Glamour*, pp. 260–265.

Greenfeld, L. A. (1996). *Child victimizer: Violent offenders and their victims*. Washington, DC: U.S. Department of Justice.

Greenfeld, L. A. (1998a). *Alcohol and crime*. Washington, DC: U.S. Department of Justice, Bureau of Justice Statistics.

Greenfeld, L. A. (1998b). *Violence by intimates*. Washington, DC: U.S. Department of Justice.

Greenfield, P. M. (1997). You can't take it with you: Why ability assessments don't cross cultures. *American Psychologist, 52*, 1115–1124.

Greenhouse, L. (2000, February 29). Progam of drug-testing pregnant women draws a review by the Supreme Court. *New York Times*, p. A12.

Greenwood, P. W., Rydell, C. P., Abrahamse, A. F., Caulkins, J. P., Chiesa, J. R., Model, K. E., & Klein, S. P. (1994). *Three strikes and you're out: Estimated benefits and costs of California's new mandatory-sentencing law*. Los Angeles: RAND Corp.

Grove, W. M., Eckert, E. D., Heston, L., Bouchard Jr., T. J., Segal, N., & Lykken, D. T. (1990). Heritability of substance abuse and antisocial behavior: A study of monozygotic twins reared apart. *Biological Psychiatry, 27*, 1293–1304.

Guerra, C. (1998). Neuoranatomical and neurophysiological mechanisms involved in central nervous system dysfunctions induced by prenatal alcohol exposure. *Alcohol Clinical and Experimental Research, 22*, 304–312.

Gurr, T. R. (1976). *Rogues, rebels and reformers*. Beverly Hills, CA: Sage.

Hagan, F. E. (1993). *Research methods in criminal justice and criminology*. New York: Macmillan.

Hagan, J. (1985). The assumption of natural science methods: Criminological positivism. In R. F. Meier (Ed.), *Theoretical methods in criminology* (pp. 75–92). Beverly Hills, CA: Sage.

Hagan, J. (1989). *Structural criminology*. New Brunswick, NJ: Rutgers University Press.

Hagan, J., & Bumiller, K. (1983). Making sense of sentencing: A review and critique of sentencing. In A.

Blumstein, J. Cohen, S. Martin, & M. Tonry (Eds.), *Research on sentencing: The search for reform* Vol. II (pp. 1–54). Washington, DC: National Academy Press.

Hagan, J., Gillis, A., & Simpson, J. (1987). Class in the household: A power-control theory of gender and delinquency. *American Journal of Sociology*, *92*, 788–816.

Hagan, J., Hefler, G., Classen, G., Boehnke, K., & Merkens, H. (1998). Subterranean sources of subcultural delinquency beyond the American dream. *Criminology*, *36*, 309–342.

Hagan, J., & McCarthy, B. (1997). Anomie, social capital, and street criminology. In N. Passas & R. Agnew (Eds.), *The future of anomie theory* (pp. 124–141). Boston: Northeastern University Press.

Hale-Benson, J. E. (1986). *Black children: Their roots, culture, and learning styles.* Provo, UT: Brigham Young University Press.

Hamlin, J. E. (1988). The misplaced role of rational choice in neutralization theory. *Criminology*, *26*, 425–438.

Haney, M., Noda, K., Kream, R., et al. (1990). Regional 5-HT and dopamine activity: Sensitivity to amphetamine and aggressive behavior in mice. *Aggressive Behavior*, *16*, 259–270.

Hansen, E. J., & Reekie, L. (1990). Sex differences in clinical judgments of male and female therapists. *Sex Roles*, *23*, 51–64.

Hardie, E. A. (1997). Prevalence and predictors of cyclic and noncyclic affective change. *Psychology of Women Quarterly*, *21*, 299–314.

Harding, S. G. (1979). Is the equality of opportunity principle democratic? *Philosophical Forum*, *10*, 206–223.

Hare, R. D. (1996). Psychopathy: A clinical construct whose time has come. *Criminal Justice and Behavior*, *23*, 25–54.

Harries, K. D., & Stadler, S. J. (1989). Assault and heat stress: Dallas as a case study. In D. J. Evans & D. T. Herbert (Eds.), *The geography of crime* (pp. 38–57). London: Routledge

Harrington, M. (1984). *The new American poverty.* New York: Holt, Rinehart, and Winston.

Harris, M. A. (1998, November). *Neighborhood disadvantage and violent delinquency: The buffering effect of religious involvement.* Paper presented at the Annual Meeting of the American Society of Criminology, Washington, DC.

Hart, S. D., & Dempster, R. J. (1997). Impulsivity and psychopathy. In C. D. Webster & M. A. Jackson (Eds.), *Impulsivity: Theory, assessment and treatment* (pp. 212–232). New York: Guilford.

Haskins, R. (1989). Beyond metaphor: The efficacy of early childhood education. *American Psychologist*, *44*, 274–282.

Hay, C. (1998). Parental sanctions and delinquent behavior: Toward clarification of Braithwaite's theory of reintegrative shaming. *Theoretical Criminology*, *2*, 419–444.

Hayner, N. S. (1933). Delinquency areas in the Puget Sound region. *American Journal of Sociology*, *39*, 314–328.

Heimer, K., & DeCoster, S. (1999). The gendering of violent delinquency. *Criminology*, *37*, 277–318.

Heller, M. S., Traylor, W. H., Ehrlich, S. M., & Lester, D. (1984). The association between psychosis and violent crime: A study of offenders evaluated at a court psychiatric clinic. *Journal of General Psychology*, *110*, 263–266.

Henry, S., & Milovanovic, D. (1993). Back to basics: A postmodern redefinition of crime. *The Critical Criminologist*, *5*, 1–2, 12.

Henry, S., & Milovanovic, D. (1993). *Constitutive criminology: Beyond postmodernism.* London: Sage.

Herbert, D. T. (1980). Urban crime and spatial perspectives: The British experience. In D. E. Georges-Abeyie & K. D. Harries (Eds.), *Crime: A spatial perspective* (pp. 26–46). New York: Columbia University Press.

Herbert, D. T. (1989). *The geography of crime.* London: Routledge.

Herman, J. L. (1988). Considering sex offenders: A model of addiction. *Signs*, *13*, 695–724.

Herrnstein, R. J. (1988a). The individual offender. *Today's Delinquent*, *7*, 8–9.

Herrnstein, R. J. (1988b, Winter/Spring). *Crime and human nature* revisited: A response to Bonn and Smith. *Criminal Justice Ethics*, *7*, 10–15.

Herrnstein, R. J., & Murray, C. (1994). *The bell curve: Intelligence and class structure in American life.* New York: Free Press.

Hess, B. B., & Ferree, M. M. (1987). Introduction. In B. B. Hess & M. M. Ferree (Eds.), *Analyzing gender* (pp. 9–30). Newbury Park, CA: Sage.

Hetherington, E. M., Stanley-Hagan, M., & Anderson, E. R. (1989). Marital transitions: A child's perspective. *American Psychologist*, *44*, 303–312.

Hilliard III, A. G. (1984). IQ testing and the emperor's new clothes. In C. R. Reynolds & R. T. Brown (Eds.), *Perspectives on bias in mental testing* (pp. 139–169). New York: Plenum Press.

Hindelang, M. J. (1970). The commitment of delinquents to their misdeeds. *Social Problems*, *17*, 502–509.

Hirschi, T. (1969). *Causes of delinquency.* Berkeley: University of California Press.

Hirschi, T. (1996). Theory without ideas: Reply to Akers. *Criminology, 34,* 249–256.

Hirschi, T., & Gottfredson, M. R. (2000). In defense of self-control. *Theoretical Criminology, 4,* 55–70.

Hirschi, T., & Hindelang, M. J. (1977). Intelligence and delinquency: A revisionist review. *American Sociological Review, 42,* 571–586.

Hirst, P. Q. (1975). Marx and Engels on law, crime and morality. In I. Taylor, P. Walton, & J. Young (Eds.), *Critical criminology* (pp. 203–232). London: Routledge and Kegan Paul.

Hoffman, J. P., & Cerbone, F. G. (1999). Stressful life events and delinquency escalation in early adolescence. *Criminology, 37,* 343–374.

Hoffman, J., & Miller, A. (1998). A latent variable analysis of general strain theory. *Journal of Quantitative Criminology, 14,* 83–111.

Hollingshead, A. B., & Redlich, F. C. (1958). *Social class and mental illness: A community study.* New York: Wiley.

Holmes, S. A. (2000, April 16). Look who's questioning the death penalty. *New York Times,* p. WK3.

Hooton, E. (1939a). *The American criminal.* Cambridge, MA: Harvard University Press.

Hooton, E. (1939b). *Crime and the man.* Cambridge, MA: Harvard University Press.

Horn, J. M. (1983). The Texas Adoption Project: Adopted children and their intellectual resemblance to biological and adoptive parents. *Child Development, 54,* 268–275.

Hoyenga, K. B., & Hoyenga, K. T. (1993). *Gender-related differences.* Boston: Allyn and Bacon.

Huff, C. R. (1998). *Criminal behavior of gang members and at-risk youth.* Washington, DC: National Institute of Justice.

Humphries, D. (1999). *Crack mothers: Pregnancy, drugs, and the media.* Columbus: Ohio State University Press.

Hutchings, D. E. (1993). The puzzle of cocaine's effects following maternal use during pregnancy: Are there reconcilable differences? *Neurotoxicology and Teratology, 15,* 281–286.

Inciardi, J. A., Lockwood, D., & Pottieger, A. E. (1993). *Women and crack-cocaine.* New York: Macmillan.

Innes, C. A. (1988). *Drug use and crime.* Washington, DC: National Institute of Justice.

Jensen, G. F. (1990, November). *Power-control vs. social-control theories of delinquency: A comparative analysis.* Paper presented at the Annual Meeting of the American Society of Criminology, Baltimore, MD.

Jensen, G. F. (1999). A critique of control balance theory: Digging into details. *Theoretical Criminology, 3,* 339–343.

Johnson, J. G., Cohen, P. & Bernstein, D. P. (1999). Childhood maltreatment increases risk for personality disorders during early adulthood. *Archives of General Psychiatry, 56,* 600–606.

Johnson, R. E. (1986). Family structure and delinquency: General patterns and gender differences. *Criminology, 24,* 65–80.

Johnson, R. E., Marcos, A. C., & Bahr, S. J. (1987). The roles of peers in the complex etiology of adolescent drug use. *Criminology, 25,* 323–340

Jonassen, C. T. (1971). A re-evaluation and critique of the logic and some methods of Shaw and McKay. In H. L. Voss & D. M. Petersen (Eds.), *Ecology, crime and delinquency* (pp. 133–146). New York: Appleton-Century-Crofts.

Jones, C. (1994, July 8). Test scores show gaps by ethnicity. *New York Times,* pp. B1, B3.

Jones, T., Lea, J., & Young, J. (1987). *Saving the inner city: Broadwater Farm strategy for survival.* London: Middlesex Polytechnic Centre for Criminology.

Jurik, N. C. (1999). Socialist feminist criminology and social justice. In B. A. Arrigo (Ed.), *Social justice, criminal justice* (pp. 30–50). Belmont, CA: Wadsworth.

Jussim, L. (1989). Teacher expectations: Self-fulfilling prophecies, perceptual biases, and accuracy. *Journal of Personality and Social Psychology, 57,* 469–480.

Kamin, L. J. (1986, February). Is crime in the genes? The answer may depend on who chooses what evidence. *Science,* 22–27.

Kaplan, H. B. (1975). *Self-attitudes and deviant behavior.* Pacific Palisades, CA: Goodyear.

Kaplan, H. B. (1980). *Deviant behavior in defense of self.* New York: Academic Press.

Kaplan, H. B., Johnson, R. J., & Bailey, C. A. (1986). Self-rejection and the explanation of deviance: Refinement and elaboration of a latent subculture. *Social Psychology Quarterly, 49,* 110–128.

Kaplan, H. B., Johnson, R. J., & Bailey, C. A. (1987). Deviant peers and deviant behavior: Further elaboration of a model. *Social Psychology Quarterly, 50,* 277–284.

Kauzlarich, D., & Kramer, R. C. (1998). *Crimes of the nuclear state: At home and abroad.* Boston: Northeastern University Press.

Kelling, G. L., & Moore, M. H. (1987). *From political reform to community: The evolving strategy of police.* Cambridge, MA: Harvard University, JFK School of Government.

Kennedy, L. W., & Baron, S. (1993). Routine activities and a subculture of violence: A study of violence on the street. *Journal of Research in Crime and Delinquency, 20,* 88–112.

Kennedy, L. W., & Forde, D. R. (1990). Routine activities and crime: An analysis of victimization in Canada. *Criminology, 28,* 137–152.

Kennedy, M. C. (1976). Beyond incrimination. In W. C. Chambliss & M. Mankoff (Eds.), *Whose law, what order?* (pp. 34–65). New York: Wiley.

Kessler, S., & Moos, R. H. (1970). The XYY karyotype and criminality: A review. *Journal of Psychiatric Research, 7,* 153–170.

Keyes, D. (1982). *The minds of Billy Milligan.* New York: Bantam Books.

Kick, E., & LaFree, G. (1985). Development and the social context of murder and theft. *Comparative Social Research, 8,* 37–58.

Kifner, J. (2000, May 19). A state votes to end its death penalty. *New York Times,* p. A16.

Kilborn, P. (1997, March 11). Revival of chain gangs takes a twist. *New York Times,* p. A18.

King, D. R. (1988). Multiple jeopardy, multiple consciousness: The context of a Black feminist ideology. *Signs, 14,* 42–72.

Kitsuse, J. I., & Dietrick, D. C. (1959). Delinquent boys: A critique. *American Sociological Review, 24,* 208–215.

Klein, D. (1980). The etiology of female crime: A review of the literature. In F. R. Scarpitti & S. K. Datesman (Eds.), *Women, crime and justice* (pp. 70–105). New York: Oxford University Press.

Kleinmuntz, B. (1982). *Personality and psychological assessment.* New York: St. Martin's Press.

Klockars, C. B. (1979). The contemporary crises of Marxist criminology. *Criminology, 16,* 477–515.

Koeske, R. (1980). Theoretical perspectives on menstrual cycle research. In A. Dan, E. Graham, & C. P. Beecher (Eds.), *The menstrual cycle* (pp. 8–24). New York: Springer.

Kohn, M. (1965). Social class and parent-child relationships: An interpretation. *American Journal of Sociology, 68,* 471–480.

Kohn, M. (1976). Occupational structure and alienation. *American Journal of Sociology, 82,* 111–130.

Kohn, M. (1977). *Class and conformity.* Homewood, IL: Dorsey.

Kold Kash in Kalifornia. (1999, August 28). *Boston Globe,* p. A18.

Koren, G., Shear, H., Graham, K., & Einarson, T. (1989). Bias against the null hypothesis: The reproductive hazards of cocaine. *Lancet, 340,* 1440–1442.

Kornhauser, R. (1978). *Social sources of delinquency.* Chicago: University of Chicago Press.

Koss, M., Gidycz, C., & Wisniewski, N. (1987). The scope of rape: Incidence and prevalence of sexual aggression in a sample of higher education students. *Journal of Consulting and Clinical Psychology, 55,* 162–170.

Kozol, J. (1991). *Savage inequalities: Children in America's schools.* New York: Crown.

Krisberg, B. (1975). *Crime and privilege.* Englewood Cliffs, NJ: Prentice-Hall.

Kristof, N. D. (1996, April 14). Asian childhoods being sacrificed for prosperity's lust. *New York Times,* pp. 1, 8.

Krohn, M. D., & Massey, J. L. (1980). Social control and delinquency behavior: An examination of the elements of the social bond. *Sociological Quarterly, 21,* 529–543.

Krouse, J. P., & Kauffman, J. M. (1982). Minor physical anomalies in exceptional children: A review and critique of research. *Journal of Abnormal Child Psychology, 10,* 247–264.

Kuhn, T. S. (1970). *The structure of scientific revolutions.* Chicago: University of Chicago Press.

Lamiel, J. T. (1987). *The psychology of personality.* New York: Columbia University Press.

Larzelere, R. E., & Patterson, G. R. (1990). Parental management: Mediator of the effect of socioeconomic status on early delinquency. *Criminology, 28,* 301–323.

Laub, J. H., & Sampson, R. J. (1988). Unraveling families and delinquency: A reanalysis of the Gluecks' data. *Criminology, 26,* 355–380.

Lawmaker's rape view stirs ire. (1995, April 20). Raleigh, NC: Associated Press. (Internet).

Lea, J., & Young, J. (1984). *What is to be done about law and order?* New York: Penguin.

LeBlanc, M., & Kaspy, N. (1998). Trajectories of delinquency and problem behavior: Comparison of social and personal control characteristics of adjudicated boys on synchronous and nonsynchronous paths. *Journal of Quantitative Criminology, 14,* 181–214.

Lee, F. R. (1997, October 23). Young and in fear of the police. *New York Times,* pp. B1, B10.

Lefton, L. A. (2000). *Psychology.* Boston: Allyn and Bacon.

Lemert, E. M. (1951). *Social pathology.* New York: McGraw-Hill.

Lemert, E. M. (1964). Social structure, social control, and deviation. In M. B. Clinard (Ed.), *Anomie and deviant behavior* (pp. 57–97). New York: Free Press.

Lemert, E. M. (1967). *Human deviance, social problems, and social control.* Englewood Cliffs, NJ: Prentice-Hall.

Lerner, G. (1993). *The creation of feminist consciousness.* New York: Oxford University Press.

Levitan, S., & Johnson, C. M. (1984). *Beyond the safety net: Renewing the promise of opportunity in America.* Cambridge, MA: Ballinger.

Lewis, N. A. (1993, November 24). U.S. restrictions on adult-TV fare are struck down. *New York Times*, pp. A1, A20.

Liebman, J. S., West, V., & Fagan, J. (2000). *A broken system: Error rates in capital cases, 1973–1995*. Washington, DC: The Justice Project.

Lim, L. L. (1998). The economic and social bases of prostitution in Southeast Asia. In L. L. Lim (Ed.), *The sex sector* (pp. 1–28). Geneva: International Labour Organization.

Limandri, D. J., & Sheridan, D. J. (1995). Prediction of internal interpersonal violence: An introduction. In J. C. Campbell (Ed.), *Assessing dangerousness* (pp. 1–19). Thousand Oaks, CA: Sage.

Lindesmith, A. R., & Gagnon, J. (1964). Anomie and drug addiction. In M. B. Clinard (Ed.), *Anomie and deviant behavior* (pp. 158–188). New York: Free Press.

Lindner, R. (1996). *The reportage of urban culture: Robert Park and the Chicago School*. New York: Cambridge University Press.

Linhorst, D. M. (1998, November). *The unconditional release of mentally ill offenders from indefinite commitment: A study of Missouri insanity acquittees*. Paper presented at the Annual Meeting of the American Society of Criminology, Washington, DC.

Linnoila, V. M. I., & Virkkunen, M. (1992). Aggression, suicidality, and serotonin. *Journal of Clincal Psychiatry, 53*, 46–51.

Lippen, L. B. (1989, November). *Incarcerated women: Personality differences by race*. Paper presented at the Annual Meeting of the American Society of Criminology, Reno, NV.

Liska, A. E., & Reed, M. D. (1985). Ties to conventional institutions and delinquency: Estimating reciprocal effects. *American Sociological Review, 50*, 547–560.

Lively, K. (1997, March 21). Campus drug arrests increased 18 percent in 1995; Reports of other crimes fell. *Chronicle of Higher Education*, pp. A44–A46.

Lizotte, A. (1978). Extra-legal factors in Chicago's criminal courts: Testing the conflict model of criminal justice. *Social Problems, 25*, 564–580.

Lodhi, A. Q., & Tilly, C. (1973). Urbanization, crime and collective violence in nineteenth-century France. *American Journal of Sociology, 79*, 297–311.

Loehlin, J. C., & Rowe, D. C. (1992). Genes, environment, and personality. In G. Caprara & G. L. Van Heck (Eds.), *Modern personality psychiatry: Critical reviews and new directions* (pp. 352–370). Herts, England: Harvester-Wheatshaft.

Lombroso, C. (1876). *L'uomo delinquente*. Milan: Hoepli.

Lombroso, C. (1895). *The female offender*. New York: D. Appleton and Co.

Lombroso, C. (1912). *Crime: Its causes and remedies*. Montclair, NJ: Patterson Smith.

Longshore, D. (1998). Self-control and criminal opportunity: A prospective test of the general theory of crime. *Social Problems, 45*, 102–113.

Lorber, J. (1993). Believing is seeing: Biology as ideology. *Gender & Society, 7*, 568–581.

Lorber, J. (1998). *Gender inequality: Feminist theories and politics*. Los Angeles: Roxbury.

Loring, M., & Powell, B. (1988). Gender, race and DSM-III: A study of psychiatric behavior. *Journal of Health and Social Behavior, 29*, 1–22.

Lou, H. C., Hansen, D., Nordenfelt, M., et al. (1994). Prenatal stressors of human life affect fetal brain development. *Developmental Medicine and Child Neurology, 36*, 826–832.

Love, A. A. (1998, June 9). Wage gap between the sexes narrowing. *Atlanta Constitution*, p. 1.

Lutiger, B., Graham, K., & Einarson, T. R. (1991). Relationship between gestational cocaine use and pregnancy outcome: A meta-analysis. *Teratology, 44*, 405–414.

Lynch, M. J., & Groves, W. B. (1986). *A primer in radical criminology*. New York: Harrow & Heston.

Lynch, M. J., & Stretesky, P. (1999). Marxist criminology and social justice. In B. A. Arrigo (Ed.), *Social justice, criminal justice* (pp. 14–29). Belmont, CA: Wadsworth.

MacKinnon, C. (1986). Pornography: Not a moral issue. *Women's Studies International Quarterly, 9*, 63–78.

MacKinnon, C. (1989). *Toward a feminist theory of the state*. Cambridge: Harvard University Press.

MacLean, B. (1992). A program of local crime survey research for Canada. In J. Lowman & B. MacLean (Eds.), *Realist criminology: Crime control and policing in the 1990s* (pp. 336–365). Toronto: University of Toronto Press.

Maguire, P. (1987). *Doing participatory research: A feminist approach*. Amherst, MA: Center for International Education, University of Massachusetts.

Mankoff, M. (1971). Societal reaction and career deviance: A critical analysis. *Sociological Quarterly, 12*, 204–218.

Mann, C. R. (1989). Minority and female: A criminal justice double bind. *Social Justice, 16*(4), 95–114.

Mann, C. R. (1993). *Unequal justice: A question of color*. Bloomington: Indiana University Press.

Mann, C. R. (1995). Women of color and the criminal justice system. In B. R. Price & N. J. Sokoloff (Eds.), *The criminal justice system and women* (pp. 118–135). New York: McGraw-Hill.

Mann, C. R., & Zatz, M. S. (Eds.). (1998). *Images of color, images of crime*. Los Angeles: Roxbury.

Mannheim, H. (1965). *Comparative criminology*. Boston: Houghton Mifflin.

Maris, P., & Rein, M. (1973). *Dilemmas of social reform*. Chicago: Aldine.

Marshall, R. J. (1983). A psychoanalytic perspective on the diagnosis and development of juvenile delinquency. In W. S. Laufer & J. M. Day (Eds.), *Personality theory, moral development and criminal behavior* (pp. 119–144). Lexington, MA: Lexington Books.

Martin, J. L., & Dean, L. (1993). Developing a community sample of gay men for an epidemiological study of AIDS. In C. M. Renzetti & R. M. Lee (Eds.), *Researching sensitive topics* (pp. 82–99). Newbury Park, CA: Sage.

Martin, R. (1985). Perceptions of self and significant others in assaultive and nonassaultive criminals. *Journal of Police Science and Criminal Psychology, 1*, 2–13.

Martin, R., Mutchnick, R. J., & Austin, W. T. (1990). *Criminological thought*. New York: Macmillan.

Marx, K., & Engels, F. (1845). *The German ideology*. Moscow: Progress Publishers.

Marx, K., & Engels, F. (1948). *The Communist manifesto*. New York: International Publishers.

Marx, K., & Engels, F. (1962). *Selected works, Vol. 1*. Moscow: Foreign Language Publishing House.

Matsueda, R. L. (1988). The current state of differential association theory. *Crime and Delinquency, 34*, 277–306.

Matsueda, R. L. (1989). The dynamics of moral beliefs and minor delinquency. *Social Forces, 68*, 428–457.

Matsueda, R. L. (1997). "Cultural deviance theory": The remarkable persistence of a flawed term. *Theoretical Criminology, 1*, 429–452.

Matseuda, R. L., & Anderson, K. (1998). The dynamics of delinquent peers and delinquent behavior. *Criminology, 36*, 269–308.

Matseuda, R. L., & Heimer, K. (1987). Race, family structure, and delinquency: A test of differential association and control theories. *American Sociological Review, 53*, 826–840.

Matthews, R. (1987). Taking realist criminology seriously. *Contemporary Crises, 11*, 371–401.

Matza, D. (1964). *Delinquency and drift*. New York: Wiley.

Matza, D., & Sykes, G. M. (1961). Juvenile delinquency and subterranean values. *American Sociological Review, 26*, 712–719.

Mauer, M., & Hurling, T. (1995). *Young Black Americans and the criminal justice system: Five years later*. Washington, DC: The Sentencing Project.

Mawson, A. R., & Jacobs, K. W. (1978). Corn consumption, trytophan, and cross-national homicide rates. *Journal of Orthomolecular Psychiatry, 7*, 227–230.

Mazerolle, P., & Maahs, J. (1998, November). *General strain and delinquency: An alternative examination of conditioning influences*. Paper presented at the Annual Meeting of the American Society of Criminology, Washington, DC.

Mazerolle, P., & Piquero, A. (1997). Violent responses to strain: An examination of conditioning influences. *Violence and Victims, 12*, 3–24.

Mazur, A., & Lamb, T. A. (1980). Testosterone, status, and mood in human males. *Hormones and Behavior, 14*, 236–246.

Mazur, A., Booth, A., & Dabbs Jr., J. M. (1992). Testosterone and chess competition. *Social Psychology Quarterly, 55*, 70–77.

McCarthy, B., Hagan, J., & Woodward, T. S. (1999). In the company of women: Structure and agency in a revised power-control theory of gender and delinquency. *Criminology, 37*, 761–788.

McCarthy, J. D., & Hoge, D. R. (1984). The dynamics of self-esteem and delinquency. *American Journal of Sociology, 90*, 396–410.

McCord, J. (1991). Family relationships, juvenile delinquency, and adult criminality. *Criminology, 29*, 397–417.

McCord, W., & McCord, J. (1964). *The psychopath: An essay on the criminal mind*. Princeton, NJ: Van Nostrand.

McCrate, E., & Smith, J. (1998). When work doesn't work: The failure of current welfare reform. *Gender & Society, 12*, 61–80.

McDonald, L. (1982). Theory and evidence of rising crime in the nineteenth century. *British Journal of Sociology, 30*, 404–420.

McDowall, D., & Loftin, C. (1992). Comparing the UCR and NCS over time. *Criminology, 30*, 125–132.

McEachern, A. W. (1968). The juvenile probation system. *American Behavioral Scientist, 11*, 1–43.

McGill, H. G. (1938). The Oriental delinquent in the Vancouver juvenile court. *Sociology and Social Research, 22*, 428–438.

McGinley, H., & Paswark, R. A. (1989). National survey of the frequency and success of the insanity plea and alternate pleas. *Journal of Psychiatry and Law, 17*, 205–221.

McGregor, R., & Lawnham, P. (1993, August 5). Japan apologizes to sex slaves. *The Australian*, p. 8.

Media Report to Women. (1993, Fall). Canada cracks down on TV violence: U.S. Programmers, advertisers resist restrictions. pp. 1–3. Silver Spring, MD: Communications Research Associates, Inc.

Mednick, S. A., Gabrielli Jr., W. F., & Hutchings, B. (1987). Genetic factors in the etiology of criminal behavior. In S. A. Mednick, T. E. Moffitt, & S. A. Stack (Eds.), *The causes of crime: New behavioral approaches* (pp. 74–91). New York: Cambridge University Press.

Megargee, E. I. (1972). *The California Psychological Inventory handbook.* San Francisco: Jossey-Bass.

Megargee, E. I., & Bohn, M. J. (1979). *Classifying criminal offenders: A new system based on the MMPI.* Beverly Hills, CA: Sage.

Menard, S. (1992). Residual gains, reliability, and the UCR-NCS relationship revisited: A comment on Blumstein, Cohen and Rosenfeld. *Criminology, 30,* 105–113.

Menard, S., & Morse, B. J. (1984). A structuralist critique of the IQ-delinquency hypothesis: Theory and evidence. *American Journal of Sociology, 89,* 1347–1378.

Menard, S., (1997). A developmental test of Cloward's differential-opportunity theory. In N. Passas & R. Agnew (Eds.), *The future of anomie theory* (pp. 142–186). Boston: Northeastern University Press.

Menzies, R., Chunn, D. E., & Webster, C. D. (1991, November). *Risky business: The classification of dangerous people in the Canadian carceral enterprise.* Paper presented at the Annual Meeting of the American Society of Criminology, San Francisco, CA.

Menzies, R. J., Webster, C. D., & Sepejak, D. S. (1985). Hitting the forensic sound barrier: Predictions of dangerousness in a pretrial psychiatric clinic. In C. D. Webster, M. H. Ben-Aron, & S. J. Hucker (Eds.), *Dangerousness: Probability and prediction, psychiatry and public policy* (pp. 115–144). New York: Cambridge University Press.

Mercer, J. (1972, September). IQ: The lethal label. *Psychology Today,* p. 44.

Merton, R. K. (1961). Social problems and sociological theory. In R. K. Merton & R. A. Nisbet (Eds.), *Contemporary social problems* (pp. 775–823). New York: Harcourt, Brace and World.

Merton, R. K. (1975). *Social theory and social structure.* New York: Free Press of Glencoe.

Merton, R. K., & Montagu, M. F. A. (1940). Crime and the anthropologist. *American Anthropologist, 42,* 384–408.

Messerschmidt, J. (1986). *Capitalism, patriarchy, and crime.* Totowa, NJ: Rowman & Littlefield.

Messerschmidt, J. (1993). *Masculinities and crime.* Lanham, MD: Rowman & Littlefield.

Messner, S. F., & Tardiff, K. (1985). The social ecology of urban homicide: An application of the "routine activities" approach. *Criminology, 23,* 241–268.

Michalowski, R. J. (1977). Perspective and paradigm: Structuring criminological thought. In R. Meier (Ed.), *Theory in criminology* (pp. 17–39). Beverly Hills, CA: Sage.

Michalowski, R. J. (1985). *Order, law and crime: An introduction to criminology.* New York: Random House.

Michalowski, R. J. (1993). (De)construction, postmodernism, and social problems: Facts, fiction and fantasies at the "end of history." In J. A. Holstein & G. Miller (Eds.), *Reconsidering social constructionism* (pp. 377–401). New York: Aldine.

Miczek, K. A., & Tornatzky, W. (1996). Ethopharmacology of aggression: Impact on autonomic and mesocorticolimbic activity. *Annals of the New York Academy of Science, 794,* 60–77.

Miethe, T. D., & Moore, C. A. (1986). Racial differences in criminal processing: The consequences of model selection on conclusions about differential treatment. *Sociological Quarterly, 27,* 217–237.

Mifflin, L. (1998, April 17). Increase seen in number of violent TV programs. *New York Times,* p. A16.

Miller, S. L. (Ed.) (1998). *Crime control and women.* Thousand Oaks, CA: Sage.

Miller, S. L. (1999). *Gender and community policing: Walking the talk.* Boston: Northeastern University Press.

Miller, W. B. (1958). Lower class culture as a generating milieu of gang delinquency. *Journal of Social Issues, 14,* 5–19.

Miller, W. B. (1962). The impact of a "total-community" delinquency control project. *Social Problems, 10,* 168–191.

Minor, M. W. (1980). The neutralization of criminal offense. *Criminology, 18,* 103–120.

Minor, M. W. (1981). Techniques of neutralization: A reconceptualization and empirical examination. *Journal of Research in Crime and Delinquency, 18,* 295–318.

Minor, M. W. (1984). Neutralization as a hardening process: Considerations in the modeling of change. *Social Studies, 62,* 995–1019.

Moffitt, T. E. (1997). Adolescence-limited and life-course-persistent offending: A complementary pair of developmental theories. In T. P. Thornberry (Ed.), *Developmental theories of crime and delinquency* (pp. 11–54). New Brunswick, NJ: Transaction.

Monachesi, E. (1955). Pioneers in criminology IX: Cesare Beccaria (1738–1794). *Journal of Criminal Law, Criminology and Police Science, 46,* 439–449.

Monahan, J. (1996). *Mental illness and violent crime.* Washington, DC: National Institute of Justice.

Monahan, J., & Steadman, H. J. (1984). *Crime and mental disorder.* Washington, DC: National Institute of Justice.

Montagu, M. F. A. (1968, October). Chromosomes and crime. *Psychology Today*, pp. 42–49.

Moore, A. M. (1997). Intimate violence: Does socioeconomic status matter? In A. P. Cardarelli (Ed.), *Violence between intimate partners* (pp. 90–100). Boston: Allyn and Bacon.

Moore, D. B., & McDonald, J. M. (2000). *Transforming conflict*. Sydney: Transformative Justice Australia.

Moore, J. (1991). *Going down to the barrio*. Philadelphia: Temple University Press.

Morash, M., & Chesney-Lind, M. (1991). A re-formulation and partial test of power control theory. *Justice Quarterly*, 8, 347–377.

Morgan, M., Rapkin, A. J., & Goldman, L. (1996). Cognitive functioning in premenstrual syndrome. *Obstetrics and Gynecology*, 88, 961–966.

Morris, W. (1981). *The American heritage dictionary of the English language*. Boston: Houghton Mifflin.

Mullen, P. E., Burgess, F., Wallace, C., Palmer, S., & Ruschena, D. (2000). Community care and criminal offending in schizophrenia. *Lancet*, 355, 614–617.

Mumola, C. (1999). *Substance abuse and treatment, state and federal prisoners, 1997*. Washington, DC: U.S. Department of Justice, Bureau of Justice Statistics.

Murray, C. A. (1976). *The link betwen learning disabilities and juvenile delinquency*. Washington, DC: U.S. Government Printing Office.

Myers, S. L., & Talarico, S. M. (1986). The social contexts of racial discrimination in sentencing. *Social Problems*, 33, 236–251.

Nagel, S., & Weitzman, L. J. (1972). The double standard of American justice. *Society*, 9, 171–198.

Nasar, S., with Mitchell, K. B. (1999, May 23). Booming job market draws young Black men into fold. *New York Times*, pp. 1, 24.

National Institute of Mental Health. (1985). *Mental health, United States, 1985*. Washington, DC: U.S. Government Printing Office.

Nature of clothing isn't evidence in rape cases, Florida law says. (1990, June 3). *New York Times*, p. 30.

Neisser, U. (Ed.). (1998). *The rising curve: Long-term gains in IQ and related measures*. Washington, DC: American Psychological Association.

Newman, G. (1983). *Just and painful*. New York: Macmillan.

Newman, G., & Marongiu, P. (1990). Penological reform and the myth of Beccaria. *Criminology*, 28, 325–346.

Newman, L. S., Duff, K. J., & Baumeister, R. F. (1997). A new look at defensive projection: Thought suppression, accessibility, and biased person perception. *Journal of Personality and Social Psychology*, 72, 980–1001.

Newman, O. (1972). *Defensible space*. New York: Macmillan.

New Zealand judge: Rape as exciting. (1996, July 7). Wellington, New Zealand: Reuters. (Internet).

Nichols Jr., W. W. (1980). Mental maps, social characteristics and criminal mobility. In D. E. Georges-Abeyie & K. D. Harries (Eds.), *Crime: A spatial perspective* (pp. 156–166). New York: Columbia University Press.

Niehoff, D. (1999). *The biology of violence*. New York: Free Press.

Nikolic-Ristanovic, V. (1999). Living without democracy and peace: Violence against women in the former Yugoslavia. *Violence Against Women*, 5, 63–80.

Nye, F. I. (1958). *Family relationships and delinquent behavior*. New York: John Wiley.

Offen, K. (1988). Defining feminism: A comparative historical approach. *Signs*, 14, 119–157.

OJJDP model programs 1990: Preserving families to prevent delinquency. (1992, April). *Juvenile Justice Bulletin*.

Olewus, D. (1987). Testosterone and adrenaline: Aggressive and antisocial behavior in normal adolescent males. In S. A. Mednick, T. E. Moffitt, & S. A. Stack (Eds.), *The causes of crime: New biological approaches* (pp. 263–282). New York: Cambridge University Press.

Ondrovik, J., & Hamilton, D. (1991). Credibility of victims diagnosed as multiple personality: A case study. *American Journal of Forensic Psychology*, 9, 13–17.

Orcutt, J. D. (1987). Differential association and marijuana use. *Criminology*, 25, 341–358.

Orne, M. T., Dinges, D. F., & Orne, E. C. (1984). On the differential diagnosis of multiple personality in the forensic context. *International Journal of Clinical and Experimental Hypnosis*, 32, 118–169.

Osthoff, S. (2001). When victims become defendants: Battered women charged with crimes. In C. M. Renzetti & L. Goodstein (Eds.), *Women, crime and criminal justice: Contemporary perspectives* (pp. 232–242). Los Angeles: Roxbury.

Owen, D. (1985). *None of the above: Beyond the myth of scholastic aptitude*. Boston: Houghton Mifflin.

Park, R. E., Burgess, E. W., & McKenzie, R. D. (1967). *The city*. Chicago: University of Chicago Press.

Parlee, M. B. (1982, September). New findings: Menstrual cycles and behavior. *Ms.*, pp. 126–128.

Parlee, M. B. (1983). Changes in moods and activation levels during the menstrual cycle in experimentally naive subjects. *Psychology of Women Quarterly*, 7, 119–131.

Passas, N. (1997). Anomie, reference groups, and relative deprivation. In N. Passas & R. Agnew (Eds.),

The future of anomie theory (pp. 62–94). Boston: Northeastern University Press.

Passas, N., & Agnew, R. (Eds.). (1997). *The future of anomie theory*. Boston: Northeastern University Press.

Paswark, R. D. (1986). A review of research on the insanity defense. *Annals of the American Association of Political and Social Sciences, 484,* 100–114.

Paternoster, R. (1987). The deterrent effect of perceived certainty and severity of punishment: A review of the evidence and issues. *Justice Quarterly, 42,* 173–217.

Paternoster, R. (1989). Decisions to participate and desist from four types of common delinquency: Deterrence and the rational choice perspective. *Law and Society Review, 23,* 7–40.

Paternoster, R., & Mazerolle, P. (1994). General strain theory and delinquency: A replication and extension. *Journal of Research in Crime and Delinquency, 31,* 235–263.

Paternoster, R., Saltzman, L. E., Waldo, G. P., & Chiricos, T. G. (1983). Perceived risk and social control: Do sanctions really deter? *Law and Society Review, 17,* 457–479.

Paternoster, R., & Triplett, R. (1988). Disaggregating self-reported delinquency and its implications for theory. *Criminology, 26,* 591–625.

Peeples, F., & Loeber, R. (1994). Do individual differences and neighborhood context explain ethnic differences in juvenile delinquency? *Journal of Quantitative Criminology, 10,* 141–157.

Pepinsky, H. (1999). Peacemaking criminology and social justice. In B. A. Arrigo (Ed.), *Social justice, criminal justice* (pp. 51–70). Belmont, CA: Wadsworth.

Pepinsky, H. & Quinney, R. (Eds.). (1991). *Criminology as peacemaking.* Bloomington: Indiana University Press.

Perlez, J. (1991, July 29). Kenyans do some soul-searching after the rape of 71 schoolgirls. *New York Times,* pp. A1, A7.

Peterson, R. D., Krivo, L. J., & Harris, M. A. (1997, November). *Disadvantage and neighborhood crime: Do local decisions matter?* Paper presented at the Annual Meeting of the American Society of Criminology, San Diego, CA.

Petrill, S. A., Plomin, R., Berg, S., Johanson, B., Pedersen, N. L., Ahern, F., & McClearn, G. E. (1998). The genetic and environmental relationship between general and specific cognitive abilities in twins age 80 and older. *Psychological Science, 9,* 183–189.

Phillips, M. R., Wolf, A. S., & Coons, D. J. (1988). Psychiatry and the criminal justice system: Testing the myths. *American Journal of Psychiatry, 145,* 605–610.

Phillips, P. D. (1980). Characteristics and typology of the journey to crime. In D. E. Georges-Abeyie & K. D. Harries (Eds.), *Crime: A spatial perspective* (pp. 167–180). New York: Columbia University Press.

Piquero, A. R., & Hickman, M. (1999). An empirical test of Tittle's control balance theory. *Criminology, 37,* 319–342.

Platt, T. (1975). Prospects for a radical criminology in the USA. In I. Taylor, P. Walton, & J. Young (Eds.), *Critical criminology* (pp. 95–112). London: Routledge and Kegan Paul.

Plomin, R., Fulker, D. W., Corley, R., & DeFries, J. C. (1997). Nature, nurture, and cognitive development from 1 to 16 years: A parent-offspring adoption study. *Psychological Science, 8,* 442–447.

Pogrebia, M. R., & Poole, E. D. (1989). South Korean immigrants and crime: A case study. *Journal of Ethnic Studies, 17,* 47–80.

Polk, K. (1991). Review of *A General Theory of Crime. Crime and Delinquency, 37,* 575–581.

Pollack, S. (1998, November). *Social constructions of women in conflict with the law: Challenges to victimization and self-esteem discourse.* Paper presented at the Annual Meeting of the American Society of Criminology, Washington, DC.

Pope, K. S., Butcher, J. N., & Seelen, J. (2000). *MMPI, MMPI-2 & MMPI-A in court: A practical guide for expert witnesses and attorneys.* Washington, DC: American Psychological Association.

Poussaint, A. F., & Comer, J. P. (1993). *Raising Black children.* New York: Plume.

Pruss, R. C. (1975). Resisting designations: An extension of attribution theory into a negotiated context. *Sociological Inquiry, 45,* 3–14.

Punishment is 18 months for killing cheating wife. (1994, October 19). *New York Times,* p. A20.

Quinney, R. (1970). *The social reality of crime.* Boston: Little, Brown.

Quinney, R. (1973). *Critique of the legal order.* Boston: Little, Brown.

Quinney, R. (1980). *Providence: The reproduction of social and moral order.* New York: Longman.

Quinney, R. (1991). *Journey to a far place.* Philadelphia: Temple University Press.

Quinney, R. (1998). *For the time being.* Albany: State University of New York Press.

Quinsey, V. L., Rice, M. E., & Harris, G. T. (1995). Actuarial prediction of sexual recidivism. *Journal of Interpersonal Violence, 10,* 85–105.

Radford, J. (1987). Policing male violence, policing women. In J. Hamner & M. Maynard (Eds.), *Vio-*

lence and social control (pp. 30–45). Atlantic Highlands, NJ: Humanities Press International.

Radzinowicz, L. (1966). *Ideology and crime: A study of crime and its social and historical consequences.* London: Heinemann Educational Publishing.

Rafter, N. H. (1992). Criminal anthropology in the United States. *Criminology, 30,* 525–545.

Raine, A. (1993). *The psychopathology of crime.* New York: Academic Press.

Raine, A. (1996). Autonomic nervous system factors underlying disinhibited, antisocial, and violent behavior. *Annals of the New York Academy of Sciences, 794,* 46–59.

Raine, A., Venables, P. H., & Mednick, S. A. (1997). Low resting heart rate at age 3 years predisposes to aggression at age 11 years: Evidence from the Mauritius Child Health Project. *Journal of the American Academy of Child and Adolescent Psychiatry, 36,* 1457–1464.

Rankin, J. H., & Wells, L. E. (1990). The effect of parental attachments and direct controls on delinquency. *Journal of Research in Crime and Delinquency, 27,* 140–165.

Rapp, D. (1981). *Allergies and the hyperactive child.* New York: Simon & Schuster.

Rebellon, C. J., Thaxton, S., Kaufman, J., & Agnew, R. (1999). *A general strain theory of the race/crime relationship.* Unpublished manuscript, Emory University, Atlanta, GA.

Reckless, W. C. (1961). A new theory of delinquency and crime. *Federal Probation, 25,* 42–46.

Reed, G. E., & Yeager, P. C. (1996). Organizational offending and neoclassical criminology: Challenging the reach of a general theory of crime. *Criminology, 34,* 357–382.

Regoli, R. M., & Poole, E. D. (1978). The commitment of delinquents to their misdeeds: A re-examination. *Journal of Criminal Justice, 6,* 261–268.

Reiman, J. (1995). *The rich get richer and the poor get prison.* Boston: Allyn and Bacon.

Reiss, A. J. (1951). Delinquency as the failure of personal and social controls. *American Sociological Review, 16,* 196–207.

Reiss, I. L. (1986). *Journey into sexuality: An exploratory voyage.* Englewood Cliffs, NJ: Prentice-Hall.

Renzetti, C. M. (1992). *Violent betrayal: Partner abuse in lesbian relationships.* Newbury Park, CA: Sage.

Renzetti, C. M. (1998). Connecting the dots: Women, public policy and social control. In S. L. Miller (Ed.), *Crime control and women* (pp. 181–189). Thousand Oaks, CA: Sage.

Renzetti, C. M. (1999, March). *Private violence in public housing: Violence against women public housing residents.* Paper presented at the Annual Meeting of the Academy of Criminal Justice Sciences, Orlando, FL.

Renzetti, C. M., & Curran, D. J. (2000). *Living sociology.* Boston: Allyn and Bacon.

Renzetti, C. M., & Curran, D. J. (1999). *Women, men and society: The sociology of gender.* Boston: Allyn and Bacon.

Renzetti, C. M., Edleson, J. L., & Bergen, R. K. (Eds.). (2001). *Sourcebook on violence against women.* Thousand Oaks, CA: Sage.

Renzetti, C. M., & Lee, R. M. (Eds.). (1993). *Researching sensitive topics.* Newbury Park, CA: Sage.

Report: NYC cops search Blacks more. (1999, December 1). Associated Press on-line.

Reuter, P. (1999, April). Drug use measures: What are they really telling us? *National Institute of Justice Journal,* pp. 12–19.

Rice, M. (1990). Challenging orthodoxies in feminist theory: A Black feminist critique. In L. Gelsthorpe & A. Morris (Eds.), *Feminist perspectives in criminology* (pp. 57–69). Philadelphia: Open University Press.

Richie, B. (1996). *Compelled to crime.* New York: Routledge.

Riding, A. (1993, January 9). European inquiry says Serbs' forces have raped 20,000. *New York Times,* pp. 1, 4.

Rimer, S., & Bonner, R. (2000, May 14). Bush candidacy puts focus on executions. *New York Times,* pp. 1, 30–31.

Ripper, M. (1991). A comparison of the effect of the menstrual cycle and the social week in mood, sexual interest, and self-assessed performance. In D. L. Taylor & N. F. Woods (Eds.)., *Menstruation, health and illness* (pp. 19–33). New York: Hemisphere.

Ritzer, G. (1980). *Sociology: A multi-paradigm science.* Boston: Allyn and Bacon.

Robertson, J., & Fitzgerald, L. F. (1990). The (mis)treatment of men: Effects of client gender role and lifestyle on diagnosis and attribution of pathology. *Journal of Counseling Psychology, 37,* 3–9.

Robison, S. M. (1936). *Can delinquency be measured?* New York: Columbia University Press.

Rogers, J. W., & Buffalo, M. D. (1974). Fighting back: Nine modes of adaptation to a deviant label. *Social Problems, 22,* 101–118.

Rose, D. R., Clear, T. R., & Scully, K. (1999, April). *Incarceration and social disorganization: Rethinking residential mobility.* Paper presented at the Annual Meeting of the Southern Sociological Society, Nashville, TN.

Rosenau, P. M. (1992). *Postmodernism and the social sciences: Insights, inroads and intrusions.* Princeton, NJ: Princeton University Press.

Rosenbaum, J. L., & Lasley, J. R. (1990). School, community context, and delinquency: Rethinking the gender gap. *Justice Quarterly, 7*, 493–513.

Rosenfeld, R., & Messner, S. F. (1997). Markets, morality, and an institutional-anomie theory of crime. In N. Passas & R. Agnew (Eds.), *The future of anomie theory* (pp. 207–224). Boston: Northeastern University Press.

Rosenthal, R., & Jacobson, L. (1968). *Pygmalion in the classroom.* New York: Holt, Rinehart, and Winston.

Rowe, D. C. (1986). Genetic and environmental components of antisocial behavior: A study of 265 twin pairs. *Criminology, 24*, 513–532.

Rowe, D. C. (1994). Genetic and cultural explanations of adolescent risk taking and problem behavior. In R. D. Ketterlinus & M. E. Lamb (Eds.), *Adolescent problem behaviors* (pp. 109–126). Mahwah, NJ: Lawrence Erlbaum Associates.

Rowe, D. C. (1995). Biosocial models of deviant behavior. *Population Research and Policy Review, 14*, 301–313.

Rowe, D. C., & Gulley, B. L. (1992). Sibling effects on substance use and delinquency. *Criminology, 30*, 217–223.

Rowe, D. C., & Osgood, W. (1984). Sociological theories of delinquency and heredity: A reconsideration. *American Sociological Review, 49*, 526–540.

Rowe, D. C., Rodgers, J. L., Meseck-Bushley, S., & St. John, C. (1989). Sexual behavior and nonsexual deviance: A sibling study of their relationship. *Developmental Psychology, 25*, 61–69.

Rubin, P. N., & McCampbell, S. W. (1995). *The Americans with Disabilities Act and criminal justice: Mental disabilities and corrections.* Washington, DC: National Institute of Justice.

Rubin, R. T. (1987). The neuroendocrinology and neurochemistry of antisocial behavior. In S. A. Mednick, T. E. Moffitt, & S. A. Stack (Eds.), *The causes of crime: New biological approaches* (pp. 230–262). New York: Cambridge University Press.

Russell, D. E. H. (Ed.). (1993). *Making violence sexy.* New York: Teachers College Press.

Sampson, R. J., & Groves, W. B. (1989). Community structure and crime: Testing social disorganization theory. *American Journal of Sociology, 94*, 774–802.

Sampson, R. J., Raudenbush, S. W., & Earls, F. (1998). *Neighborhood collective efficacy—Does it help reduce violence?* Washington, DC: National Institute of Justice.

Sanday, P. R. (1981). *Female power and male dominance.* New York: Cambridge University Press.

Sarbin, T. R., & Miller, J. E. (1970). Demonism revisited: The *XYY* chromosome anomaly. *Issues in Criminology, 5*, 170–195.

Sarri, R. C. (1986). Gender and race differences in criminal justice processing. *Women's Studies International Forum, 9*, 89–99.

Sattler, J. M. (1992). *Assessment of children: Revised and updated.* San Diego: Author.

Savelsberg, J. J. (1999). Human nature and social control in complex society: A critique of Charles Tittle's *Control Balance. Theoretical Criminology, 3*, 331–338.

Savitz, L., Turner, S. H., & Dickman, T. (1977). The origin of scientific criminology: Franz Joseph Gall as the first criminologist. In R. Meier (Ed.), *Theory in criminology* (pp. 41–56). Beverly Hills, CA: Sage.

Scarr, S., & Weinberg, R. A. (1983). The Minnesota adoption studies: Genetic differences and malleability. *Child Development, 54*, 260–267.

Scarr, S., & Weinberg, R. A. (1994). Educational and occupational achievements of brothers and sisters in adopted and biologically related families. *Behavior-Genetics, 24*, 301–325.

Schalling, D. (1987). Personality correlates of plasma testosterone levels in young delinquents: An example of person-situation interaction. In S. A. Mednick, T. E. Moffitt, & S. A. Stack (Eds.), *The causes of crime: New biological approaches* (pp. 283–291). New York: Cambridge University Press.

Schauss, A. (1980). *Diet, crime and delinquency.* Berkeley, CA: Parker House.

Scheff, T. J., Retzinger, S. M., & Ryan, M. T. (1989). Crime, violence, and self-esteem: Review and proposals. In A. M. Mecca, N. J. Smelser, & J. Vasconcellos (Eds.), *The social importance of self-esteem* (pp. 165–199). Berkeley, CA: University of California Press.

Schiff, M., Duyme, M., Dumaret, A., & Tomkiewicz, S. (1982). How much could we boost scholastic achievement and IQ scores? A direct answer from a French adoption study. *Cognition, 12*, 165–196.

Schmidt, P., & Witte, A. (1984). *An economic analysis of crime and justice.* New York: Academic Press.

Schoenthaler, A. (1983). Diet and crime: An experimental examination of the value of nutrition in the control and treatment of incarcerated juvenile offenders. *International Journal of Biosocial Research, 4*, 25–39.

Schoenthaler, A. (1984, November). *Nutrition and crime: A quasi-experimental time-series reanalysis of the Virginia Diet-Behavior Program.* Paper presented at the Annual Meeting of the American Society of Criminology, Cincinnati, OH.

Schuessler, K. F., & Cressey, D. R. (1950). Personality

characteristics of criminals. *American Journal of Sociology, 55,* 225–235.

Schumann, K. F. (1976). Theoretical presuppositions for criminology as a critical enterprise. *International Journal of Criminology and Penology, 4,* 285–294.

Schur, E. M. (1965). *Crime without victims: Deviant behavior and public policy.* Englewood Cliffs, NJ: Spectrum.

Schur, E. M. (1973). *Radical nonintervention.* Englewood Cliffs, NJ: Spectrum.

Schwartz, M. D. (1988). Ain't got no class: Universal risk theories of battering. *Contemporary Crises, 12,* 373–392.

Schwartz, M. D. (1991). The future of critical criminology. In B. MacLean & D. Milovanovic (Eds.), *New directions in critical criminology* (pp. 119–124). Vancouver: Collective Press.

Schwartz, M. D., & DeKeseredy, W. S. (1997). *Sexual assault on the college campus.* Thousand Oaks, CA: Sage.

Schwartz, M. D., & Friedrichs, D. (1994). Postmodern thought and criminological discontent: New metaphors for understanding violence. *Criminology, 32,* 221–246.

Schwartz, M. D., & Pitts, V. (1994, March). *Toward a feminist routine activities theory on campus sexual assault.* Paper presented at the Annual Meeting of the Academy of Criminal Justice Sciences, Chicago, IL.

Schwendinger, J., & Schwendinger, H. (1983). *Rape and inequality.* Newbury Park, CA: Sage.

Sellin, T. (1938). *Culture conflict and crime.* New York: Social Science Research Council.

Selva, L., & Bohm, R. (1987). A critical examination of the informalism experiment in the administration of justice. *Crime and Social Justice, 29,* 43–57.

Serbin, T. R., & Miller, J. E. (1970). Demonism revisited: The XYY chromosomal abnormality. *Issues in Criminology, 5,* 195–207.

Shaw, C. R. (1930). *The jackroller.* Chicago: University of Chicago Press.

Shaw, C. R. (1938). *Brothers in crime.* Chicago: University of Chicago Press.

Shaw, C. R., & McKay, H. D. (1942, rev. 1969). *Juvenile delinquency in urban areas.* Chicago: University of Chicago Press.

Shaw, C. R., & McKay, H. D. (1971). Juvenile delinquency in urban areas: Theory. In H. L. Voss & D. M. Petersen (Eds.), *Ecology, crime and delinquency* (pp. 87–99). New York: Appleton-Century-Crofts.

Sheldon, W. (1949). *Varieties of delinquent youth.* New York: Harper and Brothers.

Shelley, L. (1981). *Crime and modernization.* Carbondale, IL: South Illinois University Press.

Sherman, L. W., Gartin, P. R., & Buerger, M. D. (1989). Hot spots of predatory crime: Routine activities and the criminology of place. *Criminology, 27,* 27–56.

Sherry, A., Lee, M., & Vatikiotis, M. (1995, December 14). For lust or money. *Far Eastern Economic Review,* pp. 22–28.

Shoemaker, D. J. (1984). *Theories of delinquency.* New York: Oxford University Press.

Short, J. F., & Strodtbeck, F. L. (1965). *Group process and gang delinquency.* Chicago: University of Chicago Press.

Shulman, A. K. (1980). Sex and power: Sexual biases of radical feminism. *Signs, 5,* 590–604.

Shumsky, N. L., & Stringer, L. M. (1981). San Francisco's zone of prostitution, 1880 to 1934. *Journal of Historical Geography, 7,* 71–89.

Siegel, L. (1992). *Criminology: Theories, patterns and typologies.* St. Paul, MN: West.

Silver, E., Cirincione, C., & Steadman, H. J. (1992, August). *Demythologizing inaccurate perceptions of the insanity defense.* Revised version of a paper presented at the Annual Meeting of the Society for the Study of Social Problems, Pittsburgh, PA.

Simcha-Fagan, O., & Schwartz, J. E. (1986). Neighborhood and delinquency: An assessment of contextual effects. *Criminology, 24,* 667–703.

Simon, R. J. (1975). *Women and crime.* Washington, DC: U.S. Government Printing Office.

Simon, R. J., & Landis, J. (1991). *The crimes women commit, the punishments they receive.* Lexington, MA: Lexington Books.

Simons, R. (1978). The meaning of the IQ-delinquency relationship. *American Sociological Review, 43,* 268–270.

Singleton, R., Straits, B. C., Straits, M. M., & McAllister, R. J. (1988). *Approaches to social research.* New York: Oxford University Press.

Skinner, B. F. (1953). *Science and human behavior.* New York: Macmillan.

Skogan, W. G. (1990). *Disorder and community decline: Crime and the spiral of decay in American neighborhoods.* New York: Free Press.

Smart, C. (1982). The new female offender: Reality or myth? In B. R. Price & N. J. Sokoloff (Eds.), *The criminal justice system and women* (pp. 105–116). New York: McGraw-Hill.

Smart, C. (1987). Review of *Capitalism, patriarchy, and crime. Contemporary Crises, 11,* 327–329.

Smelser, N. (1989). Self-esteem and social problems: An introduction. In A. M. Mecca, N. J. Smelser, & J. Vasconcellos (Eds.), *The social importance of self-esteem* (pp. 1–23). Berkeley, CA: University of California Press.

Smith, D. A., & Paternoster, R. (1990). Formal processing and future delinquency: Deviance amplification as selection artifact. *Law and Society Review*, *24*, 1109–1131.

Smith, S. K., & DeFrances, C. J. (1996). *Indigent defense*. Washington, DC: U.S. Department of Justice, Bureau of Justice Statistics.

Snodgrass, J. (1976). Clifford R. Shaw and Henry D. McKay: Chicago criminologists. *British Journal of Criminology*, *16*, 1–19.

Snodgrass, J. (1982). *The jackroller at 70*. Chicago: University of Chicago Press.

Snodgrasse, R. M. (1951). Crime and the constitution human: A survey. *Journal of Criminal Law, Criminology and Police Science*, *42*, 18–52.

Snyder, H. N., & Sickmund, M. (1999). *Minorities in the juvenile justice system*. Washington, DC: U.S. Department of Justice.

Sommer, B. (1983). How does menstruation affect cognitive competence and psychophysiological response. In S. Golub (Ed.), *Lifting the curse of menstruation* (pp. 53–90). New York: Haworth.

Sontag, D. (1993, September 27). Women asking U.S. asylum expand definition of abuse. *New York Times*, pp. A1, A13.

Sparks, R. F. (1980). A critique of Marxist criminology. In N. Morris & M. Tonry (Eds.), *Crime and Justice, Vol. 2* (pp. 159–208). Chicago: University of Chicago Press.

Spear, S., & Akers, R. L. (1988). Social learning variables and the risk of habitual smoking among adolescents: The Muscatine Study. *American Journal of Preventive Medicine*, *4*, 336–348.

Spitzer, S. (1975). Punishment and social organizations. *Law and Society Review*, *9*, 613–637.

Spitzer, S. (1983). Marxist perspectives in the sociology of law. *Annual Review of Sociology*, *9*, 103–123.

Spohn, C., & Holleran, D. (2000). The imprisonment penalty paid by young, unemployed Black and Hispanic male offenders. *Criminology*, *38*, 281–306.

Stanko, E. A. (1985). *Intimate intrusions*. London: Routledge and Kegan Paul.

Stanko, E. A. (1996). Warnings to women: Police advice and women's safety in Britain. *Violence Against Women*, *2*, 5–24.

Stark, E. (1990). Rethinking homicide: Violence, race, and the politics of gender. *International Journal of Health Services*, *20*, 3–26.

Steadman, H. J., McGreevy, M. A., Morrissey, J. P., Callahan, L. A., Robbins, P. C., & Cirincione, C. (1993). *Before and after Hinckley: Evaluating insanity defense reform*. New York: Plenum.

Steele, C. (1997). A threat in the air: How stereotypes shape intellectual identity and performance. *American Psychologist*, *52*, 613–629.

Steffensmeier, D. (1989). On the causes of "white-collar" crime: An assessment of Hirschi and Gottfredson's claims. *Criminology*, *27*, 345–358.

Steffensmeier, D. (2001). Female crime trends, 1960–1995. In C. M. Renzetti & L. Goodstein (Eds.), *Gender, crime and criminal justice* (pp. 191–211). Los Angeles: Roxbury.

Steffensmeier, D., Kramer, J., & Streifel, C. (1993). Gender and imprisonment decisions. *Criminology*, *31*, 411–446.

Steffensmeier, D., Ulmer, J., & Kramer, J. (1998). The interaction of race, gender, and age in criminal sentencing: The punishment cost of being young, Black, and male. *Criminology*, *36*, 763–797.

Stein, M. B., Yehuda, R., Koverola, C., & Hanna, R. (1997). Enhanced dexamethasone suppression of plasma cortisol in adult women traumatized by childhood sexual abuse. *Biological Psychiatry*, *42*, 680–686.

Steinberg, M. (1995). *Handbook for the assessment of dissociation: A clinical guide*. Washington, DC: American Psychiatric Association.

Stephens, R. D., & Arnette, J. L. (2000). *From the courthouse to the schoolhouse: Making successful transitions*. Washington, DC: Office of Juvenile Justice and Delinquency Prevention.

Sternberg, R. J. (1986). *Intelligence applied: Understanding and increasing your intellectual skills*. New York: Harcourt Brace Jovanovich.

Stitt, B. G., & Giacopassi, D. J. (1992, July-August). Trends in the connectivity of theory and research in *Criminology*. *The Criminologist*, pp. 1, 3–5.

Straus, M. A. (1993). Physical assault by wives: A major social problem. In R. J. Gelles & D. R. Loseke (Eds.), *Current controversies on family violence* (pp. 67–87). Newbury Park, CA: Sage.

Straus, M. A., & Sugarman, D. B. (1997). Spanking by parents and subsequent antisocial behavior. *Archives of Pediatrics and Adolescent Medicine*, *151*, 761–767.

Suddath, R. L., Christison, G. W., Torrey, E. F., Casanova, M. F., & Weinberger, D. R. (1990). Anatomical abnormalities in the brains of monozygotic twins discordant for schizoprhenia. *New England Journal of Medicine*, *322*, 789–793.

Sudman, S., & Kalton, G. (1986). New developments in the sampling of special populations. *Annual Review of Sociology*, *12*, 401–429.

Sudman, S., Sirken, M. G., & Curran, C. D. (1988). Sampling rare and elusive populations. *Science*, *240*, 991–996.

Sullivan, R. F. (1973). The economics of crime: An introduction to the literature. *Crime and Delinquency, 19,* 138–149.

Sutherland, E. H. (1931). Mental deficiency and crime. In K. Young (Ed.), *Social attitudes* (pp. 357–375). New York: Holt.

Sutherland, E. H. (1937). *The professional thief.* Chicago: University of Chicago.

Sutherland, E. H. (1947). *Principles of criminology.* Philadelphia: J. B. Lippencott.

Sutherland, E. H. (1949). *White collar crime.* New York: Holt, Rinehart and Winston.

Sutherland, E. H. (1951). Critique of Sheldon's *Varieties of Delinquent Youth. American Sociological Review, 18,* 10–13.

Sutlive, V. H. (1991). *Female and male in Borneo.* Williamsburg, VA: Borneo Research Council.

Swanson, J. W., Holzer, C. E., Ganju, V. K., & Jono, R. T. (1990). Violence and psychiatric disorder in the community: Evidence from the epidemiologic catchment area surveys. *Hospital and Community Psychiatry, 41,* 761–770.

Sykes, G. M., & Matza, D. (1957). Techniques of neutralization: A theory of delinquency. *American Sociological Review, 22,* 664–670.

Sylvester, S. F. (1982). Adolphe Quetelet: At the beginning. *Federal Probation, 46,* 14–19.

Tanioka, I. (1992, November). *Social control theory at* [sic] *Japanese society.* Paper presented at the Annual Meeting of the American Society of Criminology, New Orleans, LA.

Tanioka, I., & Glaser, D. (1991). School uniforms, routine activities, and the social control of delinquency in Japan. *Youth and Society, 23,* 50–75.

Tannenbaum, F. (1938). *Crime and the community.* Boston: Ginn and Company.

Tarde, G. (1912). *Penal philosophy.* Boston: Little, Brown.

Taylor, B., & Bennett, T. (1999). *Comparing drug use rates of detained arrestees in the United States and England.* Washington, DC: U. S. Department of Justice.

Taylor, I., Walton, P., & Young, J. (1973). *The new criminology.* New York: Harper Colophone Books.

Taylor, R. B., Gottfredson, S. D., & Brower, S. N. (1980). The defensibility of defensible space. In T. Hirschi & M. Gottfredson (Eds.), *Understanding crime* (pp. 53–71). Beverly Hills, CA: Sage.

Taylor, R. B., & Harrell, A. V. (1996). *Physical environment and crime.* Washington, DC: National Institute of Justice.

Taylor, V. (1990). The continuity of the American women's movement: An elite-sustained stage. In G. West & R. L. Blumberg (Eds.), *Women and social protest* (pp. 277–301). New York: Oxford University Press.

Taylor, V. (1996). *Rock-a-by-baby: Feminism, self-help and postpartum depression.* New York: Routledge.

Tennenbaum, D. J. (1977). Personality and criminality: A summary and implications of the literature. *Journal of Criminal Justice, 5,* 225–235.

Teplin, L. A. (1985). The criminality of the mentally ill: A dangerous misconception. *American Journal of Psychiatry, 142,* 593–599.

Teplin, L. A. (1990). The prevalence of severe mental disorder among male urban jail detainees. *American Journal of Mental Health, 80,* 663–669.

Terry, R. M. (1978, August). *Trends in female crime: A comparison of Adler, Simon, and Steffensmeier.* Paper presented at the Annual Meeting of the Society for the Study of Social Problems, San Francisco, CA.

Thornberry, T. P. (1973). Race, socioeconomic status, and sentencing in the juvenile justice system. *Journal of Criminal Law and Criminology, 64,* 90–98.

Thornberry, T., Moore, M., & Christenson, R. L. (1985). The effect of dropping out of high school on subsequent criminal behavior. *Criminology, 23,* 3–18.

Thys-Jacobs, S., Alvir, J. M. J., & Fraratacangelo, P. (1995). Comparative analysis of three PMS assessment instruments—The identification of premenstrual syndrome with core symptoms. *Psychopharmacology Bulletin, 31,* 389–396.

Tittle, C. R. (1995). *Control balance: Toward a general theory of deviance.* Boulder, CO: Westview.

Tittle, C. R. (1997). Thoughts stimulated by Braithwaite's analysis of control balance theory. *Theoretical Criminology, 1,* 99–110.

Tittle, C. R. (1999). Continuing the discussion of *Control Balance. Theoretical Criminology, 3,* 344–352.

Tittle, C. R., Burke, M. J., & Jackson, E. F. (1986). Modeling Sutherland's theory of differential association: Toward an empirical clarification. *Social Forces, 65,* 405–432.

Tittle, C. R., Willemeg, W. J., & Smith, D. A. (1978). The myth of social class and criminality. *American Sociological Review, 43,* 643–656.

Toby, J. (1957). Social disorganization and stake in conformity: Complementary factors in the predatory behavior of hoodlums. *Journal of Criminal Law, Criminology and Police Science, 48,* 12–17.

Toby, J. (1979). The new criminology is the old sentimentality. *Criminology, 16,* 516–526.

Toch, H., & Adams, K. (1989). *The disturbed violent offender.* New Haven, CT: Yale University Press.

Triplett, R. A. (1990). *Labeling and differential association theory*. Unpublished doctoral dissertation, University of Maryland.

Turk, A. (1975). Prospects and pitfalls for radical criminology: A critical response to Platt. *Crime and Social Justice, 4,* 41–42.

Turk, A. (1980). Analyzing official deviance: For nonpartisan conflict in criminology. In J. Inciardi (Ed.), *Radical criminology: The coming crisis* (pp. 78–91). Beverly Hills, CA: Sage.

Turner, S. P., & Turner, J. H. (1990). *The impossible science*. Newbury Park, CA: Sage.

Upham, F. K. (1987). *Law and social change in postwar Japan*. Cambridge: Harvard University Press.

Ursel, J. (1991). Considering the impact of the battered women's movement on the state: The example of Manitoba. In E. Comack & S. Brickey (Eds.), *The social basis of law: Critical readings in the sociology of law* (pp. 261–288). Halifax: Garamond.

U.S. Department of Commerce, Bureau of the Census. (1996, 1997, 1998, 1999). *Statistical abstract of the United States*. Washington, DC: U.S. Government Printing Office.

U.S. Department of Justice, Bureau of Justice Statistics. (1994). *Violence against women*. Washington, DC: Author.

U.S. Department of Justice, Bureau of Justice Statistics. (1997). *Criminal victimization in the United States, 1994*. Washington, DC: Author.

U.S. Department of Justice, Bureau of Justice Statistics. (1998). *Sourcebook of criminal justice statistics*. Washington, DC: Author.

U.S. Department of Justice, Office of Juvenile Justice and Delinquency Programs. (1997). *Juvenile offenders and victims: 1997 update on violence*. Washington, DC: Author.

U.S. Department of Labor, Bureau of Labor Statistics. (1998). *Employment and earnings*. Washington, DC: Author.

U.S. Department of State. (1994). *Country reports on human rights practices for 1993*. Washington, DC: U.S. Government Printing Office.

U.S. General Accounting Office. (1990). *Death penalty sentencing: Research indicates pattern of racial disparities*. Washington, DC: U.S. Government Printing Office.

Van Erp, A. M. M., & Miczek, K. A. (1996). Prefrontal cortex dopamine and serotonin: Microdialysis during aggression and alcohol self-administraion in rats. *Society for Neuroscience Abstracts, 22,* 161.

Van Goozen, S., Frijda, N., & Van de Poll, N. (1994). Anger and aggression in women: Influence of sports choice and testosterone administration. *Aggressive Behavior, 20,* 213–222.

Van Voorhies, P., Cullen, F. T., Mathers, R., & Garner, C. C. (1988). The impact of family structure and quality on delinquency: A comparative assessment of structural and functional factors. *Criminology, 26,* 235–261.

Vaughn, D. (1997). Anomie theory and organizations: Culture and the normalization of deviance at NASA. In N. Passas & R. Agnew (Eds.), *The future of anomie theory* (pp. 95–123). Boston: Northeastern University Press.

Verhovek, S. H. (1998, January 1). As woman's execution nears, Texas squirms. *New York Times*, pp. A1, A12.

Virkkunen, M. (1987). Metabolic dysfunctions among habitually violent offenders: Reactive hypoglycemia and cholesterol levels. In S. A. Mednick, T. E. Moffitt, & S. A. Stack (Eds.), *The causes of crime: New biological approaches* (pp. 292–311). New York: Cambridge University Press.

Virkkunen, M., Nuutila, A., Goodwin, F. K., et al. (1987). Cerebrospinal fluid monoamine metabolites in male arsonists. *Archives of General Psychiatry, 44,* 241–247.

Vivian, J. (1993). *The media of mass communication*. Boston: Allyn and Bacon.

Vold, G. B. (1958). *Theoretical criminology*. New York: Oxford University Press.

Vold, G. B., & Bernard, T. J. (1986). *Theoretical criminology* (3rd ed.). New York: Oxford University Press.

Volkow, N. D., & Tancredi, L. (1987). Neural substrates of violent behavior: A preliminary study with positron emission tomography. *British Journal of Psychiatry, 151,* 673–688.

Vowell, P. R., & May, D. C. (2000). Another look at classic strain theory: Poverty status, perceived blocked opportunity, and gang membership as predictors of adolescent violent behavior. *Sociological Inquiry, 70,* 42–60.

Walby, S. (1990). *Theorizing patriarchy*. Cambridge: Basil Blackwell.

Waldo, G. P., & Dinitz, S. (1967). Personality attributes of the criminal: An analysis of research studies. *Journal of Research in Crime and Delinquency, 4,* 185–202.

Wallerstein, J. S., & Blakeslee, J. (1989). *Second chances*. New York: Ticknor and Fields.

Walter, G. D. (1992). A meta-analysis of the gene-crime relationship. *Criminology, 30,* 595–613.

Walters, G. D., & White, T. W. (1989). Heredity and crime: Bad genes or bad research? *Criminology, 27,* 455–485.

Warr, M., & Stafford, M. (1991). The influence of delinquent peers: What they think or what they do? *Criminology, 29,* 851–866.

Warren, M. Q. (1979). The female offender. In H. Toch (Ed.), *Psychology of crime and criminal justice* (pp. 444–469). New York: Holt, Rinehart and Winston.

Webster, R. (1995). *Why Freud was wrong: Sin, science, and psychoanalysis*. New York: Basic.

Weisel, D. L., Gouvis, C., & Harrell, A. V. (1994). *Addressing community decay and crime: Alternative approaches and explanations*. Washington, DC: National Institute of Justice.

Wells, L. E. (1989). Self-enhancement through delinquency: A conditional test of self-derogation theory. *Journal of Research on Crime and Delinquency, 26,* 226–252.

Wells, L. E., & Rankin, J. H. (1983). Self-concept as a mediating factor in delinquency. *Social Psychology Quarterly, 46,* 11–22.

West, D. J., & Farrington, D. P. (1977). *The delinquent way of life*. London: Heinemann.

Wexler, D. B. (1981). *Mental health law*. New York: Plenum.

White, J. L., Moffitt, T. E., & Silva, P. A. (1989). A prospective replication of the protective effects of IQ in subjects at high risk for juvenile delinquency. *Journal of Consulting and Clinical Psychology, 57,* 719–724.

White, M. (1987). *The Japanese educational challenge*. New York: Free Press.

Whitehead, J. T., & Boggs, N. N. (1990, November). *Control theory and felony probation: An empirical test*. Paper presented at the Annual Meeting of the American Society of Criminology, Baltimore, MD.

Whitney, C. R. (1992, November 13). East Europe's frustration finds target: Immigrants. *New York Times,* pp. A1, A8.

Wiatrowski, M. D., Griswold, D. B., & Roberts, M. K. (1981). Social control theory and delinquency. *American Sociological Review, 46,* 525–541.

Widom, C. S., & Ames, A. (1988). Biology and female crime. In T. E. Moffitt & S. A. Mednick (Eds.), *Biological contributions to crime causation* (pp. 308–331). Dordrecht: Martinus Nijhoff.

Wilbanks, W. (1987). *The myth of a racist criminal justice system*. Belmont, CA: Wadsworth.

Williams, F. P. (1984). The demise of the criminological imagination: A critique of recent criminology. *Justice Quarterly, 1,* 91–106.

Williams, W. M., & Ceci, S. J. (1997). Are Americans becoming more or less alike? *American Psychologist, 52,* 1226–1234.

Wilson, J. Q., & Herrnstein, R. J. (1985). *Crime and human nature*. New York: Simon & Schuster.

Wilson, J. Q., & Kelling, G. (1982). Broken windows. *Atlantic Monthly, 211,* 29–38.

Wilson, W. J. (1996). *When work disappears: The world of the new urban poor*. New York: Knopf.

Winfree, L. T., Fuller, K., Vigil, T., & Mays, G. L. (1992). The definition and measurement of "gang status": Policy implications for juvenile justice. *Juvenile and Family Court Journal,* 29–37.

Witkin, H. A., Mednick, S. A., Schulsinger, F., Bakkestrom, F. E., Christiansen, K. O., Goodenough, D. R., Hirschhorn, K., Lundsteen, K. C., Owen, D. R., Phillip, J., Rubin, D. B., & Stocking, M. (1976). XYY and XXY men: Criminality and aggression. *Science, 193,* 547–555.

Wolfgang, M. E. (1973). Cesare Lombroso. In H. Mannheim (Ed.), *Pioneers in criminology* (pp. 232–291). Montclair, NJ: Patterson Smith.

Wolfgang, M. E., & Ferracuti, F. (1967). *The subculture of violence*. London: Tavistock.

Wonders, N. A. (1999). Postmodern feminist criminology and social justice. In B. A. Arrigo (Ed.), *Social justice, criminal justice* (pp. 109–128). Belmont, CA: Wadsworth.

Woodman, D., Hinton, J., & O' Neill, M. (1977). Relationship between violence and catecholamines. *Perceptual and Motor Skills, 45,* 702.

Wright, R. A. (1991, November). *The failure of nonintervention*. Paper presented at the Annual Meeting of the American Society of Criminology, San Francisco, CA.

Wright, R. A., Logie, R. H., & Decker, S. (1995). Criminal expertise and offender decision making: An experimental study of the target selection process in residential burglary. *Journal of Research in Crime and Delinquency, 32,* 39–53.

Young, J. (1987). The tasks facing a realist criminology. *Contemporary Crises, 11,* 337–356.

Young, T. R. (1985). *A Marxian theory of crime*. Paper #108, Transforming Sociology Series, Red Feather Institute.

INDEX